Understanding and Nurturing the Missionary Family

Understanding and Nurturing the Missionary Family

Compendium of the
International Conference on Missionary Kids
Quito, Ecuador, January 4-8, 1987
Volume I

Edited by
Pam Echerd and Alice Arathoon

William Carey Library

PASADENA, CALIFORNIA

Published by WILLIAM CAREY LIBRARY
a Division of WCIU Press
P.O. Box 40129
Pasadena, California 91114

Cover art by Jonathan Gregerson
Cover design by Paul Merrill

ISBN 0-87808-224-7
Library of Congress # 89-083398

PRINTED IN THE UNITED STATES OF AMERICA

To our parents,

Dale and Vivian Sheetz

and

Scotty and Ann Burger,

and

to all grandparents who creatively find ways to show their love to
their grandchildren living in another country

Contents

Part I MK: Nurtured by Communities

Part II Parenting Missionary Kids

Part III   When Special Care is Needed

Part IV   Educational Options for Missionary Kids

Part V   MK Identity Formation

Part VI   MK Re-entry

Part VII   The Adult MK

Foreword

The setting was Quito, Ecuador in January 1987. Five hundred people representing the Christian missionary endeavor from every continent had gathered to interact, listen, share, learn, and discuss the issues facing the missionary kid. This two-volume compendium of the second International Conference on Missionary Kids (ICMK) is prepared to remind us of things said and to facilitate our response to those issues.

The original idea that grew into the ICMK centered on bringing together a "critical mass" of concerned and capable people who would identify the needs of missionary kids and their families and begin to work toward solutions. Fifty to seventy-five people seemed like a reasonable assembly to those who initiated the idea. When instead 336 people attended ICMK Manila in 1984 and 523 attended ICMK Quito in 1987, it became clear that the issues facing missionary families are indeed high priorities in the missions community.

We have watched with deep delight as God has blessed the original intent of the ICMK. Since that first conference, agencies have reviewed and revised policy and appointed specialized personnel to care for MKs The academic community has responded with the encouragement of research and the promotion of teaching in overseas schools through the Christian College Teacher Education Coordinating Council. Others have developed models for transition and re-entry seminars, a prefield training program for MK teachers and dorm parents, MK hostels, and multitudes of both individual and corporate activities.

ICMK came into being as a cooperative effort in *thinking*, with the expectation that *doing* would follow. We hope that the doing will be an expression of love focused in several directions, first to the MKs themselves in caring for their needs. Secondly, to the parents of MKs in helping and encouraging them in their role as both parents and missionaries. And thirdly, to the world by developing and releasing the potential of the MK. It is my intense desire that in hearing and reading we shall become doers.

David Pollock
Chairman, ICMK Quito

Preface

If you went to the Quito ICMK, we're sure one of your lasting impressions was of too much in too little time — too many people to talk with, too many seminars to choose from, and too many ideas to process. This volume will provide you the opportunity to "attend" many of the sessions you had to miss for lack of time, as well as review what was presented in those you did attend. Perhaps you took home a stack of papers and a selection of tapes to process more slowly at a later date. If so, reading these abridged versions of the presentations may be just the inspiration you need to get out your originals and think them through in their entirety.

If you did not go to the Quito ICMK, there are many things you missed which this book will not provide — all the sights, sounds, tastes, smells, feelings, and friendships which contributed to making the conference an unforgettable experience. However, this book allows you to benefit from the insight of those who presented papers or participated in the discussions.

Ninety presentations, even when abridged, make a very thick stack of paper, so we have divided the presentations into two volumes. This first one is intended as an overview for anyone interested in missionary families. In the second volume we have included presentations that would be of more interest to professionals working with missionary children — teachers, counselors, school principals, house parents, mission board administrators.

The list of addresses at the back of each volume are there to be used. One of the most important outcomes of the conference was the chance to make new friends who share similar interests. By writing to the author of a paper which interests you, you may make a friend and learn of others who share your interest. You may also learn how the presenter has modified his position in the intervening years.

The words "his position" lead us to a small clarification. The editors are two women who grew up in the days of androcentric generics (before there was such a fancy name for the use of male pronouns to stand for anybody) and were unscarred by the experience. Although a friend has told us that there is some justification from Middle English for using the plural form *they* as the generic form, we have in general chosen to use the masculine as the generic when editing was needed to clarify pronoun references.

Editing a compendium such as this is a balancing act between the right of the speaker to have what he said accurately represented (but not so accurately as to include every false start, misstatement, repetition, or rabbit trail), and the rights of the readers to have available the contents of the conference in a form that is easily readable and not overly redundant. We hope we have struck an acceptable balance.

When we agreed to edit the compendium, we had no idea of the magnitude of the task ahead of us. However, the year we spent doing it was a highlight in both of our lives. It was wonderful to spend a year working together on a project which we knew would be of benefit to people around the world. Every presentation brought us new insights on topics we had discussed together over the years or else introduced us to new topics we had never even thought about. We know that you will also be enriched by your reading.

For us, in addition to what we learned by from the presentations, there were many other learning experiences, as well. For one thing, we both advanced technologically. Pam learned the intricacies of Microsoft Word, and Alice got the courage to tackle her Apple computer.

We have learned more about the shoulds and should-nots of public speaking from transcribing and editing those tapes than we ever did from a speech class. In fact, we think editing a transcript of one's own public speaking would be a valuable exercise in any speech class.

There is, however, a great difference between oral and written speech. We learned more about those differences while trying to turn the one into the other than we ever did in our linguistics classes. Sentences that made perfect sense to Pam when she transcribed them were subject to multiple interpretations by Alice, who did not have the intonation to guide her through the written form. So sentences had to be reworked.

We learned why quotations in the New Testament do not match quotations in the Old Testament. In talk after talk, even though they were not translating from one language to another, speakers tended to paraphrase quotations in order to emphasize their point. When, then, do you use quotation marks? The punctuation and spelling rules we learned in school were not always adequate for the task of making spoken language "lie flat."

We have come to appreciate more deeply the power of books and tapes to transcend the limitations of time. As we have had occasion to talk with some of the speakers from the Quito ICMK and ask them questions about their talks, we have seen them stretching to recall an event which for them occurred two years ago, but for us was occurring in the present as we listened to the tapes and edited their words.

So, while the Quito ICMK is "ancient history" for those who were there, it is a present-tense source of encouragement and insight to anyone who chooses to read this compendium.

We would like to express our appreciation to Mercedes Muñoz for her many hours of transcribing tapes and keyboarding edits, and also to our husbands, Steve and Hilary, and our sons, Daniel, Jonathan, Andoe, and Peter for their encouragement and patience during the year we worked on this book.

Pam Echerd and Alice Arathoon
Guatemala City, July 1989

P.S. I need to add a new technological skill to my list of things learned through doing this book—producing photo-ready copy using a laser printer. And I also have a whole new list of people to thank for helping me achieve that goal: Dan Tutton, Dave Linton, Joyce Nies, Carlene Grant, and my mother, Vivian Sheetz.

Pam Echerd
Dallas, TX, September 1989

Part I

MK: NURTURED BY COMMUNITIES

1

MK: A Person in Perspective

Cliff Schimmels
Wheaton College

I'm excited to be here because I sincerely believe there are some kids somewhere in this world who are going to profit because we are here this week. I'm excited any time I think that kids profit.

We talk about hostages and get all excited about hostage situations. In the United States alone this morning there are forty-four million Americans being held totally against their will in institutions called schools. I get excited about anybody who will do anything to make it a little better for those kids.

Jim — A Spiritual Leader

I hope we spend some time this week talking about my friend Jim. I first met Jim when I went to Wheaton College. He was in my first class — the first MK I had ever known. He was outgoing, personable, bright, a school leader. He was very much an asset in my class. Jim and I developed a natural friendship. We jogged a lot, and at the speed I jogged, we talked more than we exercised. I got very well acquainted with Jim. In all my years of dealing with other people's kids, I'd never been around a young man who had received more inspiration or direction from his father, or who was closer to his father than Jim was. I was astounded by that. Then one day, I discovered that Jim had lived in boarding schools all of his life, and he was only around his father three months a year. I was really startled.

One day Jim stuck his head in my office door. I could see that he was perplexed. He said to me, "Do you need money?"

I said, "What kind of a question is that? I've been a school teacher all my life. Yeah, I need money."

3

"No," he said, "Do you have some kind of an emergency need for money?"

I said, "Well, no. Why do you ask?"

He said, "Well, the Lord just gave me $200, and I don't know what to do with it."

"Wait a minute. The Lord gave you $200?"

"Yeah. I went down to pay my bill, and it was $200 less than it was supposed to be. There was $200 in the account that shouldn't have been there. So the Lord has given me $200, and I don't know what I'm supposed to do with it. I'm supposed to give it to somebody, but I don't know who."

I said, "What's the possibility that the Lord intended the $200 for you?"

He said, "No, I don't think the Lord works that way."

So he went off down the hall on his mission. Strange situation. That night Jim's roommate's father had a heart attack. The roommate had to fly home. Would you care to venture how much it cost to get the roommate home? Exactly $200.

I've kept up with Jim since then, and he lives his life completely in tune with the Holy Spirit. If the Lord has a couple hundred dollars and doesn't know what to do with them, he'll give them to Jim, because Jim will have the right idea. He is that kind of a person.

How in the world did he learn that? Who taught it to him? Who was his model? Let's talk a lot about Jim this week. Let's talk about those kids who come out of our missionary schools and our missionary homes and become spiritual leaders.

Last night I was reading about a despicable guy in the book of Genesis, a fellow named Isaac. He had to go down to Egypt because of a famine, and when he got there he told his wife, "Tell everybody you're my sister so they won't kill me." Isn't that a despicable thing? Where in the world did Isaac learn to do that? Well, maybe from his dad who did it twice, same lie. Where do we get our models? Where did Jim get his model?

Dan—Honoring Commitments

Let's spend some time this week talking about my friend Dan. Dan graduated from college two years ago. At that time, he decided what his abilities were, what his desires were, what his likes were, and what his calling was. In his mind, he visualized the perfect job. He looked around for a couple of years, and did some other things, but he was unable to find that perfect job. So about six months ago, he took another job. The company trained him a little, and he immediately became successful. They liked him and he liked them.

But after working for them for about six weeks, he got a telephone call from people who offered him the perfect job. Isn't that a blessing? Not really. It threw him into a state of depression and anxiety. Blessings sometimes do that because they force us into making decisions. He deliberated for a week—sheer agony. "This is the perfect job. This is what I've been praying for. But can I leave the company that's already been good to me?"

After a week of agony, he finally called the people with the perfect job and said, "No, I can't come. I'd like to tell you that this offer is the Lord's will. But I don't know that for sure. The one thing I do know for sure is that it is the Lord's will that I honor every commitment with integrity."

Where in the world did he learn that? He grew up in a missionary home; grew up in a missionary school. What is there in our curriculum that teaches that kind of integrity? What teaches that kind of honoring a commitment? Where was his model?

Do I find these two gentlemen strange? The man who lives his life according to the Holy Spirit? Yes. I think anybody who lives his life according to the Holy Spirit is a little strange. He's exactly the type of person I think we all ought to try to be. I find him uniquely normal.

Do I find Dan, who will make that kind of a commitment to integrity a little strange? Yes, nowadays somebody who commits himself to integrity is a little strange. I find him exactly the kind of person I hope my son grows up to be. I find him uniquely normal.

Sally—Self-Reliant

Let's spend some time this week talking about my good friend Sally. Every day people living in very isolated situations make the kinds of decisions about life and death that most of us never get an opportunity to make in a whole lifetime. I get the idea that Sally's parents are that kind of independent people. Sally was home schooled through the eighth grade. She went to a boarding high school for four years, and while she was in high school, decided her lifetime ambition was to be a high school history teacher.

She chose a college in the United States without a whole lot of counseling and direction. After attending the college for about six weeks, she found out they had dropped their teacher education program the previous year. She couldn't get to be a high school history teacher at that college. But rather than transfer, she took some courses, did what she thought she wanted to do, and transferred to our school after three years.

I've got news for you. We are never kind to you when you transfer to our school at any stage. And we definitely are not kind to you when you transfer to our school after three years. We weren't kind to her. I would guess that in the first year she was in our school she heard the words "No, you can't," more than she had heard them in all the rest of her life put together. She butted heads with the system all the time. She didn't make major requests, just minor ones where the system couldn't budge. She never got much counsel. She didn't seek much. She didn't come to see us. As a result, she made some wrong decisions. We forced her into taking two more years of course work. But she ran out of money before that was over. She had to drop out to go to work, never asking for a dime from anybody. She was too independent for that. She would go out to work, make enough money, come back a semester. It took her three years to complete those two years. But she didn't get her bill paid in time, and we wouldn't release her grades for her transcript, so her teacher certification was delayed.

Finally she got to be a high school history teacher, but she's very bitter and very disillusioned. She doesn't want anything to do with Christians any time, any place, not even her own family.

Let's talk about these kids who grow up in missionary communities and develop a certain kind of self-reliance. We put fifteen- or eighteen-year-olds on a plane and ship them clear across the world without much supervision. We really do teach them a certain kind of self-reliance, and we need to take that self-reliance and turn it into a great asset. But let's remind ourselves that self-reliance is just one step away from isolation. A self-reliant person is just one step away from being a terribly frustrated, isolated person when they hit the system. Let's teach these kids somewhere along the line that it's not a sign of weakness to ask a question. Let's spend some time talking about these kinds of people.

Expectations Regarding Social Relationships

Let's spend some time concentrating on the missionary community's development of expectations and social relationships which may never happen anywhere else in the world except in the missionary community itself. Let me illustrate that. It seems to me that people in missionary communities really care about each other, and they interact with each other on a day-by-day basis. I show up in a missionary community, and within fifteen minutes every kid is calling me Uncle Cliff. I like that. I have lived in the same house on the same street in Wheaton, Illinois, for twelve years, and no kid dares call me Uncle Cliff. I am Mr. Schimmels, and don't you forget it. I don't have an Uncle Cliff relationship with a single kid in Wheaton, but I have one with missionary kids all over the world.

I think the same thing is true with peer relationships. The friendships between missionaries are some of the finest, most significant, intense friendships there are. These kids grow to depend on those friendships, and they are very unlike other friendships.

I spent six weeks trying to be a high school student a few years ago. The first thing that surprised me was there's not a whole lot of socialization in American high schools. I was fortunate. They found my spot. They put me in a remedial science class. I was fortunate to have at least one class with remedial kids, because they socialize with each other. That might be one of the reasons why they're remedial. I don't know. The nice thing about remedial kids is that their membership is open. "Hey Cliff, come be a part of us." They got a thrill out of that.

I also had classes with the elite, the kids who wear badges on Friday afternoons—football jerseys and cheerleader costumes. They socialize a little bit, but with each other. Their membership is closed.

In between those two groups, you have sixty or seventy percent of the high school students in America who don't socialize a bit during the day. They don't have any friends at all. Basically, life for them is a pretty lonely, isolated life. Don't deceive yourself. I was in class with one student who was there for six weeks, and at the end of six weeks he knew four other students by name.

The missionary kid comes into this community with a lot of expectations about friendships. Then the missionary kid says to me, "I don't fit in." If we listen to that, we want to say, "Our community is rejecting the student." I don't think that's true. They're never going to have as close friendships as they left.

My son graduated from high school four years ago. He played on a state championship football team where those guys spent a lot of time together — suffered together and bled together. He came home for two weeks at Christmas and never went to see a single high school friend. That's not going to happen with MKs. When they come back, and there's a high school friend within three hundred miles, they go to see him.

We need to talk about these very special characteristics. These are positive things, but we need to teach kids how to use them as such.

Brian — Not Academically Motivated

I'd like to spend some time this week talking about my good friend Brian. But we're not going to. Let me tell you about Brian. He grew up in Africa. Good fellow. Conscientious, hard worker. He's just not real academically sound. Brian doesn't like to read. He doesn't read very well. One of those is a cause and the other is a result, and I don't know the difference between the two. He just doesn't have a lot of academic motivation. He graduated from high school. Everyone else was going to college — not Brian. He didn't know what to do with his life, so he came to Wheaton. He didn't come to the college. He just came to live in the community. He tried junior college a little; that didn't work. He went down and got a job as an apprentice auto mechanic. I talked to his employer. He liked Brian. Brian was a good fellow, learning quickly. But he was one of the loneliest, most isolated human beings I have ever known. He stayed two years, and I don't know how he did it. After two years, he went back to Africa. He's a twenty-six-year-old man wandering around Africa looking for a definition of his life.

You know why we're not going to talk about Brian? Because we all refuse to admit that he exists. We're trying to deny that he lives. You college people are sitting there with a smirk on your faces. "We've got a great re-entry program at the college." That doesn't do Brian any good. He's not going to your college. And you mission reps, you guys come to my class and you think I'm not paying attention sitting back there yawning, but I hear what you say to these young teachers. "How would you like to teach a whole school full of highly motivated, challenging kids? Come be a missionary teacher." Most of your kids are that way. But my student goes out there, and she runs into Brian, who's not particularly motivated academically, so she just refuses to admit that he exists. We pretty well ignore this

guy. What's even worse, his parents deny that a problem exists.
When Brian was a kid, they gave him the Narnia Chronicles for
Christmas. You give books to a nonreader. He wanted a hammer.
You don't dare give this kid a hammer.

If it's any consolation, Brian's just about as well-off in missionary
schools as he is back in the States. You don't have a curriculum for
him; you don't have much for him to do; and you deny that he exists.
But the same thing would be true back home.

Schools are about words. Have you ever noticed that? We
speak words. We write words. We talk words. We think words.
People who like words get along well in school. People who don't
like words don't get along very well in school. I dare you to walk into
an American high school and go to the art department. You take
your life in your own hands down there, because that's where the
mean bunch is—in art and automobile mechanics.

I am more concerned about the Brians than the kids who are
coming back to college. College is a nice cushion between missionary
life and wherever they're going to go. Brian doesn't have a cushion
at all. We need to talk about him a little bit.

Helen—Adolescent Adjustments

I'd like to spend some time talking about my good friend Helen.
I actually don't know Helen, but her father came to see me the other
day with a serious problem about her. They were missionaries in
South America. They got reassigned to the home field and are living
in Wheaton. They moved to Wheaton when Helen was in the seventh grade. No problem. She made the transition. Things were
going well. But she entered ninth grade this year. All of a sudden,
we've got a whole bunch of missionary kid re-entry adjustment problems. Her father spilled those out to me for two hours. She comes
home from school, goes in her room, slams the door, stays there,
doesn't interact with the family. She cries a lot. When she comes
out, you don't know how she's going to be. She may be really hyper
and loving, or she may cry and get mad at everybody. Her grades
have gone down. She complains all the time that nobody likes her.
This is a serious missionary re-entry problem.

I did some research. In the city of Wheaton, we have 476 ninth
grade girls, and 471 of them are going through missionary re-entry
problems. You know what? There is a disease that sweeps the West
called adolescence. There are some physical signs. Somebody told
me the other day that his son grew five inches in five months. Look

at the bottom of the pants. If the pants fit, the kid's not an adolescent.

Regardless of how much we care, and regardless of how much time we spend, there is a missionary kid somewhere in the world this week who is going to get a pimple. And there's not a whole lot we can do about it. I'm not trying to make light of this, but I do think we need to tell ourselves that going through childhood, going through adolescence, and going through that terrible time when you leave adolescence and go into adulthood is a normal progression of life.

Do any of you remember that transition? I remember. I left the country farm and went off to college. I got terribly homesick and went home. That first morning I felt so great about getting home, and I got up and went in the bathroom and my toothbrush wasn't there. Do you remember the first time you went to the bathroom and your toothbrush wasn't there? It occurred to me, "You don't live here any more." There was terrible pain knowing that.

There are transitions in our lives, and we all go through them, and I have a notion that very few of us escape without some scars. I've got a blue spot in the middle of my forehead. I went out for track when I was in high school. I was so slow, the coach shot me with the starter pistol. We've all got some scars from growing up.

I think we need to be very concerned that we distinguish between the petty and the profound. Sometimes problems are very profound, and sometimes they're relatively common.

Helen's Father

The other person I want to talk about this week is Helen's father. I'm not sure we've got enough seminars about Helen's father. I find him a pretty typical parent. I've heard stories ever since I got here about how the poor child felt when the Daddy left her at the gate. Did you ever think about how the parents felt when they left her at the gate? I think we need to do some thinking about how parents feel.

I'm going to say something controversial here, but the more I'm around, the more I believe that I'm telling you the truth. I hear about good parents and indifferent parents. I'm not sure there are very many indifferent parents. There are parents who don't know how to handle their own emotions. There are parents who don't know how to handle their own anxieties. And there are parents who don't know how to handle their own challenges as parents. But I'm not going to call them indifferent. I'm just going to call them inexperienced and uneducated, and they need help.

Let me tell you something about being a parent. I had a college professor one time who said, "The choice to bring a child into the world is taking out a twenty-year mortgage on your life, your time, your emotions, and your money." I thought that made sense until my oldest became twenty-two. It occurred to me the professor didn't know what he was talking about. The decision to have a child is to take out a lifetime mortgage on all of your emotions. I have a notion there are very few parents in the world who don't go through a day when most of their emotional thought isn't spent on their children.

Those of you who are parents know what I'm talking about. I get most of my identity from my children. I get most of my emotional fulfillment from my children. And if things aren't right in my home, my life suffers. We need to bear this in mind when we raise other people's children. Those of us who have been in the position of dealing with other people's children are in an interesting position, almost a selfish one. We see kids in such fine ways that parents will never be able to see.

Parents can't see them the same way we do. I meet parents every day, and it seems they have two anxieties: (1) Is my child unique? and (2) Is my child normal?

"I dare you to tell me my child is not normal." I run into this every day.

"Hey, Mrs. Jones, your child has a little reading difficulty. We've got a reading class that's just right for him."

"What do you mean my kid's not normal? I don't want him in that dummy reading class." They'll fight you all the way. "Don't suggest to me that my child is not typical and normal."

We need to understand the anxiety that comes up. I think those of us who rear other people's children have been very derelict in our duties to tell parents what we know.

Do you know that as a parent I can never know how my own child relates to his peers? The only time I see him around peers is when they are at my house, and then he's different. The only way I can know how he relates to peers is if his teacher or dorm parent tells me. I never know how he relates to other adults.

Andy—No Longer British

I'd like to spend some time this week talking about my friend Andy. Andy grew up on a South American mission field. His parents are British. Andy went to missionary school, which means, whether you want to admit it or not, he basically went to an American school. He was basically taught by American teachers. He was basically taught to think the way Americans think.

Andy grew up thinking like an American. When it came time to go to college, he didn't bother with the A levels; he didn't bother with the O levels. He came to Wheaton. We're glad he did because he can kick a soccer ball farther and better than most people can. But he spent his four years in Wheaton, and went back to South America.

The tragedy is he'll never be British. One generation and his roots are gone. I think that's a tragedy. We need to talk about that.

Julie — Story Teller

I'd like to spend some time this week talking about my friend Julie. Julie doesn't have an exciting story. She's an MK from Africa and spent her early life listening to African preachers. Because she did, I ask her to give devotions in my class as often as I can get her. Her stories are always so funny. Let me tell you one of the stories that Julie told us in class the other day.

It seems there's one branch growing out of the side of a mountain, thousands and thousands of feet above the rock below. Here an eagle came and built her nest. She laid her two eggs, and two little birds hatched. She sat on them, and she nurtured them, and she cared for them so gently. She would go and get them food and bring it back to the nest. These little birds grew and grew, and they were happy. It was a nice family. The birds loved their mother so much, and she loved her children. Then one day she flew down and sat on the branch and ushered each of the little birds out of the nest. She grabbed that nest in her beak and she started swirling her head, and she tore that nest into a thousand pieces. It fell all the way down thousands of feet to the rock below. The little birds sat there and looked at her and said, "Mom, have you gone crazy?"

Pretty soon she edged over to one of those little birds and started nudging him with her wing. He said, "Wait a minute. This is uncomfortable."

She nudged him a little more. "Mom, you're cramping me here."

She nudged him again. "Mom! Mom!"

In a moment he fell off that branch and went tumbling down the face of the mountain, thousands of feet to the rock below and to sure death. He closed his eyes and thought, "Why did she do this?" And he hated his mother with a passion he'd never known before. He waited and he waited, and right before he thought he was going to hit, he felt something under him very soft and gentle. He opened his eyes, and it was his mother's wing, lifting him back to the branch.

Then she did it with the other bird. She did it over and over again until both of them could fly.

You want some Scripture for that story? Deuteronomy is the book, as best as I can tell, for third-culture kids. These people had been away from home for awhile. They were getting ready to come back. They anticipated re-entry problems, so the leader sat down and gave them a whole list of re-entry suggestions. In the thirty-second chapter he tells them, "Like an eagle that stirs up its nest and hovers over its young, that spreads its wings to catch them and carries them on its pinions, the Lord alone will lead you."

There comes a time when we're going to have to stir the nest. But the one thing we can make sure our children know is that before they hit the rock, their hope is the nail-scarred hand of the resurrected Lord which will reach out and grab them.

2

MK: A Person in Communities

Ron Cline
World Radio Missionary Fellowship

I have with me a box that reminds me of myself. I'm fairly strong, secure and solid. A lot of me is closed to other people. A lot of me I don't want you to see. Sometimes it's really hard to get inside me and know what I think and how I feel. Sometimes it's really hard for me to be open and honest. This box probably represents each of us. Here we are, a whole bunch of boxes. We need a realistic view of ourselves.

Being Open about Ourselves

Isn't it a little frightening to come to a conference full of experts? Some of you are very threatened by that. You're sure your question is a dumb question. There's no way you're going to ask that question. There are some things you violently disagree with that the expert is saying, but you're so threatened you can't respond to them. You look around and say, "Man, their school is bigger and better. He's got a bigger title, more education."

Others of us feel like experts. We're not here to learn anything. We're here to answer questions. We have come with a whole bagful of answers. All we need is the right question. And if it doesn't come up, we'll make our answer fit whatever question happens to come. We have ceased to be learners. We strut around with a superiority complex and look for those people who are terribly threatened and bless them with a little bit of fellowship.

What MKs in your community need are people who are honest and open. People who don't have all the answers. They need to interact with adults who are willing to say, "I don't know. I don't have that answer, but I'll help you find it." or "That's a real problem for me, too."

14

I've spoken at a lot of your school chapels. When I ask for testimonies, it's always the kids who respond, never the teachers. However, no one, not even the kids, ever seems willing to share their spiritual problems. I've never heard a teacher stand up in school and say, "Would you pray for me? I'm not making it spiritually. I have trouble reading my Bible. I have trouble keeping Quiet Time. I don't share my faith. I haven't foamed at the mouth to testify to anybody for years." So, when kids have those thoughts, they feel like there's something wrong with them. They feel like they're sick, so they won't admit their weaknesses either. We teach them well, not by what we say, but by what we do.

What we need to realize is that we're all just pilgrims on a journey. We adults just happen to be a few years ahead of the kids. We need to be good guides.

Maybe this is a good time for you to think about what you have to offer MKs. What do you bring to their community? Phoniness? Rightness? Perfection? Or the example of a growing adult, learning from his mistakes, and trusting God.

Maybe this is the time to ask a dumb question. And when you've asked it, you're going to find a lot of people who say, "Hey, thank you. That's the question I had, too."

You can be honest. You can be helpful if you're willing to work at it, but sometimes we're so threatened or so proud that we give our kids total phoniness. We need to be open about who we are.

Being Open about Our Mission

Let's talk about mission or purpose. Why are you involved with MKs? Because you're called to? Nothing else you could do? Somebody had to do it? It was a way to stay in the city?

I think sometimes we get into a situation because we have taken the easiest track. Even in missions, we sometimes lose sight of our purpose. We need to be honest about this.

We have a lot of world citizens we call MKs who are trying to figure out what to do with their lives. They're looking for people who have found life. There you are. How are you doing? Bored? If you're not going to spend time with them as a caring person, who is? What is your purpose? What's your mission? What are you doing?

Be sober

Paul told Timothy, "Timothy, you've got to be aware of four things: First, in everything be sober." I think we've lost that skill. That doesn't mean not to smile and not to have fun. That means to be aware of what's going on around you. Why? Peter tells us in I Peter 5:8, "Be sober because the devil, your adversary, is seeking whom he can devour." Do you think you're doing the kind of job the devil would want you to stop doing?

See what you're doing for the kingdom. Do the MKs see a person who is on guard against the devil, who is concerned about sin in his own life, not in somebody else's? We don't need any more of those guys in referee shirts going around blowing the whistle on other Christians.

MKs are sick and tired of inconsistency. We don't need compromise. We need commitment.

Endure hardship

Then Paul told Timothy, "Endure hardship." I think we've lost that skill, too. We've stepped aside from that. "I'll serve you Lord, but I want to be comfortable. My classroom has to be comfortable; my school has to be comfortable; my home has to be comfortable." We are more committed to comfort than we are to service. We don't know what hardship is. I'm making generalizations, but most of us aren't involved in hardship.

Do the work of an evangelist

Then Paul said to that young man, "You have to do the work of an evangelist. I know you haven't been trained to be a great evangelist, but that's your purpose."

What kind of models are we in that area? I was a youth minister in the good old Campus Crusade days. We used to have this habit of taking young people down to the beach to witness. It was great. I sat on the blanket, and had the kids go out and hand out tracts. I got a great tan that way, but never thought about it as far as being an example, until later.

There are parts of me that really do not want to be opened. I've learned what I like and what I don't like about ministry. I've learned what I want to do and don't want to do. I've kind of defined my own life. I'm not a great deal different down here than I was in the States. God says, "I want you to be available and be used." I want to be available. Sure, I'll sponsor kids going out and handing out tracts. But I don't want to do it. I don't want to go out and sleep on the ground, eat rice and fried bananas, cope with mosquitoes and bugs. But Paul says, "Do the work of an evangelist. Be willing to do those things that aren't easy to do."

Fulfill your ministry

Then Paul said, and this is a tough one, "Fulfill your ministry." Don't quit doing what you're called to do. Most of our mission organizations have a disease in them called "Climb the Ladder." We take somebody who is doing a good job and move them up on the ladder until they are out of their place of ministry. We're really good at taking a guy who knows nothing about administration and putting him in administration and then criticizing him when he doesn't do a good job. Then he gets discouraged and somebody comes along and offers him another job and he takes it. He leaves the mission and we say, "What's wrong with that guy? He's lost his faith." He was doing what he came to our mission to do, but we wouldn't let him.

We don't go out and find administrators because we get threatened by them. It's our fault. We don't want outsiders coming in and telling us what to do. It's a family business. We own it. So we promote people inside who can't do a good job and who can't fulfill their ministry. Then they make decisions that keep us from fulfilling our ministry, and we get really mad at them, but it's not their fault.

You've got to figure out what your mission is. Why are you doing what you're doing? Communicate it to those people. Let them know what you're involved in. Bring that as a contribution to your community.

Being Open in Our View of MKs

I want you to open your life in one other area, too, and that is your view of MKs. Some say that MKs are disadvantaged. Poor, poor kids. I'm not knocking people who believe that, because they've probably known those kinds of kids.

The best thing that ever happened to my life was coming to the mission field. I remember when we told our friends that we were taking our three kids, ages ten, twelve, and fifteen, out of public school and moving down to South America. They told us our kids would hate us forever, and we would ruin them. I want to tell you, it's the best thing we ever did for our family.

I remember when three missionary kids committed suicide in the same year. It sent ripples. "We've got to do something Our kids are really in trouble!" But that same year seven thousand kids of the same age in the United States committed suicide. I didn't hear anybody talking about that. Four hundred thousand attempted suicides that same year!

We can't get locked into the box that says that MKs are disadvantaged. At the same time, we can't afford to lean back and say, "Haven't we done a good job?" MKs are MKs. They're kids. They're people. Some are disadvantaged. Some are advantaged. The world's changing. Countries are changing. The MKs are changing. We, hopefully, are changing.

When we talk about missionaries and MKs in community, I want you to realize that that MK is in your community for a reason. If your community has an MK it will never be the same. I believe a community with an MK in it is blessed of God, whether that MK is disadvantaged or advantaged.

Now, may I ask you a very personal question? What are you giving to that MK? When you leave this conference, what will you take with you that will make you a blessing to the MK? What will you give to his life? What will you bring to your community? A person who says, "I have arrived. I am the way I am, and I'll always be this way. Don't try to change me. I'm right. My mission is right"? Is that what they're going to get? Or are they going to get a person learning, searching and trusting God. Are they going to find a person who knows why he's where he is? A person who regardless of what happens is going to fulfill his ministry? A person who is going to do the work of an evangelist? A person who will show them how to share their faith, not tell them how to share it? A person who will take them out and show them that he's not just a teacher in a classroom but an ambassador of Jesus Christ?

Are you going to go back with your little folder full of notes and sit back and say, "Ask me any question. I've got the answer"? Or are you going to go back and look at those MKs and say, "These are individuals, creations of God, people put in my pathway by design. We are a God-designed community."

There were some areas of my life that were painful to open. You're going to find the same thing. The first time you say to a kid, "I'm sorry. I was wrong," or, "You may be right. I may be wrong," it will be hard. But boy does it feel good when it finally gets done.

My life is kind of like my hand. When I say to God, "Fill me," and I'm hanging onto everything that's mine, there's no way he can. But when I open it and say, "Fill me," he's got a little room to work.

I really believe the most important people in all of missions are the people working with MKs, because MKs are the next generation of missions. They are the people who understand.

The world is closing off so rapidly. Sixty-six percent of the world is closed to any missionary activity at this point, and by the year 2000, eighty percent of the world will be absolutely closed to any kind of missionary activity. We've got a big job to do, folks, and I believe we have maybe one or two generations left to do it. Our resources sit in your classroom, and live in your dorm. All those MKs need are people who are authentic, real people who understand the calling of God and who treat them with a degree of dignity.

3

Abram, the First Missionary

Alfredo Smith
Pastor, Christian and Missionary Alliance Church, Quito, Ecuador

Whenever I go to the States, they ask me, "Are you British?" When I'm in England, they ask me, "Are you French?" When I've been in Canada, they've asked "What part of the world are you from?" And in Argentina they call me "El Inglés." I know what it is to be a man in the middle. When it comes to national constituencies, I'm not a national. When it comes to missionary staff, I'm not a missionary. So I think I can quite understand what you're dealing with. We served in Argentina for many years, then in Peru, and now in Ecuador. But the Lord is good, and he has accompanied us throughout all these years.

I'd like to share with you Genesis 12:1 and 4. "Now the Lord had said unto Abram, Get thee out of thy country, and from thy kindred, and from thy father's house, unto a land that I will shew thee . . . . So Abram departed as the Lord had spoken unto him."

When we speak about Abram, we are speaking of what I'd like to call the first missionary. He was called of God to fulfill a divine task, to raise a new race for God. He was living at ease in Ur of the Chaldees. It was a promising home town. Ur was a densely populated, very active seaport city. Its holy shrines were a center of great attraction to the peoples of the ancient East. People would go to Ur on account of the famous graveyards that were under the protection of the goddess of the night. It had a tremendous library.

Separation from Place

Abram was seventy-five years old—no time to move around really. Then the Lord stepped on the scene to tell Abram, "Get thee out of thy country." While everybody was thronging to Ur, the Lord

20

was telling Abram, "Get out. Leave. I have a special task for you." Abram was deprived of what I'd like to call his own little corner.

In exchange for this stability, we read in Genesis 20:13 that he became a wanderer. What a word! A wanderer. Always on the road, never at home. We read in Acts 7:5, "And he gave him none inheritance in it, no, not so much as to set his foot on." Think about it—leaving his little place, his comforts, to start a pilgrim's life. The removal of a basic need was decreed by God. That which becomes essential to what we would call a normal life was abruptly plucked out of the life of Abram. He was in for a very hard time. He had to learn spiritual principles. This natural element was taken out of his life in order to have him assimilate new elements that were super-natural. This is something that applies to us. We're working for the Lord under the pressures that are proper for our situation.

I ponder when we read in Hebrews 11:9, "By faith he sojourned in the land of promise, as in a strange country, dwelling in tabernacles with Isaac and Jacob, the heirs with him of the same promise." So this principle of depriving him of his little corner was applied to Isaac and to Jacob. They had to go uphill, learning what it meant to live as pilgrims. That's hard. There's only one instance in which I believe there was a little bit of self-pity. It was at an early stage. When he states, "When the Lord made me go as a wanderer," I believe there's a little bit of self-pity behind that statement. But then he starts growing and building his character on a knowledge of God. These spiritual principles are instilled in his heart in such a way that he becomes a joyous man of faith in spite of not having his little corner.

Separation from Family

In Genesis 12 we find he had to leave his kindred and father's house—not only his country and his little corner. Now here we come to a very touchy point.

Abram had to leave his kindred and his family, his father's house. Remember that many a time family ties can hinder God's purposes for our lives, if we are men called from God. Remember Saint Paul's statement in I Corinthians 7:33? "But he that is married careth for the things that are of the world." Have you ever pondered that text? I am married, and fortunately, my wife cares for the things that are from above. But Paul was wise and enlightened by the Holy Spirit in such a measure that he could state, "He that is married, careth for the things that are of the world, how he may please his wife." There you have a clear instance in which blood links can really affect our calling from God. They can deviate our loyalties. Remember Matthew 10:37? "He that loveth father or mother more than me is not worthy of me, and he that loveth son or daughter more than me, is not worthy of me." Deviation of loyalties. "Abram, I have a special task for you. Leave your kindred. Leave you father's house. We have a special job to carry out."

When we come to this point, we now have someone else stepping on the scene, an MK—Lot. Abram is a missionary. He was called. What was Lot doing there? I don't know. He simply attached himself to Uncle Abram, and off he went. I've been pondering this. We could probably point out six or seven instances regarding Lot. With one exception, they are all negative. It has to do mainly with attitudes. A lack of spiritual insight characterizes that first MK.

In Genesis 13:10, when the parting moment approaches, the attitude that characterizes Lot is one of selfishness. I remember looking from the heights of the midlands in Israel right down to the Valley of Jordan. It's a beautiful sight—green pastures. What a contrast with the surrounding dry lands! And there we have Lot looking down from the heights, and he saw that fertile land. He didn't adopt the right attitude. He should have said, "Abram, you are the oldest; you have to choose." No sir, not Lot. He was in for business. So he chose, as the Scripture says, the plain of Jordan.

Then we find this first MK of ours starting to pitch his tents near Sodom, disregarding the evilness of the men of Sodom.

In chapter 18, we find him sitting at the very gate of that evil city of Sodom. This is interesting. We find Abram sitting at the gateway of his tent, while Lot is sitting at the gate of Sodom. Isn't that eloquent? Something was going wrong, drastically wrong with this MK of ours.

Next he raises a very questionable family. I don't know where he met his wife, but you know the story of Lot's wife—a divided heart; children that were reared in a very questionable way. What a family! Sons-in-law that were unbelievers and could not be persuaded of the coming judgment of God. Daughters that in an emergency will resort to incest in order to obtain a descendancy. Something was going wrong with this MK.

There is only one instance in the whole Scripture we find a positive thing mentioned about Lot. That's in II Peter 2 where we are told that he was a righteous soul, and he was in anguish seeing the evilness of those that were surrounding him. It's the only positive thing we find about Lot.

I believe Lot is in heaven. I believe he's a saved man. I believe that Abram managed to instill some of the spiritual principles that he had discovered in his relationship with God. Lot's attitudes were wrong attitudes that brought a lot of sorrow and tears.

Truth can be taught, but not necessarily assimilated. Spiritual principles are not learned merely by the mind. How we need to understand this! They have to be grasped and assimilated by the spirit.

I've been in many conferences and I've heard, for example, Dr. Graham speaking about the need of having Spirit-filled evangelists. I've been in seminars, and I've heard about the need of having Spirit-filled pastors, but allow me to say that we badly need Spirit-filled teachers, men that understand the moving and the promptings of the Spirit. We need people not only with the capacity that modern sciences are giving us, but people that will have the charismas of the Holy Spirit—discernment, knowledge, wisdom, faith. These elements are essential to reach those who are under our care. Many of our kids are perfectly familiar with all that has to do with biblical vocabulary. Are they familiar with the Holy Spirit? Can they realize the prompting of the Spirit? In other words, are they coming along in the knowledge of the Almighty? That's our task.

Separation many times can be the best thing possible. I always remember a missionary colleague of ours, who has already gone to the presence of the Lord. He had just come for his first term to Argentina, so I asked him, "Myron, don't you miss your family?" He looked at me with that big smile that was so characteristic of him, and said, "You know, Alfred, we are at the right distance." Ten thousand miles away! I didn't grasp it at that moment. Then I realized what he meant. He was fully persuaded there was a God-given task weighing on his shoulders, and family ties could hinder him. God is at work. He's building a character for eternity, and consequently he has to break blood links. That's painful.

Acting with Wisdom from Above

Third and final point, we are told in verse 4 that Abram departed as the Lord had spoken to him. Have you ever pondered how he departed? We are told how he departed in Hebrews 11:8. "He left without knowing whither he went." That's the way the Bible puts it.

The Lord put Abram to the test. "Now, Abram, I want you to rely fully on my guidance. You'll have to renounce your common sense, your experience, all that is filed and stored in your mind, and simply trust in me." That's faith.

This is one of the most difficult things for us to do. It's very hard for me to deny what I know, what I believe, and what I feel. There's such a thing as a wisdom from above that has to be placed in us by the Holy Spirit of God. When we have to trade the wisdom with which we were born that's from below—earthly, sinful, and devilish—for the wisdom that comes from above—pure, gentle, and full of God's truths—a tremendous operation has to take place. It's going to be painful.

When Abram received God's gift of wisdom from above, he marched to Mount Moriah. It's interesting how God puts it. "Take now thy son, thine only son Isaac, whom thou lovest, and get thee into the land of Moriah; and offer him there for a burnt-offering." There he went with Isaac, hand in hand, ready to offer him on the altar of sacrifice. Abram was graduating with honors. He was yielding; he was surrendering the very blessing for which he had waited for twenty-five years.

He had reached that point of maturity in which he could sacrifice his son. He had reached the point in which self-pity was left behind. Speak about traumas, they were completely overcome. Abram was walking hand in hand with God. He could even surrender his own son with a great hymn of victory. He knew in whom he was trusting.

I do ask God that he may help us to understand these spiritual principles. They're essential. Spiritual wisdom instilled by the Holy Spirit through Spirit-filled teachers will do the supernatural work that our kids are needing. Let us not lean on technical resources, good as they may be. We have to discover that spiritual dimension in which God is at work. And that's where the old-fashioned times of prayer and fasting come in. That's when we realize that we have to discover new dimensions in our spiritual warfare. Pray. And now the second responsibility of ours, instill spiritual principles. It's the work of the Holy Spirit of God. May the Lord bless.

4

MK: A Person in Process

Ruth Van Reken
SIM International

When I went to the ICMK in Manila, the most important discovery I made was that I was still an MK. One of the things we have to realize is that the MK process does not stop when you graduate from college or when you get off the mission rolls.

I think, because I left the field even before high school, I tried to put my MK experience in the background. It was like my life was disconnected. I was in America doing my thing. I had put aside my Africa experience. You can't explain what you've been.

I adjusted well in high school, but when it was time for my daughter to go to high school, I suddenly was faced with an enormous number of feelings that were coming from some place I had no remembrance of. I prayed, "Lord, I have to go somewhere with these feelings. I have to sort them out." I was thirty-nine at the time. That's a long time to have carried around a lot of baggage you don't even know about. God had been working in my life, but when I came to this particular crisis point, I started to sort out my emotions by writing my parents what I really felt.

Some people have said, "Why didn't you write cheerier letters? You should spice the book up and make it happier."

I said, "I already wrote the letters about the happy part. It was this other part I could never write at the time."

Two years ago I got a questionnaire for the first ICMK asking me, as a missionary parent, to fill out information on education and so forth. I found myself feeling very angry. I thought, "What about me?" Everything I saw was about the kids in grammar school, high school and college. I thought, "We didn't have that. And here I am thirty-nine years old, all by myself, sitting in Africa trying to figure out what all this meant in my life."

I'm Not Alone

I wrote Dave Pollock a letter asking if I was the only one who ever experienced this long-term process of having to sort out my separations. (I was really a model MK. I never rebelled. I did everything the way we were supposed to. My family was a model family. My parents have six kids who all love Jesus. I thought I was fine.) Dave nicely wrote me back and said he'd look at my letters. I sent them to him, and he told me that I wasn't alone. He invited me to come to the last ICMK and share my experiences.

On the plane over there, I was terrified. I thought, "I may find out in truth I'm the biggest turkey that ever was an MK. I'm not just talking now to people who don't know about it. I'm talking to people who have been there. And if they haven't been there, and I'm the only one, my aloneness is going to be compounded forever." It was scary. But praise God, many others of you told me you understood. I found out that I hadn't *been* an MK, but that I *am* an MK. The *kid* part of it is what's tricky, because I'm not a kid any more. The grey hair is showing. My kids think I'm over the hill.

Now I've had the chance to examine what it is to be an adult MK. The first thing is that I am not alone. The TCK definition was helpful originally in letting me know that people are identifying a group of us that are anomalies of some sort. But there is something about it that still leaves me alone. That's when you say that I take from my host culture, which for me was Africa, and that I take from my home culture, which was America, and that somehow I make up my own culture. My experiences are totally different than everybody else's. So if I'm the one taking from here and there and putting it together, I still don't belong anywhere.

Last year I was asked to be with a group of people that were MKs married to "OKs." I said, "What do you mean they're an OK and I'm an MK?"

They said, "OK means ordinary kid." Right off the bat I felt that same old feeling of not being OK.

A researcher wanted to examine what our TCKness had done to our marriages. Somebody said, "My mother had a maid, so it was hard for me to do my housework." All of us nodded.

We were talking about these things and everybody there understood. The researcher kept saying, "No. That's your missionary part. What about the other country?"

Every one of us was from a different country, and yet every one of us understood each other. We didn't have to explain. We were laughing and crying. Things were clicking.

Finally I said, "You know what? It's the missionary part that's the third culture."

I thought, "I do belong somewhere."

I don't care what you want to call it; you can define it all you want. But I do belong. I belong to whatever this culture is that is missions. It's mine. That's my roots. I belong to every MK here and they belong to me, and when we talk, we know it. We don't have to explain it.

It's been good for me to realize I belong to such a big group. I am not strange. I am not alone. I belong somewhere.

Differences between MKs and Other TCKs

The other thing you have to figure out is TCK. I identify with other people who have lived overseas faster than I do with someone who has always lived in the States. But we have some very definite differences.

Where we lived is considered a hardship post for somebody in the embassy community. They're there for two years so their career can be advanced. The whole point is that they're representing another culture. They try to be British, Dutch, whatever they are, in that other culture. That's their job. We go to live. We are supposed to amalgamate.

The business community is different than both of us. That community totally invests. When we had a coup, a friend who is a businessman said, "You guys can leave. You have no investment here. My whole life, all my savings, everything is in this business. I don't have the choice of picking up and leaving." We have differences.

There's one basic, absolute, underlying difference. We have an underlying principle of faith that affects our decisions and is the reason for our decisions. That makes an enormous difference in both positive and negative ways. In the positive, I thank God for the fact that my life is tied to eternity. There is tremendous strength in that for me. I have seen life in the raw.

When Scripture says, "Feed the hungry," I don't have to try to decide if I am supposed to join my hands across mid-America and give to Farmer's Aid. There's somebody at my door who needs a cup of rice. It's simple. They need rice. The Bible says, "Feed them." Give them rice. It says, "Clothe the poor." And there are people who have nothing, absolutely nothing. It says, "Don't store up for yourselves treasures on earth." That's easy in Africa. We have just taken a leave of absence, and I am struggling with how to live as an American Christian where choices are not so well defined.

The greatest thing about being an MK is seeing that God is universal. The body of Christ is big. I like traveling; I like being a world citizen; but what really makes me happy is seeing that Jesus works.

An African brother, Willy Brown, said to me, "Sister, I'm so poor here, but I've got so much treasure there." A month later he was dead, and I thought, "Yes, Jesus, he's living where his treasure is. Thank you Jesus."

I see people in my church who are from all walks of life, who are from all races, from all countries, and I say, "Jesus, you are big, and we understand each other in you." That's the greatest joy of being an MK for me, knowing that part of God.

How Dare We Mind the Pain?

Because there is so much good about the missionary experience, and because we've done it for Christ, where do we go with our pain? That is the thing that has caused me the most struggle. When I went to boarding school at age six, it wasn't easy for me. But what missionaries were told then (and I hope they're not being told now), was, "Don't let your kids know how bad it makes you feel." So parents, in the name of being helpful (and I have good parents) encouraged us and cheered us up and did everything to let us know how happy we were going to be, how much fun it would be.

You thought, "Wow, this is really neat." You got all excited about going on the airplane. Then the moment came to step on the airplane and something else hit you. You were about to say good-bye to your mother and father. There was a reality that wasn't there before. But they were not crying. They were waving good-bye. I remember getting on the airplane and my heart was breaking.

Since one of the criticisms people give me is that this is only me, I'm going to read you two other quotes. I have lots of quotes, but I won't read them all today.

One person said, "The first few years I would miss my parents desperately for days to weeks. Eventually I became numb and inured."

Maybe a lot of you will relate to this one:

I don't remember much from my early years at school. I blocked most of it out, I suspect. However a vivid early memory is one of my parents driving down the long road away from the school while I stood watching their car disappearing in the distance. I was only five and I thought I would never see them again, and I didn't know why they were leaving me. There must have been some adults around, but I don't remember any of them. I only remember the loss and the terrible feeling of being alone. Today my heart breaks for that little boy, I wish I could go back and hold him and tell him how much I love him and that I care. I can't write this without crying. It still hurts so. The man may be forty-five, but the little boy is still there and still frightened.

No one has ever helped him deal with that loss. I think the greatest problem is, if the loss is for Jesus' sake, as we know it is, how in God's name can we mind? When God asks you something and you love him (and I did love him as a little girl, and I believe you did, too) how dare you mind?

Of course, I cried the first night, and people cheered me up again and told me about the picnics and all the wonderful things we were going to have. If it's so much fun, guess whose fault it is that you feel so alone? It's yours. We begin to develop a tremendous denial of our feelings. We don't understand that it's OK with God that we have pain.

Another experience that I never dealt with until I wrote these letters was when my folks left for four years. I know that's not going on now, but there are a lot of us who went through that. One girl wrote:

> The next separation was at age thirteen for me and six-
> teen for my sister. I can see this as yesterday, a video before
> me. Such love for Christ, yet such pain. I remember that
> dreading the separations, I had already started chewing my
> nails. Determined to quit, I chewed on my hankie, often wet
> with tears. That day at Grandma's we watched the truck disap-
> pear around the corner, waving frantically at our parents, my
> sister and I on the curb, then on the street, then the other side
> of the street, tears flowing like waterfalls, hearts simply break-
> ing in pieces. It seemed like death had grabbed our hearts,
> trying to snuff them out. My poor hankie got chewed so
> severely that there were holes in it. It was a time of loneliness I
> had never experienced. Relatives really didn't meet our needs,
> for we were shamed for tears of loneliness and pain.

That's happened to a lot of us. How could we mind when it was done for Jesus?

Jesus Cares about the Pain

I want to tell you a little of what Jesus has done for me regarding that. In the first place, I'm not saying we can't have separation. I think Scripture does not give us the option to say that categorically. There's a paradox in Scripture which I learned from Gene Garrick. Gene helped me realize that there are some things that we can't resolve fully. The Bible teaches us we are responsible for families. The Bible also says there is cost. I can't sort out here theologically all the whys and wherefores of how it works. But I'll tell you what Christ did for me.

During our first term in Liberia, my uncle was a missionary there, too. He had a motorcycle accident. My cousin was also on the motorcycle. His head had been crushed, and it was obvious that he was not going to make it. While I stayed at the hospital, my husband went home. He called me in the morning and told me our house had been robbed. I had a real hard time with God right at that moment. "Here we've come to serve you, and where have you gone?" I had a tremendous crisis of faith. Yet I was hanging onto God, because some part of me knew that God was still in control, and he was the answer.

As I sat at the hospital, I said, "God, I can't make any sense out of this. Life has turned into a major disaster." I had never had a loss experience like that, that I had acknowledged. For the first time, there was permission to say that there was pain, because when you see an accident, everyone can acknowledge that you have a right to grieve. The community was allowing me to grieve. I was allowing myself to grieve, because it was legitimate. It wasn't anybody's fault. I wasn't going to be blaming anybody if I said, "This is painful."

I've never had the same experience of Christ lifting me up. He took me to the Garden, and he sat me beside him there. He said, "Ruth, I know what it is not to want the Father's will. I understand. Sometimes the Father's will is very painful, but there's an answer. It's 'nevertheless.' Because I understand the pain, I am going to carry you. I'm not going to push you."

It was a great comfort to me that I was allowed to grieve and that he would hold me in my grief. Because of that, the Lord has given me permission to go back and grieve for my other losses. When I do that, people say I'm being negative. I'm not being negative. I just need to go back and tell the Lord that it hurt. In doing that, there are tears, but somehow tears are very cleansing.

The thing that has grieved me the most in the last two years is that some people feel very nervous if we talk about pain. It's like we're denying God. I think the reason I couldn't talk about it for so long was because I was afraid if I discussed the pain that God had allowed, I would lose Him, so I didn't want to take the risk of exposing the pain even to myself.

People have said things to me like, "Ninety-five percent of the kids did fine. Why don't you talk about them?" Or "It's a battle, Ruth. There are going to be people wounded in battle. You just have to expect it." Or "If you'd had a different personality . . . "

That's probably true. I'm sure some of you did not experience what I did. But each time I feel alone, and each time I think, "I should just quit," Jesus reminds me of a wonderful chapter about percentages in Luke. First, there were ninety-nine sheep that made it and one that didn't. He said, "Go look for the one." It was only one percent, but it was worth looking for. After that, there is a story about ten coins. One of them got lost. That's only ten percent, but he said, "Go look until you find."

After that, there's a fifty-percent story. There was a prodigal son who decided he wanted to go try life on his own. The father let him go and never blamed himself. He didn't try to figure out what happened, but he waited for that son to come back. And as we know, the son did return.

The other part of the story is that someone was vexed that so much attention was given to the returning son. "I made it on my own. Why bother about him?"

We have to be careful. A lot of us who are here "made it," but God says there are a lot of people who aren't here, who got hurt in the process. He says, "Don't forget them." We need to find them. They belong to us, too. Their roots are in our system. Their hurts were often in our system. The Lord says, "You are to be my hands and arms and look for them."

I want to share a letter I got from one of them and comment as I read.

Dear Ruth,

I don't think I know you, but what I'm about to tell you seems too personal to call you Mrs. Van Reken. I am sure you would be surprised if you could have seen my reaction to your letter *[the questionnaire I sent out for the seminar]*. Great sobs. Although I left the host country twenty-seven years ago, the pain from the separation and the loss I felt, not of leaving the country, but of being separated from my family, and what I thought they felt. *[Many MKs thought their parents didn't care because they never saw them cry. This resulted in great pain for them. The healing has come when they can find out as adults that it mattered to their parents that they were left. That is a story revealed in questionnaire after questionnaire. Be very careful to let your children know it matters to you, too. They may have to go, but they need to know that it matters to you.]*

My strongest feeling over the years has been one of neglect. No one really cared. *[That's not true in terms of absolute fact. Those were her feelings.]* They never cared how I felt about being an MK, because I certainly did not ask to be one. No one ever told me that my feelings of anger were normal and not bad. There wasn't something wrong with me because of how I felt. Fortunately I sought professional help four years ago, and I can now at least admit to people that I am an MK. I had often told people my parents were in government service. I suspect I am not typical for an MK. *[All kinds of MKs, by the way, kept saying "I'm the only one probably," and then wrote lines which at least ten thousand other people have probably felt.]* I also suspect there are a number of others like me, and all of us are, perhaps, a little ashamed to admit how difficult some parts of life have been for us.

Somehow, being an MK was supposed to be special, but it never worked for me. I can't say how many of my personal problems arise from being an MK, how many come from other things. *[She had some other severe losses that she mentions.]* What I learned, even before I became an adult, was that you really couldn't count on other people to be there if you needed them. Consequently, it didn't pay to form close, warm, caring relationships, because somewhere along the line, the other person would be gone, leaving me alone, hurt, and grieving. *[Thirty-nine percent of the people who wrote back from that survey say specifically that they have trouble with close relationships because of the fear of loss.]*

I think if someone had been open with me, able to accept my questions about why I felt so rotten if God wanted my parents to do what they did, instead of speaking platitudes about God taking care of everything if you trust him, I might have found an easier way through these years. *[That's community— accepting.]* Instead I ended up feeling I had been conned and fed a line that was an easy way out for adults around me. I suspect I had questions they couldn't really answer. So easy—my pain was a consequence of my failure to trust in God. But I didn't know how to trust any more than I was. And the pain didn't go away.

So the second lesson I learned was, you can't count on God, either. And that is a very lonely place, and it's a scary place to be, not able to trust people or to trust God.

It has only been after several years of therapy that I am able to talk of my feelings as I have here. I have finally been able to return to church and to a relationship with Jesus Christ. I tried other things — alcohol, marijuana, tranquilizers — but none of them stopped the pain. At last the pain is only a sometime thing. *[That's important, too. In a process, we are always growing. I haven't arrived yet. I wish I had, but that's life.]* There are still areas of my life that I don't want to share with my parents. I don't want to see the hurt in their eyes. I truly believe they did the best they could and what they thought was right.

My parents' mission now has a ministry to MKs, and I hope that helps ease the transition for them. I certainly have never felt totally American, even today, and often as a teenager and young adult felt I really didn't belong anywhere. People say to me, "How neat to live in another culture and see a different life firsthand." I wanted a big white house with an attic for all my outgrown toys, and a place to go that would be safe and welcoming.

The theme of your conference, "MKs Nurtured by Communities," struck me as perhaps a key. I never felt nurtured — not at the boarding school, not at the hostel where I lived with other MKs through my first two years of high school. I felt orphaned and abandoned. I was seven years old when my parents began their missionary service. Maybe that's an important age. Certainly my sister who was younger has not had the same feelings of hurt, loss, and anger. *[She had a brother who was killed, so she says she doesn't know how he would have come out, but he had struggled greatly at the time of his death.]* I've written more than I planned, and hope my sharing my life with you will help you as you work with others. If you ask me what I would say, this is what I would say to people working with MKs:

Be accepting of their feelings, even, or especially, the bad ones, the difficult ones.

Don't answer questions with platitudes, especially the ones that can generate guilt so easily.

Give lots of love, hugs, caring gestures, special recognition when the going is rough, and extra attention.

Don't give up. It may take a long time, but we can come back to the family after a long absence, and we need to know you're waiting for us. *[Isn't that beautiful! Isn't that a challenge!]* During my adult years I often wrote my parents only once or twice a year, but they never stopped writing every week or so. They kept the line open so that when I was ready, I knew they were there just waiting for me. They welcomed me with open, loving arms.

Are we as a community ready to open our arms to those who have embarrassed us? To those who have given us a bad name?

Are you willing to be the arms of Jesus, to say, "We're willing to weep with you and accept the pain because of the fact that Jesus loves you."

It has been wonderful to listen to *The Messiah* this year. The very first words are "Comfort ye, comfort ye, my people." I've been struck anew with the fact that it's OK with Jesus to say there's pain because that's what redemption is all about. That's what resurrection is all about.

Jesus is the redeemer. He takes the very things in our lives that have been painful. He turns them into the things that bring glory to Him. He uses them in my life to reach other people, to love other people, to make me open to other people, because I understand that it's OK for them to hurt, too. I also understand that Jesus is a healer who brings something else to life when we are willing to accept His comfort and healing, that we might be more complete and more his children.

Father, I thank you for this conference. I thank you for everyone who cares. I thank you for everyone who has walked the same path that I have and who is in every way my brother and my sister. I thank you for our parents who have cared, and I pray, Lord, that we will not forget them also, for many of them have been hurt as they have watched their children suffer. They have wondered where your promises are, Lord, that you will return to them a hundredfold in this life that which they gave up for you.

Lord, may we be the instruments in bringing part of that hundredfold to them, and of restoring the hurts, and of reaching out to those who were wounded in the battle. Give us hearts of compassion and not judgment, Lord, and give us insights that we don't even know we need, that we might be useful to you in this work. In Jesus' name, Amen.

5

Counting the Cost
Reaping the Reward

In commemoration of the thirtieth anniversary of the martyrdom of Nate Saint, Jim Elliot, Pete Fleming, Roger Youderian, and Ed McCully, participants watched *Through Gates of Splendor* and listened to reports by people who were directly affected by the tragedy.

Kathy Saint Drown

I didn't want to come to this conference to tell you about the loss of my dad. I hesitated because I have lived quite a fishbowl existence. But I asked, "Do I really have the right to be selfish enough not to let you see that I'm real and human?" I experienced a loss and a hurt, but it was the kind of hurt that people know how to relate to. They know how to walk up to you and say something significant. But I'm concerned about that guy who's thinking, "Yeah, she had people put their arms around her. They understood her loss, but I'm sitting here wondering if my dad loves me as much as he loves his work." That's a sort of loss, too, and it causes pain and it causes hurt. I want to speak to those kinds of losses, the kind of losses that I think most MKs experience.

Peter and James had the audacity to say "Suffering is a privilege." Can you imagine? I can honestly look you in the eye, and say, "Suffering really is a privilege." I haven't always been able to say that with a smile on my face. There were many times when I said it that my teeth were clenched; my fist was too, sometimes, and my heart was breaking, because not only had I lost my dad, but I was also experiencing the pain of guilt that comes from having had wonderful examples all around me, and sometimes not measuring up.

There were times when I felt, "I just do not want to be in MAF." (MAF doesn't stand only for Mission Aviation Fellowship. It stands for Move Again, Friend.) That has been the trial of my life. But is that the kind of pain that you blurt out? Is that the kind of pain that is put up on a screen and brings tears to people's eyes? No. There are other pains that I know all of you have.

If James and Peter really said it is a privilege to suffer, then doesn't it seem logical that if we prevent people from experiencing the suffering that God allows, we might in actuality be thwarting the ministry of Christ in their lives? That's a question I ask myself and Ross as we raise our two MKs. Having experienced pain, I want so badly to spare them any hurt. I want to smooth the road for them, but I have to ask, "Is it right for me to prevent pain?" Certainly I don't want to promote it.

What are we to do? I think the answer is almost too simple. I think we're to come alongside those who are growing spiritually through pain, allow them to experience suffering, and to just say, "I'm here with you while you go through it."

There were many people who so lovingly and kindly met our needs in very practical ways after we lost dad. There were two people in particular who not only did practical things like taking the boys fishing and fixing things around the house for Mom, but included us in family vacations. This couple did even more than that for me. You know them as Dave and Kay Landers. I know them as Uncle Dave and Aunt Kay. They did something for me that you can do for other MKs. They seemed to say to me, "Kathy, we're here, and it's OK to hurt, not just over your dad's death. It's OK to hurt about anything. You're one of the bunch. You're normal. Just because you had an unusual experience doesn't make you any different." They didn't say this in words. They said it with their actions. "We know that you're going to face more pain ahead, living without a dad, and all the publicity. We're not going to try to prevent that pain in your life, but we're going to be there."

I remember one time when I returned from college. I came back here to Quito, and my mother got a phone call. She said, "Dave and Kay want to take you out to dinner."

I was so sure she meant the family; we always did so many things together. She said, "No, they just want to take you."

As I reflect back on what they would consider such a small gesture, I'm sure, I cannot thank them enough. They were saying to me, "Kathy, we really care about you. It has nothing whatsoever to do with how spiritual you are. We just care. We'll listen. You can fail in front of us. You can blow it. We know you don't inherit spirituality from anybody, much less your father."

And that is what I think we all need to do. Be there. Let those of us who are MKs expose our hearts to you. As Ruth said this morning, "Let us experience pain and hurt in front of you openly."

I trust that as an older MK (I'm almost thirty-eight), I now can speak to you on behalf of the young MKs. Help us see that we're normal. Help us to be transparent. Don't deny us the stage that we are at in our spiritual growth. Support us as we learn all about being Christlike through pain. Don't mold us into any predesigned shape, but let that wonderful creative God shape us into very unique and different individuals. That may even mean lowering your expectations for us. Finally, do what the pastor this morning said. I almost find it hard to say because it's a bit trite. Pray. Amazing how simple that word is and how many of us who are in ministry full time put that at the end of the list. It's not visible. It's not easy to do, and you don't get credit for it. Those are my goals in relating to MKs, and I trust they will be yours, too.

Rachel Saint

You have seen the part of the film of the men on the beach with the Auca Indians. I had been working with Dayuma, an escaped Auca Indian, on a jungle hacienda. When Marj saw that film, she said, "Bring Dayuma in to Quito, and we'll show her the film."

Dayuma almost crawled right through the screen. I remember physically holding her. She said, "I think that young woman on the beach is my younger sister." She couldn't be sure. She had fled ten years before. She hadn't had any word of her family since then.

She looked at the young man, and she named him. She missed. It was his brother.

She looked at the older women and said, "That's my Aunt Mintaka." If anybody doubted it, Aunt Mintaka had an earlobe that was eaten away by a jungle infection, and Dayuma knew all about it. There was only one Aunt Mintaka.

She listened to the story. She turned to me and said, "Where were those gift drops being made?" I told her. She knew the place. She knew the way in. Aucas were closer than they had ever been to civilization when they were where those gift drops were being made by my brother Nate.

Then she looked at me and said, "My family has killed your family." Nobody else believed it, but Dayuma knew her people.

They said it was a tragedy, but those pictures opened the way for Dayuma to take me back to her people. I had talked to her about it before. She had said, "There's no way. That's a vast jungle. How can I find my people? My people wander around. Besides, I don't know whether any of my family survived the attack that killed my father and my grandfather when I ran away. There's no way. But if you go and find my mother, you come back and tell me."

This film, bought with the price of blood, gave her the first hope she ever had of going back to her people to communicate the gospel which I had been able to teach her in her own language, and which she had latched onto because she had been searching since she was a little girl.

Including family in the work

I found out after Nate was killed that both Kathy and Steve (Phil was too small) had been briefed about what Father was going to do down on that beach. They had been taught about the Aucas' need for the gospel, how nobody had ever gone to them, and how Father, with his four friends whom the children also knew, was going to try to reach them.

If there's anything I can contribute to this congress, it's to beg you who are real parents, and you who are dorm parents, and you who are stand-ins, like Kay and Dave Landers were, to share your missionary work with your children.

This is what Nate and Marj had done, so we didn't have any big trauma at that point. We had a few later, but these little children took it in their stride that Father had gone to be with Jesus, because their parents had shared their missionary service. If you're a missionary on a foreign field, your children are part of that mission, and their prayers will reach the throne maybe faster than those of some of us who are older.

They also had briefed my parents, and so the trauma for my parents was less. They wanted the prayers of their parents, and they let them know. So when the word came, my parents had an idea of what had been going on and why.

Nobody briefed me except the Lord. The week before they went to the beach I was in Nate's house. There were Auca spears in that room. I looked at them. For five years I had been trying to get into that tribe. I said, "Lord, I'm ready for any sacrifice if you'll just reach these unreached Waorani Auca." Little did I know that before the week was out, God would ask of me the life of a precious brother that I had raised from the time he was little. I, too, had been prepared by the Lord. Preparation of children for life, I insist, is not just the school's responsibility.

Loving enemies

The day came when little Stevie was twelve years old, and he wanted to come out and live with Auntie Rachel for the summer and play with the Auca children. I did some tall thinking before I decided that the Aucas now had come to the point where I could say, "Yes, Stevie, you may come and live with me." It broke my heart to see him playing happily with the children of the killers.

One day they were playing with little toy spears, trying to see how many times they could spear a banana root as it went down the rapids. When they came back to the house, Stevie still had his little spear in his hand. He sat in the hammock and poked it at one of the teenage girls, and the place blew up.

They came to me and they said, "He poked his spear at Nyaeno." I suddenly realized that poking spears at people was "fightin' talk" among the Aucas. So I talked to them and simmered them down.

Then I called in Stevie and I told him what had happened, and he began to bawl. I told him, "I've explained to them. Just don't ever do it again. It's all right."

But he didn't stop crying, and I finally got a little provoked, and I said, "Now, Stevie, this has gone far enough. You've got to stop crying and tell the Lord you'll never do it again. They all know you didn't mean any harm."

He just sobbed and said, "But Auntie Rachel, now they'll think I don't love them."

Who taught him that? Auntie Rachel hadn't taught him that. His mother, who had lost her husband, raising those three children alone, had taught him to love his father's killers.

Kathy came out, too. She helped me while I finished the Gospel of Mark in the Auca language.

She came in one day and said, "Auntie Rachel, Dayuma's sister is telling me something. I can't get a clue."

I finally went out and asked, "Oba, what did you say?"

"I told her that my father was speared, too."

That was the first time I had seen Kathy react at all to the fact that her father had been speared. I said, "But Kathy, it was not only her father, it was her mother, too."

I ran a survey around that group, and with very few exceptions, all of the adults in the group had lost both father and mother to Auca spears, as well as grandfathers, uncles, and children. The world was upset by the death of five American missionaries. But that tribe, with their lack of the gospel, had reduced their own family group which Dayuma estimated at two hundred, to forty by actual count, in sixteen or eighteen years. Even a primitive Auca Indian could project that out and say, "If you hadn't come when you did, there would have been none of us left."

When we had the dedication of the Gospel of Mark, little Phil, who was the smallest and didn't remember his father, came with the others. Phil sat on Kimo's lap. Kimo was our pastor, one of the killers. And when Kimo, with the printed Gospel in front of him, stumbled on a scripture verse, little Phil prompted him because he could read those letters and get it close enough for Kimo to finish the verse. This is a miracle — children taught to love their enemies.

Aucas today

We tried to teach the Aucas that, too. We succeeded. It was recently my privilege for the thirtieth anniversary to take three of those former killers to Guayaquil to give their testimony before one thousand Christians standing in the civic center, and to hear Aucas tell how the grace of God had saved them. Gikita, the lead killer said, "I used to be hateful, I did. I used to be hot. But God has healed my heart."

Minkayi said, "The blood of Jesus has washed my heart, and it's clean."

Kimo said, "I see by your faces that you know how to pray. God has told me to go to that last remaining group of savage Aucas. It's dangerous work. But if you all pray, and God spares my life, I'd like to come back to Guayaquil and tell you what God has done."

It was a great privilege to be the interpreter on that occasion. Now lest you think that everything is lovely and the job is done, just let me end by saying that we have new circumstances, new problems. We need new prayers. Many of my own faithful prayer partners have gone home to glory. The Aucas today need your prayers. As you teach MKs, I hope you'll teach them that Aucas out there need their help, too. I find myself praying that I, at this point, will have the same faith to believe that God can meet the problems of the Auca today, as I had the faith to believe that he could take care of the spearing problem of thirty years ago.

The Aucas now have trails to the outside. Outsiders' sins are being channeled in. Liquor is being bought. Oil money is rampant. The younger people think that they have to buy liquor and drink it to be civilized. The school that started out being taught by Christians now has two out of three teachers who are rank leftists.

They ran a campaign to get rid of me, lying about me. My first reaction was just that, a reaction. Before that I would have said any Auca would give his life to save mine. But things had changed.

I went back home and I prayed about it. One verse of Scripture just jumped out of my Bible: "And I will gladly spend and be spent for you though the more abundantly I love you, the less I be loved." It has been there for my seventy-three years and a lot longer. I said, "Who am I to fuss? Paul had problems like this."

Gikita, the lead killer of Palm Beach, was the oldest living man then, and he's still the oldest living man thirty years later. He walked four hours over the trail to get to the Sunday morning service. He said, "I say, how can we throw out Nimu? She is one of us, one of our in-group. She has come and brought us the gospel." The Aucas simmered down.

It takes guts

I have one more thing to say. As you teach missionary kids, young or old, in college or out, tell them that Rachel Saint said, "It takes guts to be a missionary these days." When I went to the field it was an honor to be a missionary. Everybody looked up to you in your home church and your community. Of course the neighbors said you should stay home and take care of mother, but it was an honor and a privilege. Today nobody wants you on the mission field. Nobody in the national country thinks that you have any right changing the cultures. Your fellow students think you're crazy to throw away your life like this. It takes guts.

Others Who Were Affected

Dave Landers: I'm Uncle Dave. My contact with Ecuador came through the Saints. Nate married my cousin Marj and eventually took her off to South America. Their California visits during furlough were spent at our family home. One of those visits took place while I was a sophomore at the University of California, Berkeley. I was able to accompany Nate to several off-campus meetings, where he would share about his missionary experience and work and about being a Christian. I'm a people watcher, and frankly I was very much impressed with Nate's solid and honest commitment to God. He was truly a keen Christian. I had been floundering in my own life direction, and God used that particular visit to straighten me out.

I remember vividly, while I was crossing the San Francisco Bay Bridge, hearing the first radio news about Nate's death in the Oriente of Ecuador. To say I was deeply moved is a gross understatement. Two years later my cousin Marj, on behalf of HCJB, invited Kay and me to work in Ecuador. I have been here now close to twenty-eight years as a dorm parent and teacher and have had the opportunity to minister to third culture young people and be ministered to by them. It's been super.

Carol Cathro: When I was growing up in New Zealand we used to listen to radio HCJB. I remember sitting by a crackly radio and listening to Aunt Bea, who used to come in from Quito, Ecuador. We used to write letters to Aunt Bea and sit by our radio receiver and listen for our letters to be read over the radio. It was a real thrill to sit there as little kids and hear our names being spoken from a radio in South America. I'm not sure at that time I knew where South America was, but it was an awful long ways away. You could tell that by the noise on the radio.

It was through listening to HCJB that we first heard of the death of the five guys. I remember our family being shocked. We hurt for those people. I remember praying for those in the families that had been left.

It was two years after their deaths that Marj Saint and Nancy Wilnor came to New Zealand. Because of our listening to HCJB, we went to hear these women speak. As a ten-year-old, I was so impressed by Marj Saint. The fact that she would stay in Ecuador and minister to the people who had killed her husband seemed unbelievable to me. They showed us slides. We saw many of the pictures that you saw on the screen tonight. They also showed us a slide of a patient lying in a hospital bed with a radio lying above the bed. Marj told us that through the HCJB broadcast these patients could hear of the love of Jesus and be saved. As clearly as if it was yesterday, I can remember walking out from that meeting, looking at my mother, and saying, "One day I am going to be a nurse and work at that hospital."

Never underestimate the power of the Holy Spirit in the lives of children. I was ten, and I really believe I had my first call to Ecuador. There were many times in those following years when I didn't think I'd ever make it, but God was faithful. He had chosen me, and I came. As you minister to kids all over the world, I pray that you'll be honest with them, be open with them, be sincere, because that's what shows, and that's what will help them to model themselves after people of God.

John Brawand: After I had served with the United States Army in the Second World War, I enrolled at Wheaton College in January of 1947, just forty years ago this month. While there I knew Nate Saint, Jim Elliot and Ed McCully. Nate Saint and I were in the same English class. I can still see him there in blue jeans. In those days, very few fellows wore blue jeans. He was a very friendly, personable fellow. Then later I was in class with Jim Elliot. Jim was a tremendous fellow, too. He graduated with highest honors. He was collegiate middleweight wrestling champion for the state of Illinois. He was a gifted preacher. I still recall his speaking in chapel.

Ed McCully was an outstanding track and football athlete. I recall that he entered the William Randolph Hearst National Oratorical contest and won. He went back to Wheaton College and delivered that winning oration in Pearce Chapel. I have never forgotten it. It was a tremendous speech. I say this just to show you the calibre of those fellows.

I didn't know the other two, but I am sure that they were equally fine Christian fellows. Their deaths had a tremendous effect on our lives. As I recall, January 9, 1956, news of their deaths was on the front page of the *Chicago Tribune*. I was deeply stirred as I read that story. Somehow Alice and I felt in our hearts that we should join Wycliffe Bible Translators. We went to Guatemala, and it was our privilege to serve among the Rabinal Achi Indians for twelve years. We're now in our twenty-eighth year with Wycliffe.

Praise God from whom all blessings flow. God does indeed move in mysterious ways his wonders to preform. Rachel didn't know it, but that verse that she mentioned also had a tremendous impact on our lives. "I will very gladly spend and be spent for you, though the more abundantly I love you the less I be loved."

Alice Brawand: I'd like to remind us that the story goes on and on, as we pass the torch down to our MKs and they serve the Lord wherever God calls them.

I was very moved when I realized that the martyrdom that called us into full-time missionary service with Wycliffe happened in the very country where God called our precious daughter. She's now here with her dear husband and their son, the child of an MK. Now that I'm a little older, I can see a little bit of God's perfect plan from one generation to the other, on to the other. God never makes a mistake.

6

Jesus as an MK

Alfredo Smith
Pastor, Christian and Missionary Alliance Church, Quito

Our text is Hebrews 5:7-9:

> Who in the days of his flesh, when he had offered up prayers and supplications with strong crying and tears unto him that was able to save him from death, and was heard in that he feared; Though he were a son, yet learned he obedience by the things which he suffered; And being made perfect, he became the author of eternal salvation unto all them that obey him.

One of my colleagues made a statement from the pulpit. "I have already settled with the Lord all that has to do with my life. I'm ready to die for my faith." It was only a matter of a few years after he made that statement that his authority in the church he was pastoring was challenged. It was a big church. He was quite an important man, but when he had to face the challenging of his authority, he "cracked up," as the Americans say. He just couldn't take it. Sometimes we don't realize what it means to be on the altar ready for the sacrifice.

Service and nobility of purpose seem to be vanishing rapidly in our days. Heroism and that old spirit of adventure for great causes are giving way to mercantilism. High ideals and spiritual goals are viewed as nonsense. In our Christian circles we are being surrounded by these pressures, and we're not very much aware of it. Concepts of sacrifice are giving way to a sense of professionalism and well-being. I think about our children. Have you noticed the trend? Those of us who are already graying remember a few decades ago, when kids would think in terms of history, literature, geography. No more. Now our young folks think in terms of computers and commercialized mathematics. They are thinking in terms of gain. And all this indicates a drift. Missionary endeavor is being threatened by this. A sense of well-being seems to be governing the choosing of careers.

The call of the Christian faith to carry the cross seems to be alien to our generation.

Suffering Loss of Identity

I'd like to glance into the life of the greatest MK that ever set his foot in this world, Jesus Christ. Think about a few little things we have in Isaiah 53 about the Lord Jesus Christ. In verse 2, he had to face an identity crisis. "For he shall grow up before him as a tender plant, and as a root out of dry ground: he hath no form nor comeliness; and when we shall see him, there is no beauty that we should desire him." Completely lost in the crowd.

Especially in the secular world, people seem to brag about their backgrounds. They have their coats of arms and so forth. When we go to the Bible, we realize that there's no such thing as identity when a man is not in Christ. Remember Acts 19 when those exorcists were dealing with that demonized man? And the evil spirit answered them, "Jesus I know, and Paul I know; but who are ye?" Speak about identity—what identity? "Who are ye?"

Remember in Matthew 7 those great people who had been performing tremendous miracles, healing the sick, and prophesying? The Lord says, "And I will profess unto them, I never knew you." Again the same thing. An identity? What identity? "Who are you speaking about? You have no identity. You have no name, no father, no lineage, no nothing."

Jude 13 says they are "wandering stars, to whom is reserved the blackness of darkness forever." Erratic stars doomed to an anonymity forever!

We have one who has an identity, and what an identity! In Isaiah 9:6 we have a cluster of names that identify him fully. We have no name, but he has names. The first one in Isaiah 9:6 is Wonderful, to be admired. He's called Counsellor, to be admired in his wisdom, The Mighty God, to be admired in power, The Everlasting Father, to be admired in immortality, The Prince of Peace, to be admired in equity and harmony. He is the Morning Star. He is the Lord of Lords. He is the King of Kings. Speak about identity—he has identity. And yet in Isaiah 53:2, we find he is losing his identity. "He hath no form, no comeliness; and when we shall see him, there is no beauty that we shall desire him."

Suffering Loss of Personal Dignity

Secondly, in Isaiah 53:3, he has his personal dignity trodden down. We are told that "He is despised and rejected of men; a man of sorrows, and acquainted with grief: and we hid as it were our faces from him; he was despised, and we esteemed him not."

Could we take that? I seem to sense that behind that dedication of ours to the missionary endeavor, there's a subtle spirit behind the scene that is saying, "Well, I'll take this job if I have some kind of guarantees."

The Lord didn't have guarantees. He was born in a manger. He died on a cross. The cross was reserved for the worst — violators, robbers, thieves, and traitors. Speak about exposure to traumas!

Verse 5: "But he was wounded for our transgressions, he was bruised for our iniquities: the chastisement of our peace was upon him, and with his stripes we are healed." Wounded, chastised, bruised, and not because of himself, because of others. I must confess that whenever I have to pay for something I have not taken or take the blame for things I have not done, I find it very difficult. Jesus was paying a price for things he had not done.

The tremendous thing in all of this is that he had the power to avert these circumstances. "Thinkest thou, that I cannot now pray to my father, and he shall presently give me more than twelve legions of angels?" When I think of a single angel killing 185,000 Assyrian soldiers, I just can't help wondering what twelve legions of angels could do. He had those angels at hand, but he did not call on them.

Verse 8: "He was taken from prison and from judgement." All legal rights denied. Rome at fault. Jewry at fault. These great institutions were of no avail whatsoever.

Verse 9: "And he made his grave with the wicked." Who would you like to be with when your hour of parting comes? Your wife? Your children? Your loved ones? "He made his grave with the wicked." Thieves. Violators. Traitors.

When I come to verse 10, I'm just astonished. "Yet, it pleased the Lord to bruise him." Is the Lord sadistic? When I get to this scripture, and I look at the generation to which I belong, I feel as if there's a tremendous gap. Are we where we should be?

"It pleased the Lord." Men's redemption is painful. We are born in pain, and we die in pain. We must never forget it. We have devised a whole system that says we are always supposed to smile.

Everything has to be positive. Nobody can cry. We are living in deep hypocrisy.

Sin is tragic; life is solemn; death is devastating. And when we speak about Jesus, we are speaking of a man of sorrows, acquainted with grief. He wasn't pessimistic, but he was in the mortar. Under those grinding stones, he was being crushed. He wasn't pessimistic; he was realistic.

I think about Hebrews 10:7, "Then said I, Lo I come to do thy will, O God." And verse from 5, "But a body thou hast prepared me." The Lord received a body prepared in eternity for one single purpose—to suffer and die.

We read in Hebrews 5:7 that his praying was with strong crying and tears. Have you been in those prayer meetings where there are coffee and cookies? I've been to many of them. I don't find the Lord in a prayer meeting like that. I find the Lord in the mortar being crushed. His prayer was a soul-draining experience.

He feared. We are told by those who know Greek that this word *fear* has to do with cautiousness, awareness. He knew about the powers with which he was dealing. He feared.

Suffering in Order to Learn

And he had to suffer to learn. Verse 8: "Though he were a Son, yet learned he obedience by the things which he suffered." It's a fact, there's no conversion without suffering. There's no knowledge of God without suffering, and there are no efficient servers without suffering. It's part and parcel of our program.

Many times I've dealt with people who want to know the Word of God and know Christ, but who are not willing to open up in that critical experience we call repentance and conversion. Suffering— there's no such thing as salvation without suffering.

Let me wind up with the encounter between the Lord Jesus Christ and Peter in Matthew 16:22-23. The Lord is sharing with Peter the fact that he's going to suffer. He's going to be rejected, despised, and killed. We read in Matthew 16:22-23, "Then Peter took him apart and began to rebuke him saying, Be it far from thee, Lord: this shall not be unto thee." That's our response. That's the mind pattern that is governing our life and our conduct. "No sir, no suffering for me."

What was the Lord's response? "Get thee behind me, Satan." What a statement! "Get thee behind me, Satan: thou art an offense to me: for thou savourest not the things that be of God, but those that be of men." Have you ever tried to maintain status quo, prevent those bitter experiences, and evade all that has to do with pain and sacrifice? "Now no chastening for the present seemeth to be joyous, but grievous: nevertheless afterward it yieldeth the peaceable fruit of righteousness unto them which are exercised thereby." I think these words are alien to our present ways of thought.

Human nature in Jesus was at its highest expression, yet it had to be crushed. Flesh and blood cannot inherit the kingdom of God, nor does corruption inherit incorruption.

Painful discipline is life. To shun discipline is death. That's Solomon's teaching.

7

The MK's Advantage: Three Cultural Contexts

Ted Ward
Trinity Evangelical Divinity School

I hold a very positive view of intercultural experience as foundational in the development of fulfilled personhood in the modern complex world. Consequently I view the MK growing up experience as very positive and very valuable, in comparison with the experiences available to their cousins who are stuck back home.

Advantages of Growing Up Overseas

Growing up overseas represents at least three kinds of head start: First of all, one of the most predictably difficult problems in every Western society is the problem of coping with interpersonal relations. More jobs are lost, more people drop out of school, and more people seek psychiatric help over that issue than any other. I submit that the intercultural experience carries with it the kind of flexibility and the kind of rolling shift that allows well-balanced young people to get a head start in coping with interpersonal relations.

Beyond that, the overseas experience provides a concrete awareness of what the world is really like. Much tension and conflict in this world arise out of an ethnocentrism that is totally unaware of, and unconcerned about the rest of the world.

There's another kind of head start, which is so dear even to many American missionaries. That is, "What will my kid do to make money in life?" There is an absolutely overwhelming trend toward an increased demand for internationally experienced young people to go into international careers, if they have broken the language barrier. International experience and multilingual capability are more valuable than degrees in today's marketplace.

Scars from Growing Up Interculturally

Growing up leaves damage. Growing up leaves scars and it leaves hurts. Let us not be maudlin about this. Life is like that. But there is nothing wrong with us getting together to talk about those scars and about ways to offset them. I refer to what I think of as the two key scars predictable in the intercultural growing up experience, whether missionary or other. I think they are inevitable, and to some extent they are painful and damaging, but so is life in any society.

Disorientation

I refer to the scars that are left by disorientation. There's a lot more that we can do about that than we're currently doing. Take a moment to conceptualize an experience that you and I could have together. We are both together in a large city. Neither one of us knows the city. You stand on one street corner, and out of sight of you I stand on another street corner. We each decide that we will just stand on those street corners for four hours and see how we feel at the end of the experience. Everyone walking by is a stranger, with the exception of one friend who walks by your street corner every thirty minutes and winks. At the end of those four hours, I will be miserable; you will be comfortable. What made the difference? The reorienting experience that comes from involvement with other people, no matter how slight, through which we reaffirm our identity and reestablish our sense of who we are, and even, if you please, where we are.

We can do far more than we do today if we really come to understand what disorientation is and take more seriously the need for periodic orientation. When we were travelling a lot with our small children we would wake up in a strange place and say, "Where is it today?" We knew jolly well our kids were going through a whole day of wondering where they were and why. Periodically we would sit at breakfast in a strange place and say "Let's go through this. Here's where we are. Here's why we're here. And here's what's likely to happen." So far as my wife and I could make out, our kids never really suffered much from disorientation.

Racism

The other scar that is perhaps inevitable is the scar left by racism. Much that we do as expatriates is ultimately ethnocentric and racist. We need to name it. We need to work on it because it's part of the sinful tendency of human beings.

These scars are worth the price, but we should do what we can to reduce them and to reduce their negative effects.

Our Goals for MKs

However, we're after something far more significant than simply the reduction of scars. We're after the power in life that comes from disciplined resourcefulness. I will give you three to one any time on a missionary kid over anybody else in terms of disciplined resourcefulness. American kids today sometimes don't even know how to change the tire on a car.

Another of the great positives we're after is culture-learning skills themselves—the capacity to learn culture. Just as surely as you can learn how to do other things in life, you can learn how to learn culture. That's a tremendously powerful skill. It makes a person much more able to cope with the range and variety of situations that life holds.

The third of these great bottom lines is flexibility—the capacity to identify with the great figures of history who were able to move internationally and interculturally and influence the world. Our young people have this benefit.

Negative Stereotype

There's a terrible negative stereotype that has developed around this whole business of growing up overseas. It is partly because of the misunderstandings of some of our novelists, James Michener, for example.

James Michener doesn't understand the missionary community, and he understands MKs even less. His book *Hawaii* is deeply resented by the native Hawaiian population. I happen to know this because I am involved with them. His premises are that the missionaries did damage, and he makes even more of the fact that the MKs went bad. One of the first great missionary activities, sponsored by a church in the United States, Park Street Church, the Sandwich Island Mission, began as a response to a very practical request from a ship captain's cabin boy who had jumped ship in Boston in the 1820's. Cold and disheveled, he found himself in the basement of Park Street Church. The people of Park Street became interested in him, and through him became interested in his people. They sent out several waves of missionaries.

These missionaries took their families. That is an old American habit. Once they got the kids out there and they started growing up, they got kind of a second thought that said, "Oh, oh. What are we supposed to do now?"

You know what they did? That first group of Sandwich Island missionaries built a high school for their kids in order that they would have social interaction with nationals — there's a word! They quickly reduced the Hawaiian language to print, put together enough Hawaiian language books to get a number of other kids ready, and within the fourth year of that mission, in an illiterate society, they had some native kids ready to go with their kids to the first MK school ever established overseas. That school stands today in Maui and is called Lahai High School. It is a public high school and has been in continuous use since it was first built. The MKs didn't go home to Boston, because the families thought that the very people that Jesus Christ had called them to were worthy to be lived with and worthy to be included in the humanity that is the whole of God's universe.

Many of those MKs made the dreadful mistake, according to Michener, of intermarrying with Hawaiians. Do you know that the great first families of Hawaii have missionary grandmothers? Yes, indeed, the MKs became involved in commerce, in shipping, and in agriculture. They transformed that group of islands. They haven't done half the damage that the tourists have done, and the Hawaiians know it. They entered into society as the co-parents of the emerging culture in the turbulent overflowing nature of human change.

I think even as Michener misunderstood missionaries, sometimes missionaries misunderstand culture. I've heard the word *culture* used in some very strange ways, mostly used as a static term to mean a kind of a thing that sits there. Look folks, culture, whatever else it is, is not static. Competent people in the world move with competency among shifting patterns of culture. The issue is not trading in one culture for another, like you'd trade in one car for another. It's not a thing. It's not sitting over here and then sitting over there. It's being human and moving in and out from here to there, and being able to competently function in varieties of situations. Human cultures are not to be abandoned so that we can become third culture or anything else. Our cultures always profit from being expanded and blended. Would that the missionary community could accept the validity of expanding and blending their cultural ways with others.

Cultural Contexts of the MK

The MK is especially benefited by having three cultural contexts. Let me point out that I am talking about three cultural contexts, not three cultures.

Now the originator of the term *TCK*, third-culture kid, was a colleague of mine in the same department. We worked together for many years. In her original paper when she coined the term, Ruth Useem was talking technically, about the cultural variables that are not definable in terms of *ours* and *theirs*. She was talking about the dynamic of that which is different because people from outside settings residing in an inside setting do not take their primary identities ultimately from either, but they take it from the commonness that they have with others who are doing the same thing. Now we have popularized and seriously misused the term *TCK*.

This technical vocabulary may indeed have drawn us off the trail, but let me take a moment to deal with it. The first culture is one's own native base culture. Second culture is the culture into which one is knowingly adapting by virtue of being somewhere else—though in many cases rejecting particulars of that culture, nevertheless living willingly within it. The third culture, and this was Ruth's insight, is that different little culture that's created by a whole bunch of people who are doing that second culture thing. When the whole bunch of people are doing it at the same place, same time, same space, they create their own community. She had in her original paper no reference to anything like what we would call the MK.

You may be interested in knowing that she and her husband, John, spent most of their lives in Asia studying the overseas intellectual communities of Western European and American people in the sciences and technology. Those transplanted technologists and scientists in Singapore would seek their friendships not among Singaporeans, but among others from Germany, from Sweden, from Denmark, from Brazil—who were also technologists in Singapore. That was what she described as the third culture. I think we've seriously misused that term, and in the process, we've created a static term. Then we've given it some standard values, and made generalizations about it which lead us to the wrong questions.

What are some of the wrong questions? They are nonsense questions. "Is it OK to be an MK?" "What are the problems of being an MK?" They're dumb questions, but they're the questions that a static view of culture leads you to.

Then you get preoccupied by rootlessness. Oh, come on. Millions of people in the world are rootless. Don't get paranoid about thirty thousand kids when ten percent of them are rootless.

Separation. Look, if you want to see separation do some real damage, go back to your home churches and take a look at the kids of the divorced Christians. They've got a separation problem.

It used to be that the American family moved once every seven years. It's down to once every 2.7 years. You're from a society in the West of moving people. That's what urbanization is all about. All the kids of Americans are moving too much. In fact, missionary families typically move less than American families move.

First cultural context

We should understand the cultural contexts in which we operate. First of all, every one of us operates as a child of some kind of community. For the MK, this is as a child of the missionary community. What is the culture base culture, or starting place culture, of that child? It's the culture of that base community. Now if you believe that the starting place culture of the missionary community of Quito, Ecuador, is exactly like the starting place community of white middle class Americans of Toledo, Ohio, you are wrong. It is not exactly like it. It has a lot in common, however.

Think of it in terms of communities, not cultures. We all can understand *community*. The goal of that community is to produce an aware citizen with a sense of identity. But, by golly, we've got a problem. Many people in American society today, and to some extent in some of the other Western societies, are not learning enough about the distinctives of their own culture. They don't even know what they are. If I were to ask the typical man on the street in the United States, "Name five values that are distinctly American values," he would give me a very quick one-word response, and it would be "Huh?"

One of the problems that the overseas family has is the need to really comprehend at a fairly specific level what makes that base culture coherent. For example, we need to understand and be ready to help our children understand what our rituals are. You've got to come to grips with the rituals that give your culture texture. What is the Fourth of July? What does it stand for? Why are there holidays on Presidents' birthdays? What was the Thanksgiving idea? Where did it come from? Why do Americans celebrate Christmas differently? Why is Christmas so mercantile? We need to understand that that's part of our value system.

Now you say, "Well, I'm not proud of part of it." Well, that's all right. That's known as maturity, and people in any culture can come to a level of maturity that says, "Not everything about the way we are is glorious, but we understand it. We appreciate it. We value it, and sometimes we even defend it irrationally." That's part of a base culture.

What is it that we pick out to pass on to our kids? It's possible as a critical Christian to come to grips with the positive side of our culture and our history. What are the events that have shaped us?

A crucial issue in missionary kid education at this conference is the willy-nilly application of American propositions, American values, American notions, without even understanding what they are.

We must be in our society in order to help develop the culture of that society. That's part of the business of the gospel. And the business of the gospel involves Americans in being in the American culture, and it involves Canadians in being in the Canadian culture, etc.

In every society you can find some values that have their origin in some biblical premise. There's one that I find very interesting to reflect on. Americans tend to derive their identity and draw their self awareness from a contemporary "who we are," rather than, as true in many other Western societies, "who our family has been and where our family came from."

"We know who we are." Americans like to say that. It's important we know who we are—not who we were, but who we are. There are Europeans who like to keep pointing back and saying, "Here is where we came from." They look back. Americans always look in the present, and that is strangely a Christian view. The core of that idea is that we are, as Christians, what we are because of what God is doing.

So there is a strangely Christian root in that cultural value. But in a fallen world it goes sour. It turns into a kind of repression of our consciousness of our worldly heritage, the denial of our past. It turns into an excessive preoccupation with "me" and "here and now" and "my thing." Very American. We even turn around and coin pejorative language to desecrate some aspects of our cultural past, especially our willingness to blend. I'm particularly sensitive to some language like "half-breeds." In rejecting our unique sources, white Americans have formed a whites-only thing they call a melting pot. They became very self-satisfied over time with that "now" identity and in the process became racist. Good news and bad news.

The core of many of our value ideas are sound, if we can help our kids peel them apart like the banana and find the good inside. We could do our culture a great deal of good if we knew how to do that, and if our kids were doing that competently. Americans overseas are typically more concerned about those things than their cousins in the States. That's good. That's a benefit of a first, or base culture, context of the overseas growing-up experience.

Second cultural context

But there's a second cultural context, and this gets even better, because our second context is carved out of being friendly, voluntary participants in a host society. The goal of this process is becoming sojourners who learn. In any culture, we gain perspective on our own base culture as we see it from outside. Even a tourist can get this. The only problem is that tourists too often don't know how to do it.

The biblical models that are outstanding to me are: Abraham in the Old Testament, who through his sojourning experience came to know what God was; Jesus as a focal person in the whole of God's plan, a tremendous example of a sojourner; and of course, Paul, who was the nomad of nomads. The great model missionary, don't forget, was an itinerant. These people were conforming to culture, but being transformed by that which is greater than culture, and using cultural experience as part of that transforming process. It really does work.

One of the greatest goals that I see in experiencing culture two is perspective. That perspective helps us see our own base culture more clearly. In the context of the culture of the other, we have the experience that is unavailable to the fish. The fish is never asked in as a consultant on how it feels to live in the water, for the simple reason that the fish has absolutely no way of comparing living in the water with living anywhere else. One reason that Americans can't tell you what it means to be American is because so few Americans have ever experienced it from a second cultural context.

I find more MKs understanding the nature of American society than people who are raised wholly within it. Would that we could get that message across to parents. Paranoid parents have got to be helped.

They think they've hurt their kids. They think God goofed. They think somehow God has to separately call everybody at every minute at every hour to every altitude, latitude, longitude, and attitude. That has got to be a lot of bunk. Our God has called all of us into this world to be ministering persons in cultures. Whether I'm locked into some goshawful subcultural context in North America or some other in the world, what's the difference?

Notice the frequency of the word *survive* in reference to other culture living. "How do you survive?" Every time you hear the word *survive*, replace it with the word *thrive*. It will at least rhyme, and it sure does a lot for your spirits. Words like *culture shock*—good grief! Talk about popularization of some bad research! Culture shock—for the most part largely exaggerated poop! Incompetency, yes, but incompetency comes in all kinds of forms. Don't talk about survival kits. Anxieties for parents and children are far less if we use our second cultural context to better understand our first cultural context.

Third cultural context

The beauty of growing up overseas is that there is a third cultural context that can come into clarity, and is actually looking forward into what I see as twenty-first century Christianity. Today's Christian has the possibility of being called by God into service as a member of the international community of the body of Christ. *World Christians*, a common, almost cliche term, really has a lot of substance underneath it. The problem is we haven't gotten serious enough to get together to talk about what we mean by *world Christian*. There are a lot of things that could happen if we were to take a conference such as this and just focus it on some of the distinctively evident characteristics of being a world Christian in the missionary kid community. Let me just give you a couple of examples.

Characteristics of the MK as World Christian

A characteristic of the overseas missionary child is this extended family that even goes beyond blood lines. You've experienced it—Uncle Pete, Aunt Mary. It is representative of a third cultural context that I think we haven't named properly, partly because we've been hung up on this notion of the third culture. We live in a culture of the Christian in the internationalizing world, and that is a cultural context. Think about it.

Another characteristic is the loyalty to Christian values, even above the social pragmatics that we deal with in any society. There are characteristics of the internationalizing community of Christ that may very well, in this increasingly shrunken world, become characteristic of the church in general in the twenty-first century. One of my propositions is that the missionary kid of the nineties will be the prototype of the Christian of the twenty-first century.

We're coming to understand now that people don't just move out of their nation in order to get education and then come back home again. Missionaries haven't quite come to grips with this. You may be interested in knowing that the term *brain drain* has almost disappeared from professional literature, because we know very well that people who get higher levels of education generally don't go home again in the old-fashioned, maudlin sense of going back to their own community and their own people. They become part of an internationalizing set of people.

Many of the people in this room originally may have gone into missions for a three- to five-year stint. However, now, even if they were to leave missions, they would probably remain in some kind of international community in some kind of international work. This is a very important transformation occurring in modern societies.

The Peace Corps veterans who were so strongly in demand in the late sixties and seventies have largely disappeared because of the de-emphasis of the present administration of the Peace Corps. Therefore, the MK community once again may become the popular source for internationalists to take responsibilities overseas.

It's an old notion and is probably true in historical perspective, that the missionary community has produced a number of illustrious people. That was back in the days when the missionary community was raising up kids who had their eyes on the national or international societies in which they were serving. Today's paranoia among American parents overseas causes them to fix their eyes and their kids' eyes back home on re-entry without asking the question, "Why re-entry?"

Now I think the reason for re-entry is valid. Don't get me wrong. But why should we predispose ourselves to direct our kids? I heard at least one of the MKs on this platform say, "Don't push us into your models of our future." And I heard a mature, experienced, MK mother of MKs say a very comparable thing about her childhood.

There's a vacuum in the world that can be filled by MKs who are freed by their parents and by their communities to be whatever it is that God wants them to be. More important, the world Christian as a cultural model can be founded and grounded in Romans 12. I would strongly urge you to understand all that Romans 12 holds. We see the image there of the living sacrifice, yes. But then we see the qualitative descriptions: not egocentric; not ethnocentric; transformed, not conformed; and committed to a body-life concept of community.

Now I ask you, "Could that be characteristic of the community of Christianity on the world scene in the twenty-first century?" I believe so. The problem is that missions are in transformation. Mission strategies are changing. Missionary deployment patterns are changing. The nature of the missionary vocation is changing. A career missionary today does not get buried in China at age forty-seven under great mounds of Chinese soil. He gets buried at age forty-seven at a North American mission office desk under mounds of paper. That's called a career missionary.

The problem is that we see the cracks. We see the flaws. We see the lumps. We see the bumps. We're aware that there are real problems in the missionary community today. Let's back off and look at the bigger picture as God sees it. Sure there are problems. Sure there are cracks; there are flaws; there are bumps; there are lumps — but God is in control. God is doing his thing. The trouble is that it is our stubbornness sometimes that insists on being able to see exactly every step. Again, that is a value that is very Western. "I gotta know where I'm goin' or I don't wanna go."

The sad fact is that most North American churches, your supporting churches, are painfully monocultural. They need your help to get out of that. Wow! What thirty thousand MKs could do by just going home, to help transform those churches that just don't see anything beyond the back fence.

Once upon a time a very marvelously learned man who was culturally flexible, who knew how to work in that second context and third context, said these words, "Though I am free and belong to no man [sounds like an American, doesn't it?], I make myself willingly a slave to everybody [begin to know who I'm reading from?] to win as many as possible. To the Jews I became like a Jew to win the Jews. To those who were under the law I became like one under the law. To those not having the law I became one not having the law, so as to win them. To the weak I became weak, to win the weak." Here's the ultimate statement of third context flexibility: "I have become all things to all men, so that by all possible means I might save some. I do this for the sake of the gospel, so that I may share in its blessings." That's what I mean — the MK as the prototype of the twenty-first century Christian.

Would that we would integrate our Christianity in the whole of our experience. Being a Christian, you see, ultimately is a cultural matter, not just an other-worldly experience. We need to synchronize our families, our communities, and our schools to this culture three, the context of Christian internationalism.

Role of the Schools

Schools need to carefully articulate what it is that parents are and who it is that parents are becoming. There is no excuse for any institution allegedly serving missions making things harder for missionaries or for missions.

I do know my repertoire of horror stories pretty well. I could elect to use this hour to do some muckraking, but I promised myself and the good Lord I wouldn't. But he allowed me to put this one line in here, and I'm going to read it so I won't embellish it:

"I am sick of the stories of last minute teachers arriving in a state of real shock within cultural enclaves attempting to teach children and projecting racist overtones. MKs deserve better. Missionaries must demand better. And God's name must be better served." We need to put "Christianity" in our Christian schools in something other than the required course in Bible.

Defaults in "Christian" education

There are four defaults in much that passes as Christian education that a truly Christian education would come to grips with.

Ethnocentrism is a kind of learning impairment. If you knew you were doing something to kids that was making it harder for them to read, you would do something about it. Ethnocentrism makes it harder for kids to learn from the environments in which they live. It's a learning impairment. We ought to recognize it and put our heads together on it.

Fear of the unknown produces hostility and anger and a lot of other nonglorifying fruits, that are hardly fruits of the Spirit. We need to help people with fear.

Superiority syndrome is the notion that might makes right, and our way is the best way. These are not the ways of Christ. Simply helping children see how much better they are than their fellows and their siblings is no way to encourage them. Most of us as parents know that, but we turn around and do that in our communities.

Social distance and isolation. We can learn to accept culture as an encounter, a walk of life, dynamic and changing; to learn and to teach the skills of learning culture; and not to fret over whether or not I want my kid to marry a national. That's a secondary question, and if it becomes a haunting obsession early in life, it guarantees all negative outcomes. Furthermore, it guarantees to put children into schooling environments that are totally abstracted from the societies in which you're living. The Christian community, in addition to our schools, needs to be helped to develop the support structures that make real this community of Christ. The Christian community needs to acknowledge its cultural difference.

We need at the same time to relate acceptingly in the spirit of the Gospel to people to whom we are ministering even though their ways are culturally alien from ours. Our good Lord was criticized for keeping company with people of a culture that was unfitting in the eyes even of the Pharisees. "You hang around with these publicans and sinners and fallen women and all the rest of the rabble."

He said, "I have come for that purpose."

Do we need research in this field? Yes, I think we do. We need a better understanding of our context, and a clearer understanding of ourselves and the dynamics that are impacting MKs because of who we are. Do we need analysis? Yes, I think so, because to see more clearly is to be better in touch with realities and better able to cope. Respect and perspective are the keys to Christian development.

Having said all that, I am very much afraid that a preoccupation with diagnostics and with therapies can get us into a great deal of trouble. We need to think bigger than the MK as our unit of analysis in the first place. There is nothing wrong with having two or three conferences focusing on the MK. I am thankful for the way the good Lord has raised this consciousness at this time. But we need a bigger unit of analysis. We need to look beyond our schools and our families. We need to look at the whole nature of the Christian community in a given context and all that it can be for the glory of God. Anxious parents, defensive schools, isolated communities — these are remediable to the glory of God.

We are the people of hope. I Corinthians 13:13 is still there, and our major strength lies in that word *hope*. It sits between faith and love. The greatest of these is love. Indeed, in the genius of the gospel, that's the crux of it. But in the serving of the communities of Christ, we must be careful to keep the centerpiece, hope, in its place. Growing up as an MK should always be approached by any of us — parents, professionals, community members — in terms of its positive values, especially in light of the needs of a world in which Christians with global interests, concerns, and competencies will serve well their Lord and Master who reigns.

Part II

PARENTING MISSIONARY KIDS

8

Young Adults/Young Children: Coping with Competing Needs and Demands

Joyce Bowers
Social Worker, Former Missionary, Lutheran Church of America

My husband and I went to Liberia as newlyweds. Both of our daughters were born there. We traveled back and forth for eleven years, finally returning to the States when they were eight and nine years of age. While we were in Liberia, I frequently experienced mild depression. I felt overtired and needed a lot of sleep. Many times I experienced difficulties with cultural adjustment and marital stress. At the time I really didn't recognize what was going on and thought, "I'm a Christian, and I'm called by God to be here. This is the right place for me to be." Many times we can ignore problems and just go on. However sometimes they become so great that we can't.

Since our return, I have entered a masters program in social work and have begun studying some of the issues. It has been a personal pilgrimage to look back at the years I spent in Liberia as a new bride, as a mother of infants and as a mother of children being sent away to boarding school. I have been answering the questions that I didn't know enough to ask at the time that I was actually living them. My personal sense of satisfaction at this point comes in being able to make other people aware of what I wish I had been aware of when I was a young mother and a young wife.

There are many things about missionary life and other kinds of foreign service that are tough. But we can identify the pressure points so that when people face them, they know there is not something wrong with them, but that it's a normal, expected part of being a missionary and being overseas.

There are predictable life stages for adults as well as for children. Typically people who are twenty-two to thirty are starting their families and have preschool children. I want to look at the needs and issues of young adults and preschool children and how they interact.

The social and emotional needs of young children can be organized in many different ways but I've chosen to look at trust versus mistrust, autonomy versus shame and doubt, and initiative versus guilt.

Most psychologists say the basis of trust is developed within the first year. Within the first year, the infant learns whether the world is reliable or not. Someone I know said, "If you baby a baby when he is a baby, you won't have to baby him when he grows up." The loving response to an infant's needs begins to build trust. If that's not built in that first year, it's very difficult in later years for a person to trust.

Autonomy is the sense of "I'm a person in my own right." The terrible twos really have a positive side. In saying, "No," to whatever you want, this two-year-old is saying, "I am a person myself. I am not just your child. I am a person who can make decisions and who has needs and wants that I'm going to express." If the child has not developed basic trust in the first year and is insecure in his relationship with his parents, he may not be a terrible two. He may be a "good" child, perhaps too good, because he is not secure enough to test whether he can go against the parent.

Initiative begins to develop around age three or four. That's the wonderful time of life when they can get dressed all by themselves. This is the age of wanting to help mommy. Sometimes it seems more bother than it's worth, but if you can engage their helpfulness, which is natural at this age, then that's your best hope for it carrying over into later childhood.

One of the most important things is for the child to know he is loved. I think there are very few parents who don't love their child, but there are parents who don't know how to communicate unconditional love to their child. Two helpful books are Dr. Ross Campbell's *How to Really Love your Child* and Bruce Narramore's *Help I'm a Parent*.

Basically missionaries are strong people, and generally they form strong families. Problems arise when the parents get overburdened, whether it's actually doing mission work, or whether it's simply coping with the environment and all that is involved in moving.

Dr. Hugh Missildine has developed the concept of "the inner child of the past." He says that within all of us adults, there is still the child that we once were. He identifies a number of "parental pathogens." These are things that parents inadvertently do wrong that cause problems for their children after they reach adulthood.

The one that most often applies to missionaries is neglect in terms of not being emotionally available to their children, because they're so preoccupied with so much else that's going on. He says that neglect is:

> ...often found in homes where parents are frequently absent or busily preoccupied and where little consideration is given to the child's right to have the parents' interested assistance at each level of his development.... A child neglected in early life often lacks the ability to form close and meaningful relationships,... has difficulty setting limits on himself as an adult,... has trouble seeing himself in a healthy perspective, in establishing a self-identity that would enable him to relate to others.... He erects a barrier, making every effort to appear self-sufficient, independent of others, detached, aloof.

Developmental stage of young adulthood

Young adulthood is a time of terrific growth and decision making; it's a time of establishing patterns and building a foundation for the rest of life. It is a very important period of life. To me the stage of young adulthood is to adult life what preschool is to youth. You're just beginning, in so many different ways. You're learning tremendous amounts of material. You're learning to cope with a career, a marriage, having your first home, having your first job. There's a tremendous amount that's going on in the lives of young adults.

Men are focusing on their careers, which if they're missionaries, means their ministry. The women typically are having babies, and taking care of little ones. The young man is fulfilling what he has been preparing for. Through high school and college he has been looking forward to a career. He's been learning things that he can now put into practice.

On the other hand, the wife is plunged into the full time job of having and raising children. It is a job for which she's had almost no preparation. It is a stressful job that takes a great deal of energy.

The young man, typically, is excited. His life is just blossoming. He's got the world by the tail. Meanwhile the young wife is at home feeling overwhelmed and perhaps depressed. Very often the missionary wife is not at all sure what her role is. Maybe she had a successful college career, but what's that when you're getting up in the middle of the night with a screaming baby? It can be a time when the husband and the wife are going two separate directions. To build a marriage and to learn to work together while at the same time learning to work in the mission is a very big agenda for the young couple.

I think most of us just assume that life is going to go on and fall into place. We don't think about all of the really profound issues that we're facing. The young couple needs to talk these things over. What is the wife's role? What is the husband's role? What is his role in the home? What is her role outside the home? The role of the missionary wife needs a lot of consideration and a lot of discussion. The husband and wife, as well as the missions community, need to set some goals and make some decisions.

I don't think you can give any one answer that applies to everyone. This is something that has to be worked out for each family, or perhaps for each mission situation. Perhaps it's the choice of the couple for the wife to be at home. Her main task in life is to be a homemaker and a mother. But then, there's her next door neighbor who's teaching classes and doing things that she can write home about. The young mother who's not doing that asks, "What am I going to write home about? Well, I changed fifty-two diapers." There's a real need for affirmation of the mother who stays at home as well as for the one who does work outside the home but wonders, "What's happening to my child when I'm not there?"

When I was at that stage, I always did some activities outside the home because I got cabin fever if I just stayed home with the kids all the time. At one point my little daughter, who was about eighteen months old, wouldn't go to sleep unless the window was completely covered by the curtain, with no little cracks. Our curtain wasn't quite big enough, so we pulled it a little this way and a little that way. "No, there's a crack there." I thought she was just being difficult because she didn't want to go to bed, until she told me that her baby-sitter had told her that the moon would come and get her if she wasn't good. The Liberian way of controlling children is to threaten them.

That provided me with a few guilt feelings about leaving my child with a native baby-sitter even though it was only a couple of hours a day. There's no easy answer; there's no perfect answer to all these issues.

Alternative care

Research supports the view that it's very damaging for children to be cared for by someone outside the family. It also supports the view that it's fine to have alternative care fifty hours a week. You'll find somebody to support whatever side you take. Because of the commitment of both young parents to mission work, and from the standpoint of good stewardship of time and talents, it may make sense for young children to be cared for part-time by other people.

For infants up to age two, the ideal is care either by another person in the child's home or in another home, with a maximum of three or four children per adult.

According to Joyce Kruckeberg of the Children's Education Department of Wycliffe Bible Translators, a child between the age of twelve and eighteen months should not be away from parents more than two hours per day; for a child between eighteen and twenty-four months the maximum is three hours. By age three, however, a group care situation for half of the day may even be preferable to constant home care. It provides the child with playmates, intellectual stimulation, and opportunities to develop competence and confidence.

Popular pediatrician and author T. Berry Brazelton, believes that full-time mothering is necessary for the first four months of life but after that, children and parents can tolerate much more separation than Kruckeberg recommends so long as parents concentrate on fulfilling their child's needs during the few hours that they are together.

Many parents worry that their children will suffer if not given full-time mothering. However, the concept of the nuclear family with mother as exclusive caregiver is a recent invention of the Western middle class. In most countries of the world, throughout history, children have been cared for by extended family members and other adults, not just their biological mothers. No one has claimed fathers must be with their children twenty-four hours a day in order to have strong, healthy relationships.

Recent research regarding day care for children of working mothers shows that, given certain important conditions, day care is not harmful and is often beneficial for preschoolers. Those conditions are: (1) good day-care facilities with warm, affectionate caregivers in a safe, consistent, structured environment, (2) limited number of hours per day (Kruckeberg's recommendation is that maximum number of hours per day equals the child's age plus one), (3) attitude of the mother in using alternate care. Families who use alternate care after careful consideration of the needs of the child and the demands of the work to which God called them can do so responsibly and with a sense of peace in God's provision. Women who are happy with their lives make better mothers whether at home full time or away from home part of the time.

It is good stewardship to set up group child care wherever there are enough preschoolers to make it feasible. It may be a cooperative run by parents. Joyce Kruckeberg's *Guidelines for Mission Preschool Programs* is an excellent, detailed handbook on making group child care "much more than babysitting." Good child care frees women to use their valuable skills and gain satisfaction in doing so.

Helping young children deal with separation and loss

Much has been said about helping older MKs deal with loss and grief, but I would like to talk about it with regard to preschoolers. I believe that just as other patterns of life are being set during the preschool years, so the pattern of dealing with separation and losses is being developed and set within the family.

Preschoolers are oriented to Mommy and Daddy. One of the losses that little ones can experience is the loss of the parents even though they are bodily present. Think of what new candidates have to go through in candidate school, in language school, in orientation, and in adjustment to a new culture. There's a tremendous drain on the energy and attention of these young parents causing the child to experience a sense of loss. "Where is Mommy? Even if she's there, she's not there somehow. She's different than she used to be. She gets mad at me quicker, and I get spanked more often." There may be a real sense of loss there.

By the age of two or three, children are oriented to their surroundings. They are able to adjust, but that doesn't mean it's always going to be easy. Many children go through periods of having nightmares, not sleeping well, wanting to sleep with Mommy and Daddy.

There can be some very unique reactions by individual children to the adjustment process.

Three-year-old Julie moved with her family to Liberia in March, some years ago. Her skin was "winter white" but she quickly acquired a deep tan playing outside in the tropical sun. Surrounded by Africans and watching herself getting darker by the day, she assumed she was changing her race and becoming black.

Her parents, unaware of what she was experiencing (they were in language school at that time) were baffled and dismayed when Julie began to refuse to answer to her own name, but insisted on being called Carol. Their houseboy's practice of favoring Julie's younger brother simply because he was a boy was no help as firstborn Julie went through a full-blown identity crisis.

Fortunately Julie's parents were sensitive enough, and Julie was verbal enough to get things sorted out.

To help a child cope, prepare the child ahead of time. Your mind is so full of plans and what's going to happen, you may forget to talk about it with the child. Talk about where you're going, what it's going to be like, what you're going to do, what you're not going to do.

I don't believe that a young child should be involved in the decision of whether or not to go, but once you make the decision, you can talk to him or her about what it's going to be like, what's going to be different and give them some preparation.

A lot of people say, "Oh I don't like good-byes." But good-byes are very, very important for ourselves, as well as for the children. Over a period of time say, "Well this is the last time we're going to be doing such and such." "This is the last time we're going to go to the park." "This is the last time we're going to go to McDonald's." It gets to be draining, it's true. In a way you wish could just sneak out and be done with all of that, but the good-byes, the parties, the send-off from the church, are all very, very important. It's similar to having a funeral to say good-bye to the deceased. It's very important to go through that kind of process. Painful as it is, it really helps bring closure to one part of life before you start another part.

Let the child decide what toys and clothing are going to go with him or her; what's going to stay at home, what's going to be given away. You may say, "Oh, leave that ratty old sweater behind. We don't need that." But if that ratty old sweater is very important to the child, maybe you should take it along. Or give him a choice, "OK, you can take whatever fits in this little suitcase."

One thing I did when our children were a little bit older, was have a yard sale. If they can keep the money they get from selling their things, they will part with them much more easily than if you just say, "Well, we can't take all of this. You've got to get rid of some of it." There may be some things that really need to be packed away. Even when they get back, they may not be interested any longer, but at the time of leaving, if they can't bear to part with all the teddy bears and the dolls, maybe those need to be kept at grandma's house, so that they can know where they are.

Children go through stages of grief which are similar to what adults go through, but they're not verbal enough to say what they're feeling. Children in general act out their feelings rather than express their feelings in words. One of the biggest things that we need to do is to identify what the child might be feeling and verbalize it so that the child knows that it's OK to feel that. A book which I found very helpful is *Helping Children Cope with Separation and Loss* by Claudia Jewett.

One of the best ways for anyone, adults as well as children, to deal with loss is to talk about it. A lot of times when someone in the family of a friend dies, you don't know what to say, so you don't say anything. Not saying anything is the worst thing you can do. Say anything about the person. Reminisce. Say, "Well, I remember when..."

This is also very important for children in moving from one country to another. This can be done with an album of pictures. I did this inadvertently one time, when we came back from Liberia for furlough. I had made up a picture album for the purpose of showing people in the States what life in Liberia was like. I'd taken pictures of all the common ordinary things. Well, my daughter age two and a half spent hours and hours going through that book as we traveled. She would look at the book, and she would look out the window. Then she would look back at the book. You could just see the wheels turning around. Life in Liberia was so very different from life in the States. She couldn't verbalize it, but I'm sure she wondered, "Am I dreaming? Is this real?" She could look at the pictures and say, "Yes, it really was like I remember."

Preschoolers love bedtime stories, especially custom-made ones told spontaneously by parents; my daughter at age three or four loved stories which started "I know a little girl who..." and described in detail a typical day in the life she had left. She would squirm with delight and make corrections in the story, even though we conspired to avoid naming the main character. I did not realize at the time that I was affirming her confidence in the reliability of her own memories and observations—a confidence that is shaken in a time of loss.

We've all had some experience where we think, "Hmm, that was a little strange, I feel kind of, I don't know how to express it." Then somebody else who was also there, would put into words exactly what you were feeling. You know what a relief that brought you and it's the same with kids. They may be experiencing something, but they don't quite know what it is or how to put it into words. But if Mommy can put it into words, then it's OK. That really helps them accept it and deal with it. Being able to do that depends on being in touch with your own feelings, because what they're feeling is very much what you're feeling.

It is very important for preschool children to have routine and predictability in their lives. If there's anything that disrupts routine, it's being a missionary. Sometimes it's impossible to have a routine. But particularly at bed time, it is important to know that first we take a bath, then we get our pajamas on, and then we read a story, and then we pray. It may seem very simple to us, but to a child that is very comforting, and gives them a sense of security that everything is right with the world.

Now as a parent of older children, when I invite a young couple over they'll sometimes say, "Well, we have to leave by eight o'clock because we have to get the children in bed."

I think, "Couldn't you let that go for one night?" But really, bedtime is a priority time for little kids. It can really help if you can maintain a routine.

For children under two, who are unable to comprehend loss, it is important to concentrate on fulfillment of needs. During an infant's first year, moves are not usually traumatic unless the quality of caretaking suffers. Between the first and second birthdays, separations from parents can be very traumatic, but environmental changes are not as significant. If parents are convinced that what they are doing is God's will, and are generally satisfied with their lives (even though there are difficulties) their contentment will be communicated to the children, even to babies. But if there is uncertainty and tension, that will also be communicated and is likely to result in fussy, demanding little ones.

God comforts us, so that we can comfort others. There are a lot of difficulties and struggles in missionary life, and in life in general. If we are able to receive comfort from each other then we can pass the comfort that we receive on to our children and to others. That comfort may be in the form of an attractive tray of tea and toast with a china tea pot.

There was a lady in her sixties who went as a Peace Corps volunteer to Liberia. The orientation process was being carried on at our school, and at one point I went to the dorm where she was staying and discovered that she was nauseous and depressed and really feeling very low. I went back home and fixed up a really nice tray of tea and toast, because she couldn't tolerate the food that was being served. She told me later that was what kept her in Liberia—that tray of tea and toast. I had no idea at the time that I was doing such a service to her, but she was teetering on the edge of saying, "No, I can't hack it, I'm going back to the States." The comfort that she was able to receive from that tray of tea and toast gave her enough strength to say, "I'm going to go on." She was a terrific Peace Corps volunteer. We were very happy that she stayed.

If parents have a sense of security in their marital partnership and in trusting God's provision and protection; if they effectively communicate their love for their children; if they have a sense of humor, curiosity, flexibility, an ability to accept differences, and a deep conviction that God is leading them; then their children will largely be protected from emotional harm.   Depending on parents' attitudes, new experiences may be threatening to children or they may be a wonderful adventure.

9

Missionary Fathers and Their Responsibility Toward Their Children

John Burgess
Gordon College

I remember that before I was married, I thought that my wife and my children would have to realize that the primary task in my life was the calling of God. What God called me to was going to consume my prime time. But as I held our first child, I began to realize that my primary task was my family. He had called me to this family. He had given me this family to care for. I was to be a steward over my children.

I don't think I have shorted God in any way in any of the other commitments that I had, but to me, my family was my primary mission field, and I had best get at it.

The Importance of the Early Years

The more I have thought and read about the development of the child, the more I have come to realize that we need to be concerned about the early years of the child's life, beginning at Day One. I've become more and more convinced that it's the relationship that I as a father establish with that baby that determines the development of the future relationship I will have with the child.

Lately, there has been a lot of research going on with one, two, and three-year-olds. And some of those researchers have come to the opinion that the first two years are the most important in the development of a child.

They say that the quality of the relationship a child has with his siblings and with his parents in the first two years of life, not only influences but maybe even determines the quality of love that that child will be able to demonstrate to others and to receive as an adult.

By the end of the third year, the child's self-concept has already been formed. If we are concerned about the kind of self-concept a child has, then we need to be concerned about those early years. I think the child's awareness of God and the kind of concept he has of God are both developed during those early years.

Fitzhugh Dodson made the statement, "It is important for you to start the relationship with your child early because the first few years of his life are the most important ones. By six, his basic personality structure has been formed, and this determines to a large extent what kind of an adolescence he will have, how successful he will be in his adult life, what kind of woman he will marry, and how happy and lasting that marriage will be."

If the state of infancy is most crucial in the development of a quality person, then the father cannot postpone involvement with his child until that son can throw a football, or his daughter can ride a bicycle. The father's obligation in the nurturing process begins with the birth of the child.

Infancy is a stage of beginnings during which the father begins a relationship with his child. The quality of the beginning of this relationship will greatly influence the quality of future relationships that the child has with the father and with other people.

The period of infancy marks the beginning of personality development. Initial steps in the formation of their view of the world and life are taken. Their perception of people begins to emerge. The foundation for self-concept is laid, as well as the basis for the development of an awareness of God.

It cannot be overemphasized that the early days of infancy are extremely important in the establishment of a relationship that will support successful nurturing, and enable the father/child relationship to endure stormy periods of misunderstanding, disagreement, or even hostility.

Laying the Foundation

What can the father do to lay the foundation for a father/child relationship conducive to raising a child whose life glorifies God and conforms to the teaching of Scriptures?

Spend time with the baby

More and more fathers are doing that, but traditionally, the wife is the care giver. I would like to challenge fathers to consciously begin their love relationship with that child in the hospital, even before the child comes home. Visit the child just as you visit your wife.

My own son was present for the birth of his child. While the nurses and doctors were taking care of the mother, he had an extended time to sit and hold his little son. I think fathers today have a much greater opportunity to begin a relationship with the baby from Day One, than they did in the past.

When the baby is brought home, start immediately to develop a routine that includes talking to, playing with, caring for, loving, and enjoying your baby. The father should become involved with his infant in a variety of activities. The mother undoubtedly is still the caregiver; the father is typically the playmate. In fact, researchers say that if you take a motion picture of a child as it's interacting with the mother or father, and play it back without the sound, the researcher can tell just from the movement which parent is talking to the child.

Establish a bond of love and respect and security for your child

There should be a time every day, when a father has a significant quality time with his children. Quality time is the way you handle your child, the way that you respond to the child, the way that you notice or don't notice things that they do. The way that you accept something that they do for, to, or with you.

Establish a bond of love. Love is the necessary context enabling positive personality growth. Love is not a characteristic which is inheritable. A child loves as a result of being loved. The quality of the relationships in which the infant is involved during the first year of life has considerable impact upon the ability of the child as an adult to receive and give love and affection.

One father, even while his children were infants, would identify one personality characteristic or action each day that he appreciated. When his child was just a few days old, he would say, "I like your smile." When the child turned over from his stomach to his back for the first time, he would express his appreciation for what the child had been able to do.

Talk with the child even when he may not be able to respond, at least verbally. Establish with that child a feeling of appreciation and love. It is the responsibility of the father to provide an atmosphere in which the child may grow and develop, feeling comfortable and secure. Respect your child right from the beginning.

One day our daughter, who was in her teens, said to my wife, "Mom, you and Dad are so lucky."

My wife asked, "Why?"

She said, "Because you never had rebellious children."

She was right. I asked my daughter, "What do you think has made our relationship so good?"

She said, "It's because you and Mom respect us and always have."

Pray for your baby

I think it's appropriate to ask yourself what kind of a person you want your child to become. There are personality characteristics that the Scripture says should be in a follower of God. Pray specifically for those things to take place in your child's life.

Pray for your baby, but also pray for yourself. I remember when I was caring for my first son, and my wife was out for the evening. Everything was going nicely, until finally he began to cry. I tried to soothe him and get him to stop crying. He didn't. I checked everything that I could think of that might be wrong. Nothing was wrong. He just wouldn't stop crying. I had an inclination to shake him to get him to stop crying. I didn't do it, but it made me realize that I needed to pray for myself, maybe even more than I needed to pray for my child, in order that I might be a model for that child.

Be a model of a biblically structured life

Be able to say to your children, "Be an imitator of me, as I imitate Christ. My behavior is that which God wants and desires to see in a person." One man said, "My father didn't tell me how to live. He lived and let me watch him do it." From the earliest days of infancy, the child should observe in the father a living example of a man who honors God.

Be supportive of the mother

This will indirectly affect your relationship with the child. The father should lovingly support his wife as she assumes the responsibilities for child rearing. Understand the demands being made upon her. The involvement of the father in caregiving activities will provide a greater appreciation for the role that she plays. Meaningful support of the mother is truly a significant aspect of being a father, and provides a family atmosphere conducive to the growth of the child.

We have a friend who made it a practice on their monthly anniversary to provide a candlelight meal for his wife. Then the first child came along. The normal thing would be to forget doing that. Not him. He even hired a baby-sitter so he could still carry on their monthly anniversary celebration, when they would have that time together. He was supporting his wife, and that indirectly supported the child as well.

Create an awareness of God in your home

The Amplified New Testament translates Ephesians 6:4 this way: "That the father is to rear the child tenderly in the training and discipline of the Lord." Although the spiritual nurture of the child should be a joint effort by the father and mother, this verse definitely identifies the father as having major responsibility for the spiritual development of his children. The father needs to create an atmosphere in which the child develops an awareness of God.

In my own life, I've worked daily to create an awareness of God's presence. He is always with me, so all that I do and say is really done and said in the presence of God.

When the mother and father pray and study the Scriptures, the baby can be included in this experience. When you have your devotions together, include that child. We did from the day our first child came back from the hospital. Although it might seem the infant has no comprehension of the activity, the inclusion in worship enables the child to grow gradually into an awareness of the presence of God in your life. Later there would be no need to formalize the family worship, as the family had been at worship from the time the child came into the family.

Include the baby as thanks is given before meals. We used to even pray with our children over the bottle. It still is our practice to hold hands as grace is said before the meal. The child should be an accepted and actively participating member of family worship from the moment that child is brought into the home.

Include the infant in the worship activities of the family outside the home. Two weeks after I was born, my mother took me to church, put me in a basket at the back of the church, and that was the beginning of my church attendance.

We should bring God into our conversation as a natural expression of our daily thoughts. One father who carries his child in a front carrier said, "As we walk along, I point out what God has done in creation."

The laying of adequate foundations is emphasized in the Scripture in every way. The first two years of life is the time in which to lay the foundation for the father/child relationship.

10

Preserving the Family and Fulfilling the Ministry

Paul Kienel
Executive Director, ACSI

In 1962 I became the principal of a small Christian school in California. It tripled in size within three years, but I worked twelve and fourteen hours a day, six and a half days a week. If I had kept up that pace, I wouldn't be standing here today telling you how to preserve your family, because I wouldn't have much of a family to talk about. Song of Solomon 1:6 says, "They made me the keeper of the vineyards, but my own vineyard have I not kept." It is possible to, in effect, win the world and lose your own family. And that cannot possibly be the Lord's will.

I wish I'd heard more pastors using I Timothy 5:8 as a text. "But if anyone does not provide for his own, and especially for those of his own household, he has denied the faith, and is worse than an unbeliever." Incredible statement! It establishes the priorities of life for all of us. If I interpret that correctly, you won't go to heaven if you purposely neglect your children.

My wife and I have learned to preserve our family, and still maintain our commitment to the call of God upon our lives. The things I share come out of personal experience.

I am sure that our number one mission in this life as believers and parents is to raise our children to bring honor to the name of Christ. Almost twenty-one years ago, my wife and I sat down and determined that no matter how busy we became in this work, we were not going to, in effect, win the world and lose our children. Our children really were number one with us. We repented for the three and a half years that we had worked so hard and neglected them. We made a little course correction in our way of living that really saved our family. And I'm so glad we did.

Spend Time with Your Family

Do not allow your schedule to consume you. Through these last twenty-one years I've held pretty much to an eight-hour day. I have learned to maximize my work during that time. When I'm with my family at home, I'm totally with my family. I have to write quite a bit, and there are occasions when I bring my writing home, but if I do that, I write early in the morning before the family is up. I don't take family time to do the work. I keep Saturdays absolutely open for my family. Through the years we have almost always done something together as a family on that day.

In the evening after dinner is family scheduling time. We coordinate the family calendar with my work calendar. Through the years, if my children wanted us to attend something at school or church, or if we were planning a family outing, dinner time was the time when we orchestrated our family calendar. And that has been a key to our family togetherness.

I have learned through the years that if you don't make things happen with your family, if you don't prioritize time with your family, good things will not just happen. Never once have my wife and I allowed our ministry to break a commitment with our children. Once that commitment is on the master calendar, coordinated with our work calendar, we've never ever broken that commitment with our children.

If somebody asks me to speak anywhere in the world, and I look at my calendar, and I have a family event scheduled for that time, I simply say, "I'm already booked for that time." This commitment to time with our family has really added to my credibility with my children. They know they really are number one with Annie and me. Nothing has priority over time that I've committed to my family. Absolutely essential to your ability to govern your family is your believability and credibility with your children.

Be an Example of Righteousness

Your children are watching you live out your life, and they are patterning their life after yours. If you're a positive, joyful Christian in whom the Spirit of God dwells, your children are going to see that. But if you are negative, if you do not respond to situations in life as a Christian, and if you're not dependent upon the Lord, your children will see that, and they will develop a pattern similar to yours.

My father died when I was seven. My mother was left alone with my two younger sisters and me. But never once can I remember my mother complaining about her lot. She was and still is a joyful Christian lady. I picked up that pattern. My sisters picked up that pattern. We learned to live positively in the face of great adversity because of the parental example that we had before us.

Think about the way you live and realize you are modeling other lives. You are the model for the next generation in your household. It's amazing how much our children pick up from us. It's amazing how many children follow their parents in their church affiliation. It's amazing how many children follow the parents in their political persuasion. I'm a Republican, and my mother is a Republican, and her parents were Republicans. But never once do I ever recall my mother sitting down with me and saying, "Paul, I think you ought to be a Republican." I picked up her views on politics without ever having a lesson in politics. It's amazing all of the deep seated things we pick up from our parents. We don't realize we're picking them up, and most parents don't realize that they're teaching them.

Help Your Children Understand Your Motivation for Serving God

Show them in a variety of ways the enthusiasm that you have for your work. If you are a teacher or an administrator, let it leak out in your conversations that you feel that what you do is vital to the future of those youngsters and that you feel privileged to help young people. Give them things to read about what you do. Tell them about some of the successes of what you do. They need to learn about that.

Keep the Channels of Communication Open between You and Your Children

I believe it's absolutely essential for parents to show love and affection to their children. Dr. Tim LaHaye told me one time, "Most of the adult problems that I learn about come from a childhood where parents failed to express love to their children." Fathers especially are often guilty of not saying the words, "I love you."

When I come home to our family, I make the rounds, and I kiss everybody, and say, "I love you." If we've got any company there, I kiss the company. We just believe in family affection. Your children, my children, every one of them, need to know that their parents love them. Quite frankly, it needs to be said every day. If you're in an MK school where parents are a long ways away, you're there on behalf of those parents. You can't say it quite the same, but you can say it. Love needs to flow from you to them.

Children can face almost anything if they have a home base where they know they are unconditionally loved. Your kids need to feel your love, and your kids need to feel love from one another.

Be a Public Relations Agent for Your Children

It's very important to the emotional stability of your children that they have standing with your family and your adult friends. I can remember very well when all our family was together, my mother would show them things I made and say, "I'm really proud of my son for making this." She would do the same thing with my sisters. She would share this not only with family, but also with people that were important to her. She was actually bragging about me to them. As I grew up, I had such standing with those people that I wanted to live my life in such a way that I continued to please them. That was a great stabilizing force in my life.

I can tell you another important matter that you need to think about in this day and age. Because I was the only boy in a house full of ladies, a minister friend gave some very good advice to my mother shortly after my father died. He said, "You know, you've got a boy in the family, and he's going to need some masculine modeling. If you don't remarry, then you need to associate with some whole families, so that he can see what a father does, and how boys relate to their fathers, and so on."

My mother took that very seriously. She went on a personal friendship crusade with three very solid families in our church. Busy as she was, keeping us together, she spent many a Saturday or Sunday afternoon taking us to visit the homes of those families. My mother built bridges between us and those families. And those people helped me in my concept towards work, because all of them were very successful hard-working people. They helped me in my concept towards money management. Many of the ideals that I have today, I picked up from those families. And had I not had those masculine models, it could very well have been that I would have picked up feminine characteristics.

Much of the homosexuality in our world today comes from the fact that there are so many single-parent families. Boys are modeling their lives after their mothers, because there is no father. Even in whole families, many fathers are so weak in the leadership of the family that boys are patterning themselves after the leader of the family, who happens to be the mother.

Think about the need for your children to have standing first of all in your own family, and then in your circle of friends. Be sure that circle of friends will add strength to the lives of your children and not be a detriment to them. Something that my mother did for me, and I do for my children is pray that the Lord will send people into their lives that will make a major difference. I can't think of anything more significant in adding stability to the life of a child than to have a reason for pleasing this crowd of people.

Keep Life in Your Family Interesting

If I were a youngster in some of the families I see, I think I would say, "Life is a drag here." It's really up to you and me as administrators and managers of our families to orchestrate life in such a way that the children will say to themselves, "I'm glad to be a part of this family."

Most of us would not have the positions we do if we were not organized, creative people. But some of us spend all of our creative and organizational energies on our work and ministry, and we do not use that same creativity and that same organizational ability in keeping life interesting in our family. Think about the needs of your children and ask yourself, "If I was a child here, what would I need that I am not now receiving?" Then set about to improve the quality of life in your family.

I'm not talking about making every day a field trip. I'm not talking about spending great sums of money on your children. You can do more harm than good with that kind of thing. But when you have an opportunity for creativity, and you have an opportunity to organize something wonderful with your children, put your whole heart into it. See to it that to the best of your ability, you make it a grand occasion.

Some years ago, I purchased a camper. There's nothing quite so effective in bringing your family close together. You're close together whether you want to be or not in a camper. On the back of our camper, we carry a small motorcycle. Having three girls, I built three carts. Each cart hooks to the other cart, and then the lead cart hooks to my motorcycle. It's a ridiculous looking thing; it's twenty-three feet long, but my children's memory banks are filled with all kinds of amazing adventures that we've had through the years with that crazy motorcycle and those funny carts.

I'm not suggesting that you all go out and buy campers and motorcycles, but in your own setting, do something that is interesting to you and to your children. See to it that it happens. Schedule the time, put creativity into it, and let your children see that you love them enough to give your best energies to making life interesting in your family.

Don't allow your work or ministry to so dominate your mind that you have no room for your number one priority in this life — and that's your kids. We're not getting this message from enough sources. A lot of church pastors want to make the church the center of all things, but the first institution established by God was the family. Interestingly enough, the second institution established by God was civil government. The third institution was the church. Life should revolve around the family, and you need to see to it that you make life in your family interesting.

Establish a Pattern of Goal Setting

Establish a pattern of goal setting in your children — long-range and short-range goal setting. My mother, having to raise us alone, realized as I approached my high school years that there was no way that she could afford to send me to college, let alone a Christian college. So she said to me, "Paul, I want you to think about going to a Christian college. I feel strongly about Christian education." We were on welfare. We were so poor that poor people felt sorry for us. She said, "I believe that you can get through college if you will learn a skill or trade of some kind. That way you can propel yourself through college."

I grew up in a little town of northeast Oregon called Milton-Freewater. We had one contractor in our town; he was a Christian man named H.O. Warner. He had a cabinet shop and a construction crew. So I went to Mr. Warner and said, "Mr. Warner, I want very much to work my way through a Christian college, and I believe I can do that if I learn the carpenter trade. I would like to work for you every day after school and on Saturdays, and I will work for you for nothing, if you will teach me the trade." It's amazing how quickly you can gain employment under those terms. My heart was in this thing. I really had it in my mind that this was the way I was going to work myself out of the poverty cycle. He could see very quickly that I was serious. Every school day from 3:00 to 5:00 and all day Saturday, I would go to the cabinet shop and work. Within a few weeks, he decided that I was serious, and so he started paying me.

By the time I was a freshman in college, I was a full journeyman carpenter. I was the youngest carpenter in our trade union, and I could earn enough money in the summer to completely pay for all of my college tuition. Besides that, I drove a brand new Mercury. I dressed well. The kids in college thought I was from a wealthy family, and I didn't have the heart to tell them anything different.

The reason that happened was because my mother planted an idea in my head, and then all along the way, she encouraged me. She complemented me. She shared with her friends and her family what I was doing, and they encouraged me. The whole pattern of life that she had established made that happen for me. I worked my way through seven and a half years of college.

I believe that we have too many youngsters growing up today without any visions, without any pictures of what they're going to do with their future. We have too many kids graduating from our Christian high schools and Christian colleges who have never really established the pattern of driving a stake in the future and then breaking their neck to get there. That's what it takes. If we can help our children establish the pattern of visualizing what they can do and then working toward it, we will do them a great service.

These are just common sense things that we have learned along the way. I hope they're helpful and practical to you.

11

Raising Children Overseas

Walt Stuart
Black Forest Academy, West Germany

I am convinced that the key to raising a child is the parents. I also believe that the biblical principles for rearing children are transcultural.

Hindrances to Development of the MK's Full Potential

Not understanding that parents have a significant ministry

When my son was three, he kept asking me, "Dad, why don't you become a garbage collector?" In his eyes, a garbage collector had a good job. He rode on the back of a big truck, and he did something tangible.

What was Dad doing? One time one of my kids told me, "Somebody asked me what you do all day, and I said that you sit and read books." That's all he saw.

When MKs cannot esteem that their parents are in a significant ministry, they have problems with being overseas. "Why am I here?" If Dad and Mom are not involved in a work that has significance, they don't see any reason for their being in a foreign country.

It is important for your kids to know you are involved in an important ministry, not to brag about it, but to say, "Hey, we're here on the King's business. We're here for a reason." Especially in the initial stages when they don't know what you are doing, a lot of kids say, "Why am I going through all this?" Remember to communicate with them.

A lot of MKs are embarrassed to tell other kids their parents are missionaries. The big question in national schools is: "What does your dad do?" They're expecting to hear that he is an ambassador from the U.S.A. I explain that we are serving as ambassadors, but for the King of Kings.

I decided early in my ministry in France to get an office outside the home. Not everyone can afford that. That's not always realistic or necessary, but for me it was. I found a fantastic office—a broom closet that had electricity and a ventilating system. It was a place I could go in the morning. The kids saw Dad going to work. Dad was doing something.

We who are in church planting sometimes lack a definite structure. I found that it was important for me to structure my life. You have to bring order to your life. That's important to your children.

Finances

Another area I found to be significantly important to children is the area of finances. We feel the weight of finances as parents, because we often have to say, "No, we can't do that," and "No, you can't buy that because we don't have enough money." But finances don't have to be negative, even when we are hurting. They shouldn't be the matter of table talk in a negative sense. Too often when we are preoccupied with finances, we allow that to be the center of our whole conversation, and our children absorb that.

Many MKs today refuse to even consider the possibility of going out as a faith missionary. "I refuse to become a beggar." That's their conception of faith missions. They want to be involved in international ministries, but they want to earn their way. There's nothing wrong with that so long at they have in their hearts the alternative of being a faith missionary or a tentmaker.

I was talking to an MK in Vienna who is an international businessman. I know his family real well. They are fantastic people. He said, "My kids will never, ever have anything second-hand." I can understand his reaction.

That is one thing I had to deal with early on in my ministry. I still wrestle with finances. I wrestle when people start talking about sums of $35,000 to $40,000 to keep a family in Europe. I ask, "Am I worth it?" I had to deal with the scriptural approach to missionary finances. The more I studied the Word of God the more I came to the conclusion that it was a privilege for the body of Christ to be involved in world-wide missions. They were the beneficiaries of our finances—of giving.

We often quote Philippians 4 at the time of a commissioning service, "And our God will supply all of your needs, according to his riches." But who is saying that? It's the missionary Paul who is saying it to the sending church. He's saying, "Don't worry. If you give to me, God will supply your needs. You're the beneficiaries."

Make sure you have wrestled with the issue of finances and gotten it straightened out in order that you can positively and biblically approach the issue of money. We don't have to enter churches with the idea of being a beggar. A laborer is worthy of his hire. We need to communicate that positive sense of faith living and giving to our own children. They need to see we are thankful for what God provides. We need to thank the Lord.

Furlough

A third area that hinders our children is deputation. It can be a very positive experience, but many times it's a negative. Some of our kids are convinced the U.S. is comprised of nothing but church buildings. That's all they've ever seen. Why? Because we hit home and we jump in the car, and we go from church, to church, to church. It's a marathon.

I hear missionaries bragging about the ten thousand miles they put on the car, and the fifty-five churches they visited, and the three hundred people they saw. And I ask, "Where were your kids all that time?"

"Oh, they were in the back seat." Sure they were in the back seat. Totally out of it.

Furlough doesn't have to be a negative thing. It can be a very positive experience and an opportunity for our children to get to know some very special people in their lives.

When we went on furlough, we would not always bring our children with us to visit churches. We would sometimes leave them with a favorite cousin for two weeks, or make sure they were with their grandparents. We wanted them to know family, and to feel a part of a family.

Sure the churches were disappointed. "Oh, where are your children?" They were sincere, but they forgot about them after two minutes.

We wanted our children to be able to go back to North America and know the people that really cared about them. That takes developing. It doesn't happen overnight. You just don't fly back and say, "You are in college now, sweetie, you can go visit Aunt Jane. She said you could come any time you want."

"Mom, who is Aunt Jane?"

They feel more of a stranger with Aunt Jane than they do with their roommate's parents that they got to know on weekends. We need to cultivate relationships.

It's a time to teach them some cultural experiences. One of my wife's sisters lives right in Washington, D.C. We know the museums, the White House and the Capitol. It's become a family center of enculturation. Philadelphia is my home area. We've made sure that our kids have gotten to know some of the major cultural and historical places in the United States so they can understand a little bit about the country in which their parents were born. It's our home country. It's not theirs, but they can get to appreciate it. That's really important.

There are also some educational opportunities. We actually sent our kids to a summer school for a few weeks. They understood and spoke English, but they had to learn to read and write it. Use your furloughs in a positive way.

We decided after our first furlough that we weren't going to use our children as objects or object lessons unless they came to us and said, "Hey we'd like to do this." They've done that on occasion, but to force them to stand up in front and sing cute little French songs was something else. Mind you, our family sang a lot. We love it! When we hit the church it was natural for Mom and Dad to say, "They'll sing." That was fine when they were three, four, or five. Next furlough, forget it.

We never forced it. Once in a while we would ask them, "Would you do that?"

"Well, yeah, O.K. We'll do it." That's fine. Read their attitudes. Don't force them.

Lack of activities with Christian peers

A fourth area that can be a hindrance is a lack of Christian peers and a lack of Christian activities for their age group. I say this particularly for those in pioneer works. We were confronting this as we started a church in France. Where were the other Christians kids their age?

Right from the onset my wife and I said, "We will always have a children's group or a youth group for our children, even if we have to do it ourselves." God was gracious in answering our prayers to give our children Christian peers with whom they could grow up and interact and share Christian activities.

I remember at one point we'd have thirty to fifty kids in our living room every Saturday evening. Our children loved it. They were totally a part of it. Our kids could identify. They said "Hey, we aren't weird. We are not unique."

It's also important that your particular mission or denomination sponsor a camp that your kids can feed into. You've got to think of their peer needs on a spiritual level. If they aren't being nurtured on that level, if they don't see others of their age group who believe in God like they believe in God, they are going to begin to question the validity of your Christianity. "Why is everybody against what you teach?"

I dealt with a young man a few years ago at Black Forest Academy, who had been socially, emotionally, and spiritually isolated all his life. He was thirteen years old, and literally an emotional cripple. He had been raised by his parents in Egypt in a tutorial situation, and didn't have any Egyptian comrades. Finally his parents were going back to Canada. They sent him to school as a transition step. It was a wipeout. The guy couldn't handle it. I asked, "Hey, didn't you have any Christian friends your age?"

"No, I've never had a Christian friend my age." He didn't know how to relate to people his age. He just went into a shell.

A negative mission environment

I think another hindrance develops if you raise your children in what I call a negative mission environment. What is a negative mission environment? It's one where a spirit of criticism prevails. That doesn't mean you should never criticize your mission. We should all be in the business of constructively and positively critiquing, criticizing, and evaluating our mission organization.

When I arrived in France, all looked well on the surface. (I'm telling in-house stories perhaps. That's dangerous.) But one day my wife and I kind of took over the MKs. There was no MK ministry, and we saw all these neat teenagers. A lot of them were in isolated situations. We said, "Let's have a weekend with them, do something together."

We took them ice-skating, went skiing at Grenoble and did different things with them. One night when my wife slid into bed about 3 A.M., she was literally shaking. She said, "Honey, I don't know what we're into, but in the majority of these kids there's anger, resentment and bitterness. I think it's against their parents, or against the mission. I'm not sure."

Sure enough, what had transpired in one particular part of our mission was total negativism, jealousy, one-upmanship. Who was the brunt of all of that? Those kids. Even today I can picture in my mind every one of them. Every one of them has wrestled deeply with their spiritual life. I would say the large majority of them are believers and have a desire to serve God, but they are still deeply bruised because of what they experienced through this critical attitude. The kids were negative, because of the negativism of their parents. They had the feeling that their parents kind of hated each other. That wasn't true, but that was their conclusion. As a result there was tremendous rivalry among the kids. Part of that came because of finances.

God has called us to be peacemakers, and if we find this negativism creeping in, we need to stop it. We need to handle it biblically. Don't allow it to go on. Don't be a participant. Don't be caught up in the gossip of the mission. Stop it. That takes courage, because you won't always be popular. If somebody comes to throw another piece of garbage on, you need to turn around and say, "I don't want to hear that right now."

Multilingual illiteracy

Many of us are raising multilingual illiterates. At BFA we have children who can speak three, four, or five languages without thinking twice about it. But basically these kids are semi-illiterates, when they first hit BFA. That is, they can speak multiple languages, but they are the master of none.

We need to develop a mother tongue for our children. When our children were in the French school system, they were examined by the school psychologist as all the kids were examined. The school psychologist said, "Mr. Stuart, I've examined your four children, and they are all very intelligent, but they need to determine now which is going to be their mother tongue." We kind of brag about the advantages of having bilingual, or trilingual kids. Our kids basically speak three languages, but my older children are literate in only two languages, and my younger children are literate in only one language. That can be developed, but they need to have a base language in which to build. We're hoping that ultimately they will be literate in the three languages. But that can't happen until you start with the first.

Inadequate exposure to career opportunities

I think another hindrance is the fact that our children haven't been adequately exposed to the multiplicity of careers available to children with a third cultural experience. Many of us talk about the basics. "Well, you can be a doctor, a lawyer, a nurse, a missionary, a pastor, a teacher, an evangelist." And then what? Do other careers exist? I was looking at a career book, and I just got overwhelmed by the multiplicity of careers that exist out there. Many of them would be appropriate for our children. They would fit right in. They would have an impact in that area of discipline as well as in the world.

At BFA we've started a career day. We've contacted internationals in Europe, people from the Department of Defense and embassies, business men and professionals. We've had them come and present the possibility of other types of careers. God wants to infiltrate the world and he may want to use your child to infiltrate a very special area that you've never thought about. Your child needs to be exposed to that. If he does come to the point where he says, "I want to be a church planting missionary," he knows that God has called him to be a church planter missionary. It's not that he didn't have any other choice, "Well, since I can't be anything else I guess I'd better get back to the field and be a church planter missionary." That would be sad.

I've touched kids who have gone back to the field, and I've said, "Why are you here?"
"I don't know."
"Well, how did you get here?"
"Well, I went to Bible School."
"But why did you go to Bible School?"
"Well, my parents thought it would be a good idea."
"Why did your parents think it would be a good idea?"
"Well, that's what they did."

We are almost afraid for our children to face that world. Now I'm not opposed to Bible school at all. I went to Philadelphia College of the Bible. For me it was excellent. That's what God wanted. That's where I should have been. But for others, that's not their niche; that's not their place.

Let me encourage you to look at the particular gifts, abilities, and skills that your child has, and at the uniqueness of his third cultural context, and start offering him some alternatives. Show him there are other possibilities.

Mixing ministry with home life

The last thing I'll talk about in a negative context is the mixing of ministry with home life. God has called us to the ministry, but he has also called us to a home life. To me they run parallel. They don't run in empirical order. If I'm walking with God, I'm also walking in accordance with my wife. I'm also walking properly with my children. I'm also walking properly with my ministry.

Too often, we fail to give some unique time to the home. Too often our table talk concerns finances. That's part of ministry. Table talk can also be about what we're doing all the time.

Here's how table talk often goes: "Hey, you know so and so?"

"Yeah."

"They are an excellent contact."

Our kids look at us and say, "I thought they were our friends."

"Oh, they are our friends but they are a contact for the gospel."

That we are out to reach these people for Jesus Christ needs to be communicated, but that can be communicated without our looking at these people as ministry objects.

Around our table we pray specifically for people. We ask our kids, "Who do you want to pray for?" And we pray for that person. But, be careful when all of your lifestyle is revolving constantly around the ministry. Just a word of warning.

Parental Pluses That Promote the Development of the MK's Potential

Family memories

I think we need to constantly build family memories. Build memories and traditions. We have traditions in our family.

Christmas Eve has always had a certain traditional form for us. We always spend it with certain people that are very special to us and to our children. That's important. When we invite people in for special times, we consult our children.

I have to admit it is very difficult for me to be here today at this conference. I wanted to come, and was asked to come. My family gave me permission to come. Why is it difficult? Because every year at this time, we are on our family vacation. Right now my wife and three kids are skiing in the Swiss Alps. We have a family tradition that after Christmas we go skiing. It's skiing in the day, hot chocolate in the afternoon, book reading at night—and it's special.

I'm not a part of that right now, and neither is my daughter who is in college. I wrote her a long letter last night, and I was just about weeping as I wrote it. It's become an integral part of our lives.

My wife is already planning for Christmas when they're all back in the States. She's already saying, "We've got to get a place they can come back to." We can do that. That's how important it is.

Winter and spring were our big family vacations. In the spring we would head off to Rome. We'd head off to Greece, driving down through Czechoslovakia. One summer we did a family ministry through the eastern countries of Yugoslavia, Hungary, and Rumania. Our family will never be the same because of that. As we walked into a Rumanian church, we saw the thousand people in there literally fall down on their knees before God and cry out.

Vacations that count and build memories are very important.

Exposure to quality people

Expose your children to interesting and stimulating people. We have opportunities that many people don't have. We have access to dignitaries, mission executives, and world renowned evangelists. We need to expose our children to these people. One rule for these people when they come into our house is that they don't talk to me about business at the table. I want them to focus their attention on my children, interact with them, have something to say to them and answer their questions. I want my kids to be exposed to these people—Christians and non-Christians. I want them to grow. This will help your children develop a better world view, as well as a better God view, as they hear about what God is doing throughout the world through the lives of these individuals.

Involvement in local activities

The third thing is to encourage your children to be involved in local activities. It's easy to isolate ourselves, especially in an MK school setting. We've found that out in Germany. We're thankful that we live in a national neighborhood. Our boys are able to participate in the local team, as well as the school's soccer team, which plays in the German league. They get to know the kids. They bring them home. They can interact with them. They get involved in gymnastics and tennis and drama and music. What we are saying to our kids is, "This is the world to whom Christ has called us." We shouldn't isolate them, nor should we use our children as bait to reach the world.

Involvement in school life

As parents, be involved in your child's school life, whether your child commutes or whether you have a child who's boarding. Make some of their big events a part of your program. Mark them on your calendar. Some parents never show up for any event, not even the graduation of their children. Can you imagine what that says to the kids? The message is loud and clear, at least in their minds. The non-presence of their parents communicates a negative message. The administrative director of BFA said to some of the parents on the opening day, "You know, BFA is an institution that collaborates with the parents in process, but it is not an adoption agency."

Preparation for life in the home country

Introduce your children to some North American ways. I mentioned this before on deputation. Remember, your child is probably going to go back to North America, at least to go to college. That's not always the case, but they should feel comfortable enough that one day they can choose which culture they ultimately wish to live in without feeling they have to come back "home." Expose them to some North American colleges. Take them around. Be involved in their college application procedures. I'm amazed at how many kids right before Christmas in their senior year don't know where they are going, have not applied to a college, have not even asked for application forms. The parents expect the school to do the whole thing for them.

Learn about the scholarships and grants that are available. Money doesn't have to be an issue in college today. There are many grants and much financial aid available to make it affordable.

Your child should choose first. We said to our kids, "Shoot for a college that you think you can't get into, but that you would like to go to. Shoot for a college in the middle that you really would like to go to and you think you can make. Then choose a college you know you can get into." They've done that, and it's worked out well. We said, "We're not going to think of finances until we see the financial package. Then it can be an honest consideration."

Look for grants. My daughter went to Wheaton college this year. It cost her $2,400 for the whole year because of the school package plus outside grants that we received for her. It is possible.

If it's at all possible, plan to go back with your child to get him started in college, a job, the army, or whatever. I think a furlough would be ideal. At least they feel you're a phone call away.

It's not always possible. The next three years, we have three going back. We can't take a furlough each year. But one of us will go back with them. This next year we're going back for a six-month furlough. The following year my wife will probably accompany my daughter back. The following year we'll go back again on a short furlough. It's important.

When my wife was at Wheaton for the freshman year of our daughter, she saw a number of kids sitting in a corner weeping, and she found out that many of them were MKs who had just been flown over, gotten off the plane, and walked into the college. They had never been on the college campus before, had hardly touched base in North America before. There they were, alone.

We can buffer where it's important to buffer.

12

Parenting Spiritual Values

Lester and Jo Kenney
Assemblies of God, Southeast Asia Area

Jo Kenney: Whether you are working alone, and there's no one else to help your child grow in the Lord, or whether you're in a big city surrounded by many people, you still have the major responsibility to impart to your children spiritual values that you hold dear.

We're going to talk about four ways of parenting spiritual values: (1) by understanding our children, (2) by praying for and with our children, (3) by teaching our children, and (4) by being an example or modelling our spiritual values for them. One of the most profitable things we thought we could do was to get together a good list of books that would help you in this role.

Opportunity to Understand Our Children

Recommended book:
Campbell, Ross. *How to Really Love Your Child.* Wheaton: Victor Books, 1977. ($2.95, $4.95).

This book helps you to understand the differences in your children and know better how to work with those differences. The very first chapter talks about how each child has a unique temperament from birth.

Why should we as parents struggle to change an extremely active child into a docile, listening child, if these traits are already clearly identifiable at such an early age. We just need to accept that each child is different and recognize their differences. The author tells you how a nurturing parent makes the difference in whether the child, even a difficult child, will succeed in life. How many of us have said when the second child comes along, "Now if I had just done this differently, how much easier it would have been with the first one." That's probably not true. That was just a different child.

Understand that the parents' relationship is the most decisive factor in building the child's self-esteem. Understand the child's need to feel unconditionally loved, and understand how to convey your love to your child. There is a chapter on each of these subjects in the book.

The Opportunity to Pray for and with Our Children

Recommended books:

Shelley, Judith. *The Spiritual Needs of Children.* Downers Grove, Illinois: Intervarsity, 1982.

Gray, David and Elizabeth. *Children of Joy.* Wellesley, MA: Roundtable Press (Readers Press), 1975.

Prayers for a parent to pray continually until answered

Lester Kenney: Here are some things you might like to put on your prayer list. I don't have a rosary as such, but I have certain things that I pray about every day.

We all want to pray that our children will accept the Lord as their Savior and Lord. We don't want to conquer the world for the Lord and lose our own family. I prayed every day since my boy and girl were born that they would be saved until the Lord answered that prayer in a wonderful way. Pray that your children will follow Christ's teachings, no matter what culture they're in.

I'm not shy to tell my children that I've prayed for them all their lives that they'll marry the partner that's God's choice for them. To me, that's very, very important. The right vocation and the purpose in life are also things we pray for all the time.

It's good that children know we are praying for them. You don't have to tell them, "OK, I pray for you, now you better produce," but in a loving way say, "I love you. I care for you. And I'm concerned for you in these areas."

Prayer for a parent and child to share regularly

It's a wonderful thing that we can pray together. Mealtimes were a great time for us to pray together. Noontime was our family's key time. Family time can be whenever you want it. Just be sure you have it sometime.

Asking God's blessing on family members is a good way to remember those that aren't there. Get the children involved; have them pray for God's protection or God's strength, or God's healing. I know this is the father's responsibility, but God also hears children when they pray.

Pray for the family's ministry to others. Mom and Dad are there for a reason. Why are the kids there? A tearful missionary parent told us one time that their son came with tears in his eyes and asked, "Dad, why didn't you tell us about some of the problems, so we could have understood you, and prayed with you about them?" We don't want to tell anyone about some of our problems, but there are a lot of problems that we can talk about. We can ask our children, "Why don't you pray with us for our Bible school, because we need a revival?" Or, "Why don't you pray for that pastor down there?"

Get the children to pray, and God will answer their prayers. They can be a tremendous blessing.

Prayers for specific needs

There are times when you need to pray for specific things:

- Adjustment to a new culture.
- Adjustment during re-entry to the home culture.
- Adapting to a new school situation. Tell your children what their new school will be like and say, "Let's pray right now that as you go to this new school, you'll fit right in." There will be problems, but they can be a matter of prayer.
- Forgiveness and reconciliation. These are so important. When you teach your child to pray for forgiveness and reconciliation, then give them a role model.
- Healing and strength during illness.
- Safety in political crises. Many of us have been through riots and revolutions. Sometimes it puts a very heavy burden on children. I was away preaching when a riot broke out. I came back the next day into a city that was under a total curfew. It wasn't until many months later we realized our son had carried a heavy burden during that time wondering how he, as a little child, could take care of his mother and sister. He thought that was his responsibility. I wish he had told us earlier, so we could have prayed about it and reminded him of Jesus' love and care for us wherever we are.

- Bereavement.   This may concern the sickness or death of somebody overseas, or maybe somebody very close.   In our situation, one of our son's closest classmates was suddenly killed in a bicycle accident.   I remember a very precious time of prayer with my son in that hour of bereavement.   Actually I don't think I said much.   We just sat and wept together and felt the wonderful presence of God.

Opportunity to Teach Our Children

Recommended books:

Strauss, Richard.   *Confident Children.*   Wheaton: Tyndale, 1975.
Gray, David and Elizabeth.   *Children of Joy.*

Teach from a scriptural basis

Jo Kenney: We as parents need to be sure our children have the opportunity to express their feeling about accepting Christ as Savior. I talked with a missionary kid who was seventeen.   She said, "I don't think I was ever saved."   She was in church all her life, but kids can just let things flow over their heads and not really understand.   It is very important that we parents, in a casual way, make sure our children understand what it means to accept Christ as their Savior, to commit their lives to the Lord, and then to build the Word of God into their daily lives.

Teach in the "dailyness" of every day living

Because our lives are so varied with one going this way and one going that way, many of us don't take time for daily devotions.   So we need to seize the moment to teach the Word of God.   The Bible says "When you rise up (as the day begins), when you sit in your house (at mealtimes), when you lie down (at bedtime), and when you walk by the way" (when you travel), are good times to teach your children. For example, when you're on deputation, when you're going back and forth on those long journeys, you can make that a useful time for teaching.

But of course the most important thing is just having the answer when the question comes.   Our most important teaching is in unplanned sessions with our children.   If we're going to teach in those moment-by-moment times, we've got to be prepared with an answer. That's the secret of teaching your children.   Be prepared to give them the Word. Give them an answer from the Word of God when they need that answer. We can do that only as we live it and as we know it ourselves.

Teach through the activities of special days

Children of Joy is such a good book. It not only deals with special times such as Advent, Christmas, the twelve days of Christmas, and Holy Week, but also with difficult times. This book talks about how to teach your children when they are sick. You teach children the love of God when they're in a period of convalescence. Maybe your children don't have a Sunday School class, or a Bible club they can go to but you can give them a class at home. You don't have to have it on Sunday. Have it on Wednesday, Thursday, whenever. But be sure that they have a formal time of learning as well as what you give them day by day.

Children of Joy lists at the end good books for parents and for children.

Opportunity to Model Spiritual Values

Recommended books:

Kenney, Betty Jo. *The Missionary Family.* Pasadena: William Carey, 1983.
Richard, Strauss. *Confident Children.*

Lester Kenney: Several years ago our denomination arranged a program whereby a missionary on furlough would teach for one year in one of our colleges in the United States. I had the privilege of being the first teacher in the missions program at Northwest College.

One of the most important courses I thought we could have was "The Missionary Family." It dealt with the family overseas. The reason I chose this was that in our early days of teaching in Malaysia, a young man from India came up to us and said, "I have been watching you day and night for several months to see what a Christian family looks like. I have never seen a Christian family before in my life." Until then, we had not realized that we had been teaching what a Christian family looked like.

It was a privilege then to begin teaching "Christian Family" in the Bible Institute in Kuala Lumpur, Malaysia, realizing that the Christian family was one of the most important things we could put in the agenda of the Bible school. I began looking for texts on the missionary family and couldn't find any. So, doing the logical thing that any normal missionary would do, I asked my wife to write one. She did. *The Missionary Family* has been printed three times. One of the exciting things to me is that my wife receives letters from around the world telling how it has been a blessing.

Model our value of spiritual experience (I Cor. 11:l)

All of us believe that our children need spiritual values. They need to accept Christ themselves. Our religion is not their religion. It must be reborn in their hearts. We need to know Jesus intimately and allow him to make us what he wants us to be.

Model the fruits of the Spirit

It is so important that we are positive (Proverbs 22:6), calm (Psalm 37:8; Ephesians 4:31), consistent (Proverbs 19:18), and loving (Ephesians 5:1-2). We don't want kids to say, "My mom and dad are missionaries, but if you could see the way they live at home, or the way they do down at the market, or the way they drive in traffic..." The fruit of the Spirit relates to correcting our children, but let's also include that in our total life, in our life with each other.

Model our trust in scriptural examples for dealing with a wayward older child

Be persistent in prayer (Matthew 15:22,28). Observe the actions of the prodigal son's father (Luke 15:11-32). The father did not forcibly restrain his son from leaving home (Proverbs 22:6). The father let his son bear full responsibility for his actions (1 John 9-10). When his son repented, the father welcomed him with true forgiveness (Matthew 6:12).

Model our moral standards in daily life to help our children

I've always wondered at the boldness of Paul when he said, "Follow me as I follow the Lord." We say, "Don't look at me. Just follow the Lord." What a man, who could go to that culture and say, "You follow the Lord as I do"!

Model our value of the father-child relationship (John 13:34-34)

The father-child relationship is so very, very important.

We are thankful that we can, with the help of God, have Christian homes wherever we are. We can raise our families to know and love the Lord. We serve him because we love him and we want our families to love him and also serve him.

Other Helpful Books

Jo Kenney: These are other books that I have found helpful:

Devin, Edna M. *Garlic in the Flower Bed*. 1820 Dabob P.O. Road,
   Quilcene, WA 98376. ($3.00).

> This is a book of poetry written by a missionary who
> raised six children in Indonesia. While it may not be wonderful
> poetry, it is from the heart of a missionary mother, who was an
> effective missionary on her own for many years after her young
> husband died.

Ferber, Richard. *Solve Your Child's Sleep Problems*. NY: Simon and Schus-
   ter, 1985.

> Bedtime is such a wonderful time to build up your child
> spiritually, but if you're struggling with a child that you can't get
> to bed night after night, and you're getting angry and frustrated,
> it's hard to impart spiritual truth.

Graham, Ruth Bell. *It's My Turn*. Old Tappan, NJ: Revell, 1982.

> In this very small book, Ruth Graham talks about differ-
> ences in children and how you can react to them. She faced
> many of the problems that missionaries do: separation, much
> time away in the ministry, etc.

Johnson, Barbara. *Fresh Elastic for Stretched Out Moms*. Old Tappan, NJ:
   Revell, 1986.

> This is for parents who have suffered great heartache in
> their relationship with their children: drugs or death or some
> really traumatic thing.

LeBar, Lois. *Family Devotions with School-age Children*. Old Tappan, NJ:
   Revell, 1977.

Schulman, Michael and Mekler, Eva. *Bringing up a Moral Child*. Reading,
   MA: Addison-Wesley, 1985.

> It's totally secular. It is not related to the church at all,
> but it teaches you how to teach your child to be kind, to be
> caring, to be unselfish. I find it to be an excellent book.

13

Families in Transition: Preserving the Family in the Midst of Change

Dave Sanford and Ray Chester
Arizona College of the Bible

Ray Chester: Some of our statements may seem somewhat radical to you; they may not. We are going to allow you to draw conclusions. We are speaking from an intensely biased position which comes from the deep convictions and values we share.

We were asked to speak on "Families in Transition: Preserving the Family in the Midst of Change." Since this is not our title, we feel we have the privilege of dismantling it. We want to take a look at the overall philosophical statement that is being made by this title.

Relation between Transition and Disintegration

Dave Sanford: Maybe I should ask a question first. Is transition the cause or root of family disintegration? That's what the title says, isn't it?

Sometimes it's easy to transfer some of our own personal responsibilities to something inanimate. If we're having a problem in making this transition into the new society or culture, we say the transition is the problem. We're having a difficult time making adjustments so we say it's the transition that's the problem and ask how we preserve our family in the midst of the transition. That gets a little bit dangerous. All of a sudden we use experience to determine our theology.

We're "transisting" all of the time, from childhood all the way through life. It is a normal, common, everyday experience for all of us.

Chester: Therefore, it is not making a transition that is the problem.

Sanford: When families move from one society to another, from the States to a more primitive setting, the transition is a large one. But if there is not a motivation, something deeper than just the transitional part of it, we are no different than anyone else. This topic could be addressed at a SIETAR conference or Mobil Oil executive meeting.

There's nothing necessarily wrong with addressing these issues. But we want to see if there is anything beyond the transition that the family should be aware of. As we looked at the title, it implied to us that there is something we must do as a family, an isolated family, to preserve ourselves from disintegrating in the midst of this event of "transisting" from one culture to another.

The Family in Community

We also had to ask, "Who is the family? What family are we talking about here?"

Chester: Do you realize there are multiples of families involved in "transisting"? We want to look at those.

Sanford: The nuclear family is one. My wife, my son, and I came to Ecuador twenty-seven years ago; we did go through some changes. Change of environment, language, climate, friends—a lot of things changed drastically.

Chester: What about the extended family? Do they go through the transition?

Sanford: I can still remember getting on the plane in Cleveland, Ohio. I think more about it now that I'm a grandad. I didn't think about the transition that my in-laws were going through as they saw their young daughter taking their grandson and going off to this far land. I didn't give that a thought. The extended family was also affected by our leaving.

Chester: What about your Christian family that you left? What about your local body? Are they affected? Yes, they are, because there is now a vacancy in that local body. What did Paul say? "If one member suffers, all suffer."

Sanford: It was not solely my responsibility to endeavor to preserve my nuclear family as we moved to Ecuador. There was a whole supportive community that helped in this preservation.

There is an interdependency, a reciprocity within these supportive communities that helps us make our transitions.

Chester: Reciprocity involves a back and forth. Is there reciprocity in this?   What about the transitional family, and what about the receiving family? Remember, the family is not the nuclear unit.

Sanford: There's both a sending family, the community from which you came, and a receiving family, the missionary community into which you go. We don't stop to realize that we go into a different cultural context when we leave home. We have developed a subculture in the missionary community in the countries we have gone to. There are certain rules and regulations. If someone doesn't fit in to those, the same thing happens here that happens back home. Either someone takes care to bring you in and explain it to you and bring you into line, or you're outside.   So there is within the missionary community, a responsibility and reciprocity.

There's also the national church community. They give support, and we enter into their community life. We're making a transition into a whole new kind of experience. I would trust that most of us are very much involved in the new community, the national community.   There is a large community in which this particular event is happening.

Preventing Disintegration of Missionary Families

Chester: Yet we still see disintegration and problems. We still see people going from point A to point B and somewhere along the way falling apart.

What can be done? As Dave and I have talked about this with hundreds of missionary families, we've come up with a very brief statement about what may be going wrong. There are some basic issues we have refused to look at.

Conviction of the sovereignty of God

Sanford: Our whole value concept of the supernatural is very skewed. Who is the God that we serve? Do we genuinely know, believe, and base our life upon the fact that our God is sovereign?

American values concerning the supernatural have infiltrated the Christian community and have disastrously changed our attitude toward God and who he is.

Chester: Do you really believe in the sovereignty of God? One of my greatest concerns as I travel around the United States among evangelicals, is that we have zero need for God or his Word. We have become so sophisticated, so intellectual.

We evangelicals have no assurance in the sovereignty of God in our lives. Therefore we look at other areas like "transisting" and preserving. We set ourselves up as God and try to accomplish the task, and we wonder why everything disintegrates.

Sanford: We are not taking away from the responsibility of man. A genuine understanding of the fact that God is God will produce a genuine personal holiness.

As we've talked about the difficulties in making transitions, the problems of loneliness, and so forth, a question came to my mind. Are MKs not reflecting the very models they are watching us present? Is their confidence in a sovereign God?

What do they hear at home as we talk about our personal needs, as they hear us talk about our physical needs, as they hear us talk about our economic needs? Do they hear, do they see, do they sense a personal holiness that is expressing the very character of Jesus Christ through these transitions?

If somebody asks you a question, where does the response come from? What forms your response to any question, no matter how trivial? Do you constantly, diligently seek to have every thought in your mind centered in the will of God and the Word of God?

What forms your thoughts? It's not just an understanding of certain data. Our kids at school like an answer for every question they might raise. Ray and I never answer questions. Our purpose is to raise interest and thought.

We tell our students, "We don't have answers for everything. We want you to begin learning the process by which you are going to come to conclusions. On what data do you make those conclusions?" It's amazing to me that we spend a tremendous amount of time putting into our minds and hearts data that will not help us come to biblical conclusions.

> **Chester:** My students had an assignment to read *Man of Vision, Woman of Prayer* and write a reaction paper. One young MK sat down fuming, and I asked, "Is anything particularly wrong today?"
>
> She said, "I'm so mad."
>
> I said, "Why?"
>
> She said, "That turkey left his family to fall apart."
>
> I said, "How did you come to that conclusion?"
>
> "Well, if he would have stayed home, everything would have been OK."

"But how did you come to that conclusion?"

"I know it."

"Let me help you with a few words. In your personal experience, in all of the families where the husband has travelled, you have seen problems."

"Yeah. That's it."

I said, "Do you know all the fathers who have travelled?"

"Of course not."

"Is it possible that there are some fathers who travel and go through changes and everything remains well at home."

"Yes, it's possible."

"But in your experience it doesn't exist."

"No, in my experience it doesn't exist."

"When you are eighty years old, will you then have experienced all travelling fathers?"

"Of course not."

"You're making a life decision based on your experience. Is there any other standard, any other measuring rod you may want to look at other than your own personal experience?"

She looked at me and said, "You mean the Bible?"

"Good possibility." We looked up Ephesians 4:13 where Paul stated that Jesus Christ is the measuring rod.

Sanford: Why don't we have a standard other than our own personal experience which dictates our theology?

Chester: I was touring a Christian mental health facility, and near the end of the tour I happened to ask the director, "What is it you do here?"

He said, "We endeavor to help Christians cope with their problems."

I said, "I'm sorry to hear that."

He said, "What do you mean?"

I said, "Because I can't find anywhere in Scripture where it tells me to cope."

Did you ever think about that? Where does that word come from? Coping is nothing but existence from point A to point B. Usually we break down about two-thirds of the way through it. "We are more than copers in Christ." Is that what that verse says?

No, "We are more than conquerors." That doesn't mean that problems mysteriously go away. It also doesn't mean denial. What does it mean? It means in the midst of our problem, there is an attitude of victory, not because of who I am or because I've gone to some seminar that taught me how to have a better view of myself. I have victory because of Christ.

Why don't we believe that? Why do we get trapped into saying, "I'm coping"? I hear that constantly.

We have a little card we give out: "Why cope? You were born to conquer."

Sanford: This is another area where our personal experience colors our theology. When I don't sense victory I have to somehow reinterpret Scripture in the light of my personal experience. Be very careful of that. God still is sovereign. God still is absolute. God still is true. That doesn't mean we're always going to feel victorious, but nevertheless, we do have victory in Christ. There is the possibility and potential of being able to make the transitions victoriously, expressing the character and person of Christ in doing so, IF the data that we are drawing on is biblical.

Even in times of failure, discouragement, and distress, he is the one who will express himself through us. We must live knowing God to be God, and allowing our children and those we impact in our communities to recognize that. As we go through these times, by his grace, he has given us those skills and abilities to do it victoriously.

An articulated purpose in life

Sanford: I wonder how many personally have a stated written purpose of life. For those of you who are married, how many of you with your spouse have a stated, articulated, written purpose to life?

Chester: We've asked some people this. We teach a group of pastors at Moody's Graduate School. We've never yet had one who has had a purpose in life.

Sanford: That's not to say that you don't have a purpose of life wrapped in some theological jargon like, "The purpose of life is to glorify God and enjoy him forever."

Chester: If you don't glorify God, then that's not your purpose in life. That's your *stated* purpose in life. What is your purpose in life? We've talked to people with forty-eight ThD's behind their names, and they can't answer this. What is your purpose in life? Why are you here?

Sanford: I would sense that of all of God's creation, those who are in his leadership position should know why we're here. We talk about a purpose of life—not just a goal or objective. We are talking about the more fundamental, ultimate question of why you exist. You live by that whether you articulate it or not.

You came here because of your purpose of life. Some of it may be very much tied in with the whole value system of society. Why are you here? It is an expression of your purpose of life. As I have worked this through with my family, we have asked "Why do we exist?"—not singularly, because we do not live singularly.

A director of a mission agency wrote me after we had been talking about this, and said, "My wife and I had never done this. Here we are, the directors of a mission agency, and we never sat down to see if she is going the same direction I am, if our purposes are the same." How can two walk together unless they agree? They were not as dynamic a team as they could have been. They found it exciting to begin to understand what God's purpose for them in this world is—a sense of the ultimate that controls all of their decision making.

Some of us get in trouble because we're always saying yes to everything. Why? Maybe because we don't really know why we're here. It's a way to fulfill some of those insecurities we have when people need us. What is my purpose in that? My purpose is a controlling, ultimate purpose that God has burned into my heart by his Spirit through his Word.

Chester: Can you think of any examples of people in Scripture who had a stated, written purpose in life?

Paul said, "This one thing I do." How many things did he do? He did one thing. He had a lot of activities. He was diversified. But he had one purpose in his life.

Sanford: David, do you remember? "One thing have I desired of the Lord. That will I seek after." Consequently he was called a man after God's own heart. Seeking diligently the heart of God.

Your purpose does make a difference in your decision making. The decisions you make, you make because of your purpose of life—your decision to come here; the decision on how to discipline your children; the decision of what you are going to study, what you are going to do, how you live. Those decisions are based upon your purpose of life.

It also controls or limits your behavior. If you have a broad, humanistic purpose of life, then you are going to do and seek things which fulfill that. But if it is one for your own personal holiness because of the Sovereign God you serve, your behavior is going to be limited. These guys going to the Olympics decide to be an Olympic gold medalist. Their behavior is limited considerably. There are things they don't eat. There are places they don't go. They may even move from one location to another to be closer to whatever they're doing in their process of getting ready. Their time schedules, their mental training—everything is brought under the control of that limiting aspect of their purpose of life.

It helps us to focus our energies. Maybe some of us are totally burned out because we have no place to focus our energies. They are being dissipated in all kinds of things for some purpose that we don't even know, and we're being consumed by it.

Motivation

Chester: Another category in here is motivation. If my motivation for doing what I'm doing is a motivation the world can match, then I'm no different from the world.

> A former student who had transferred to a state school to get a degree in psychology came back with some questions. He said, "Ray, I've got some questions about a few things that are going on."
>
> I said, "Probably rightfully so. Why do you think you want to be a counselor?"
>
> "Well, I'm a good listener."
>
> "Sorry. I know some godless pagans who are great listeners."
>
> He said, "Yeah, but I'm real empathetic."
>
> "Sorry. I know some godless pagans who are real empathetic."
>
> He said, "I really think that I can help."
>
> "Strike three. I know some godless pagans who really help pretty well. You haven't told me one thing that is different from any godless pagan. Nothing. Your motivation for doing what you're doing is a motivation any godless pagan can have. What's different about you?"
>
> He said, "I guess I haven't thought through this too well, have I?"
>
> I said, "No, I don't think you have."

Why are you doing this? You have a purpose in life. If somebody comes along with a request, why would you do that? What's your motivation? Why would you "transist"? Why would you come here? Have you ever wrestled with issues like that? Is there any difference between your decision and any godless person's?

Observation and thinking skills

Give your kids and family some tools and skills to enable them to make transitions. We should be alert to the fact that we all teach. I was speaking with a missionary this morning who said, "I didn't realize that when we came to Ecuador, we were actually modelling a way of making this transition to our children." Fortunately, their children saw a good model and they enjoy their international status. She said, "We were young, and we didn't even think about it." Yet God gave them grace to be able to present that kind of a model, and their children were able to make that transference from their parents going through it to their process of making transitions back into the United States society.

As we come into a new situation we can observe it. Some of us are very poor observers, or we are very biased observers. It is fascinating to see what people who have not been out of the States too often see when they travel. If this is your first time in Ecuador, maybe you have been shocked by some of the things you have seen.

When we find people viewing a culture in a very negative way, we say, "What are you looking at? I don't see what you are seeing." How do we teach our children to observe? They observe as we observe. When your children listen to your feedback on what you are seeing, they are going to observe the same thing. Their vision is going to be biased by your reactions. We must act creatively in the way that we observe and make sure that we are objective in the things that we see.

We can train others from our own personal experiences in our own families, in the process helping them to establish skills of creative analysis and creative action. This can happen in the States. It can happen as you travel from one community to another. It can happen on deputation. It can happen in the classroom. Give them the skills and help them to think. Don't give them the answers. What did you see? What does this mean? What do you draw from this? If it is true here, will it happen there?

Avoiding spiritual entropy

Looking at the continuing process of life can present to the Lord and to the communities around us a healthy, vigorous, dynamic, growing family. I believe that is the basis of ministries, particularly in third world countries, where the family is such an important institution within their society. Our mission family must express Christ as we make that jump into their society, like Christ, not holding onto what he had. No transition we can make in this world will come near going from the glories of heaven to a dirty stable. Even if we were to go from the United States with all of its comforts and conveniences to the inner part of Mexico City and live with the poor, that transition would be a mini-step. Christ didn't hang onto the glory, but became part of their society. As Paul said, "All things to all men that by all means I might save some."

A missionary couple had a difficult time in a foreign country for five years. We had talked with the husband one time while he was on the field. He said, "I'm so depressed here that every Sunday after I preach, I spend the whole afternoon crying. This has been the worst, most traumatic thing that has happened in my life."

When they came back on furlough last year, his wife didn't even want to hear the name of the country where they had been serving. It had been that traumatic for her.

Toward the end of the furlough he called me and said, "We have one week to decide whether we are going to return or not." They had had all year to decide, but all of a sudden the deadline was one week away.

He said, "All this year we've been seeking counsel and help about who we are and what we're doing and why we're there, from our pastor, from the missions committee, from our friends, and counselors around Phoenix. The message that we have heard is 'If you don't like it, don't do it.'"

He was a seminary graduate, a phenomenal guy in the languages, and had a tremendous ministry in that country. He said, "Somehow that doesn't fit the reason why we should go or not go — my personal comfort."

I said, "No, Christ would not have gone to the cross if that were the issue. It wasn't too comfortable hanging there between heaven and earth."

We went back to his purpose. Then the two of them together, searched their hearts before God. They returned. Now they have a totally different perspective and purpose for being there. The transition has been phenomenal.

They have school-aged children who are going to be going to national schools. They are responding in a totally different way than that first term when they were fighting being there. They had reflected their parents' attitude in the transition. Now that issue was settled.

The wife said to me, "Dave, thanks for helping us to think it through and to see why we are here."

Chester: The root of the disintegration within the transition process seems to us to be the existence of a spiritual entropy.

Sanford: It's that process of decline, of wearing down. If the family disintegrates through the transition, it is probably evidence that there is already in process a spiritual entropy. This is our bias.

Part III

WHEN SPECIAL CARE IS NEEDED

14

Parents: Needs/Problems
and Mental Health

Marjory Foyle
Psychiatrist, Missionary Health Service

I have been asked if I will speak about problems, therefore I will. But at the outset, if it sounds a little bit negative, remember this sentence: Parents of missionary children are wonderful. They have a quality of handling their children, of caring, and of training which is admirable. Congratulations to all of you.

Parents and children form a community. Problems between the parents will have an influence on the health and the well-being of the children. You see, children are like sponges. They will automatically absorb the atmosphere around them. Sometimes if either parent has a problem and tries to hide it, the children are made anxious and uneasy. Unfortunately they usually rationalize it wrongly. The child who is aware that there is unhappiness or anxiety at home will automatically think, "It has to be my fault." It is very important, if parents are having problems between themselves, or if they are concerned about their work, that the child understand just a little bit about the problem in order to understand it isn't his fault.

I am going to talk about three groups of problems: First, problems before the parents decide to go abroad; secondly, problems during expatriate service; thirdly, problems during re-entry.

Problems before parents decide to go

Missionary parents obviously have to think carefully before they decide to go abroad. Good parents are going to ask themselves:

1. Is it right to expose my children to the health problems of third world countries? This is an important question. Children have died in third world countries. Children have been

injured.   Children have been blinded because of diseases in
the third world countries.   Therefore, caring parents will sit
down and ask themselves if are they right.   It's even worse if
the grandparents are strongly against the move.   They can
even accuse the parents of being uncaring of their own children.   How that can hurt!

2. Is it right to expose the children to multicultural life?   Recently I have been reading articles which speak about the
enlarging aspects of being an MK.   However, all of us know
of wounded MKs, MKs who have had great problems in
adjustment, problems in working out their experiences, and
particularly problems at re-entry.   Wise parents think about
these problems.

3. Is it right to endanger the children's educational, financial,
and social security by giving them an expatriate childhood?
About two years ago, one of my friends was weeping.   He
was a doctor and a professor in a college in Asia.   His son
had had a dream of being a doctor, but because his education
had been unavoidably messed up, it became impossible.   That
is the kind of impact that the parents' calling can have upon
the children.   This, of course, can often stir up a large
amount of resentment.

What Can the Parents Do?

Seek a consensus of trusted opinion

I don't know if it has happened in America, but certainly in
Britain and in the continental parts of Europe, lots of people are
joining house churches.   Quite often these are rather closed, strict
groups.   Some of these house churches have appointed elders.   And I
have discovered that in some, the elders have become increasingly
dictatorial and will tell the young people what to do.   These aren't
the kinds of trusted opinions that I'm speaking about.

I'm speaking about a group of prayerful people who will help
these young people decide if it is right for them to go abroad.   That
was the pattern of the church in Antioch, where Paul and Barnabas
prayed and the church discussed.   They ultimately arrived at a consensus of agreement.   We don't read anywhere that the church
refused Paul and Barnabas.   It was a consensus of opinion, which is
extremely important.

Look carefully at opposition

Most people think that if they're interested in expatriate service and if people oppose it, the origin of that opposition is the devil. That isn't always so. I think that the most important cause, which is rarely spoken about, is the psychological needs of the candidates' parents, the grandparents of the children. This can be a wonderful time when God works good out of evil. Supposing the grandparents are violently opposed and accuse the parents of being uncaring and unfeeling, "Who will look after us?" "What happens if the children get ill?"

I don't think candidates are ever taught to wonder if their parents have problems. I think they have to be taught. It may be that the desire of these children to go abroad provides the first opportunity for the grandparents to come to terms with their own deep psychological needs. Candidates must take the opportunity that God is presenting to them to help their parents have a look at the reasons why they need to keep hold of their children. This is an important opportunity for a ministry of God's healing to all the people concerned. However, on occasion the opposition of these grandparents remains implacable. Of course, the candidate couple has to decide before God if their parents come first or if the calling of God comes first. I think you and I have to stand carefully with them, because this is a terrible dilemma. Certain things can help.

- Make arrangements for substitution. If the children decide to go, perhaps members of the church can act as substitute children. It is wrong for the children to simply storm off and not take care of the needs of the parents, but let them try to work out patterns of substitution.

- Work out communications. If the grandparents remain implacably hostile, ask them to come over and see where their children live. Glamorize it a little in order that the parents have an interest. If the parents won't hear of it at that time, then ask them six months later, and perhaps it will work out. Even though the opposition's been implacable, relationships have to be preserved in small and practical ways—calling up, if possible; correspondence; picture postcards; and telegram cables on the parent's birthday.

Involve the children

The children, as appropriate, should be involved in making the decision. If the children are younger than three years old, it isn't really important to have their involvement. By and large the kids are happy where the parents are. But I think they ought to be told that they're going to move, and that all their playmates won't be quite the same.

The children who are over three, but aren't yet adolescent, have to know everything about the proposal, but they don't have to be asked to decide. They've got to be taught. You have to explain where they're going; teach them about the country by relating it to some of the things they've learned at school.

The problem arises when an adolescent is going out for the first time. I am of the implacable view that if the adolescent says persistently, "I will not go," then you do not go. They have quite enough to handle with puberty without adding on adjustment to a third world culture as well. However, sometimes that implacable view is based on pure ignorance. That can be solved quite easily. Take them on holiday to that country where you're hoping to go. Perhaps you can't get out to the jungle, but you can take them to that country. Let them have a look around. Show them the good and show them the bad. It will help, perhaps, to break down their negative feelings about it.

In England recently, I discovered that the U.S. Navy has a policy exactly like that. When teenage kids are involved, they allow them to go and have a good look first. Same in big business. Oil companies do it. It is worth thinking about if these teenage kids have an implacable opposition. However, if they still remain totally negative, I do not think this couple ought to go. If the couple does go and after twelve months their adolescent child has not adjusted well, I think they definitely need to consider returning home.

Problems during Expatriate Service

Marital relationships are the cornerstone of the family after the Godward relationship. They are of extreme importance. In the mission situation, couples are subject to special stresses such as unavoidable separations, changing roles of the partners, and sexual conflicts. I have selected three areas which can cause problems.

Lack of sensitivity to each other's roles

Due to a constantly changing situation, this can be a major problem. For example, a husband and wife are working quite happily in a Hindu culture. They both have equally important roles. They're both equally fulfilled. The husband is then transferred to a Muslim area, and the role of the wife is inadequately discussed. Consequently the wife hasn't really got any idea of the enormous change in her role which is to come.   The role of the husband will be more or less the same.   But the role of the wife will change one hundred percent because of the Islamic culture.

Here I would like to add a plug for selection techniques.   I am tired to death of talking with couples in which the wife has never been interviewed separately.   One wife told me, "I was taken along like a piece of baggage, but mercifully I wasn't checked in the hold.   I had a seat."   She had no separate interview at all.   I recently was talking with a group of husbands and wives.   One hundred percent of the wives had never been interviewed separately.   They are separate candidates.   They're people.   Will you please see that they're interviewed and treated as separate candidates?   When I interview candidates for psychological suitability, I spend a day on one couple.   It's exhausting, but I spend two-and-a-half hours with the husband, two-and-a-half with the wife.   Then I interview the husband and wife together, and then the kids come in.   We need to be careful of our wives.   Excuse me that I'm quite obviously angry, but I pick up the pieces.

Lack of sensitivity to roles applies not only to selection but to location.   The officers in charge of locations must discuss it alone with the wife.   An unhappy wife destroys the home, as does an unhappy husband.

Sexual problems

It is not always known that sexuality changes with the period of expatriate life.   Sexual problems aren't the same at the beginning of the career as they are as the career goes on.   When couples arrive initially, well established sexual patterns are often disrupted.   A husband is immediately taken out by the bigwigs to have a look at his proposed job.   He's shown the hospital or something, and he's introduced to the colleagues, and he has a look at his operating room and all the rest of it, and he's scared.   He looks at what he's got to work with.   It's totally strange.   His training hasn't prepared him for it.   He comes home to his wife a very anxious man.   And an anxious man will often turn urgently to sex relations because he needs to be reassured and be re-established in his personal identity.

Conversely, his wife, who is also new to the country, has been trying to set up a home.   She's got the kids screaming.   She's got servants she doesn't understand.   She doesn't understand you have to strain milk and then boil it.   She finds cockroaches in her flour.   She's totally exhausted.

Her husband comes home and all he wants to do with this gorgeous lady is go to bed with her. But all she wants is a hug and a kiss, "Darling, I think you're wonderful. Good night." Consequently, if that pattern goes on for too long, it can cause friction. It hadn't been like that at home. There's got to be a great deal of basic trust to handle that kind of situation.

As time goes on, one major issue which turns up is contraception. Perhaps the parents have settled it early on in the marriage, but when they go over as expatriates, psychological needs change. Once again the issue comes up. Now it may be that if the wife's role isn't fulfilling, she wants more children. I saw an example of this recently where there was rivalry between two couples. One couple that was reasonably well-established had a child. The person who was really anxious and unfulfilled immediately told her husband, "We've got to have a baby." But the husband was worried already about finances. He was having a good look at the budget. They had three children and he couldn't see any way at all that they could financially support a fourth kid. Also, he was forty-plus and wasn't wanting to start with diapers and bottles again. Consequently, there was a stress placed upon the whole sexual aspect of the marriage.

Or conversely, I have met husbands who were longing to have a child again. Perhaps they had all girls and wanted a boy, or perhaps they had boys and wanted a girl. The husband begged his wife to have more children. But the wife was overloaded and she felt she just couldn't cope. Without adequate support systems, it's very difficult for couples to handle the stresses and strains of that particular aspect of marriage.

It is also of great importance that the husband and wife communicate constantly about their single work relationships. It has to be brought into the open. Single people and married people must be taught in orientation how to behave toward each other.

Lack of agreement in family matters

I've seen more conflict about raising children than about almost anything else. Perhaps the best example I can give is on matters of discipline. Supposing the background of the husband is rigid. He expects his children to be rigidly disciplined. I have known a household that at exactly 8:00 A.M., BBC time, these children were to be standing behind their chairs, all dressed, ready to pray. The wife of the household came from a very easygoing home in one of the southern states of Ireland, where time is unimportant. Consequently, the trumpet was blowing with an uncertain sound in that household. The

children didn't know what to do. As we all know, children like to
have things all cut and dried. They can't handle uncertainty. By
adolescence, it's all right. They get more able to handle certain kinds
of uncertainty. But younger children really need an understandable
pattern. Parents really do have to handle this matter in a way which
is going to prevent confusion for their children.

Disagreement on eduction is equally traumatic. This is rarely
mentioned, but the children have strong views about where they want
to go to school. How often are they asked in expatriate households?
It's very important that the wishes of the child are understood.

There was a household where I had to talk this over with the
parents. Their child, aged nine, was longing to go to boarding school,
but because of the needs of the parents to have a permanent baby,
they couldn't send the kid. The child was frustrated, and the parents
were guilty.

If the child isn't certain what is best, I would take the child to
see the options. For example, if the parents think a boarding school
is best, then spend a vacation in the area. Supposing parents think
home education is best. Take the child to stay with somebody who is
having home education. It helps to pictorialize the problem.

If the child has gone to for some time and doesn't want to go
back, provided his academic or dorm performance is OK, and his
health is OK, and he's sleeping OK and eating OK, I would explore
to see what is behind it. If he isn't wanting to go back because he's
declining totally, then I think that is serious. If his academic performance is OK and his dorm parents are happy with him, then he's
probably indicating, "I don't want to be bereaved again of my parents." Then it would be wise for you to go to school with him. Take
him yourself.

It's not always understood that every time the children go away,
the parents have an actual experience of mourning. It's often short,
perhaps two days. But the experiences of bereavement are com-
pressed into that period. First there can be denial. "I can't believe
that the kids are going in two days. It's impossible." Then anger.
"Why do we have to work here, God, where I have to keep being
bereaved of my children?" Then gradually there's a period of
adjustment. But there will be mourning.

Here I want to give a piece of clinical advice. If that mourning
is prolonged, and it becomes a great problem in the home, everybody
must ask themselves, "When should we terminate these people's service?" There was one group that I worked with where a couple
mourned for six months every time the kids went back to school,

because communications were cut and it was impossible to have access to the children. What I said was, "Give it a try for three semesters. If they haven't resolved it by then, their stay has to be terminated."

Sometimes the mourning can be relieved by substitution. It's often possible by being interested in national children, or having a work involvement. All parents have to work out what is wise in that area, but to leave it blank is so dangerous.

Practical advice on marital relationships

First of all, the marital relationship must be examined before the candidates are accepted. Once again let me explain why I've got grey hair.

> Candidates are selected. Then six weeks before they're flying off to Timbuktu, they are sent to me with a longstanding marital problem. "Will you please straighten it out in six weeks, Doctor?"
>
> I write back and say, "I'm awfully sorry. It's impossible."

Missions are sometimes a bit naive. They think that because this couple is Christian, the marriage is automatically fine. It may be. But it may not be. Therefore it has to be examined with a view either to pre-acceptance counseling or an enrichment course, but it must be before acceptance is finalized. If there's doubt, I would suggest these candidates be delayed for twelve months to receive further counseling and evaluation.

After they are accepted, the marriage must be regularly reinforced. I think missions are wise to take great pains that serving missionaries have regular opportunities to strengthen their marriage. It is discussed in furlough counseling, and courses are arranged.

Pastoral care in the early stage is of vital importance. Wise language schools now have pastoral counselors on their staff whose only duty is to care for language students in all aspects of their lives. If you haven't got such a program in the group you work with, start urging it, because it is of great help.

Pastoral counseling on the field is of equal importance. Sometimes your missionaries are nervous about talking to someone from their group, and it's good to have an alternative arrangement. If they want an outside person, that person should be appointed.

Whatever else we teach couples, teach them to keep on communicating. If they have quarreled at 8:00 at night, they must resolve it before they go to bed. How wise the Bible is: "Don't let the sun go down on your anger." I knew a missionary couple who for two years communicated only through their cook. It is very important that we teach them to keep on communicating.

We need pastoral-care people who will try with tact and care to find out what is wrong when they hear rumors of a conflict in the marriage. It is of special importance for the experienced missionaries. All the care and attention goes to the new people, and experienced missionaries are often neglected. Perhaps they have started quarreling. Perhaps the wife is menopausal or the husband is menopausal, and everything is going wrong. They must have great care also.

Problems during Re-entry

The circumstances of re-entry have a direct bearing on the relationships between the parents and between the parents and the children. I have discovered that if the parents come home because of the educational needs of the children, re-entry is easier. This is a joint decision which they have expected and planned for, and the whole family has accepted that when Johnny is fourteen we'll all have to go. They've planned for it and have mourned in advance. They have prepared. As a rule, although there is grief at the parting, it really doesn't cause a large amount of problems.

Illness or handicaps

But problems arise when one person is ill. Here is an area where anger, grief, bitterness, and resentment are experienced, but as a rule they are not verbalized. The parents feel ashamed even to talk about it to God. It is of the greatest importance in this area that the parents are helped to talk.

For example, supposing a child is born on the field. The parents have wanted the child and have prayed for the child, but the child is badly handicapped. They all have to go home. What a confusion! There is guilt. There is bitterness. There is resentment. There is confusion about the calling, and there is anger at God. "He called us. We asked him for a child, but now we have a handicapped child who has destroyed our calling."

It is a terrible situation which causes all sorts of problems. I have known parents who have been torn in pieces with this kind of problem. They've held onto God in blind faith, the faith of Job. "Though he slay me, still will I trust him." But they have endured agonies with their guilt and their bitterness. In reality, the child has destroyed their career prospects. The child has spoiled all the work that has been carefully built up. That is reality. The parents have to come to terms with that reality and the purposes of God.

In a situation of that kind, I've come to the conclusion that the big task that we have is to be with the parents and help them to talk about it. They're dead scared of talking, because they think we'll think they're unspiritual or they're ungodly or whatever. I have told them, "I don't care a tuppence if you're ungodly. I want you to talk about your pain, because I believe God wants you to talk about it. I am his servant." That's an occasion for hugging and kissing, and of verbalization of anger and bitterness. I am always relieved when one parent is able to say, "God, today I hate you, but I know that as we work it out, that you will explain." If they can verbalize their guilt and their hatred, then it is a great strength.

Parents who are experiencing emotions of that kind have got to be released to talk about them. It is important that they acknowledge their feelings in some way. It is dangerous if they deny their emotions because they have been made to feel Christians should not experience those feelings.

Rates of adjustment

Another problem concerns rates of adjustment. Please remember, these vary. Sometimes children are slow to adjust and the parents are fine. Or one of the parents has a problem and the other parent and the kids are fine. Don't ever hold the other person up as a model. Don't ever say, "Look at Johnny. He's not having a problem. What's wrong with you?" Remember, we're all made differently, and therefore we all have different rates of adjustment.

It is good in these areas if it's talked about openly at the family prayer time. For example, one can pray, "Dear Lord, please help Daddy who is finding it hard to be back in America." Then everybody's involved. It isn't a secret to be scared of.

15

Depression and Suicide

Esther Schubert, Family Practice and Emergency Medicine, Indiana
John Powell, Counseling Center, Michigan State University

Depression

Esther Schubert: By depression I am not referring to a low mood or a bad day, but a clinical illness, biochemically based, that occurs in Christians as well as in non-Christians. At any one time in the United States, 5 percent of the U.S. population is clinically depressed. That makes me think that at least 20 percent have been depressed at one time or another.

We have Biblical examples of depression—Jeremiah and David. Later on Martin Luther was depressed. J.B. Phillips, who was so productive for so much of his life, had a serious ongoing problem with endogenous depression. So we see that there are people who are very productive and yet have had a problem with this illness.

There seem to be three predisposing factors to depression: (1) genetic susceptibility, (2) early traumatic experiences, and (3) psychological stress later in life that echoes early loss and places unusual demands on the already vulnerable system.

The MK's greatest stresses seem to fall into two general categories, separations and cultural pressures. MKs often find themselves in situations of repeated pressures created by multiple separations and transitions involving persons, places, things, and ideas. Not only are separations a problem, but their timing in the child's life is a problem. These separations create a sense of rootlessness, and probably contribute to that unresolved grief mentioned by Dr. Pollock. The vulnerable MK may have reached the limit of his tolerance by adult life. Another series of separations that remind him of or symbolize the earlier losses may tip the scales in the direction of depression or other illnesses.

We can't ignore the fact that some MKs are subjected to exceptional stress, and that other MKs are vulnerable to average stress. These are the ones that I'd like to address.

I'll be discussing depression as an illness, not a sin. It is possible to be down emotionally because of sin in our lives. There are consequences to behavior, and we do reap what we sow. That is not, however, what I am referring to here.

Depression, by definition, is a biochemical illness in which the emotional pain is so severe that the pain of living is worse than the pain of dying. At this point suicide is a possibility. Crisis intervention addresses two issues: (1) gradual relief of severe emotional pain, and (2) immediate prevention of suicide.

We are going to discuss two primary types of depression, endogenous unipolar biochemical depression, in which suicide is a possibility, and exogenous or reactive depression. The endogenous tends to be more involved with chronic stress, and the exogenous tends to be more reactive and more related to acute stress.

Another type of endogenous depression is bipolar depression. This is manic depressive illness. This individual, when he is sick, can be either extremely high or extremely low. Untreated, the pattern usually runs about six months of being very manic and being very high, and then about nine months of very deep-seated depression. We're not going to discuss it in detail, but you should be aware that there is such a thing.

Endogenous Depression, or Major Depressive Disorder

What we are going to discuss now is unipolar endogenous depression. That means that whenever a person has this illness, he is depressed. He does not have a manic phase. The chemical model of endogenous unipolar depression is a central nervous system dysfunction involving neurotransmitters, primarily norepinephrine, dopamine, and serotonin. These chemicals become depleted, and in the process the individual can become severely depressed.

It's important to rule out physical illness. For those of you particularly in tropical countries, we see depression with malaria, and dengue. I think we see it with mono and anemia, and there are probably other illnesses. You want to be sure there's not a physical illness causing this. If you have ruled that out, there are five primary etiologies of depressions:

- Prolonged chronic stress.

- Pathological grief, anger, or guilt (unresolved negative emotions).

- Idiopathic biochemical depression. I call this no-fault depression because these are usually the situations where there is a family history of depression. There may be an aunt, uncle, cousin or parent who has it. Now the kid has it. He was raised right; he had all the right opportunities; there don't seem to be any great tragedies in his life, and yet he develops a problem with endogenous depression.

- Hormonal. We see this with premenstrual syndrome and menopausal problems.

- Medication such as for high blood pressure can precipitate depression.

The newer terminology for this is major depressive disorder. Most endogenous unipolar depressions fall into the category of major depressive disorders.

Exogenous Depression, or Minor Depressive Disorder

Exogenous depression is more reactive. It's a reaction to real or perceived loss—loss of a person, possessions, pride, self esteem, job, or status. Grief is an excellent example of exogenous depression. This is what you feel when you're holding the hand of your best friend who's dying of cancer.

Culture shock is another example. Missionaries tend to peak in their culture shock at about eight months. I believe culture shock is a type of grief reaction. You can have someone who is still immobilized six months to a year after they've come back to their home country or gone to a foreign country. I don't think that's any longer culture shock. You'd better start thinking about an endogenous component. If it's exogenous, it's self limited and usually does not last much longer than six months or a year. The person may have feelings after that time, but he's able to function.

I am not saying that as missionary kids we are ever going to be exactly like everybody else. There will always be changes in our lives and differences in the way we think, because we're missionary kids. But we will be able to function after six months to a year, even after reverse culture shock.

The treatment for exogenous depression does not include medication in most cases. Tincture of time is a major factor, as well as support systems and counseling.

These are generally considered, in the new terminology, minor depressive disorders. They are not minor to the individual who is involved. There is nothing more intense than to lose a loved one to death. But they are classified as minor from the perspective that they are usually not life threatening.

Most depression is mixed. You can have an exogenous event that precipitates an endogenous depression, such as the culture shock victim who is still culture shocked four years down the road.

Symptoms of Major Depressive Disorder

With the major depressive disorder, the individual has a loss of interest or pleasure in almost all usual activities. In addition, you need four of the following eight symptoms present for at least two weeks:

- Appetite change, either up or down.
- Sleep change. The classic sign of endogenous unipolar depression is early morning awakening. I've had patients come to me as adults and say, "I wake up at four o'clock every morning, and I'm not jet lagged. I can't get back to sleep. I'm tired all day long." They don't look depressed. They don't feel depressed. But when you describe the symptoms, these people will tell you, "I meet those criterion." So when somebody comes to you, or you hear of somebody who, for weeks and weeks in a row, is waking up early, and there doesn't seem to be any reason for it, the flag ought to go up in your mind that we may be talking about an endogenous depression.
- Psychomotor excitation or retardation.
- Decreased energy.
- Worthless feelings or excessive guilt.
- Thoughts of death, suicide, wish to be dead, or suicide attempt.
- Decreased concentration.
- Decreased sexual interest or drive.

If they come in at ten days having these symptoms, you don't say, "Wait four days and I'll see you." They need intervention. But it should not be something that just occurs on a bad day. It should be longer than that.

These individuals may or may not be psychotic. (By psychotic I mean, they're out of touch with reality.) In most of my experience they are not psychotic. They know what's going on, but they're in such emotional pain that they don't care.

By comparison, the person with a minor depressive disorder is not suicidal. He is performing adequately. He is never psychotic, and he tends in general to have a more situational and milder form of depression. It's important to distinguish between these, because a person with a minor depressive disorder can usually be kept at school and at work with time and support and counseling. But the endogenous unipolar major depressive disorder must be intervened with, and it must be done fairly quickly. Most depressions have some components of both.

Masked Depression in Adults

Marjory Foyle: These symptoms are most common in missionaries. If you don't know about them then you won't ask the right questions.

- In women, the most common symptom of masked depression is pain in the face. These people have their teeth taken out. As a rule it is depression if there is early morning wakening and if the pain is worse in the morning.
- People with chronic problems in the colon—spastic colons and all kinds of episodes of diarrhea or chronic amoebic dysentery.
- The third complaint in men is commonly impotence. They will often come to the MD complaining of impotence with anxiety about it. That anxiety is worse in the morning, and they've got early morning wakening.
- Headache, which will be worse in the morning. If you get missionaries complaining endlessly of headache, ask them how they sleep, and you will pick up early morning wakening.
- Constant complaints of weaknesses of all kinds. The blood is normal; chest X-ray is normal; the urine is normal; it's all normal. But they're worse in the morning, and they have early morning wakening.

Adolescent Depression

Schubert: Until about ten years ago, most of us thought that depression only occurred in adults. Now we realize it can occur in teenagers and even younger children. Depression, of course, is an affective illness, and we have seen a fivefold increase in major affective illness in older teenagers in the past forty years. We are realizing as we counsel adult depressives, that many of them, in retrospect, showed the first signs of depression when they were teenagers or children. Some adults have told me that they remember having some of these symptoms as early as seven or eight years of age. Unfortunately, the earlier the onset, the more severe the disease, particularly if it is not intervened with.

The general signs of depression in adolescence are similar to adult depression in contrast to the younger childhood depression. The adolescent will tend to have a dysphoric mood and low self-esteem. He may have a change in his concentration. He used to be able to do his homework in an hour, and it takes him two hours now. He has sleep changes, appetite changes, somatic complaints such as headaches, stomachaches, and backaches that you can't find a reason for, and suicidal preoccupation. Often he withdraws. His withdrawal, unfortunately, is often interpreted as resolution, and that's usually not the case. Often that is a prelude to suicide. When he seems to suddenly get better for no reason, you better start looking and see what's going on. This kid may be suicidal. He may have made up his mind that he's going to do it. Acting out may be a sign of depression in the adolescent.

The problem with kids is that they often don't see that their unusual behavior relates to how they feel. In the U.S. in the past twenty years, there's been a severe erosion of sources of external sense of self-esteem, particularly the loss of religious identity, family cohesiveness, and patriotism. Then there are three other characteristics in the United States which also apply very specifically to MKs. These are a transient society, loss of the extended family, and rootlessness. In the United States culture, we have seen this be associated with an increase in adolescent depression.

Adolescence at best is a chaotic time of life. At age twelve, we see kids normally being dependent on their parents. By thirteen or fourteen the peers become all important to them. They must have a mob identity. They want someone to hang out with at school. They want to be sure that they have a gang or a group. By fifteen or sixteen, they begin to think (although they may not do anything about it) more in terms of a single heterosexual friend, and by seventeen, hopefully we begin to see some maturing in the area of their super ego and identity.

Because of the importance of peers, I think the ages of thirteen to fifteen are a difficult time to make a permanent move as a family. If you uproot a child at that age, you have to be sure that you are available and that there are other peers available to give that kid a support system. I'm not referring to furlough. If a kid gets back to his home country and doesn't like it, he knows he'll be back on the field in a year, and he can exist for a year. What I worry about are families who make a permanent move when they have kids between the ages of thirteen and fifteen, because you can't take the peer group with you.

For some kids the loss of peers can cause them to assume that all is bleak, nothing is worthwhile, and life is not worth living. If severe depression goes on long enough, there may be permanent biochemical damage. An adult who was not treated when he had adolescent depression may need to be treated repeatedly or for a very long time as an adult, because what needed to be dealt with in the child was not dealt with.

By the time he gets into severe depression, he now has a thought disturbance. He loses his ability to think and communicate in a clear and rational way. Counseling becomes less and less effective. He becomes self-destructive, or he may run away. Severe depression may progress to suicide.

You, as adults, are faced with decisions regarding hospitalization or twenty-four-hour-a-day supervision to avoid that. You need to know when to intervene and how aggressive to be.

Girls attempt suicide three times more frequently than boys. This is often because they use less lethal means such as pills. But, as women are becoming more assertive, they're starting to use more lethal methods.

Boys succeed at suicide three times more often than girls. They use more violent and lethal methods such as guns, knives, hanging, and jumping. There is usually less chance for intervention with these methods.

In teenagers, we have to be careful about two things. One is masked depression. This is a kid who is depressed and doesn't know it. Secondly, we need to be careful of smiling depression. This is the kid who looks fine when he's with his peers, but when he gets off by himself, he looks sad. Remember that chronic stress, even in teenagers, can cause depression.

Compliant children are particularly prone to depression. They may be depressed just because there are problems in the world. We had a college-age missionary kid who stayed with us in the summer. She had a problem with depression. She was a classic compliant child. She would not eat cereal for breakfast because the milk carton had pictures of missing children, and she couldn't deal with that. There were problems in the world, and she was depressed because of it. This may be an extreme case (she is doing fine now, by the way) but that is an example of a compliant child who could not deal with the fact that the world just plain had problems. She couldn't in any way divorce herself from that situation.

The reverse is also true. We see some depressed kids who try to cope with their depressed mood through compliant behavior. This kid may be genetically vulnerable to stress. He may be compliant to avoid the stress of confrontation. He may seem fine until he is in his late teens or at boarding school faced with separation from the family. At this point, he may be unable to cope without the support of the family. This can precipitate depression or suicide.

Above all else, we must not assume that adolescent depression is a phase. Rather it is an illness, and it must be intervened with before it causes death or potentially permanent debility.

We've seen some connection statistically between depression and acid rock music, mind games (Dungeons and Dragons, the occult), drugs, alcohol, and family instability. I don't know which is the chicken and which is the egg, but I do worry about a kid who spends ten hours a day listening to acid rock music. I don't know if he gets depressed and then he listens to that stuff, or if he listens to it and it makes him depressed. Whatever it is, there certainly is an association, and I think it's a maladaptive association.

Remember, the adolescent may have to be severely depressed before his depression is apparent to his parents, to himself, or to others.

A number of studies have been done in the area of depression. We don't experiment with children, so there are times when, for better or worse, we have to extrapolate some statistics from studies done on higher primates. There are limitations to these studies, but let me share with you one study with monkeys that I think is valid. Young monkeys with a high genetic tendency toward depression, placed with extremely nurturing mothers in the colony, responded well to the nurturing environment. In most cases it was felt that genetic susceptibility could be overcome.

What that suggests to me is that the susceptible, vulnerable child, if discovered early enough, can be helped. The MK who fits the category of the vulnerable child, either by nature or by lack of nurture, needs to be placed with particularly nurturing dorm parents or teachers.

Adolescent Suicide

In the U.S., suicide is now the second leading cause of death among teens. Suicide is when the individual plans to kill himself and succeeds. A suicide attempt is when he plans to kill himself, but he does not succeed. A suicide gesture has nothing to do with death. This individual has a goal to modify someone else's behavior or to manipulate.

Statistically, suicide attempts occur 8 to 100 times more often than completed suicides, and suicide gestures occur between 50 to 220 times more frequently than suicides. The tragedy is that approximately eight out of ten of these completed suicides, in retrospect, left warning signs that nobody picked up on. My purpose today is to let you know what the warning signs are.

In the U.S., the most prominent personality characteristics associated with suicide attempts in adolescents are the following nine:

- A tendency to react severely to loss. I worry about any kid who reacts severely to loss, but I worry less about the kid who reacts outwardly. The kid who sobs and carries on and grieves it out is a lot easier to deal with than the kid who goes to the airport, sees all of his friends off over four or five years, and never sheds a tear. Nobody knows what is going on in this kid's mind. He may be a loner, an internalizer, or a kid who simply doesn't display his emotions. But there are problems there that need to be dealt with. Dobson says, "Keep your troubled child talking," and I think that's very valid advice.
- Poorly controlled or expressed rage or guilt.
- Impulsivity.
- Major depressive disorder.
- Drug abuse, alcohol.
- Personality disorders, especially borderline.
- Specific reading disorders.
- Learning disability with hyperactivity.
- Reactive disorders, adjustment disorders

Suicide in Christian teenagers

According to Bill Blackburn, Christian teenagers seem to commit suicide for all the usual reasons, plus a few of their own.

- An intolerable situation. This can be real or perceived. If the kid is depressed enough, he perceives that there is no other way out.
- To join a loved one in heaven.
- A noble, romantic view of death.
- A distorted Christian view of heaven as an escape.
- Confusion about the unpardonable sin.
- Immaturity or impulsivity.
- Mental illness.

MK high schools have consistently been below the U.S. average in the area of suicidal behavior because (1) we provide a complete support system in most MK schools, and (2) suicide is not considered an appropriate coping mechanism in those schools.

Let me qualify that by saying that if depression is severe enough, suicide can result, regardless. So don't just assume that because a kid is a Christian that he won't do something to harm himself if he gets depressed enough.

In any case, we need to be alert to signs when they occur, either at high school age or later. One danger most MKs face is that they tend to be very achievement oriented.

MKs are also subjected to a lot of expectations — their own expectations and other people's expectations of them. Somewhere along the line missionaries and MKs must learn that no amount of achievement can substitute for loss of early love and noncontingent approval.

Maris in his book, *Pathways to Suicide*, published by Johns Hopkins, has an excellent discussion of Luther, Calvin, the Reformation, and the development of the so-called Protestant work ethic. Secular, occupational success is not just one goal in American culture. It is the outstanding trait. The fruit of that is that we identify standards of personal excellence with competitive occupational achievement. Unfortunately, we have carried this philosophy into the third culture, and if there is an indictment of our MK schools, I believe that this is it.

In all fairness, some of this may result simply from putting a bunch of extremely intelligent kids into one setting. They do compete against each other. But we as adults in the third culture setting are not guilt-free. Somehow we must communicate that our self-esteem is based on our relationship with Christ, not on our performance academically, athletically, or even spiritually.

What Can You Do?

In the area of crisis intervention, what can you do? Often you are in a position to pick up on things that need to be picked up on before they become serious.

- Understand endogenous and exogenous depression and their overlap.
- Suspect depression. Understand those symptoms and pick up on them if someone is having some of those symptoms.
- If you suspect suicide potential (and if you suspect depression, you had better be suspecting suicide potential) you need to ask three questions:

  1. How hopeless is this individual? Is he giving things away? Is he talking like he's not going to be here next week? Is he writing last notes? Is he a basketball star, yet doesn't care if there's a tournament next week? Is he a kid who talks like he has no future?

  2. "Have you thought about suicide?" Ask him straight out. There is a myth that says "I don't want to ask anybody, because I might put it in their mind." That is wrong. If they are depressed, they have thought of suicide. You are not putting anything in anyone's mind. What you communicate if you ask them about it is, "I understand how sick you are, and I understand how much help you need, and I will take over and get you that help." If they're depressed, they can't get it on their own.

  3. Find out how he would do it. Find out if he has a plan. Find out what keeps him from doing it, how well thought out his plan is, how lethal he thinks his method is, or how lethal it really is. If he thinks the method that he is planning on using will kill him, you'd better intervene. Remember, forethought and planning are ominous.

- Make a decision about hospitalization. If you come to the conclusion that the kid or adult is fairly well compensated and that he will be able to get by without hospitalization, that he is not an immediate danger to himself, you must make a verbal contract with him. A verbal contract is not good for all time. You cannot say, "You must promise me you will never commit suicide." He cannot make that kind of a commitment. What you say is, "I will see you every day," or "I will see you every two days, and between now and nine o'clock tomorrow morning when I see you, I have to have a commitment from you that you will not harm yourself, and if you get to the point that you think you may, you will contact me." Then I have to be available or have somebody else available if he does make that contact. In the meantime, we start medication and we start outpatient counseling.

- If he cannot make a commitment to you that he will not harm himself, he must immediately be gotten into the hospital. If you're on a field where there is not hospitalization, he must have twenty-four-hour-a-day supervision. This is difficult to do. You take away his belt; you take away his shoe strings; you don't let him in the kitchen where the knives are; you go to the bathroom with him. You are with him twenty-four hours a day.

It takes three to four weeks for antidepressants to start working, so we're talking about a pretty major commitment. You need a team of discreet people who will not talk about what's going on and who will take care of this individual until the medication kicks in and he begins to turn around.

Treatment for Endogenous Biochemical Depression

The treatment for endogenous biochemical depression begins with the biochemical medication. What we use initially are the tricyclic antidepressants. Counseling needs to be very basic initially. You're not going to get anything in depth for the first few weeks.

I'd like to make a comment about the use of Scripture early on in severe depression. Scripture is great. We base our lives on it. But if you have a severely depressed individual and you quote Scripture to him, you will lose his involvement in your intervention. It's like offering a steak to somebody who is vomiting from the flu. There's nothing wrong with that steak, but he's not ready for it. Later on, he's going to be ready for it, and it will be great for him, but early on in depression, do not quote Scripture; do not use platitudes; do not use quick answers because there are no quick answers. Get that person medicated. Get him into intensive care, and get things started.

Later on in more intensive counseling you can start getting involved in the scriptural basis for the help that he needs.

Tricyclic antidepressants are really excellent. They can be used in adolescents or adults. People say, "I don't want to be dependent on drugs." They are not addictive drugs. I think people who are placed on them need to be on them for six months to a year at least. If they're taken off too soon, we often see a recurrence.

In the initial phase of treatment, it takes three to four weeks to see improvement. Be sure your patient knows this. Don't let him assume he's going to feel better after he's taken a couple of pills.

A danger point is when the individual first starts improving. He may be at greater risk for suicide, because his energy level may improve in the first part of recovery, and he may then have the energy to act on his suicidal wishes. Even with the best emergency room intervention in the United States, people die from overdoses of tricyclics. They're great antidepressants, but just be sure that somebody else is taking responsibility for dispensing the medication.

I don't know how to deal with the fact that Christians commit suicide. I don't think I can address that theologically. It's a real puzzle in my mind. It seems to me that most of what I see is sickness and not sin. I think we put tremendous guilt on our Christians who are depressed when we imply to them that if they were right with the Lord, they would not be depressed. I would like to counsel us to utilize the gift of mercy within the body of Christ a little more appropriately in this setting.

Treatment of Severe Endogenous Depression on the Field

You need four things to treat anybody with severe endogenous depression:

1. Access to a hospital with a psychiatric ward where people can be kept from hurting themselves or twenty-four-hour-a-day supervision for several weeks while the antidepressant is taking hold. This usually needs to be instituted immediately if the depression is severe.

2. A medical doctor. You need a doctor who understands how this medication works who is comfortable prescribing it.

   Christians often tend to deny the need for medication. They want to do it without medication. There seems to be a humiliating aspect to taking medication. That really is not the case. We have great results with these medications. Depression is one of the best psychiatric illnesses to treat. In almost all cases, it can be treated effectively, and we can return people to active, productive work.

Cross-cultural psychiatry is difficult. If there is a missionary doctor or a third culture doctor who is comfortable prescribing the medication, I would prefer using him rather than a national doctor. There are exceptions, but it is something to think about.

3. Someone who will do long-term counseling. This needs to be somebody who is really sophisticated. I don't know if it matters what degree is behind their name, but it needs to be somebody of the caliber and with the capabilities of a psychologist. Some psychiatric social workers are particularly good.

You just need to have somebody who can counsel in depth. If you do it too superficially, then you lose the opportunity of dealing with this while the person is vulnerable and available for treatment. You want to change thought patterns. You will have less recurrence if you can change thought patterns in the process of counseling.

4. Support systems. There must be people who will be support systems for that individual once he or she is treated.

It doesn't always work out that you have all four of these, so let me share with you what we have done in Taiwan. This is not ideal. I would love to have a full-time psychiatrist on the island. I would love to have ten psychologists available to do counseling. I would love to have a psychiatric hospital. We don't have it. But here's what we have done.

Treatment in Taiwan

1. If an individual is not suicidal, and if he can make a verbal commitment, we get support systems of his choice who will be involved in supervising or just being available, people who can keep their mouths shut. Discretion is appropriate. Somebody else keeps the medication. Out of fifteen or twenty patients, I've only had to send one to the home country because they were too suicidal to deal with on Taiwan.

2. With regard to the MD, I'm only in Taiwan two or three times a year, but I'm the most comfortable in prescribing antidepressants, so it has fallen to me to be involved in most of the cases of depression we have on the field. I have an excellent school nurse at Morrison Academy who manages

these people. They're in touch by phone frequently, sometimes on short notice. It's not ideal, but we're doing OK.

3. There's a good Christian psychologist on the island and Morrison Academy is currently recruiting a full time counselor, psychologist, or psychiatric social worker to be on campus to minister to the expatriate community.

4. Support systems. In Taiwan we have educated the expatriate community. Dave Brooks, the superintendent at Morrison Academy, has repeatedly brought in speakers to share about the fact that depression can occur with Christians, and that it can be medicated and treated. Every time we have one of those speakers, about five depressed individuals from different parts of the island come and want to be treated. Most of those people have been treated effectively.

Childhood, or Preadolescent, Depression

Acute childhood depression tends to last days to weeks. This kid is usually crying. This most often is exogenous depression. He needs a support system. He often can be treated on the field.

By comparison, the chronic preadolescent childhood depression is less common. These kids are often dry-eyed. They tend to be endogenous or biochemical. This is a much more serious situation, and I recommend that, if possible, these kids be treated in the home country. They not only need a psychiatrist and a counselor, they need a child psychiatrist. The whole family, in most instances needs to be counseled along with them. If you're dealing with a chronic childhood preadolescent psychosis, get this kid help, and if you can, get it in the home country where you can have a subspecialist who can take care of him.

Let me list the fourteen signs of chronic preadolescent childhood depression: You can have a number of these; it does not have to be every single one.

- The kid appears sad or unhappy.
- He's withdrawn socially or can go to the other extreme and be hyperactive.
- He may say, if asked, that he feels unwanted or unloved.
- He perceives himself in a negative light. He calls himself stupid or mean.
- He often has difficulty in controlling aggressive drives: fighting, biting, destructive behavior against persons or things.

- He often is involved in excessive bullying or teasing.
- He engages in public defecation.
- He may wet the bed long past the age when we think he should.
- He may have insomnia, not especially early morning awakening, but he may have trouble getting to sleep, or he may have trouble later on in the night.
- He may be involved in excessive auto-eroticism or masturbation. I know this is a controversial issue, but I think most kids are involved in masturbation occasionally. What you're worried about is the kid who does it excessively.
- He has psychosomatic symptoms.
- Often one or both of the parents are depressed.
- The child may have been abused physically or emotionally in the past.
- He may have separation anxiety, even to the point of school phobia occurring.

This child may have had repeated disruptions in important relationships. There may be a family history. There may be clinging, or he may go to the other extreme and be cynical and have difficulties in relationships. The family must be treated as well as the child. I don't know how many of these symptoms of childhood depression have to be present for diagnosis. We don't know much about childhood depression, and that's one reason I'm very hesitant to treat chronic childhood depression on the field. But you ought to be suspicious. If you get a cluster of these symptoms, you need to start getting involved.

Preadolescent Suicide

With regard to childhood suicide, age is very much a factor. Up to the age of five, children consider death to be reversible. They think the guy is going to wake up. They don't really think he's dead. Part of this may be immaturity, but part of it comes from seeing cartoon caricatures like Br'er Rabbit fall off the end of the cliff, flatten out, and then get up and walk away. The kid gets the feeling there's nothing you can do that's going to kill you.

Between five and nine, children consider death to have both good and bad attributes. Between nine and twelve he develops a mature concept of death. Between twelve and fourteen it is a gray area.

Generally we consider that a child under the age of twelve is in the suicide latency age. There are very few intentional suicides that occur in this age range. But they can occur. There is about 1 per 100,000 population, compared with about 12 per 100,000 population in the adolescent age range.

Adolescent Suicide

John Powell: The area of adolescent suicide has been increasingly alarming to us on college campuses. Statistically there has been an increase in the number of successful suicides on college campuses over the last five years. And we are seeing in our own mental health services a dramatic increase in the number of suicide attempts. It is not uncommon at all for the crisis team in our center to be busy in one way or another each week.

We need to realize that suicide is very seldom a sudden event. As you talk with someone who has attempted suicide, you realize that not only were there cues early on, but there were predispositional factors that played into this decision. One of these is depression. Many times there will have been many ways that this depression has shown itself that no one, sometimes not even the person himself, has picked up as having any particular significance.

Mild Depression as a Normal Reaction to Stress

It is important to realize that some of the experiences of depression, and particularly reactive depression, may occur within the normal band of behavior that each of us experiences in day-to-day life. For example, many of the separations we experience are accompanied by stress, and many times our response to that stress is to have some kind of a mild or perhaps moderate exogenous depressive reaction. Let me give you an example from my own life:

> Not long ago we made a substantial change in some of our activities. As a result, I had begun to experience three of the symptoms that were pointed out earlier. I was not endogenously depressed, but I had, for example, the classic symptom of early waking and some of the other symptoms that told me I was not functioning at all in the way I should.
>
> As I shared this with my wife, she said, "I notice that you haven't been working that effectively lately and you have

seemed kind of down." I'm not normally a person who gets depressed, so this had more significance for me than it might have had for some people whose moods go up and down.

Because she knows me very well, she was able to talk with me about feelings I had been experiencing, but that I was not aware of. As I expressed those feelings, I began to have some sense of release from some of the threat that I was feeling in making this major change in administrative responsibilities.

I use that as a baseline to realize that that is a pretty normal response to stress, even though you might also think of it as a mild to moderate depression.

When you put this in the adolescent's frame of reference, they have not had the life experience that gives them the perspective that allows them to have some kind of meaningful understanding of this particular set of events. Therefore, they're much more vulnerable to some of their own misunderstood internal mechanisms and much more susceptible to a more severe pathology than we as adults would experience.

The Missionary Context

We realize that many of the situations missionaries are faced with—the entry, the re-entry, the change of school, the moves between jungle location and base camp—will cause situational stress.

It's important to understand that this series of events that leads to depression, and perhaps to suicide, starts within the normal area. They're exacerbated as stresses in a number of situational and normal developmental situations. Then if they're not handled properly, or if the person doesn't have the capacity, or if the stress is too severe, we may see the development of some of these other disorders.

Many times suicide is related to the experience of loss and unexpressed grief. It takes many different forms. We are unique in how we experience all of these different things. In many respects we expect loss to be a part of the life experience. Life is filled with losses. Yet we find that because there often has been a caring community, the adolescent MK may hit a major loss for which there has been no prior experience and perhaps very little preparation. That may trigger off a lot of small unresolved losses that may cause the MK to at least consider suicide.

When we look at loss and grief, we have to realize that there are responses that look kind of strange but are really quite normal.

There may also be a category of responses that look quite normal but really are strange in the sense that they're maladaptive.

Many times we in the Christian community are guilty of assisting adolescents in developing maladaptive or pathological response to loss and grief by the Christian platitudes that we give them: The Lord will take care of it; it's God's will; Romans 8:28.   It's true, but it's probably not that helpful at that moment.   We may be building in, through unintentional life interpretations, an experience that leads the adolescent to believe that one does not talk about loss, pain, anger, or hurt.   Rather, all that will be taken care of in some mystical way.   If you just affirm that it will be taken care of, then it will be OK.   That is an example of telling people to look normal about these things in a pathological way.

On the other hand, we find the fourteen-year-old who has moved back to the States permanently at that critical period in the development of peer relationships, many times will repress a lot of those feelings and not really be able to understand what he or she is experiencing.   A lot of times the response of the Christian community is, "But look at these opportunities that you have here.   Bring the memories forward from the field and share them with your friends." That sometimes does not work, and although the child may look very normal, there is a lot of abnormal, maladaptive behavior taking place underneath.   It may show itself later on when there's a severe crisis that can't be coped with simply.

Those are areas one needs to be quite sensitive to in looking at the adolescent experience.

In another sense, the missions context may provide some unique things that create this kind of depression.   For example, one of the things we find generally in Christian communities is a little less understanding of the place of anger.

In my counseling and psychotherapy, a large percentage of the Christians have at the base of their problem anger that has not been expressed or resolved.   Many times adolescents have not learned to live with anger, express it, or in the sense of Ephesians 4:26, deal with it and move forward.   Many times, because they can't deal with it, the anger gets turned in, and many times that will precipitate an attempt at suicide.

Loneliness is also important to mention in the missions context. I don't know how many grown MKs I've talked with who have talked about their early boarding school experience and the abject loneliness they felt there that they didn't know what to do with.

An experience I had a few years ago with new young mission-aries points out this kind of an experience.

It was the end of the orientation program, and these mis-sionaries had been together for three months. As they were sharing some of their experiences, one of them got up to say that she had been extremely lonely and depressed, but everyone else had seemed so happy that she had not dared share her loneliness with anyone else.

She said, "It was as though some great set of claws went down into my very being and grabbed something that was deep and well rooted and pulled it out so that I was empty. I was so depressed and so lonely, but I didn't want anyone to know, so I would go down the hall to the bathroom and lock the door and just weep and weep and weep." This went on for three or four weeks.

"Then," she said, "I went down there one night and someone else was in the bathroom so I had to wait. I stood outside weeping and sobbing, and between sobs I thought I heard someone in the bathroom also weeping and sobbing, so I knocked on the door. We found that both of us were having exactly the same experience. We just clung to each other."

They discovered that despite whatever had been pulled out of them by the great claws of loneliness, they did have something to fill each other with. They began to meet and share and cry and pray and fellowship together.

You see, the missions context is filled with the possibility of pain. We need to be teaching our adolescents to cope with depres-sion and suicide in a preventive way. They need to know not only that other people care, and that other people experience similar kinds of things, but also that many times God is there in the person of another who is also experiencing pain. In that sense of Christ expressed in relationship with others can be a deep sense of hope, a sense that even though they don't know how they're going to get through that depressing suicide-possibility experience, they will make it.

I hope that is a point of view that we can talk about both as treatment and as preventive for suicide and depression.

Discussion

Concerning good-byes and closure, if a child does not have a
lot of friends, should we manufacture good-byes?

Powell: I think we should arrange some kind of a formalized good-bye. It is so important to close experiences. Many of the events that result in a depressive reaction later on are because of an experience that has failed closure somehow.

One thing you can do is to develop a ritual, with the expectation that everyone participates in the ritual. That allows everyone to express individual differences, but they've all participated together.

How do you deal with the ten-year-old child who tends to be
unemotional, and yet when things don't go perfectly, he cries.

Powell: Around that age, that can be a normal developmental sort of thing. In the late childhood years children test what kind of impact they can have on the environment, and many times there will be that kind of disappointment. It's not the way the child hoped it would be. Listening to them as they tell you how they're experiencing what they perceive as the failure will help them move through that developmental sequence.

What about the child who expresses hatred of God because
of the death of someone close?

Schubert: There are normal phases of grief. One is anger. We have to allow people to go through those phases without criticizing them or making them feel rejected in the process. If a child has a period of time when he hates God because of what happened, what he is saying to you is, "I acknowledge God is in charge."

Powell: At the risk of oversimplification, I'm going to suggest three steps that are helpful.

- Do not be threatened by hearing God attacked and denigrated. If there's one failure that's frequent for Christians, it's hearing God being attacked and needing to either defend or move back. God can take care of himself.
- Help the person express. Give him words that you may hear underneath the other words. Let him get it out. Don't be worried by whatever language he chooses. Stay right with him and facilitate it. Do clarification and reflection, some of the good old-fashioned counseling techniques.
- Stay close enough to the situation that you can observe the process. It's a predictable process, but it's also very ragged.

You'll go forward awhile, then jump back, then go forward. It has to be cycled and recycled. You may think you've gone down four steps and all of a sudden you're hearing even worse words. That's OK. It's part of the process. Trust that, stay with it, and be consistent.

Schubert: Keep your troubled child talking. If it's not something you're comfortable with, then find another significant adult in that kid's life who he doesn't feel like he has to protect. He may feel he has to protect you from the grief of whatever occurred, so he may not express himself as clearly, except when it gets so extreme that it bursts out in this angry demonstration. Another adult who relates well with this kid who can keep him talking, can hug him, and can be the additional support system.

Do you recommend talking to teenagers as a group about suicide?

Schubert: I feel much more comfortable talking about suicide to adults who may be able to intervene with adolescents than I do talking to a general adolescent population. There is a certain copycat mentality. I will not renege on my statement that if someone is depressed enough and you ask them about suicide you don't put it in their mind. But in the general population, kids are impulsive. Kids are likely to pick up on things and sometimes get involved in things on an impulsive nature. I am very careful. There was a docudrama on suicide just before the Manila ICMK, and across the country there were a bunch of copycat suicides.

16

Adjustment Disorders

John Powell
Counseling Center, Michigan State University

I'd like to talk about some general areas of stress and focus on general adjustment disorders, because it is in that area we are most likely to see symptom development in the MK community.

We need to begin with an assumption that none of us are going to be able to avoid stress. It comes with living. It is a matter of learning how to assist others who may be experiencing stress, as well as learning better ways of managing stress ourselves.

I ran across a statement the other day: "Often people are upset or damage a relationship or don't find much meaning, or are going too fast, or have lost something important. Pretty soon they get so they don't feel so good any more. And they get sick. So they go to the doctor, who looks at them and fixes them and gets them back on their feet, and then because they haven't learned why they got sick, some people go home, and they get upset again, and they damage a relationship, and still don't find much meaning, and they go fast again, or they lose something important again, and not too long, they get so they don't feel so good any more. So they get sick again. It's kind of wasteful and painful, but sometimes people go like this, getting up and down forever. That is, until one time they get sick and can't get gotten up again."

I think that's a very clear, though simple, description of what happens with some of these disorders that we're talking about. The concept of stress is a very important one. We all experience it. Most of us have some range of adaptability to meet and manage it. But inevitably, we will run into some stressful situation that will cause us to respond in such a way that shows we do not have the adaptive processes. That's the point at which it may become pathological.

Many times a stress will cause a crisis. Whether it is a crisis or not depends a lot on the way in which the person interprets this particular event or series of events and the actual capacity the person has for meeting that particular stress experience or series of stress experiences.

Many times when a person is experiencing some kind of a response to stress, one of the important things to know first is whether this person is interpreting it as crisis. Imagine a nine year old who has been counting on a picnic for two weeks and then finds it cancelled because it rains. She may interpret it as a severe crisis. For you as a parent it might be a relief because you didn't want to go. It's the same event, but the interpretations are quite different. Another person, who is used to managing a high degree of stress, may be able to handle several different rather stressful events at one time. For that person it's no crisis whatsoever.

When we consider some of the stress-related or general adjustment disorders in adolescence, we need to realize that we are seeing the development of a disorder in response to some kind of a development stage or a traumatic event. It can be either. Many times, if it is an adjustment disorder, the person will have tremendous difficulty attaching his actual feelings to the specific event. Generally there will be a fairly clear precipitating factor or event, and a response to the event in a maladaptive way. This will result in a disruption of ongoing personality functioning or growth functions, and there will be a persistence of this for at least three months.

Adjustment Disorders in MKs

If we look at the MK experience, we can identify six or eight common places where we might be sensitive to these general adjustment disorders. For both MKs and kids at home, school is often one of the places where we can see the precipitating events that may result in a stress reaction or a general adjustment disorder. Many times the school-related events will relate to issues that have to do with achievement. In other words, "Am I doing well?" And not only, "Am I doing well in getting my work done?" "Am I doing well in pleasing the teacher?" or "Am I doing well in social activities?" "Am I being accepted by my peers?" or "Am I doing well in non-academic activities such as athletics?" A lot of times disappointment, changes in relationships or failure to make achievement will be the precipitating event for a general adjustment disorder.

Many times with MKs there will be conflict with authority. This may be with parents, dorm parents, or teachers. In adolescence, there may be a strong sense of needing to test the limits, which is a normal adolescent function, but the mission environment may provide very little opportunity to do that in a constructive way. The MK then may act this out in some way that may not be tolerated within the mission situation, but that in the States would not be considered unusual. If that happens two or three times without satisfactory resolution, it may eventually precipitate a more full blown stress reaction or adjustment disorders in the MK.

There's a latent rebellion that we see in MKs. Some of the things Ruth Van Reken mentions would be explained in part by some people as a delayed or latent adolescent rebellion. In counseling adult MKs in their thirty's and even early forty's I've seen them express a tremendous surge of anger at the church, at the missionary community, or sometimes at specific people. It's because the person has moved to a certain point in his development where he can let it through now. It can be tremendously disturbing. That's more an example of a delayed response syndrome. Nonetheless, you can look at it as having been the result of a general adjustment disorder occurring in adolescence that was never dealt with. So some years later it shows up again.

Another common precipitating event with MKs is some kind of disappointment or conflict or uncertainty in both same-sex and heterosexual relationships. Many times there is not occasion to develop many friendships. One or two persons will become very important. Then some rejection by that person will often be a precipitating event for this kind of stress reaction.

There are two other general categories that we might look at. One is work responsibility. As we see a person growing, we expect that he will be able to take increasing degrees of responsibility for his work, and accept an increasing degree of independence. Yet some kids simply do not feel they are able to handle that new step of responsibility.

> I think of a thirteen-year-old daughter of some friends of ours. Not long ago she was supposed to have memorized a long reading for a school function. It really taxed her. It was a little beyond what she could do. She began talking with her mother about it. Her mother kept encouraging her and then pushing her. Pretty soon the thirteen year old just stopped and said, "I won't do it." I think she was wise. There was some conflict about that, but I think the daughter was wise enough to know that she was having to take three steps in a developmental sequence when she was only ready for one.

One other area that I've already referred to but want to emphasize is the area of relationships. Many times this will be one of the most traumatic. For MKs, especially in adolescence and young adulthood, to find that a trust has been broken, a confidence has been betrayed, or that a person one looked up to as a model has misled them as well (particularly where relationships have not been that available and only two or three people were really counted on) can be a very traumatic precipitating event that can cause a general adjustment disorder. I'd like to talk about what we see in the Scriptures about some of the common features of adjustment disorders or stress reactions.

Example of John Mark

If we look at the Scriptures, we can find a number of experiences where there was something like a general adjustment disorder or stress reaction.

Let's take the case of a young missionary named John Mark. Here is a person who evidently had potential and skill, and was actually included as a member of the group in the first missionary journey with Paul. We also know that he left the group and went back home, with the implication that the going was just a little too tough for him.

Many times the weight is on the side saying, "Look, that guy couldn't make it." There are some people who shouldn't be on the mission field, and they ought to be encouraged to go home, but they ought to also be nurtured because they're still members of the body, and there's still a place for them, even though it may not be in mission service. We see, though, that John Mark went home.

Then the occasion for his re-entrance into another missionary journey took place down at the dockside, we might say, where Paul and Barnabas were meeting for their second journey. Barnabas evidently had strong feelings that John Mark should accompany them. Paul, on the other hand, had a strong sense that it would not be appropriate to take along somebody who was not fit and who would probably require a lot of care and nurture along the way.

Put yourself in John Mark's place. What kind of reaction would you have to that sort of stress? You want to go. There's one person you really respect who says, "I would like for you to go. I'll help you out." There's another person you respect who says, "You can't go. You can't cut it. You're a loser. We don't want you." It's very tempting to think all kinds of bad things about Paul, and maybe that's appropriate. Maybe that's adaptive at that point. It's also important to realize you've got at least one ally.

Sometimes we don't look so much at the MK, or in this case John Mark, and what his needs may be. We look at who's right and what's going to take place. How's the mission going to go forward? Here we have found two men of impeccable Christian integrity who had very different views of one person. If we simplify these views a little bit, we can take Paul's and say, "There is a view designed for program and productivity, and that's what counts. People, by implication, matter less." On the other hand, we can take the view that Barnabas seemed to be encouraging; that is, that the person is important. What we do with each other is going to have a greater impact than the finest tuned program.

Who was right? I hope you haven't chosen sides. That's the tendency in a conflict situation. I'd like to suggest that both of them were right. Both acted out of a sense of integrity, and John Mark was taken care of.

To go one step further, in terms of having a comforting, encouraging community, we have to have a community that has some sense of in-touchness with the larger perspective, and tries to give some attention to both. We don't know a lot about what happened to John Mark, but let's say that he had some kind of a stress reaction, or maybe he was still having something like a posttraumatic stress disorder after knowing how badly he had failed on that first journey.

What's the first thing a person needs when they fail? Forgiveness and some sense that somebody is on their side to help them be repaired, to help them overcome, and to the extent that they can do it, make restitution. That was the role that Barnabas took. It's the role that we take as we minister to MKs. It's the role that God gives us if we have a concern in working with people that have been damaged as a result of their response to stress.

So we find that John Mark probably spent some time with Peter, another mentor, and if anybody could teach John Mark about forgiveness, Peter wasn't a bad choice. He knew about it. You can imagine John Mark walking along and saying, "Peter, I've been thinking a little about forgiveness. Do you know anything about that?"

"Well," he says, "Yeah, as a matter of fact, there was one night some time ago when something happened to me. It was the most deadly thing I've ever done, and I figured it was over. I denied the Lord himself."

And John Mark eagerly asking, "What happened? Did he forgive you?"

"Yeah, he forgave me."

And underneath that you can hear John Mark's question, "Do you think I can be forgiven? Do you think that God will forgive me and maybe Paul could forgive me?" and Peter's answer, "Yes. There's a place for forgiveness, reconciliation, and healing."

Then what happens? Barnabas and John Mark have a successful journey. Silas goes with Paul. They have a successful journey. Later on, seeing the maturity of this young man, John Mark, Paul writes and says, "Send him to me. I have need for him." The cycle was complete.

The wonderful thing about this classification is that there's a tremendous possibility for recovery.

Discussion

Do you always look for a Christian counselor?

Schubert: There are situations where we think, "This individual is a Christian, so he must be a good counselor." But not everybody who considers himself a counselor who is also a Christian has real skill. I tend to prefer a good non-Christian psychologist who is not anti-Christian and who understands my philosophy to an incompetent Christian. On the other hand, everything else being the same, I'd sure go with the Christian if there's a choice.

Powell: I'd feel very much the same way. Dedicated incompetency is still incompetency.

What are some practical things that might be done for a seventh grade girl who is resisting being in the boarding home, and presumably on the mission field?

Powell: I would want to find out if that was the issue or if it was a reaction to some things having to do with the parental home or some history she has experienced. If it really is a situational event, there is a better than fifty percent chance that a person of that age will make an adaptation if she can be attended to and listened to in rather careful ways over a period of time.

Schubert: Kids are tremendously adaptive. Most kids who are relatively healthy tend to get happy eventually wherever they go. If she is having difficulty with the transition, we just may find out that she was unhappy before the transition.

17

Posttraumatic Stress Disorder

Esther Schubert
Family Practice and Emergency Medicine, Indiana

Posttraumatic stress disorder is not really a new phenomenon. In the Civil War they had a syndrome called shell shock. Towards the end of the last century when railroad accidents began to occur, there were a number of people who had tremendous reactions to the trauma of those events. Psychiatrists didn't exactly have a name for it, but they started seeing a type of reaction. In World War I, it was called war neurosis. In World War II, the whole syndrome was made famous by Patton's slapping of the battle fatigued soldier who was brought to the hospital. Patton couldn't quite tolerate the fact that this guy wasn't on the front. After World War II, a fellow named Archibald wrote about gross stress reactions to combat in which a clear-cut picture emerged of a severely debilitating, but non-schizophrenic condition involving startle reaction, sleep difficulty, dizziness, blackouts, avoidance of activity similar to combat experience, and internalization of feelings.

Vietnam seemed to have a disproportionate incidence of post-traumatic stress disorder for several reasons. It was the longest United States war; it was unpopular; there were often no heroes; there was no clear-cut enemy in many situations. Young men and teenagers were uprooted from an immediate gratification society and thrust into this combat situation. Many of them, unfortunately, were also on drugs, which made the whole situation a little bit more unstable. It was a war in which there was great ambivalence about the social and political issues.

Now, civilians are also caught in traumatic situations: hostage situations, wars, revolutions, kidnapping, rape, natural disasters, violence, and accidents. Pressures of that sort can precipitate stress disorders. That's one reason we're acknowledging and dealing with the problem here.

Howard Smith, who was a missionary in the interior of China in the 1930s, was captured by Communist guerillas in the spring of 1934. He managed to escape a month or so later, and walked overland four or five hundred miles to our mission in Wuhu, which was a hospital station on the Yangtze River. In the process, Howard developed a real severe reaction to what he'd been through.

He could not sleep at night. He had exaggerated startle reactions for a number of months. What he did during this time was take pictures all day. Then at night when he couldn't sleep, he worked in the darkroom and developed his photography.

That's just one example of posttraumatic stress disorder which can occur on the mission field under extremely traumatic situations.

Settings in Which Posttraumatic Stress Disorder Occurs

Normally we progress through life experiencing carefully titrated amounts of frustration and stress which are important to our psychological growth and often serve a vital function in stimulating movement from one developmental stage to another. Sometimes the most valuable experiences are the painful ones, since they may add depth to the personality and increase the ability to empathize with others.

However, when painful assaults become too intense and occur too frequently, the psyche may be overwhelmed. We see this in people from chronically abusive families, refugee camps, and poverty stricken communities, as well as in holocaust victims, victims of torture, and others.

To give you some background, let us look at a child who has been abused. In order to survive his abusive parental exposures, a child withdraws. But that withdrawal becomes a pathological response in the larger society. Withdrawal is no longer a good survival technique in a more predictable and rational workplace or in a healthy marriage.

In MKs, we see some chronic stresses. Frequent separations seem to create chronic stress for some MKs which may lead to unresolved grief. Cultural stresses are chronic stresses.

However, posttraumatic stress disorder tends to develop in response to situations of acute stress. If it's an absolute stress, even a strong person may succumb. A vulnerable child may succumb to posttraumatic stress disorders sooner or with less stress than someone else. We know that some MKs just seem to be vulnerable, not because they're MKs. They're just vulnerable children.

If an MK is a vulnerable child who is subjected to multiple transitions and separations, he may reach the limit of his tolerance at a
certain point in his life. This is chronic underlying stress.

If later in life, he is in a hostage situation, or perhaps a concentration camp where he is subjected to acute stress, he might be more
likely to decompensate or have posttraumatic stress disorder if the
event reminds him of those earlier stresses. For instance, if he is
separated from his fellows in that concentration camp, it might affect
him more, because the one area where he is most sensitive is the area
of separation. There is the chronic process to which he may be sensitive, and if he has reached the limit of his tolerance early in life, then
an acute event later on in life could precipitate a stress response.

Whether the situation is an absolute stress or whether you have
a vulnerable person exposed to less severe stresses acutely, we find
that stress disorders can occur. Now, not every response to acute
stress goes to a full-blown posttraumatic stress disorder. I'd like you
to think of these as a continuum.

Normal response to acute stress

There is a normal response to acute stress. It may not be possible initially to distinguish this immediate coping response from one
that may later become pathological. But it's usual for healthy people
to respond to stress first by being stunned, paralyzed, or numb; later
developing a sense of rage, guilt, unbearable sadness, helplessness, or
humiliation.

Sealey describes the usual response to stress in three stages.
First is the alarm phase. This is the adrenaline fight or flight. You
get up to fight the situation or to run from it. Secondly, resistance,
and third is the state of exhaustion. When acute stress goes on long
enough, you do get to the point of exhaustion. At this point, you may
have depletion of body chemicals, depletion of the ability of the body
and the psyche to fight the stress. Of course, at that point you may
get into the area of chronic stress more than acute stress.

Adjustment disorder response to acute stress

The second response to acute stress is a reaction that falls short
of a diagnosis of posttraumatic stress disorder. I would call it the
adjustment disorder. This is really important. I think it has the most
application to MKs. This is, by definition, a maladaptive reaction to
identifiable psycho-social pressures, with the reactions emerging
within three months of the onset of the stressor. Signs and symptoms
are not as specific as for posttraumatic stress disorder, but they

include a variety of disturbances in interpersonal functioning, work functioning, and maladaptive extremes of anxiety, depression, rage, shame, and guilt.

Adjustment disorders may be precipitated by changes in life circumstances such as divorce, difficulties in child rearing, illness, disability, financial strain, a new form of work, graduation, moving, retirement, or cultural upheaval. Missionaries and MKs are really subject to this.

Brief reactive psychosis

A third response to acute stress, we call brief reactive psychosis. This person loses touch with reality immediately following the stressful event. This psychosis lasts from a few hours up to two weeks, and no longer. There is usually at least one psychotic symptom, such as a delusion or a hallucination. It is usually self limited. I think what happens is that the reality is too horrible to deal with or acknowledge, and so the person unconsciously has a temporary flight into psychosis in order to survive, such as in rape situations where a person simply will not remember the event. The situation is so horrible, the only way to respond, even unconsciously, is to simply block it out.

Posttraumatic stress disorder

The fourth response to acute stress is the posttraumatic stress disorder. This develops in some individuals who have been subjected to an overwhelming and unusual source of acute stress. Symptoms of this prolonged pathological response to stress include recurrent images, dreams of the traumatic event, phobic avoidance of situations that resemble or symbolize the original trauma, and behavior that is indicative of generalized anxiety. The symptoms may develop right after the traumatic event, or months or even years later.

Predisposing Factors for a Pathological
Response to Stress

The predisposing factors are the following seven, and I want you to particularly note number three and number seven, because they particularly apply to MKs. Predisposing factors include:

- A rigid, immature, or socially isolated personality. Now, I suppose this also applies to MKs, particularly those who have been raised in a very isolated setting. If they have limited social opportunity, they may not develop some of the stress coping responses that they need.

- Lack of preparedness for the event.
- Similarity of the event to an earlier emotional trauma.   I think this is very pertinent to MKs. The example I'd like to share with you is of a friend of mine.

> Rusty came from a family that was in the CIA. He had travelled and moved probably every year throughout his life. He was a quiet, withdrawn individual. He was very sensitive. He, of the four kids in his family, was the least likely to interact on an intimate emotional level.

> When he was about twenty, he went back to Virginia where the family had lived, but the family was overseas. His older sisters were married and living other places. His girlfriend broke up with him while he was in Virginia for the vacation. At the same time, he was getting ready to go into basic training for ROTC. He just could not handle all of what was occurring.

> I think either the stress of attending basic training or the breakup with the girlfriend or a combination reminded him of too many separations he had had as a kid. He disappeared one day. They found his body three days later in the woods. He had shot himself in the head.

That's an extreme situation, but the point I am making is that he had some rather normal events occur in his life. However, they reminded him of some unresolved trauma from his earlier life and, in the process, precipitated severe depression and suicide.

- Lack of socioeconomic support during recovery phase.
- Presence of a disruptive environment prior to the traumatic event.
- Significant disruption to the individual, to the family, property, or community as a result of the trauma.
- Occurrence of the trauma during a particularly vulnerable stage of the individual's psychological development. I think that's something we have to deal with regarding separation for our MKs. If it occurs at a vulnerable time, it may set up a situation which later on can precipitate a stress disorder.

If the predictable emotional distress and behavioral response persist and impair social or occupational function for an unreasonable length of time, a diagnosis of adjustment disorder may be made.

By comparison, in posttraumatic stress disorder, the event that produces the stress is generally beyond the range of the usual human experience. The routine of life is not re-established despite the concrete ending of the event. It is usually an overwhelming event over which the individual has no control.

Recognizing and Treating Posttraumatic Stress Disorder

If you are in a situation in which you have some responsibility for people, I want you to be alert to this. If it occurs, you can pull out these notes and say, "Yeah, this might be happening." That's the whole point of what we are doing.

The DSM-III diagnostic criterion for posttraumatic stress disorder has four points:

- The existence of a recognizable acute stress that would evoke significant symptoms of stress in almost anyone.

- Re-experiencing the trauma as evidenced by at least one of the following: recurrent and intrusive recollection of the event, recurrent dreams of the event, sudden acting or feeling as if the traumatic event were recurring because of an association with an environmental or ideational stimulus.

- Numbing of responsiveness to, or reduced involvement with the external world, beginning some time after the trauma shown by at least one of the following: markedly decreased interest in one or more significant activities, feelings of detachment or estrangement from others, and constricted affect.

- Then you need at least two of the following six to be diagnostic. They must not have been present before the trauma. For example, if you have a person who was shy before the trauma, you can't use shyness as part of the diagnostic criteria. It has to be something new.

  1. Hyperalertness or exaggerated startle response.
  2. Sleep disturbance.
  3. Guilt about surviving when others have not, or about the behavior required for survival.
  4. Memory impairment or difficulty in concentrating.
  5. Avoidance of activities that arouse recollection of the event.
  6. Intensification of symptoms by exposure to events that symbolize or resemble the traumatic event.

Two forms of posttraumatic stress disorder

There are really two forms of posttraumatic stress disorder. There is the acute form, where the onset of symptoms occurs within six months of the trauma. The symptoms also last for less than six months. By contrast, there is the chronic or delayed posttraumatic stress disorder. Chronic is the one in which the duration of the symptoms lasts for six months or more. The delayed is where the onset of the symptoms occur more than six months after the traumatic event.

In general, the type of person most vulnerable to problems is the one who has assumed an external air of propriety and has a limited range for displaying the natural and predictable swings of emotion that occur after trauma, or can't express those feelings because he regards them as a sign of weakness or a loss of control. The person who is very much a control person might be particularly subject to posttraumatic stress disorder given the right setting.

Stockholm syndrome

One thing that often occurs in hostage situations is the so-called Stockholm syndrome. This was first identified in the 1970's following a hostage taking and bank robbery in Sweden. The hostages were freed after about 130 hours, but they shocked the public by expressing support for the criminals. Patty Hearst is another example of this. She was dragged kicking and screaming from her boyfriend's apartment, and then within a year participated with her captors in a bank robbery and seemed to have made a fairly complete conversion to their ideals. That's an example of Stockholm syndrome.

It is characterized by a feeling of affection for the captors, usually coupled with feelings of distress or hostility towards police, government, and so forth. This bizarre response which occurs in at least fifty percent of hostages, results from a combination of terror, gratitude, and infantile dependence that is much like the abused child who clings to an abusing parent. The hostage has been degraded, isolated, humiliated, and because his life is totally dependent on another, infantilized by his captor.

It is not a permanent attitude. You deal with it a little the way you deal with the resentment phase of grief. You listen, you care, you let the victims live through it, and they do get over it in most situations.

Treatment of posttraumatic stress disorder

Our treatment for posttraumatic stress disorder approaches the problem on four fronts. The first is verbal counseling in a therapeutic relationship. Secondly, the goal is to return the patient to his prior level of competence. Thirdly, occasionally we use medications. We try not to use them if we can avoid them. Fourth, there is a need for desensitization to the memories of the traumatic event in order that the ego gains mastery over the anxiety.

Missionary Experiences with PTSD

I don't personally have an example of posttraumatic stress disorder in my own life, but many of us who were subjected to rather dramatic situations when the communists came into China during 1948 to 1950 had a tremendous need to go back and find those places.

Now there is a natural tendency among missionary kids to go back and find out where they came from. I think that's important. This seemed to be more dramatic for some of us who experienced some trauma in the departure.

It was important for me, for instance, to go back to the train station from which we left. When we got there, my mother and father and I tried to get on the train. We had reserved seats but the train was packed. Everybody was hysterical. It was an absolute mob scene. My dad picked my mother up and put her through the window and sort of tossed me in afterwards. For awhile we didn't even know if my dad was on the train. I found that traumatic. It was important for me to go back as an adult and find the train station and stand on the platform and defuse those memories.

I believe that those traumatic events in kids' lives need to be defused from an adult perspective. If you're dealing with MKs who have been through something like that, they need to go back and find the grave, people, or places.

I'd like to read a prayer letter. I will disguise organizations and people, but this is an example of posttraumatic stress disorder that occurred in a young missionary.

> During the past three or four years I have been going through and recovering from posttraumatic stress disorder breakdown resulting from my time in Beirut, Lebanon. Posttraumatic stress could possibly be a fancy name for shell shock. It's a combination of depression, anxiety, intrusive and troubled thoughts, impaired memory, increased irritability, flashbacks of a very painful experience and more. I am told it is usually outside the range of normal human experience, but then what's normal about living in a war zone? A breakdown occurs when a person's emotions collapse, causing the mental and physical functions to cease or be limited. Upon returning to the U.S. after being evacuated from Beirut, I was a bit shaky, weepy, and on edge. I was told I would be jittery for awhile, and this was normal given what I had come from. I continued to carry out my secretarial responsibilities for the team until they returned overseas.
>
> When I left the organization in June, 1983, I went to another state to visit a friend and look for a job. I began

suffering from flashbacks of Beirut, and a spiral into depression to depths I had never dreamed possible. I started receiving professional counseling for depression and an overaccumulation of stress. I began suffering from other symptoms. I was advised from several sources to take a three month period of rest, and I spent the next five months on my mom's farm in the Midwest. During this time I slept, cried, and tried to replenish my physical and emotional resources.

After this period of time, I located a psychologist who had worked with Vietnam vets. Under his care I was able to understand what posttraumatic stress disorder was and to work through the flashbacks and deep emotional pain from my time in Beirut. I had struggled with guilt and a sense of being a failure for not returning to the Middle East with the rest of the team.

Portions of this era of my life are blurred, whether by inability to remember or a desire to forget, I'm not sure. Perhaps what hurt me the most is the inability of the body of Christ to minister to the needy and the hurting. A number of times I have been told, "You and you alone are responsible for your own needs." Or, "You need to depend more on Jesus and not on others." It has made me wonder if some people cut Hebrews 10:24-25 out of their Bibles. Yet Scripture tells us, "And let us consider how to stir up one another to love and good works, encouraging one another." In Ecclesiastes 4:9-10 are the words, "Two are better than one, for if either of them falls, the one will lift up his companion." Jesus himself had an emotional support group of twelve.

I have lived with the stigma of "You are not a finisher. You are not willing to obey God when the going gets rough," i.e., gutting it out in Beirut. I have since learned there is a vast difference between being a finisher and being finished off. I have also come to realize that if I choose to leave a difficult situation when the going gets rough, it does not mean I am being disobedient to God, that I'm running from a difficult situation, nor does it mean I'm not a finisher.

I have often been frustrated by people who seem to choose to spiritualize their situations instead of looking at them realistically. It is so easy to say, "I can do all things through Christ who strengthens me." However, you can't drive a six cylinder car as though it had eight cylinders without it eventually falling apart. I have had to learn what my limits are and live within them, and to prevent others from pushing me past my breaking point. Thus far, it's been the most difficult time of my life. It has also been a time of tremendous personal growth. I have sat in the darkness of deep depression, and have seen my walk with God go to new depths as I have gained a deeper understanding of scripture.

I know some of you have had breakdowns of your own and thus journeyed down this road less travelled. Others of you, I've watched teeter-totter on the fine line between emotional fatigue and a breakdown. Perhaps some of what I've shared will be of help to you.

The thing that concerns me is that I don't think it's necessarily an isolated incident. I am concerned that within the missionary community we have a certain lack of sophistication regarding the diagnosis of stress response syndromes. Secondly, I'm concerned about the lack of exercise of the gift of mercy within the body of Christ. Here was an obviously hurting individual who was put under tremendous additional stress of false guilt by people who tended to give platitudes and short answers, instead of really dealing with what she was feeling, and communicating to her that they loved her. We have an emphasis on productivity that sometimes makes us forget about the fact that we're dealing with individuals, adults or children, who may be hurting very deeply. We need to be more sensitive to their needs and exercise the gifts of the Spirit within the body of Christ, particularly the gift of mercy in situations like this.

18

Eating Disorders

Esther Schubert
Family Practice and Emergency Medicine, Indiana

We estimate anorexia nervosa is occurring in about one out of two hundred teenage girls in the U.S. Conservatively, we estimate bulimia to affect between 5 and 20 percent of teen and young adult women in the middle to upper class. It's a very secretive illness. As I talk to Dr. Powell and other people who are on university campuses, particularly secular university campuses, they tell me that in social sororities, they see a 33 percent or better incidence of bulimia. It does seem to be almost epidemic, and I believe it is related to the narcissistic, youth-oriented idealization of extreme slenderness.

You hear young women in sorority and society circles say, "You can never be too rich, and you can never be too thin." I think that is one of the underlying attitudes that precipitate this.

I think there might be a slightly decreased incidence of this in MKs compared to the U.S. population in general. I do believe that it is culturally determined. For instance, in Haiti and in Latin America it is appropriate to weigh a little more. In the U.S. and in Europe, where people want to retain the appearance of slenderness, we see more of these eating disorders.

Unfortunately, when these eating disorders occur, they may be serious. In fact, anorexia nervosa can be fatal. It has the highest mortality rate of any psychiatric illness. We don't see as high a mortality rate with bulimia, but there's certainly disability associated with it.

Anorexia Nervosa

Anorexia nervosa is really a misnomer. Anorexia means decreased appetite, but that's not the case. These people have an appetite, but they are suppressing it. It is their one area of absolute control. If they get to the end stage where they are ketotic, they have starved themselves so much that they do lose their appetite, but we do not see that in the majority of these people. This is in contrast to some depressions where appetite may decrease throughout the entire illness, and the person loses weight because he doesn't have an appetite.

Anorexia nervosa seems to occur predominantly in teenage girls or young women and is characterized by fasting and denial by the patient. This was a closet kind of illness, not very well known until the publicity surrounding Karen Carpenter's death. The DFM-II definition is: (a) intense fear of becoming obese which does not diminish as weight loss progresses; (b) disturbance of body image, that is, claiming to be fat or feel fat even when emaciated; (c) weight loss of at least 25 percent of original body weight (If you're dealing with a teen, you have to calculate this for the expected normal weight for their age.); (d) refusal to maintain body weight over a minimal normal weight for age and height; (e) no known physical illness that would account for the weight loss.

There are sociocultural factors. Anorexia seems to occur in situations where there is a real high social expectation. You see it in middle to upper class teenage or young adult women, often in families that value outward appearances, behavior, and achievement. Often these kids have high parental expectations. (We need to be sure that we have realistic expectations for our MKs. They have enough expectations in their own nature. We need to be careful that we don't add to that.) The child is usually a model child who is compliant and perfectionistic. Many families of anorexia nervosa kids have a history of affective illness (depression or something of that sort). This child tends to be obsessively in search of perfection and has an exaggerated dependence on parental and external approval. She may have difficulty reaching autonomy and independence. She rarely acknowledges personal thoughts or feelings. She needs external approval to maintain self-esteem, even at the expense of the development of autonomy. Most of us determine our food needs by our hunger, thirst, and internal feelings. For these kids, food attitudes are determined by external rather than internal influences.

Anorexia nervosa may develop if a child is afraid of maturation. I see this in three settings. (1) The child may participate in excessive dieting to avoid development of breasts and hips if she is afraid of becoming an adult. I don't think this is conscious, but it probably contributes to the feeling we used to have that many of these kids had sexual identity problems. I don't think they do. I think it is more of an autonomy problem than a sexual identity problem. (2) As maturation signals the need for autonomy, the anorexic child may feel helplessness and ineffectiveness. Excessive dieting gives her one area of absolute control. So it is an issue of autonomy, absolute control. (3) Anorexia nervosa may also be a form of rebellion. That is, a child unconsciously manipulates the family and often her mother by exercising control over what and when she eats.

In addition to fasting, this disease is characterized by physical hyperactivity, preoccupation with food (the individual may cook but not eat), marked misperception of body image, and amenorrhea (she does not have menstrual periods). It's usually secondary amenorrhea. This is a person who has started having menstrual periods, but either at the time of the weight loss or prior to that time stopped having menstrual periods. We used to think that if the body fat went down low enough, she would stop having menstrual periods. But 25 percent of these cases of secondary amenorrhea occur before the weight loss, so that is not the mechanism. We're not sure if there is a hormonal influence or not. It takes 17 percent body fat for a girl to go through menarche for the first time, so if a person begins with anorexia nervosa at an early age and never establishes 17 percent body fat, she may be a primary amenorrhea. It takes 22 percent body fat to resume.

People die from anorexia nervosa. There's a six percent mortality rate. One percent of these kids commit suicide. Other than suicide, there are four major causes of death. (1) They have a wasted myocardium. The heart muscle becomes so depleted that it can no longer pump. (2) They may have cardiac failure. (3) They may have electrolyte abnormalities from simply not eating enough to maintain the chemicals they need. (4) They may have primary arrhythmia. That means that the heart beats erratically and can't pump blood, so they die.

Treatment

If the patient meets many of the criteria for anorexia nervosa and has a normal medical exam other than weight loss, we don't do a lot of fancy tests. We get psychiatric help. We send these kids and their families, if their problem is full-blown, to the home country. I have treated one case on the field, but it was not a fully developed case. If it is, the child needs treatment in a multidisciplinary setting that specializes not just in psychiatry but in the treatment of anorexia nervosa. It's a very specialized kind of psychiatric illness. Many of these patients need in-patient treatment. They need a psychiatrist, a psychologist, a social worker, a nutritionist, and often a medical doctor as well. We don't usually medicate. We treat with psychotherapy, insight oriented behavior modification, and family treatment. Of course, if they have severe weight loss, we often need to institute nutritional and medical care. It's important to remember that the weight loss and eating problem are only symptoms. An important transition point in the development of the disease is when the child voluntarily withholds food in the face of hunger to achieve an unrealistic degree of weight loss.

Bulimia

I want you to think of these eating disorders as a continuum of sorts. Some patients start with anorexia, and as they mature, develop bulimia. There is some overlap with anorexia nervosa. In contrast to anorexia nervosa, though, these bulimic patients tend to binge and purge. These people will gorge on between 1,000 and 55,000 calories. They do it over a couple of hours of time. It is followed by an effort to undo the binge. This is done by using diuretics (water loss pills), or cathartics (that create diarrhea).

These people binge and purge rather than fast. They have an obsessive concern about body size and a fear of fatness like anorexia, but they have less distortion of their body image and less severe weight loss. They usually have normal menstrual cycles, and are more likely to realize that their behavior is aberrant. They're more episodic in their pursuit of thinness, so often they do not get into as severe trouble.

We have discovered that some of these people have decreased serotonin levels. In our discussion of depression, we talked about decreased serotonin being a problem with endogenous biochemical depression. There is overlap. About fifty percent of bulimics are also depressed. When girls have a low serotonin level, they're likely to have problems with bulimia. The hostility becomes self directed. If boys have a low serotonin level, they're more likely to be involved in externally aggressive behavior or even suicide.

The profile of the bulimic is a high achiever, usually a female. Marked parental dependence symbolizes the family relationships. Socially anxious, she has difficulty establishing personal relationships. Depression, impulsive behavior, and antisocial behavior may occur: kleptomania, drug abuse and sexual promiscuity, which is also associated with depression in girls. Often these people tried rigid dieting before the onset of binging and purging. Anxiety and depression occur in fifty percent. There is a deep sense of shame, a fear of loss of control over the eating. These patients look relatively healthy as compared with the anorexics. Many feel inadequate. They are passive. They look to other people for confirmation of their sense of worth. The binge is very secretive. It's not simply overeating. These people absolutely gorge. They get to the point where you can see their stomach reflected against their abdominal wall, it's so big. It's actually an eating compulsion. There's a failure to respond to normal fullness.

The binge-vomiting or the binge-purge cycle occurs secretly at times of frustration and loneliness and psychological distress, so we work with these kids to find more appropriate ways of dealing with frustration. The cycle may be triggered by the mere sight of tempting food items. Occasionally, you'll see these people in a grocery store. They'll take all the junk food off the shelves and buy it and eat it on the way home in the car. They can gorge on 50,000 calories at a time. It may take a couple of hours to do it, but they do it. The actual binge is very pleasurable to the patient. According to Dr. Powell, it is a symbolic filling of something that has not been filled in emotional ways.

There are historical precedents. There is a certain psychological contagiousness to it. The Romans were involved in this. I don't want to describe exactly what they did, but it was pretty gross. We find it in models and dancers today, in socialites. Families of bulimics (and these are not bad characteristics, but this is just a statistical note) often emphasize good hearty eating. The dinner table tends to be a time of problem solving and discussion. They celebrate with food and they console with food. That may be just the way our society is in general, but statistical correlation with that has been noted.

The medical problems of bulimics are secondary to the vomiting and laxative abuse. For instance, with the vomiting there are electrolyte abnormalities, sore throat, sore esophagus, parotid gland swelling, dental problems because of the acid on their teeth, occasionally esophageal rupture, and aspiration pneumonia. Interestingly enough, one of the real diagnostic criteria for bulimia is that you'll see bruises and lacerations on the knuckles from self-induced vomiting. Cathartics and emetics tend to cause the heart to beat irregularly. Myocarditis, or inflammation of the heart can occur. There is often injury to the colon from laxatives. Many of these patients are also depressed. Unlike anorexia victims, these people often realize that they have a problem. The anorexic is characterized by extreme denial. The bulimic will acknowledge, at least at times, that there is a problem.

Powell: On our campus, some of the experts are finding another category of bulimia that does not necessarily involve the purge part of the binge-purge cycle. It is characterized by addictive behavior regarding hidden food for the purposes of gorging. Many times this has been the learned response to stress that causes anxiety and pain and disruption in some way.

Schubert: Children who have depression or a distressing situation in the home, often will start hoarding food. What I'm wondering is if there's a correlation. There seems to be an inherent preparation for crisis. Maybe the bulimic is doing the same thing.

Treatment

We treat bulimics with psychotherapy, insight supportive group and behavioral therapy. We try to help them develop better coping methods, and occasionally we use some medications. We don't have a lot of statistics yet about bulimia, but I believe there are some bulimics who can be handled on the field. It depends on the skill of your counselors, the motivation of the patient, and how deep the psychological underlying stress is.

*What would be the difference between compulsive overeating
and bulimia which involves only the binge part of the cycle?*

Powell: For the person who is binging, there is a more active interest in body image and acceptability. For the compulsive eater, that's usually less of an issue. They learn to adapt and justify their weight in different ways.

19

Burnout: MKs and Missionaries

Esther Schubert
Family Practice and Emergency Medicine, Indiana

Burnout is the result of constant or repeated emotional pressure associated with an intense involvement with people over long periods of
time.   There are physical depletions, feelings of helplessness and
hopelessness, emotional drain, and the development of a negative
self-concept and negative attitudes towards work, life, and other people. Burnout is a painful realization that the individual can no longer
help people in need. Indeed, he has nothing left to give.

The mere existence of negative feelings is not the crucial element in the identification of burnout. It is the frequency and magnitude of these symptoms which are crucial.   There is some overlap
with depression. When I talk with people who do a lot of counseling,
they tell me that sometimes they can not make a diagnosis.   They
don't know if it's burnout or depression or a mixture. Burnout and
endogenous depression tend to be more the result of chronic stress
rather than acute stress.

There are three reasons why we're addressing a topic like this at
ICMK:

- We are seeing some burnout in adolescents, particularly in
  the areas of athletics and academics. But I believe we may
  also see it in the MK who has reached the point of saturation
  with regard to separations. He can easily get to the point of
  emotional burnout because he has just hit his point of saturation. He can't tolerate too many more separations without
  some outside help.

- Adult missionaries are prone to burnout, and the effect on
  their children can be devastating. If they stay on the field,
  the MK is living with burned out and depressed parents. If
  they make a premature move back to their home country,
  there's an uprooting situation for the MK. Either way, the

MK finds himself living with parents who sense that they are failures. I don't think there's anything much worse.

- There are some longer-term consequences of the expectations MKs are exposed to. Most MKs are very goal oriented, and so they have their own expectations which are very high. In addition, they are also subjected to others' expectations: the mission board, their parents, the national church, the constituency. It really adds up. The problem is that when expectations outweigh reality, burnout may occur very quickly. Consequently, at a very early age, we may be setting up the environment that makes the MKs potential burnout victims later on.

Burnout seems to happen most to people in helping professions — social workers, pastors, welfare workers, lawyers, psychologists, doctors, missionaries, and of course MKs. One of the difficulties is that missionaries cannot divorce their work from home like many stateside professionals can. That means that they're always on call. They're always involved. It's very difficult to have that kind of ongoing day-and-night stress without at least setting up the potential for burnout.

In most human service jobs, the time-frame before burnout is only two to three years. That's why you see so much turnover in areas like social work. I feel that first-term missionaries may be most vulnerable. Often they come to the field with a real level of exhaustion. They often peak in their culture shock after about eight months on the field. They're involved in language study, which could burn out anybody. We also find that they sense, "This isn't what I'm here for. I'm here to do missionary work." So there's a certain frustration inherent in their language study.

We need to be particularly alert to signs of burnout, making an effort to prevent it as much as possible. The tragedy is that it's often the individuals with the most idealism and concern who are likely to burn out. The cost to the individual, to his kids, to his team that remains, to the organization in lost talent, to the unevangelized, and to the Lord's work is incredible.

Eventually we see burnout in most workaholics, and we also see it in people whose self-esteem is based upon their productivity.

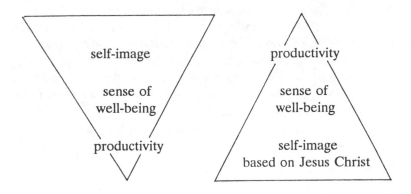

Goal Orientation Perspective   **Bible View**

What is Your Base?

I owe the illustration above to Clyde Powell from Chalet Ministries in Tennessee. The triangle on the left represents a goal-orientation perspective. It's base is productivity. This is the view of the world or the church, probably influenced by the Protestant work ethic. If the foundation for your life, for your self-esteem, for your sense of well-being, is at the bottom of a triangle like this, then you're going to have a very unstable situation. There will be times in your life when you're ill, when you're tired, when you are not productive. If productivity is your goal, you're not going to make it. You're going to burn out.

In this situation, all three of these areas are changeable. Your productivity is the foundation. It's changeable. Consequently your sense of well-being and your self-image are all changeable. They're all affected.

The Bible view, by contrast, has a right-side-up triangle. The foundation of your self-image is based upon Jesus Christ and your relationship with him. And that is unchangeable.

Above that, your sense of well-being and your sense of productivity may vary. But it doesn't really matter, because your sense of well-being is based on your self-esteem which is based on Jesus Christ.

Stress

You can't discuss burnout without mentioning stress. We have three basic ways that we handle stress: (1) Eliminate the stressor. That works real nice if you can do it, but most of us haven't managed to have that much control over where we live and what we do. (2) Modify the stressor. This works sometimes, but the most effective method is to (3) modify our response to the stressor. Remember that terminal unmanaged stress is burnout.

Link Care identifies stress as anything that worries, frustrates, annoys, angers, scares, threatens, hurts, or criticizes you, or lowers your self-esteem.

Dr. Dorothy Gish of Messiah College listed the following as sources of stress:

- Confronting others when necessary. (This was the most commonly mentioned source of stress in missionary life.) Basically getting along with other people and still getting work done.
- Communicating across language and cultural barriers
- Time and effort raising and keeping support
- Amount of work
- Work priorities
- Time for devotional life
- Progress in the work
- Need for pastoral care personally
- Making decisions affecting others' lives
- Need for a confidant. People can talk to those of us who do short-term work in other countries. They know we are going to be gone. They can unload stuff they would never dare unload to someone on the field.
- Self-acceptance
- Cultural conflicts
- Goldfish-bowl existence
- Uncertainty about my future
- Freedom to take time off for myself
- Extended family concerns
- Frequent moving
- Task orientation vs. servant attitude
- Recreation and exercise

Sources of Burnout

We have two primary sources of burnout. They fall into the category of situational or system-generated burnout, and personal or dispositional burnout.

Situational or system-generated burnout

In the area of situational burnout, I think the first subcategory is the bureaucracy. People who survive working in a bureaucracy, competent bureaucrats or executives or field leaders, avoid overload by getting to know the organization, acquiring skills, exercising autonomy, remembering goals, learning to write off things that can't be changed, and emphasizing the ones that can. Secondly, they do it with humor. (I always worry when I find a field leader who doesn't have a sense of humor.) You have to have a sense of humor. Thirdly, they develop multiple sources of rewards.

The second situational type of burnout occurs because of the type of job or the vocation. We see this especially in human service jobs because people in these vocations perform emotionally taxing jobs that require a mix of skill and emotion. They share personality patterns that encourage the choice of human service careers such as empathy, compassion, and personal experience, and they share a client-centered orientation.

The third situational burnout has to do with live-in jobs. We see this in dorm parents, counselors, and educators who live on campus. I think we see it in medical personnel—not that they live at the hospital, but they're on call twenty-four hours a day. If somebody's bleeding to death, you can't say, "I'll come after dinner," or "I'll come after family devotions." You have to go.

There are unreasonable situations where the job can't be accomplished, or the boss is totally unreasonable, but I really think these are the exceptions. Most of the time burnout comes from other sources.

Dispositional or personal sources of burnout

The dispositional or personal sources of burnout have more to do with individual traits. There are probably six personality types that are susceptible.

- Perfectionist—the person who lives with shoulds and oughts. He needs to be in control because he's insecure. He has a high energy level. He runs on nervous energy.

- Workaholic—the person who is very driven. He may be trying to live up to his own or others' unrealistic expectations.

- The goal-oriented individual. Certainly the missionary and MK fall into this category. It goes back to those triangles we talked about.

- The other-oriented person. I hope that most missionaries are other-oriented people. But these people are particularly prone to burnout. Very often we find people that have the spiritual gift of mercy or helps. They are particularly sensitive and are likely to be dragged down by other people's pain. They're likely to empathize to the point of being in pain themselves. These people need to be liked or admired. They're very sensitive to criticism. They drive themselves to avoid it. They're generous to all but themselves. They overidentify with and internalize the hurts of others. They often find themselves in a rescuer role. They are altruistic and are motivated by social and interpersonal rewards.

- People who lack assertive interpersonal skills. I would mention this along with that first characteristic in Dr. Gish's study, the inability to confront when necessary. Something simmers underneath the surface for years and years and isn't dealt with because somebody early on didn't confront gently and lovingly when it should have been done. People who lack assertive interpersonal skills have a hard time saying no. They feel guilty if they express anger or other negative emotions. They're driven by other people's expectations. Unfortunately, the other people's expectations may be unrealistic for this individual.

- The compulsive individual. This person just has to get everything done and has to get it done before he can do anything else.

Situational burnout tends to be clustered. In one organization or in one vocation or on one field or in one church, you'll tend to have repeat performances of burnout in successive personnel. If it's a pastor, for instance, you may have had every single pastor over the last fifty years burn out. If it's a group situation, you may find that several people burn out simultaneously.

By comparison, personal burnout is more likely to occur in isolated cases. Of course, you can have a mixture of the two. You'll get a person who has the personality characteristics that predispose him toward burnout in a setting which predisposes to burnout, and you've got a pretty certain burnout case on your hands within a very short period of time.

Remember, the susceptibility to burnout may be generated by the system or by the self. Most of us can tolerate prolonged intense stress at home or at work, but not in both settings.

The things that compromise our ability to cope and probably precipitate burnout are:

- A totally new situation. That probably reminds you of missionaries in culture shock.
- A completely unanticipated event.
- Any situation in which the person feels he has little or no control.
- Absence of a responsive social support system. We're trying to provide a responsive support system for our MKs when they reenter, so that if they have problems, there's somebody there who can respond to them.

The Chinese character for crisis depicts both danger and opportunity. I think that's what we're dealing with.

Behavioral Symptoms of Burnout

We need to examine burnout more closely. The behavioral symptoms of burnout include lability of mood, blunting of affect, quickness to anger, diminished frustration tolerance, suspiciousness or paranoia, increased levels of risk taking, rigidity, negative attitudes, inability to relax, constriction of recreational and social outlets, feelings of isolation, increased marital discord, and possibly drug or alcohol abuse. I don't think we're seeing a lot of drug and alcohol abuse among missionaries, but if it takes you ten cups of coffee a day to keep going, you might be doing too much.

I think our Seventh Day Adventist friends have a good point. I'm becoming decaffeinated. I wonder if we ought to be thinking about this a little bit more. Isn't that a kind of drug that we use to keep going when the Lord and our bodies are telling us to slow down? If it takes you ten cups a day, or even five cups a day, think it over.

Shank divides burnout into three stages. One is fatigue, irritability, decreased enthusiasm, somatic complaints (headaches, stomachaches, backaches that you can't find a reason for), and eating changes. The person feels incompetent, fragmented, alienated, and has unvoiced anger or frustration. It's a lot like depression.

In the second phase he becomes withdrawn. He tends to get silent. He may have a weight change, and somatic complaints increase.

The third phase is cynicism, alienation, increased withdrawal; he becomes an obnoxious escapist. At this point he may even undergo a change in values and beliefs.

Taliafaro's stages of burnout are the following five:

- Honeymoon. No matter how difficult the situation is, when you're fresh you usually can tolerate it.
- Fuel shortage. The person continues to burn the candle at both ends, but there's no oil. He keeps going by sheer self-discipline.
- Chronic symptoms. Neck, headache, stomachache, back pain that he cannot account for on a medical basis.
- Crisis. When you get to the crisis stage, things are bad.
- Hitting the wall.

Often we see people who go through stages one through three, and repeatedly go through them. They manage to back off before they get to stages four and five. But once they get to stages four and five, it's very hard to recover. At this point, things usually have to change. Unfortunately it often means a change in vocation. A person who was a missionary becomes something else. That's a tragedy, because often these things can be prevented.

It's important in burnout, just like it is in depression, to rule out any medical problem. I don't go through a lot of medical testing, because a lot of times when you do that, you distract the person from what really needs to be dealt with, which may be a driven nature or his tendency toward burnout. But I make sure they don't have malaria or dengue. I make sure they're not anemic, that they don't have mono or hepatitis or something like that. If you've ruled out a medical reason, then we need to be thinking about either depression or burnout when we get to these symptoms.

Contexts of Burnout

People are susceptible to burnout in three contexts of life.

Those susceptible in the occupational context

- The individual who is idealistic but becomes disillusioned.
- The guy who is really in the wrong career to begin with.

- The person who is trapped. In the States, when a person is trapped, it is usually by finances, but missionaries get trapped by their pride, a rash promise, or by expectations of family or friends, or even by their self-expectations. They may be trapped in a setting which is really not what the Lord called them to. MKs, of course, can feel very trapped.
- High chronic stress occupations with limited control, minimal autonomy, and many unexpected events. That's a good description of missionary medicine, or missionary work any place.
- Occupations with few rewards and a sense of futility. The nebulous aspects of being a missionary or doing any kind of spiritual work may contribute to burnout.

Those susceptible in times of transition

- Missionaries on their first term.
- Going to college is another life-cycle vulnerability. The MK is leaving his family and friends. Separation is very much involved. He's leaving a small Christian school setting. Even if he goes to a small Christian college in the States, it's going to be a lot bigger than anything he's ever been to before. He's leaving the third culture. He's making academic changes. He's put in a position where he's expected to grow up.
- MKs in their early twenties. Dave Pollock told me that there are a very small number of MKs who get stuck in the anger phase of unresolved grief. They can behave in a bizarre manner in their early twenties—maybe at other times of life, too.
- Mid-life. We find that the discrepancy between public image and private awareness can be excruciating at this point in life. MKs may have sailed through young adult life but have unresolved issues that come out in mid-life.

Those susceptible in the context of the family

The third context of burnout is the family. This can involve spouse, children, and even the extended family. We see MKs who are affected by their parents' burnout. Women who work full time and then come home wanting to be a good wife and mother are in particular danger of burning out. There just aren't enough hours in the day. The problem also involves expectations by husband, children, and the woman herself. This is something that has to be worked out.

Treatment of Burnout

We treat burnout in several ways:

- We work on monitoring individual perceptions.
- We modify family pressures.
- We modify environmental demands.

> When I was a sophomore or junior, we had already been in Taiwan four years, and I really wanted to graduate from Morrison. My parents decided that we would try to make it a six-year term so I could graduate.
>
> The summers in Taiwan are warm and can be pretty uncomfortable, particularly in the center of Taipei, so my parents got an air conditioner. We lived in China where we didn't have running water. We didn't have electricity. We didn't have a refrigerator. We didn't have anything. It was real difficult for them to get that air conditioner. But my dad was sixty-eight years old. Getting the air conditioner allowed us to stay on the field two extra years, because during the day when it was so hot, they were able to work in an air-conditioned office.

- Modify work problems.
- Detect faulty safety valves for stress. What I suggest are things like running, swimming, or biking on a regular basis to let off steam.

We try to do two or three of these things at once in treating burnout. Unfortunately, many of these people can't go back to the same job or the same place. Once burnout has occurred completely, we are talking about a situation that often cannot be salvaged, at least in the same setting.

Prevention of Burnout

It is important to prevent burnout in the first place. There are some things that can be done by organizations to prevent it.

- Allow a sense of goal accomplishment.
- People need clear-cut job descriptions if at all possible, with expectations and goals. Spiritual goals can be nebulous, and this is something that we need to work on together. I think about people who go to places like Morocco, work there for ten or fifteen years, and maybe never see any results. We need to be particularly sensitive to praying for them in the area of burnout, because they are going to be very vulnerable to that.

- Feedback and constructive criticism.
- Rewards.   In secular jobs, the rewards are things like pay benefits, security, and appreciation.   In missions we're dealing with something nebulous, so the mission board needs to carefully consider what they can do to reward people.
- Social support systems.   I think this was one advantage of being in the Orient.   We had the old mission compound. This provided a sense of community, and it gave MKs a sense of belonging.   The aunts and uncles were right next door. You may find that's not the ideal setting in an urban situation.   But it does have some advantages.   You need a social support system.   There are seven functional advantages to that: listening, technical appreciation, technical challenge, emotional support, emotional challenge, spiritual support, and spiritual challenge.

    Usually one person cannot be all of these things to you. That's why you need a team.   Let me give you an example. My husband is a great listener.   He's very supportive, but he's not medical.   So he can't offer technical appreciation or technical challenge.   I need other medical people who are going to challenge me, who are going to say,   "Look, I think you could have done better in this area," or "That was a good job."   My husband says it, but it doesn't mean anything, because he's a social worker.   The point is, you need somebody who can give you technical appreciation and technical challenge.   My husband provides emotional support and emotional challenge.   My husband gives me spiritual support and spiritual challenge, but I need other people to do that also.

- Consider the need to allow time off—not only allow it, but encourage it and require it.   I think there's a scriptural basis for one day a week.   This is very difficult when you're a pastor.   There needs to be a day other than Sunday that you have off.   You need vacations.   You need them regularly.   I am concerned as I see the tremendous pressures that first term missionaries have.   Some organizations won't let a first term missionary have a vacation until they have been there a full year or two years.   That scares me because we're talking about approaching the time when burnout is likely to occur. If people don't get a vacation for a year or two after they get to the field, I think we're setting them up for burnout.

    I appreciate what some organizations do about furloughs.   They make sure their personnel put in a certain block of time on tour, and then they make sure they have a certain block of time to be with their extended family in the United States. Intensity alone does not create burnout. But intensity without rest will.

Management needs to recognize all these things, but a person must take his own measures.

Personal Prevention of Burnout

The prevention of burnout has to do with self-examination and self-awareness.

- I think it's a good idea to keep a log and a diary so you're alert to when things are changing and when things aren't working.

- Realistic goal setting and priorities. It is my responsibility to set that for myself. I tend to blame the organization or the boss, but I find out it's really my own driven nature that's making me go the way I'm going.

- Time acknowledgement. Time off. I need to learn to vary my work routine if I possibly can.

- I have to acknowledge my vulnerabilities. A tool for anyone in the people business has to do with personal distancing. What I think that means is that we learn to establish buffer zones. This doesn't mean that you don't care, but you learn when you're in over your head. You learn when you're so emotionally involved that you are no longer objective. A lifeguard will always throw a ring or extend a pole before he jumps into the water himself. When he jumps into the water, two people are in danger. You do what you have to do, but you try to do it rationally first.

- Compartmentalization. We limit the stresses of each role to its time and place. There's a certain need for decompression. For instance, we suggest to nurses in the United States that when they come home, they get out of their white uniform, and put on something else. Make a clear break between the job at work and the job at home. I think this is one reason why live-in jobs are so difficult. There's no clear transition.

  We suggest that in your waking hours, 60 percent should be work, 30 percent relationships, and 10 percent you. It is almost a tithe. This is personal time. Do something you want to do.

- Provide your own reinforcements.

- Work to change dispositional self-attributes.
- Learn positive attitudes. Sometimes we almost need to get into cognitive therapy.
- Develop new tools for coping and improve the range and quality of old tools.

Christian Perspectives

There are some additional perspectives that are helpful in preventing both burnout and long-term chronic endogenous depression. Amy Carmichael wrote that if she was having a particularly difficult time, she would sit down and say, "Have I been sleeping? Have I been eating? How's my devotional life? How's my fellowship life?" There was a list of things she used as a checklist to make sure that she was on the beam. These are my suggestions.

- We need to be in touch with our own feelings. We need to deal with them now, not years later. This is particularly the case with MKs, or any Christian kid, who may have unresolved resentment against his parents or against God or against some circumstance. If those things simmer, they will eventually create burnout or depression in later life. We need to learn even as adults to be in touch with our own feelings right now.

- We need to eat regularly. We need to eat balanced meals.

- We need to sleep regularly. We are not God's cosmic pets. If you abuse the body and the mind that God gave you, there will be consequences. If it takes ten cups of coffee a day to keep going, there will be a price at the other end. God is more interested in us than he is in our work, believe it or not.

- We need to have meaningful relationships and fellowship. That goes back to the support system I mentioned.

- We need to have a regular devotional life. This compensates for the fact that many spiritual goals are nebulous. Our devotional life can provide the rewards that we would not otherwise have in a nebulous type of missionary or spiritual goal setting.

  There was a survey taken of a good evangelical seminary on the West Coast and tragically, 85 percent of the students there admitted that they only prayed on the run. They did not have a regular, intense, disciplined devotional life.

- Exercise. This is much more important than we previously knew. We have discovered in recent years that there are chemicals called endorphins. Their chemical composition is somewhat similar to morphine and some of the pain killers we use. These probably account for the runner's high. You feel better if you exercise regularly. There is a biochemical reason for this. I recommend three times a week at least, and if you can do more, it's great.

- Observe the law of the Sabbath. I'm not talking about the Old Testament concept of the Sabbath on the seventh day of the week. At creation God established that there needs to be one day of rest a week. Jesus said it. I believe Jesus did it. It was very difficult sometimes, but I believe it is one of the keys to dealing with our stressful lifestyle.

The consequences of not observing the law of the Sabbath are catastrophic, whether for the individual, the mission, the nation. We find this in our part of the Midwest where we have a lot of companies like Chrysler and "Generous Motors." They've been too generous too long. They have tremendous fringe benefits, and they think they can now save money by working their current personnel on Sundays. They do that so they don't have to pay additional fringe benefits to new employees. The problem is that after awhile, there's an increased incidence of illness. There's an increased incidence of mental problems. They are not observing the law of the Sabbath. They're not taking a day off a week to recuperate and rest.

Here are two scriptural examples. The Israelites were in Egypt for four hundred years. They were not seen as people, but as producers of bricks. They were slaves. When we begin to see others in terms of what they can do, not in terms of who they are, we deface humanity and breach the community. God's order is, first grace and relationship, secondly work, even his work. Without the Sabbath it is works first, and grace second. We believe in grace, but we practice works, and we communicate it to our MKs.

Later, Judah was in captivity in Babylon for 70 years after 490 years of not observing the Sabbath. It doesn't take an awful lot of math to figure out what happened. You can look up Leviticus 26:31-35 for the principle. In II Chronicles 36:21 it says, "You will be in captivity until the days of your Sabbath are fulfilled." As Christian missionaries, we have missed the boat by not insisting in our own lives and insisting in our organizational lives that we observe the law of the Sabbath.

Let me give you a personal example. We got a new pastor three or four years ago. He was a great guy. He was a person who was very sensitive to other people and very easily dragged down. When he first came, my husband and I talked to him about the absolute importance of having a day off each week and establishing that right at the beginning of his pastorate. We made an announcement to the church that, except for absolute emergencies, Monday was going to be Greg's day off.

That's hard to do on the mission field, but there are ways to be in another location for enough time each week that you are not on call twenty-four hours a day. It depends on your setting. If you are a medical doctor, you probably have to get away.

I try not to do anything medical on my day of rest. I try not to read any journals. I try to read things that are fun, because I enjoy reading. I usually ride an extra ten miles on my bicycle, or I play racquetball if it's winter. I do the things that I really enjoy doing, the things that, if I'm stressed, occur to me that I would have liked to have done.

Powell: Just to reiterate the principle, rest is what you find to be refreshing and restorative. For myself, quiet time is the best. I'm with people a lot. I enjoy people, but I'm fundamentally an introvert, at least in the Jungian sense. I get my replenishment being alone.

I can mention a couple of things that I've seen work in missionary settings. There's been some trade off with a missionary from another group for exchanging apartments or offices. Some people have found that they can go to that other place and hide out. I had a certain perverse delight when I saw how one missionary was handling it.

> He was showing me the upper rotating room on a restaurant in an international hotel. We got off the elevator, and he said, "Wait a minute. Before we go in there, let me check something." So he went in and came back and said, "It's OK."
>
> I said, "What did you do?"
>
> He said, "I just wanted to make sure there weren't any other missionaries in there before I went in. I come up here and hide sometimes. Sometimes people think I'm running around the city doing important things, and I'm really up here having a cup of coffee."

I thought, "Great!" He had found a way to get those little islands of comfort, which I think is at least a substitute if you can't observe the Sabbath in the way it was discussed.

What do you recommend that I as a principal do for a teacher who is a candidate for burnout?

Powell: One of the most helpful things you can do is simply, out of the concern you have, mention what you're seeing. Use at least some of your authority and say, "You need some time off." If you can do that in a loving way, many people will be very responsive.

In closing, let me read a brief prayer from Rev. Eric Alexander, who published it in his newsletter in 1979 from St. George's Trow Parish Church in Glasgow.

Lord, give me such a vision as will save me from mistaking a busy life for a fruitful life, of mistaking success for faithfulness or the praise of man for the praise of God. Help me not mistake organization for inspiration, or facility of speech for spiritual power, or laziness for rest, or planning for praying, or head knowledge for heart experience. Amen.

20

When Missionaries and MKs Hurt

Sharon Willmer
Counselor, Wheaton, Illinois

I begin this presentation on the following premises:

- That psychological/emotional/spiritual hurt and pain are a reality within the heart and mind of every human being, including the Christian missionary and MK.

- That there is a great need for comfort and understanding, as well as forgiveness, healing, and restructuring.

- That platitudes, pat answers, and many (if not most) of the typical ways in which we deal with hurt, pain and dysfunction prevent us from hearing and embracing the life-giving truth and message inherent in the pain itself. Further, it alienates us from God, from our self and others.

- That we are both alternately victims and victimizers, neither one negating the other.

- That we are generally afraid to look at hurt, pain, and dysfunction, and that we go to great lengths to cover it up, deny it, eradicate it (often punishing ourselves or others in the process) rather than dealing with it directly.

- That the church, though desiring to alleviate pain and suffering, is too often perpetuating the very hurt and pain it wishes to prevent.

- That there is legitimate life-producing suffering which existed before the Fall and is a part of our creaturely creation, and then there is death-producing suffering which creates chaos and disintegration, and it behooves us to know the difference.

- That in the psychological/emotional/spiritual plane as well as in the physical world there is cause and effect, and that long term abuse and hurt leaves its scars which are not eradicated at the moment of salvation, but rather must be worked out and healed in the sanctification process.

- That sanctification is more accurately understood when viewed as a divine healing process rather than a divine behavior modification program, and that such occurs by the design of God himself, not in isolation, but in community.

- That the definition of abuse is much broader than the current cultural norm, and when appropriately expanded and defined, enables us to see ourselves and others more clearly and provides us a framework which will lead to prevention and life giving support.

- That there is a model of health, a definition of personhood from which we can better understand ourselves, God, and others.

- That God is love, and his heart is towards all suffering humanity, especially, the hurting Christian.

- That there is a way of life and hope; there is a healing process which embraces and involves us all, and in which God is actively desiring to be a part.

- That God's laws have no particular significance or meaning outside of a relational context, and that the consequences of the fall are most felt and experienced in a divided self, a divided community, and alienation from God.

Identifying Your Pain

I am going to do a little describing. Some of you hurt so deeply that it cannot be expressed in tears or in words. Only a scream would come close, and then might not suffice. Others' insides may feel like a big void, an empty hole out of which you constantly try to draw life. For others, your very will to live or express yourself has been almost devoured. No scream would suffice to express such pain, for there seems like nothing left inside to even speak.

I remember a very precious woman who had been through a great deal of hurt, pain, and abuse. She had been to several therapists. One had been very helpful to her, and the others had been very hurtful. As we began to connect with the issues and experiences of intense abuse, she began to cry. The only word that I could use to describe it is the word *wail*. Some of you know what I'm talking about. It's not even a scream any more. It's something that comes from so deep within.

Occasionally, a rage for some of you seems to come from nowhere, but everywhere all at the same time. Some of you are so close to being broken down, you feel so ground down inside, that you feel like a powder that blows away with every wind. I can well remember the time in my life when I felt like this. I remember the time when I reached a place I will call utter despair. I walked around with this visual image of myself. I could see myself lying down on the ground, flat on my back, beaten up, bruised, ground down like a powder. Another part of me, standing above that broken and bruised part, was screaming at that part of me that was lying down and saying, "Get up. You have to get up. You have to go on." But that part could no longer get up. There was nothing left.

Some of you know what I'm talking about. Some of you don't. Maybe you cope and feel basically well most of the time, but can't seem to get past certain areas of hurt and pain. Maybe you have spent countless hours poring through the Scripture, meditating, memorizing, praying, practicing positive attitudes, claiming victory, begging God to change you, to fill you, loving God deeply, needing him desperately, knowing him richly in your life, but the hurt or the dysfunction seems to be getting more complicated, more confusing, more painful. Maybe you're not the one who is in such pain. Maybe it is your wife, your husband, your children, or a friend. Maybe you feel fine and can't understand why others around you seem to feel crazy, or why certain persons react so negatively to you. It's confusing to you and leaves you with feelings of frustration.

Maybe you have taken the risk to finally open up to someone about the pain and the hurt and received the following advice: "You're not trusting God enough." Have you ever heard that before? "Don't try so hard." How about, "Try harder"; "Claim victory"; "Let go"; "Take charge"? The ironical thing about all of this is that they can be said in the same day about the same incident or the same pains. Another is "Let go and let God," and at the same time, "God helps those who help themselves." You see, the hook in this is there is truth here. For some things, it is enough truth, but for others it is not, and that's the hurt. We would do well as Christians to stop handing out so much spiritual advice and do a little more listening and understanding. Philippians 1:9-10 reads (Paul is praying for these people), "And this I pray, that your love may abound still more and more in real knowledge and all discernment." Love abounds and grows in real knowledge and discernment.

Feelings toward your pain

I am wondering what it is like for you to be a Christian and have hurt and pain. Is it humiliating? Do you feel alone and isolated? Do you feel you must keep the secret? Do you spend excessive energy trying to hide it? (This is one area, incidentally, where missionaries and MKs suffer greatly.) Do you have feelings of betrayal? Are you angry with God because you try so hard and just can't seem to be OK? Do you experience continual feelings of failure and powerlessness because as a Christian you feel that it is inappropriate that you have this pain and hurt?

I'm wondering how you think God feels toward your hurting and your suffering. (I didn't say "thinks," I said "feels.") Do you think that he feels condemning and judgmental? Maybe indifferent? Maybe delighted? In fact, enjoys the fact that you're suffering? Do you think that he feels disgusted and fed up with you? Do you think he feels compassionate, comforting, and tender? Do you think he feels powerless to attend to your hurt and your pain?

I am also wondering what you think God expects you to do with your hurt and pain. And I'm wondering if you even know what hurts, if you even have the internal permission or freedom to have the hurt long enough to try to understand it. Or because you are a Christian, do you feel that you must immediately get over it in order that you may have this victorious Christian life?

And finally, I am wondering how you feel toward the part of you that hurts and is in pain and in suffering.

You see, as human beings we have this incredibly unique ability to be in ourselves and outside ourselves at the same time. We have this ability to hurt and feel pain but stand outside ourselves and evaluate it at the same time and pass judgment on it. Now most people, even in the psychological field, would describe this as the feeling side of us and the rational side of us. I don't like to do that, because that assumes that the feeling side of us is not rational. I don't think that's true. I think we are so integrated that it's not possible to separate them. We have a part of us that definitely is feeling and intuitive, and then we have that part of us that stands outside of us and judges that other part. But I find that part that stands out here has feelings too. That's why I don't like to separate the parts. This part out here that's screaming at this part in here has feelings too, and may be very angry.

I want you to do something silently for a moment within yourself. Divide your body in half. Put in the right side of you the side of you that feels basically strong and competent, in control and rational.

Then in the left side of your body, put the side of you that feels hurt, and in pain and weak. Very quietly I want you to allow the right side of you to talk to the left side of you and tell the left side of you what it thinks about you.

Now I'm going to ask you to do the opposite. Have that side of you that is in pain and frustrated and maybe dysfunctional speak to the right side of you. What does that side of you want to say to the other side ? Listen to it for a moment.

This is what some of you may have experienced. The right side of you may have said something to the left side like, "I am so sick and tired of you being this way. When are you ever going to stop giving me this grief and pain? Why don't you just stop being so insecure? Why don't you stop hurting? Why don't you do this? Why don't you do that? Shut up! Go away! I have carried you all my life. I'm tired of you. You make me hurt all the time." And the other side of you may have said to the right side of you, "Stop screaming at me. Why don't you ever listen to what I'm saying? My pain is valid. Why don't you hear me? Why don't you comfort me? Why don't you understand me?"

I'm going to ask you to do one more thing. In the right side of your body, place the adult you today. In the left side of your body place your child—you when you were a child. You pick the age. Now for a moment let the adult speak to the child. But before you do that, just take a moment to let yourself feel how you feel as an adult towards that child. Do you like her? Do you know her? Do you know him? Do you like him? And now as the adult, what do you want to say to that child? Is there anything you would like to do with that child?

I asked a woman in therapy this question one time. She said, "I hate her. I hate her. She always let me down. She didn't do well in school and now I have to live with it. She was so stupid. She'd let herself get into all of the things she got into. She didn't say no. And now I live with all of that today." She told me later in the car on the way home, "I had this image, this vision that I wanted to pick her up by the feet and bang her head against the pavement over and over and over again until her brains ran out. And I wanted to drive over them with the car." (Incidentally, I alter my illustrations to protect the identity of my patients.)

How does this child in you feel towards the adult? Frightened? Angry? Powerless? Overrun? Depressed? If your child, the child in you, could say something to the adult, what would he say? Would he say, "Stop screaming at me? Just hold me? Understand me?"

Hurt and pain can be so intrusive, so consuming and penetrating, so powerful. I don't know if there's anything more personal than our hurt and our pain. It is isolating and disorienting. It can be distracting and annoying at best, debilitating and dysfunctioning at worst. It can be draining and overpowering. It leaves us feeling vulnerable and defenseless. When we talk about our hurt, we are talking about the most private, tender, and intimate places of our lives. We would do well, when someone shares their hurts with us, to listen tenderly, intently and with great respect. For we are entering, at that moment, into the innermost sanctum of a person's being. A hurt penetrates and emanates from the deepest recesses of our soul. And it is precisely there that we all need to be embraced and loved.

Dealing with pain

How do we deal with our hurt and pain? How do we deal with others' hurt and pain?

In our North American culture of quick fixes, elaborate distractions, and high technology, and in our evangelical culture of voluminous sermons, I find that we generally rush to do any or all of the following when we find ourselves confronted with our own personal hurt and pain.

We pass judgment. That's the first thing we do. We may say something like this: "I know I shouldn't feel this way, but..." Notice?

The second thing we do is we try to push it away. We do that so well that we do that within a fraction of a second of time.

The next thing we do is build elaborate denial systems. In psychological terms, we repress, we suppress, we ignore, we deny, we disregard. I never cease to be amazed, in doing therapy with Christians, how elaborate our denial systems are. They have got to be some of the most creative in the world. And they're all biblically based.

We may panic and rush to do something. That's one of the first things we do.

A missionary child said to me, "I am a disobedient, rebellious child. Can you help me stop?"

I said, "I don't know. I think first we'll need to get at the heart of what is generating these feelings of rebelliousness and disobedience."

Immediately it was back to, "What can I do? How can I stop this?"

I knew already by the sense of her desperation that she had probably tried most everything that could be suggested for her to try, and it hadn't worked.

I'll finish that story later.

Douglas Hall, in his book, *God in Human Suffering,* makes a statement which I appreciate so much. He talks about God's omnipotence, his power, and he says in our North American culture, when we talk about power and when we talk about God's omnipotence, we talk about brute force. We think of bulldozing, whirlwinds, and tornados. When people talk about God's power, they generally think in those terms also. But he said God's power is demonstrated in his love, because it's the love that produces the lasting change in people's lives. What brute force will not do, love will do.

I think of the brilliant young man who, when we were dealing with something very, very deep in his life, put his hands to his head and said, "I can't stop the thoughts. I can't do what we're doing today, and I have to because I know it's so important, but I can't stop the thoughts."

I said, "What are the thoughts?

He said, "They're inappropriate thoughts towards you."

I said, "You mean sexual thoughts?"

He said, "Yes."

I said, "Do you feel comfortable in sharing those with me?"

He said, "No, they're too awful."

I said, "OK, can you give me an example? Have you had these before?"

"Yes, with other people all the time. I have to stop. I've prayed. I've tried. I've begged. I've memorized Scripture. And they won't stop. What can I do. Tell me. What can I do to make them stop? I've tried everything."

I said, "I bet you have. But one thing you have not yet been able to do."

He looked at me and the tears filled his eyes and began to stream down his face. That sense of despair came over his face—fear and hunger all at the same time. "Tell me, tell me," was in the face, but the fear was, "I won't be able to do it."

I said, "What I'm going to tell you, you can't do alone. In fact, an awful lot of it you're not going to be able to do. That will have to come later. But the one thing that has never been applied to this in your life is love. This part of you has never known love."

We are trying so hard to get past the hurt, pain, and dysfunction that we miss the very message that is inherent in the pain itself.

The message in pain

Physical pain exists for a purpose. It sets limits for us. Emotional pain does the same. It gives us a message. If I bang my hand against this platform and my hand begins to hurt, there is a message in that pain. Stop doing that. That's abusive. It's the same thing emotionally. There is a message inherent in emotional pain, but we try to get past it so fast that we don't take the time to hear the message that is being screamed at us from the pain itself. I don't think it is any mistake that we feel pain emotionally any more than it is a mistake that we feel pain physically. I don't try to get past the physical pain by screaming at the injured part to stop hurting. I don't condemn it and pass judgment. I feel that it's appropriate that my hand should hurt because it was abused. We don't do that in the emotional realm. And that's costing us greatly. It's especially costing us as Christians because we do this in the name of God. It becomes a double bind.

Pain is a great teacher, for it sets boundaries and limits for us. It enables us to know ourselves, to know our God, and to know each other. We make excuses and try to reduce the pain or the hurt in order that we may not have to embrace it and deal with it. Until we embrace our hurt and pain and dysfunction, we will not get past it. The more we push it away, the more we have to push part of ourselves away. The hurt and the pain and the suffering reside within us. So if we push away the hurt and pain and suffering, we push away a part of us, and that's the foundation for the divided self. We must first embrace the hurt and pain and suffering and allow the part of us that has been pushed away to come home. Then, when it comes home, we can deal with it and get past it.

The degree to which we push away hurt and pain is the degree to which we will lose truth and self. And the degree to which we become divided will manifest itself in dysfunction.

Many if not hundreds of missionaries and adult MKs are living with deep hurt and pain and levels of dysfunction. Our responses and reactions to it are varied and many. Our love and concern for them needs to manifest itself in a very real embrace of who they are as individuals, including an embrace of their hurt, pain and dysfunction. How much of their individual hurt, pain, and dysfunction is due to their missionaryness or MKness is not always clearly discerned.

Assumptions Regarding the MK

The MK as multicultural or monocultural

I want to address an area regarding MKs that I have become acutely aware of from having served on the steering committee. We have a lot of assumptions floating around about MKs. We say the MK is a third culture kid when in fact he may be monocultural. *Third culture* implies that they have taken elements from this culture over here and this culture over here and have integrated them into some internal culture. In the first place, that is contradictory to the very use of the word *culture*. Culture implies a shared experience. We don't have individual cultures. It violates the definition of the word. If we assume that the missionary child has a third culture existing within himself that is an integration of these two cultures, we have made an assumption about culture which is not correct, and thereby alienate the MK. The term *TCK* also implies integration. It implies that a person has been able to take bits and pieces of one culture, and bits and pieces of another and integrate it into some kind of whole. Whether that occurs in an MK, we don't know. Research has not been done to validate that.

We throw around terminology and define the MK and put limits and boundaries on him. That may not be him at all. If, in fact, the MK is monocultural, then the MK needs to know where his roots are and needs to be able to embrace that culture and be loved in it. The MK may, in fact, be monocultural because he exists in a missions culture. They may not have integrated home culture and host culture at all.

I'm not saying that's how it is. I'm saying that's what we don't know right now. But we're doing an awful lot of counseling and relating to persons in terms of an untested theory. As soon as we do that, we set people up for an understanding of themselves which may not be true, and then we set them on the road to dysfunction and hurt. It becomes a double bind. Your insides tell you one thing, but the outside culture is telling you another, and now you're in contradiction and pain.

The MK as exceptionally successful or unsuccessful

How many double binds are we putting missionaries and MKs in? For many and varied reasons, there seems to be a polarization in the evangelical and missions community manifesting itself in what appears to be an intense need to view the MK as either highly adjusted or as a basket case. If the MK is viewed as a basket case, there is also a prevailing attitude which assumes that it is his or her fault. He has done something wrong. He either doesn't have a good attitude; he doesn't have enough faith in God; he doesn't believe in God's sovereignty, or some such thing like this.

I call the positive side of this polarization in regards to the MK a Pollyanna syndrome. On this extreme end, there seems to be an intense need to view the MK not only as OK, but in fact exceptional, above the rest of the human race. I find when I'm doing therapy with the MK that this is one of the most hurtful things that we can do. The MK's identity and validation become too wrapped up in his exceptional cultural experiences.

The careful maneuvering that I see going on in the evangelical and missions community to make sure that everything we say or do about the MK is positive, raises very deep suspicions in my mind that we may have a cover-up going on. I have asked myself what could possibly be prompting such a driving need and extremely intense feelings. These are the three theories that I have.

- Is it possible that our basically satiated and comfortable evangelical North American culture has a need for the missionary and the MK to be their heroes of the faith, our link to a lost world?

    One of the most tragic things I deal with in therapy is when missionaries are sent home from the field with feelings of failure because there's dysfunction in them or one of their children. They are often rejected by the very church that just the year before, paraded them about in their native costumes.   .
    If they hurt or fail, we will be left to grapple with the relevancy of our own faith, our own responsibility to win a lost world. When we set them up as heroes, they have to serve as validators of our faith by their passionate allegiance to God and willingness to suffer. Thus it also eliminates our own personal need to wrestle out our own faith in this world.

- Is it possible that such a need could be masking a deeper spiritual insecurity or fear concerning God himself? Do we need the MK to be OK to assure ourselves we have not and are not missing God's will and direction in the whole missions endeavor. We have to fend off accusations of neglect, of God who would disregard his own to win the lost. Are we caught in some kind of defense of God?

- Is is possible that we are unwilling to acknowledge hurt, pain, and dysfunction in the MK because we have not embraced hurt, pain, and dysfunction within ourselves? We are thus frightened and left feeling too vulnerable to acknowledge it in them.   To embrace our own hurt, pain, and dysfunction would lead to dramatic life changes, for when one truly embraces and encounters one's own hurt, pain, and dysfunction, one comes face to face with good and evil, with God and man, and with himself.

I propose that if, in fact, we are needing to view the MK in some positive or heroic light to the point that we disregard, deny, or minimize their pain, or worse, we punish and alienate them for their pain, then we are in grave violation of them as persons.   We are grieving the Holy Spirit, we are perpetuating falseness among ourselves, and we are seriously impacting the spread of the gospel.   In so doing, we deny them their right to live honestly before God and before the world.

Now, as to why the other side exists, I suspect it is probably a reaction to the first side, and possibly it is an occupational hazard.   It can be easy for a therapist to begin to ask him or herself, "Is there any health in the land?"   I suspect that this extreme position would vanish if we could successfully avoid the first.

I propose to you that both of these positions are in error, that hurt, pain, and dysfunction are found in all of us to varying degrees, so the question is not "Is their hurt or pain legitimate?" or "Does it exist?"   The question is, rather, "Where are they hurting, and what can we do about it?" and "How does God want us to relate to them in their suffering?"   A further and more important initial question is, "Is there legitimate suffering which leads to growth and life, and is there inappropriate or illegitimate suffering which leads to death and disintegration?"   I propose to you that there is legitimate suffering and then there is that which is evil, in which God takes no pleasure. It behooves us to know the difference and to follow Christ in his redemptive work to eradicate it and to be a part of the healing process.

Illustration of the Healing Process

I'm going to give an illustration and then refer back to it because of all the dynamics it possesses.

> There was a period of two months in which my daughter's behavior became increasingly chaotic and disturbing to me.   She became increasingly angry.   I noticed that it didn't seem to matter what I did with her or how I related to her.   Nothing seemed to change the increasing disintegration that was going on within

her. She was not able to cope. She was not able to focus. Her
anger increased. Her relationships with friends were getting
into trouble. Her relationship with me was certainly disintegrating. Her relationship with her brothers was gone. I was at
a loss as to what was going on. As you can imagine, I tried
most everything I could think of to get at the heart of what was
going on, but simply could not come to it.

The thing that disturbed me the most was the lying that
began to increase. It was usually in situations that I could not
prove, so I was put in the position of being frustrated and angry
and feeling I was being deceived, but not being able to do anything about it. After about two months of this, I was ready to
call my therapist and say, "I'm coming in because I'm falling
apart in this relationship. I'm at a loss as to what to do. I need
to come in and look at myself and see if there's something
going on in me that is perpetuating this in her. I need some
outside help to look at this." But right before I made the decision to do that, at eleven o'clock one night, I was sitting on the
floor working on something. She came down to the family
room in knots. She sat on the floor, but she couldn't sit in one
spot. She was so distraught.

She said, "I am so angry."

I said, "Yes, you are."

She said, "I am so angry with God that he knows the
future."

I took it at face value at first and said, "OK honey, what
is it about the future that you're angry that God knows?"

"I don't know. I don't know."

I said, "OK. I want you to know something. Whatever it
is that's hurting you and upsetting you and generating this deep
anger, God is going to love you all the way through it, and I am
going to love you. Let's talk about it some more." So I asked
her four or five questions to try to get at the heart of what it
was. "Is it the good things in the future? Are you angry with
him for knowing the good things that you don't get to know?
Are you jealous?"

"I don't know."

"Is it the bad things in the future?"

"I don't know. I don't know. I don't know."

Then I decided I would try a little intuitive work and not
take it at face value. So I said, "You know, honey, sometimes
when we're angry about something, that's not really what we're
angry about. We're angry about something else. I'm going to
try some things on you, and you tell me if they fit. Sometimes
when we're angry with God about knowing the future, we're
really angry with him because there's something he knows about
the past. Do you think that's possible?"

And she gave me one of those looks. I said, "Would you like to talk about that?"

"Well," she said, "I've been noticing I've been lying a lot lately."

I said, "I'm glad you noticed that, because I noticed that, too."

She said, "It's not just here, Mommy. It's at school."

I said, "OK, you want to talk about it?"

She said, "About two months ago I cheated on a test. It was so easy, and I got a good grade. So then I cheated on another test, and then another test. And then I found out that I could cheat on my homework. I hate Adam and Eve."

I thought, "That's so classic. Here's this hurt and pain and frustration, and that's about as far away as you can remove yourself from it."

I said, "Why are you angry with them?"

"Because they sinned and brought this mess on me."

I said, "Well, I think you have some legitimate issues with Adam and Eve that you can take up with them when you see them. But right now that's not going to help if you focus on what they did. For you to be free of the hurt and the pain that you're feeling, you're going to need to stay with you."

Then she went through the process of confession and the tears began to come. I hadn't seen tears in two months. I loved her and held her and comforted her. Then I said, "You know what you're going to need to do? You're going to need to take the responsibility for what you have done and let your teacher know."

Then I told her three stories. The first was about when I cheated on a test in seventh grade and had to go the teacher and confess. Next, I told her about two students I had when I was teaching developmental psych. One came and confessed cheating on an exam. I told her how much I respected that student for coming to me and how close we became as student and teacher after that experience. The third case was the one she really identified with.

The third student, who I'll call Linda, failed three quarters of the exams, didn't come to over half of the classes, and didn't turn in any of the homework. I called her in about midterm and said, "Linda, you're not doing well in here. I'm wondering if I can be of help to you." She said, "Yes," and we set up a tutoring time to which she never came. So the end of the term came and I called her in and said, "It grieves me to tell you this, but I am going to have to fail you. I want you to know in advance so you can begin to prepare for it."

She screamed at me, "Do you realize that if you fail me, I am not getting into the nursing program?"

I said, "Yes, I know this is a required prerequisite course."

She said, "Do you realize what you will do to my future?"

I said, "I have an idea."

She said, "Do you realize you're doing this to me. You're going to ruin my future?"

I said, "Linda, how can you possibly assume that this is something that I am doing to you? This is what you have done to yourself."

She said, "Nobody else has ever failed me, and I've done this since junior high."

I said, "I grieve for you, because what that tells me is that no one has ever loved you enough to hold you accountable for your own growth and your own behavior. I'm going to love you enough to do this for you now."

I was in tears at that point. She was sobbing. She left, and she failed, and she dropped out of school. Two years later I saw her on campus. She had gone to a junior college, picked up skills that she needed, had returned, had taken the course over, and was in the nursing program doing very well.

My daughter, with tears streaming down her face identified with this story and said to me, "Now I'm ready, Mommy, to go to the teacher. I hope she doesn't do anything to me."

I said, "She might not, but if she doesn't, honey, it's not because you don't deserve punishment. It's what we call grace."

The teacher not only didn't do anything, but she said, "I really didn't expect you to know the material anyway. It isn't really that big a deal."

My daughter learned a very deep and special lesson, in spite of the teacher. She verbalized over the next several days what clean healing she felt inside of herself.

Two days later I picked the children up at school, and there was this hot thing going on. Some fourth grade girl had written all over the bathroom wall, the F-word and the A-word referring to the principal, and the school was hysterical. They were going to find this person and punish her for vandalism. They were going to call in the police and take fingerprints unless somebody would tell who did this."

My daughter jumped in the car and said, "You have to come to school. All of the mothers have to come to school. We have written you a letter. I will bring it home tomorrow. You have to come in and look at the F-word and A-word on the wall."

I said, "Why do I have to come to school and look at these words?"

"All the mothers have to come to see if they recognize their child's handwriting."

I looked at her and said, "Did you do it?"

She said, "No."

I said, "Then I don't need to come."

"But you have to come to see if you recognize someone else's handwriting."

I said, "I won't recognize anyone else's handwriting. I barely recognize yours."

She said, "But Mommy, you have to. You have to, or they're going to call in the police.

I said, "I'll talk to your teacher if it comes down heavy on you, but I don't have the time to go to school. I'm working all day tomorrow. Besides, honey, if you didn't do it, there's no need for me to be involved."

That night as I lay down with her at bedtime, she looked at me with a twinkle in her eye and said, "You know I didn't do it, don't you?"

I said, "Yeah, I do."

She begged me, "How do you know?"

I said, "Because you wouldn't be this peaceful."

She grinned from ear to ear and said, "Can you imagine the state I would be in if I had done that?"

I said, "I can imagine. My heart is in a great deal of pain for whatever child did this. Would you like to pray with me for her?"

Then we prayed. It was not contrived. It just came spontaneously from my own heart. So if I repeat it to you, it was not a prayer meant to teach my daughter anything. It was an honest prayer from my own heart. "God, I am incredibly aware of the hurt and the pain and the fear that must be in this child's heart as she lays down tonight to go to bed and the sense of alienation and fear from the community's response to this. I am also aware of the principal's personal hurt feelings and pray that the principal would find comforting from her own friends so that she need not continue to respond in such a hysterical fashion. Then we pray that this child may some day come to know the healing forgiveness and the joy of repentance and love from Jesus Christ."

My daughter turned over. Tears were streaming down her face. She said, "I love you, Mommy."

What was she identifying with? The child. She heard the forgiveness and applied it to herself. She felt love, and out of that love flowed love from her.

That illustration contains within it tremendous dynamics of what we are talking about: anger, hurt, pain, sin, forgiveness, repentance, love, and embracing.

Response of the Evangelical Community

When I talk about embracing hurt, pain, and suffering, I mean that we must get to the place in the evangelical community where we do not respond with hysteria over other persons' hurt, pain, anger, sin, and dysfunction. The only way that we are going to get to that place is when we ourselves have been able to hear and embrace our own hurt, pain, and suffering, and recognize that because we are fallen, we are a hurting and a broken people.

The fall does not take away our accountability and our responsibility, but it does mean that we are in a position of being less than we know we could be. And that hurts. There is a constant sense of hurt and pain. That is why we need to be aware that when Jesus Christ entered into the human race, he said, "I'm going to hold you and I'm going to embrace you with your hurt, your pain, your sin, your dysfunction. I'm going to start there with you." If we are going to follow Jesus Christ, we must start there with him and follow him and know the passion with which he lived on our behalf. To embrace hurt, pain, and dysfunction does not mean to disregard sin or responsibility, in fact, quite the opposite.

Legitimate Suffering

There is a legitimate suffering which propels us to seek those things which fulfill our human existence and purpose such as:

An awareness or sense of potential aloneness

It's within us. It's a fear, an anxiety, a suffering that exists under the surface for all of us all of the time. I propose to you that it was placed in man before the fall and that it is a legitimate suffering which propels us to bond.

The MK and the missionary also have this intense drive to belong and to bond. It doesn't change whether they're across the ocean or right next door. We have to ask ourselves, "Is it possible that an MK or missionary might be hurting because a very inherent basic human need is not being met?" It is legitimate suffering which has nothing to do with sin on their part, but has to do with something inherent in the very character of their being. It's human.

A truthful experience of finiteness

We as human beings are finite. That's part of our creation. We bump into that all the time. That produces a suffering of its own kind. For instance, we are finite and not able to make ourselves warm when we are cold, and thus we do something with the experience of that finiteness. We have limitations around us, so we build houses and heaters and fires. That finiteness drives us to think and create and build and change and develop. That's inherent within our being. I do not believe when we get to heaven that will go away. I believe that is inherent in our creaturely existence.

The MK and missionary often experience this human finiteness and their consequences greater than their North American counterparts. For example, they see suffering of a magnitude that the American child may not see or experience. One of the conflictual points for them is that when they come home and try to be American, they have experienced a knowledge of their humanness which their counterparts have not. That feels like loneliness. It is loneliness in a sense, and it is legitimate.

What can we do for the MK and the missionary? We can listen to their struggle and we can embrace it and we can say it is legitimate pain.

The reality of temptation

If we were not aware of and in touch with temptation from within, we would not know the joy of freedom. The knowledge and experience of temptation propels us to know ourselves and experience our freedom and our responsibility.

The missionary and the MK experience temptation and they fail and they conquer. I fail. I experience temptation. I have anger. I have known hate and bitterness. I struggle and will struggle until I am with him face to face. When we start setting people up in a heroic light, we promise them alienation or judgment or disappointment if they come down off that pedestal. We need to be very careful that we stop doing this to missionaries and MKs. What we need to do is embrace them fully as human beings and know that they are going to know temptation and failure. They are going to know adultery. They are going to know all kinds of sin. It is on the mission field. It is in MKs, because it is in us, because we are human beings, and that is the story of our existence.

A healthy level of anxiety

A healthy level of anxiety is inherent in us and propels us to meet our needs. Here is a classic place of double bind. Are you familiar with it? Christians should not have needs, emotional needs especially, because if you have Christ they've all been met. If there is an anxiety in us which propels us to have our needs met, we are in sin. Because if we're living for Christ, we should not in any way seek to have our needs met. What are you going to do, except be angry with yourself, judge yourself, divide yourself, get out here on the side of yourself and scream at that side of you that has needs?

I love the story when Jesus washed the disciples' feet. I love Peter. I identify with him so often. Peter was offended that his Lord should wash his feet. The typical thing we hear from that passage when we hear a sermon on it is, "Therefore go and wash each other's feet." If all we were to do was wash someone else's feet, who would ever get their feet washed? If you're to wash someone else's feet, by implication that means I must let you. There has to be dependency. When we have learned to be both dependent and independent, we are more in touch with our creation and what God intended us to be. It's an interdependent relationship.

We have to ask ourselves where we are putting the missionary and the MK in these double binds? Where are we, in essence, saying to them, "You are to be out there giving and giving, and if you need someone to care for you, then your faith is weak. You are in sin. You are not trusting God."

God-given Ability to Detect Abuse

I propose to you that abuse and violation without the intervention of love propels the human being into disintegration and chaos. The detection of abuse and violation is inherent within our being. In other words, when God made us, he created us with the inner mechanisms to discern when we are being abused. But if you hold to the pseudo-Christian teaching that we have no rights, then you have no permission to know when you are being abused. Basically, if you have no rights, then you are not being abused. If you hold to that, then you have to live in constant conflict and violation of the inner mechanisms which God gave you to know. Incidentally, the invalidation of one's perception produces schizophrenia of the highest magnitude. When a child is being abused but is told they are being loved, or when the child is being abused but is told that the abuse is appropriate, a divided self is produced, which literally makes for craziness. Unfortunately we are hooked into a lot of that.

I propose that emotions are to the spirit what nerves are to the body. Violation of our personhood registers in our emotions and our mind, and the result is emotional pain. We can also bring that pain upon ourselves by violating our own selves by sinning, going against what God created for us. I believe that it is God's desire that we listen to the inner mechanisms for the message there.

I do not believe that resentment and bitterness are one and the same. Those words are used interchangeably in our culture. I propose that bitterness has entered into sin. Resentment has not. It is appropriate to resent when you are being abused. In fact, if you do not resent it, you are in a state of ill health. If you don't resent it, where are you ever going to get the compassion to stop it for someone else? I wouldn't like it if you were to come up and slap me across the face. Frankly, I would resent it. I may not need to move into the arena of being bitter with you, but I certainly would not appreciate you doing that to me. It would be a violation.

Do you know that I was so sick at one time in my life that I could not have said that? If you had come up and slapped me across the face, my first response to myself within a split second would have been, "I should thank you for doing it." We can be so abused that we no longer recognize abuse. Incidentally, that is an issue with sexual abuse. You know no boundaries.

I remember the day when I went running down the street past an empty field and was suddenly aware that I was in a dangerous situation. I knew from the car, the person in the car, and what was going on, that this was not a situation that I should run towards. The person had passed me in the car, had turned out the lights, and was just sitting there in the car waiting next to an empty space. But I kept running in that direction because:

I felt that I had no permission to be afraid as a Christian. If I really trusted God I would not experience any feelings of fear.

If the man were to do something harmful to me, it would be because it was my opportunity to witness to him.

If he did violate me (I couldn't have used those terms at that time), it didn't matter.

I did not want to embarrass that person. That's critical. We have associated love as something that never wants the other person to hurt or own any responsibility.

I was well enough along in my life at that time to recognize that that was sick. But I couldn't, even in the recognition of that, stop. That is one of those times when God met me and spoke to me and told me to stop. It was like a high speed tape going through my mind that said, "Flee evil. Flee evil. Flee evil."

Sexual abuse is my history, so it all fit that those would be my responses. I knew that, and I knew I was sick, and I went home the next day and got into therapy.

I believe it is God's desire that we listen to those inner mechanisms, but it is possible, my brothers and sisters, for those to have been so violated that they no longer record that abuse. I believe it is God's desire to bring healing life, and part of the healing process is to restore the use of those inner mechanisms. We have to ask about the missionary and the MK. Have we taught them in this evangelical community to disregard their inner mechanisms? If they are being abused by an administrator, if they are being abused by a husband or wife, if they are being abused culturally in some way, have we taught them that it doesn't matter? Have we taught them that it's of no value or significance? Have we not even used the word *abuse*? Have we redefined terms so that it no longer is what it is, which is a violation of personhood, so that they can no longer legitimately own hurt and pain?

Dealing with Pain

I propose to you that the goal is not that we stay in hurt and pain or that we come to bitterness. Neither is the goal to eradicate suffering. We do not live in a world where we are not going to be violated or we're not going to violate someone else. The point is that we can't deal with the hurt and pain, and we cannot come to a place of healing and acceptance, until we can first embrace it and call it what it is. The majority of what I do as a therapist is identifying abuse and violation, and then taking the person through the process of comforting and healing and forgiveness that sets him free.

Remember the woman I mentioned earlier whose cry I could only describe as a wail? In that comforting process with her, I held her while she wailed through this pain, and walked with her through the incident, telling her what I would do for her in that situation and how I would respond to her need. She came back to me the next week and sat for fifteen minutes without talking, the tears streaming down her face. She kept trying desperately to say something to me. Every time she'd open her mouth, she'd start sobbing all over again. I thought it was going to be more of the deep pain and abuse issues. But that wasn't it at all. She was overwhelmed with the experience and the loss of what she had never known but had just experienced for the first time. What she wanted to say to me was, "There's something inside of me this week that has not been there before. I feel a wholeness, a substance inside, a strength that I did not know could even exist for a human being. It feels warm, and it feels so peaceful." We had just started, the abuse was so great.

There is a healing process, but you can't get there by disregarding the dysfunction, the hurt, and the violation. When we do that, we disregard the very creation of God. We basically discount how he designed us to be and be towards each other.

We need to ask ourselves, "Where are the missionaries and the MKs?"

I think of an adopted daughter of missionaries who had watched her biological parents be tortured to death. Having lost her parents, she was put into the hands of friends. Because of the religion and culture of the country, the friends ended up betraying her, and she had to flee for her life. She was adopted, fortunately by some missionaries. She is the one who, when I saw her, said, "I am a rebellious, disobedient child, and I can't love my mother."

I said, "Tell me how old you were when you were adopted?" She told me.

I said, "Where were you before that?" I knew none of that.

She evaded the question. I came back to it. She evaded the question again. So I said to her the third time, "Are you aware that you are evading the question?"

She said that she was. The tears filled her eyes, and she said, "I can't talk about that time of my life."

I said, "Honey, I don't think I can talk to you about this rebelliousness and this anger that is so strong in you without some idea of that time of your life, because I have an intuitive sense that that is where a great deal of it is coming from."

Then she began to talk about it, and went through the horrible, horrible details. She sobbed and cried. I helped her put words on what it was like for her and held her while she went through the trauma.

I said, "You miss your mother, don't you?"

She sobbed and sobbed, and said, "But I know I should be thankful because God has done all these things in my life, and I know I should love the mother I have."

I said, "Wait a minute. You miss her, don't you? You still love her. Tell me about her. What was she like?" She talked to me about her mother. I said, "I would like her, too."

Then she said, "But she's not a Christian. She's in hell. I'm so angry at God for that. But I know I should be thankful because he's had his hand on my life."

I talked it through with her and comforted her. I told her that her anger and her hurt and her fear were appropriate, and that she could take that up with God. Then I asked her, "How does your adopted mother feel towards your natural mother?"

"We've never talked about it."

"Does she know what you've shared with me today?"

"We've never talked about it."

Her adopted mother, bless her heart (I'm not passing any judgment on her), by not hearing and embracing the natural mother, was forcing the child to push away a part of herself. That creates anger and chaos from within. That chaos was coming out in a self-hatred because that was a part of her life that wouldn't be embraced. Instead, the only thing she was receiving was, "You should be thankful that God had his hand on your life," which implies, "None of that other stuff matters any more." But it does matter.

I sat and held her and cried with her for three hours and put her feelings into words. She experienced for the first time in her life that it did matter.

The next morning I gave her a hug and said, "How are you today?"

She looked up at me. Her face was radiant. She said, "Lighter."

I said, "Where?"

She said, "Right here. It feels like a boulder has been taken out of my heart."

I said, "Is there anything where that boulder came out?"

She said, "Myself."

You see, God wants us to live. He created us to live. That's part of our definition of personhood. He created us to live in relationship, in intimacy, in bonding and knowing.

We're not even touching the adopted MK at this conference. There's not one discussion that's going to take place on the adopted MK. But there are hundreds of them, and they have these issues inside. At some point somewhere in their life, someone's going to need to walk through those things.

I refer you to my talk on "Personhood, Forgiveness, and Comfort" in the *Compendium of the Manila ICMK* for a more complete picture, but I am going to pick out a part of the definition of personhood and illustrate that right now.

Learning about Ourselves from Nature

One of the places that we find out about who we are as persons is from nature itself. God's imprint is everywhere. He made nature. He made us. He's consistent with all that he does, so it should be obvious that we can find out an awful lot about ourselves by looking at the world he created for us to live in. These are some of the things that stand out to me in nature that teach us something about ourselves.

Separation of substance

In creation there is clear, honest separation of substance. The tree is clearly the tree, and not the tree and the grass mixed together. The bird is clearly a bird with clearly defined boundaries. When we talk about dysfunction, one of the greatest places of dysfunction is that the person doesn't have a sense of himself. The boundaries have disintegrated. They hardly know themselves from someone else.

If you could draw me in a state of disintegration, instead of drawing me with solid lines, you would draw me with dotted line. I was too vulnerable. I felt kind of like I had holes all over me and you or anyone else could get in me and enmesh with me. We talk about family systems that are in ill health. There's too much enmeshing going on between people. There's not clear delineation between individual persons. In nature, things are clearly defined. The bird is not bird and tree, the grass is not grass and dirt, but they are codependent. In human beings, God wants us to be clearly defined, and clearly ourselves. God has no intention or desire for us to all be little Christs or imitation heroes. He wants us to be clearly ourselves.

Unity in diversity

We see from nature that there's unity in diversity. We see that there is dependency in nature. God designed us to be dependent. We must start when we look at the missionary and the MK, from the perspective that God designed them to be dependent, not isolationist, not heroes of the faith out there living some kind of isolated life. He designed them to be dependent on us.

Cause and effect

We see from nature that there is cause and effect. I have a big bay window where I do most of my therapy. Outside my bay window there's a beautiful tree. At least it's beautiful in the spring; it drops all these messy apples in the summer. I like to use that tree as an illustration of cause and effect. If I were to go out and pour acid on the ground around the tree every day, my tree would begin to show signs of ill health.

It would be stupid of me to think that I could cure the tree by screaming at it. We try those kinds of things, though. Nor would it do any good for me to take the pruning shears and start pruning the tree; nor would it do any good for me to strip the tree of all of its leaves and leave it naked and exposed; nor would it do any good for me to isolate the tree from all the other trees around or to refuse to acknowledge the tree.

The only thing that is going to return health to the tree is if the sustenance from which the tree is drawing life contains health. So what I have to do is get down at the roots of the tree. What is the root of the tree drawing from?

When I do therapy I go back into the child, not because the past is so intriguing, or more important than the present or the future, but because it is in the child that the roots are. And it's that child that drew a certain nourishment from its surrounding environment. That child is still within us, not existing as a separate child. If you cut a tree off, you can still see the inner tree. The little tree is still a part of the big tree. We can count the rings. My child is still in me. The most significant day in my healing was the day when I could embrace that child, pick her up off the couch and put her on my lap and say, "I want to hold little Sharon. I'm going to comfort her. I'm going to listen to her and stop being angry with her and pushing her away." It would be stupid of a horticulturalist to say, "If you want to heal this tree, go and cut the inner rings out of it or ignore it."

So our focus and concern is to provide as healthy and nurturing an environment from which the missionary and MK can draw sustenance and life as possible. No one is going to be able to get a perfect environment. It just doesn't exist. But what are we going to do when abuse and violation do occur and a person does begin to show ill health? Are we going to scream at it, reject it, isolate it, or are we going to get to it?

Taking Responsibility

There are two kinds of people in the world. (Of course it's not true, but it does illustrate a point.) The ones that take all the responsibility for everything in the emotional realm, and the ones who take none or very little. When families come in for therapy, and they're in a real dysfunctional state, count on it, you're going to find that pattern. Somebody in the relationship is putting all the energy into it, and somebody is not putting very much in at all. One partner takes total blame for lack of sexuality, closeness, or intimacy, and is angry with him or herself for not being loving and kind and all of these things. However, what we find out is that often that person who is looking the best is the one who is really doing the most damage in the relationship and setting the other person up. It doesn't help to sit around blaming each other and criticizing. You have to get to the roots of each person to learn why the one is feeling totally responsible for the relationship and therefore pouring all the energy into it and assuming all the guilt, and why the other one is not doing any of it.

It's like the alcoholic syndrome. The spouse of the alcoholic typically bails the alcoholic out all the time and doesn't leave him with his pain long enough to produce change. There's message and motivation in pain. When the spouse stops rescuing the alcoholic, and he is left with his dysfunction, then he has to do something about his life or face the consequences of who he is.

In Christian homes, we have the same thing going on. On the field, I see this going on all the time. One spouse or another may be assuming all that kind of responsibility in rescuing the other, and it produces dysfunction. But since we have such wonderful denial systems in the Christian community, we can't even get close to recognizing what is really going on.

Confusion of love and kindness

We confuse love and kindness. They are not one and the same. Kindness is inherent within love, but love is not necessarily inherent in what we call kindness. You see, we have reduced kindness to a way of behaving instead of a way of being. We say it is kind to be nice and polite to people in situations where the kindest thing we could do would be to declare ourselves openly with them.

This is something that marriage partners have to learn. One partner thinks that to be kind is to not declare their own wants and needs in a situation. Instead they pretend they don't feel a certain way in order to be kind to the other person. The only problem with that is, it's not truth. The truth gets buried, but it always comes out somewhere—in snide remarks, coldness, distancing, not folding the socks right. It comes out somewhere, and often on the children.

Boarding homes

I'm not going to take up the issue of boarding homes, because I don't know for sure if they are a legitimate option. At present I assume they are, but we do have to raise the issues for MKs. Are we giving the boarding home parents enough support and nurturing so that they have plenty to give the children? Is the child load for them low enough so individual children can receive the intimate, knowing attention and love that they need?   Would a boarding parent have had time to spend three hours with a child, like I did with my daughter as she wrestled through her experience with God, life, lying, purity, and temptation?

We have to ask those questions.   And if we decide there is too great a risk involved, then instead of cringing and running away from it, we need to embrace it.   We need to provide as best we can a nurturing, loving environment.   Where we haven't done it, instead of judging, denying, and pretending the problem wasn't there, and shoving the hurt MK out of the way, we need to embrace and love him and say, "Yes, your pain is legitimate."

Part IV

EDUCATIONAL OPTIONS FOR
MISSIONARY KIDS

21

Deciding about Boarding School

Richard Fowler
LeTourneau College

"Should I send my children to boarding school?" I find this is probably the hottest issue that I have faced in talking and counseling with missionaries. It's a volatile issue because it involves self-image.

Factors to Consider

Family identity. One of the things I have found in counseling MK children who have had terrible problems in boarding school is that they feel they are needed at home to maintain Mom and Dad's relationship. When Mom and Dad are not number one with each other, the odds of a child having a problem at school increase. Sometimes a child perceives that he has to be part of that triad to keep Mom and Dad together. It may be a fact or not, but as we say in psychology circles, perception equals reality. If the child subconsciously feels that he has to be part of that triad, he or she will act up or do whatever he has to at school to get back in this triad and keep Mom and Dad together. It's very important that parents somehow indicate to their children that Mom and Dad are number one with each other; children are number two. When this happens, the children feel more secure in that relationship.

Familiar surroundings also provide a degree of security. Some psychiatric studies of army people have indicated that if a child spends at least a year in a new environment before he is sent away, he has fewer problems than if he were sent away to a boarding school sooner.

One participant said he went to the mission field when he was twelve years old. According to some research, if he had stayed at home for one year to get roots in that new setting and culture, he could have left that place knowing where home was. If a family moves to a new location just a month or two before sending their child away to another new setting, there is a degree of insecurity that tends to erupt. This is a generalization. There are some who beautifully adapt in those situations, but there are some who don't.

The ordinal position of the child in the family. Some studies have found the kids who have had the most problems in a third culture school are the first and the last child.

That might be an idea to check. Have your high school or grade school counselors start checking ordinal positions and find out which children have the most problems. See if they might indeed be the first child or the last child of a family.

Interpersonal dynamics of the family. To a small child, the family's ways are the only ways. When you get into a boarding situation, that change is going to be difficult. "Why is the way we used to do it (which is equal to the Bible in their minds) changed now?" That can cause a problem.

A family develops what we call a life script, or pattern of doing things. The transition between one life script and another is an area that needs to be studied and evaluated. Is your child compatible with the dorm parent situation? If he's incompatible, you get problems. If he's compatible, then he meshes and blends in quite well. Obviously if you have ten kids from ten different families, you have ten different life scripts. You might have two or three that fit in beautifully, two or three that don't, and the rest, by adjusting over a period of time, might develop and change.

I would suggest that if the dorm parent is secure enough in his self-image, he can dialogue with the child. Ask the child, "How different am I than your dad? What would he do differently?" Developing rapport so that they can be open and honest is a very positive factor in resolving conflicting areas and amalgamating the two families in certain ways. Children who have been allowed more independent decision making have more trouble adjusting than those from more authoritarian homes.

Parents' attitudes indirectly influence the outcome of the boarding school experience for their children. Sometimes parents harbor an anxious overconcern or resentment toward the dorm parent situation but don't verbalize it. Sometimes they will pretend there aren't any hurts. They never tell their kids, "Hey, I'm hurting. I don't want you to go." They remain aloof and afraid to reach out because they might be hurt even more. A child should never perceive his or her going to boarding school as a divorce.

The school phobia factor.   This is a resistance to going to school. This can happen in any culture, but happens even more when you put that little kid on an airplane and say, "You are going to go to school."   There are all sorts of physical ailments that can develop when it is time to leave for school, which can be the result of subconscious problems that need to be resolved.

One of the interesting factors researchers found is that a good percentage of those who have school phobia problems have a passive father and a very strong mother.

If you're sending your kids away, you need to think about the dynamics of what's happening in the family and you also need to look at what's happening at the school you are sending your children to.

Loneliness.   I've been doing a lot of research on loneliness. There needs to be an extreme amount of touching. Touching is very important for the developmental process.   If dorm parents don't touch their kids and hug them and make sure they have that contact, the odds are they're going to have a lot of problems. Dorm parents, because they are responsible for children, usually spend most of their time with those who are acting up, or the ones who are the most demanding. Their attention is diverted from this other junior who doesn't give any problems, goes to his room, does everything he's supposed to do.   However, they find he's the one who ends up with problems twenty, thirty or forty years down the road, because he's the one who didn't get that touching. Touching is very, very important.

I recommend *The Broken Heart: The Medical Consequences of Loneliness*, by James Lynch, published by Basic Books if you have to deal with this situation of loneliness. *USA Today* wrote:

> Studies by psychiatrist Mike Hollander of the University of Pennsylvania have shown more dramatic consequences of low-touch upbringings. Children who do not receive enough physical loving may grow up to shun contact or become touch junkies. Several promiscuous women, for instance, told him they use sex to entice men to hold them. Anthropologist Ashley Montague has observed that children who are inadequately loved often become physically hostile as adults. They literally rub people the wrong way.

When you see a person who people just don't like to be around, possibly you're looking at someone who was not touched much as a kid. Some children don't like touching. I would suggest that you don't suddenly become real "huggy." You start gradually over a period of time.   Just like when you adopt someone who has been abused, it takes a long time to get them to trust you. First you might just put your hand on the shoulder of a child who is acting up. In school instead of harping, just touch. Soon it becomes something that can grow. This is even more important for a teenager or young adult. This is one of the problems with American culture. We have an idea that once a child reaches adolescence, the dad should never hug his son again. You kiss your daughter, but you don't hug your boy. Many secular studies are pointing out how damaging this is.

Loneliness at an early age can cause a child to withdraw into a shell that is hard or impossible to crack. Some schools at the end of the year report, "We had a great year." They base that great year on the discipline problems that didn't happen. In reality it could have been a lousy year. The child who is lonely and starts to withdraw did not have a good year. But on the record it doesn't look like that. We need to be careful not to judge a good academic year in boarding school by just saying, "He didn't have that many problems."

Areas Where Children in the Dorm May Need Help

For children who will be raised by dorm parents, the following areas are ones with which they often need help. You can rate these on a scale of 1 to 10.

- Dealing with the loss (What would you need to do to help that child adapt better?)
- Loyalty conflicts
- Feelings of belonging
- Feelings of anger and guilt (How are they dealing with resentment of being sent away?)
- Knowing what is right
- Encounters with new siblings (pecking orders established)
- Maintaining and enhancing the child's self-identity
- New rules, new struggles

If you have a chart on each child you can set a goal for each child. You can't make number 10's out of everybody in one month, and sometimes you won't make 10's out of anybody any time. But what can you do to move a child even from 4.0 to 4.5 this semester? This chart gives you some behavioral objectives for each child that you can deal with.

Parents need to have that also. They need to work with school officials and dorm parents to find out how they will take care of these factors. It is the parents' responsibility to initiate dialogue.

An interesting phenomenon in the United States now is James Dobson's crusade against sending kids to boarding school. The new missionaries are questioning things they wouldn't have questioned ten or twenty years ago. In counseling parents, I'm saying, "You as mature Christians, who have the same Holy Spirit as anybody else, need to make sure that the decision you make is in tune with what God wants you to do."

22

National School as an Option for MKs: Factors to Consider

Dellanna O'Brien
Foreign Mission Board, Southern Baptist Convention

Any time a mission family moves to the field, deciding on the education for their children can be difficult. For many families, there may be several choices. There may be an international or a boarding school nearby. Home school programs may be available. Their mission may provide a teacher or tutor.

However, one option that is not always considered is the national school. I think there are a good number of reasons for looking at the national schools as an option. Few experiences that an MK can have can contribute to his learning and understanding of the local culture more than attending classes with children in the adoptive country. In addition, the parents have an entree into the community through the school which enables them to relate personally with adults they might not encounter in a church. Entrusting your child to a school is in essence saying, "We have faith in your system." When this can be done honestly, the very act speaks volumes about the faith missionary parents have in their new homeland. The MK's attendance in the national school places the child in a position to make friends and interact with a larger segment of his new culture.

It is often true that MKs attending an international school or studying by means of a correspondence course have little or no opportunity to interact with children of the new homeland. Missionary parents have found national schools an option which requires much less time away from their mission work in order to secure an education for their children. In areas where the only other alternative would be home study through a correspondence course, the national school may offer a very satisfactory academic environment for the MK. Even when an international school is available, the national school may remain the best choice simply because of the significant difference in the expenses of the two schools.   International schools can be tremendously costly.

Possible Negative Results

On the other hand, placing an MK in a national school can bring negative results.   First of all, by entering the national school unprepared, the child can have a devastating experience.   Isolation in a strange setting, not understanding the national language, misconstruing the intent of the missionary parent (the child may feel that he has been left to fend for himself in a new environment), or not receiving support from the parents, usually in the beginning, can be traumatic.   Frequently, too, the new missionary parents are so troubled by their own insecurities and adjustments in a new land that they miss the opportunities to help their children in their adjustment.

At the other end of the spectrum, we have MKs who have attended national schools all their lives and have so totally and completely identified with the culture that re-entry into their home country is very difficult and sometimes even impossible.   The longer the child of the third culture stays out of his homeland, and the deeper his involvement within the adoptive culture, the more difficult is his reacculturation into the social structure of his own homeland.

Another difficulty for the MK is that the curriculum offered by national schools obviously is designed to meet the needs of the citizens of that country.   Frequently, course offerings do not parallel those of the MKs own land.   Thus the MK returns to his homeland lacking courses that may be required for entrance into a college or university.   In addition, the methodology of a national school may not adequately prepare students for college or university.   In many cases, there is an emphasis on rote learning which does not prepare a student in logical reasoning and abstract thinking.

Conversely, a friend whose children had grown up in national schools said that when they came back to the states for their college education, they had never ever had an exam that was objective.   They had all been essay type.   They were totally unprepared for true-false and fill-in-the-blanks.

So methodology can sometimes be a problem. There are, however, national schools that can better prepare MKs for good college performance than some of our high schools back in the States.

Another reason that it can be difficult for the MK is that some national schools hold to a philosophy or religion that precludes the enrollment of missionary children. Exposing a young child to such teachings could be permanently damaging and therefore most unwise.

Getting Advice

After having looked at the positives and negatives, there may still be the desire to look at other factors dealing with national schools more closely. When missionaries go to a new field, they totally rely on the advice and orientation of the experienced missionaries. It is convenient and safe to follow the practices of one of your own in selecting shops, in establishing health procedures, and providing for other physical needs of the family. These new missionaries, who perhaps would be open to considering national schools, do not always have counsel from their peers in the selection of such a school.

One young missionary mother in a South American country asked an established missionary about enrolling her child in a national school. The older missionary responded, "Well, yes you can, but it just isn't done here."

Fortunately, that new missionary did enroll her first grader in the national schools and the entire family found it to be a very good and positive experience. More often, however, missionary parents, lacking familiarity with the culture, and having little or no experience in evaluating the schools, dismiss the option by default. If given specific criteria for examining a school, the missionary parents might feel comfortable with such an arrangement.

In our discussion, the term national school refers to both public and private. National public schools of many countries open their doors to missionary children. Oftentimes, private schools operated independently by a church, a mission, or by some industry or private agency may be available. In the case of both the public and the private school, instruction would be in the national language and the curriculum would be designed and appropriate for children of that nation.

Criteria for Evaluation

Is the school open to foreigners or expatriates? Most countries such as the United States open their schools to people who have immigrated. Private schools may have an open enrollment policy. Others, because of lack of provision for their own population or other reasons cannot afford to give places to guests in the land.

Are provisions for health and sanitary conditions adequate? Visiting the school can offer some impressions regarding the cleanliness and health standards of the school. I can remember when our son was in a kindergarten in Indonesia, we heard almost by accident that there were plans for a mass inoculation in his school. We knew of the lack of sterile conditions for those kinds of inoculations, and we were grateful that we could go to the school and report his up-to-date immunizations sparing him the inoculations. Bathroom facilities, water supply and any provision for food should be investigated. While we probably tend to be overanxious and too cautious about cleanliness, it does seem unwise to place our children in serious jeopardy because of unsanitary conditions.

Is the quality of education adequate? This is a value judgement, not easily made. It is especially important, for older students who must qualify for college admission. For the young student, though, it may not be all that important. If you are looking for opportunities for socialization, maybe you can combine at least portions of a correspondence course with the child's attendance at a national school, and cover both the needs for academic curriculum and for socialization.

Is religion or philosophy taught in the school, and if so, how forcefully? A child's participation in a catechism and a faith diametrically opposed to what is practiced at home can be more than confusing to the child. Giving lip service to practices not supported by the missionary family can retard the development of the value systems of the child and cause doubts as to his own beliefs. Knowing when to compromise and when to stand firm in one's beliefs requires maturity and understanding which come only with time. Placing a young child in a situation in which he must comply daily with practices he sees as contrary to what he is taught at home would probably be a compromise which we would not want to make.

I spoke with an MK from France who went through French school. Incorporated in those national schools were atheism and humanism. For her it was not a negative. It was positive because when she got something in the classroom she went home and talked to her dad about it, and they discussed in depth issues that young people don't ordinarily confront.

You've got to consider the individual child. Not every child is strong, and you just don't throw them into the water when you know they can't swim.

What Can We Do to Make It Work?

Simply enrolling the child is not enough. There are some steps the parents can take to increase the possibility of a smooth transition and ongoing satisfaction with the arrangement. First, the parent should meet with the school's administrator and the child's teacher. These things seem obvious to me now, but when I was on the field it never occurred to me to do that. It would have been so helpful to me, whether it would have been to my son or not. If the missionary parents are new and can't speak the language, perhaps an experienced missionary or national pastor can serve as an interpreter. At this time, the parents can indicate their commitment to the experience and state their willingness to do whatever is necessary to assist in the transition. Expressing an interest in the curriculum and teaching strategies employed at the school can further communicate the parents' eagerness to learn and be involved. Sensitive questioning in a spirit of cooperation can result in a broader understanding on the part of both the missionary parents and the school personnel.

If possible, the MK should have the opportunity to visit the school and meet the teacher before school begins. Knowing the physical setting and being acquainted with someone at school can relieve the MK's anxiety somewhat. Perhaps the teacher or school administrator can offer the names of other students who will be in the class, making it possible to get some of the children together ahead of time.

The parents' attitude towards the school experience is crucial. Parents' positive optimism about the whole thing is contagious, and the MK will usually look on it as an exciting adventure.

If he doesn't speak the language, anticipate the needs of the child. He will want to know where the bathroom is and the conditions under which he can go. He will need some other way of communicating with the teacher. It is true that children pick up a language quickly. But that period of time when he does not speak can seem long and painful unless there is a way of working through that transition.

It is often helpful for parents, both mother and father, to volunteer time at the school. The studies of Bible, music, art, and English are frequently areas where help is needed. Again, the missionary parents' attitude in offering help is most important. (Don't go in and say, "I want to do this grand and glorious thing for you because you have a tremendous need.") The MK's own feelings must also be assessed. For example, if there is a separation problem, maybe the appearance of the parent at school would be negative.

One of the exciting fringe benefits of an MK's enrollment in a national school is meeting and developing a close relationship with families in the school. As missionary parents take the initiative and approach other parents at school gatherings, they often develop firm friendships which form a strong base for witnessing opportunities.

Discussion

In the discussion that followed, the following suggestions were made:

- *Apply the same principles when returning to the home country.*
- *Consider setting up an English supplementary school after regular school hours.*
- *Consider hiring an English speaking teacher to work in a national school who will teach some classes to the English speakers during the school day.*
- *Consider attending national school for some subjects and home school others.*
- *Consider vacation schools to supplement the national schools.*
- *For primary education, there is probably no need to worry about the rote style of learning so common in national schools, because at that stage children learn best through rote learning.*
- *In a situation where there are nationals involved in minority ministry, it is possible to join with them in a cross-cultural home school.*
- *Choose a college that will give credit for knowledge of the national language.*
- *Community colleges can provide needed credits to fill any deficits in curriculum in the national high school.*

23

Home Teaching and School Weeks

Saloma Smith
Sind Elementary Education Program

People who live in remote areas or travel a lot have for many years taught their own children. In a home teaching situation, in the secure environment of his home with a parent whom he trusts, a child's individual needs can be met and his interests used and developed to further his learning.[1]

The MK who is home taught can have courses from his own homeland, in contrast to the mission school curriculum. Most mission schools are primarily American schools, not because of a deliberate prejudice, perhaps, but because Americans are usually in the majority, and their nation is a world power, making it quite natural that the mission schools should, almost unconsciously, become American schools. This can cause some problems for non-Americans. Sometimes, for example, historical figures who were traitors in the U.S. are heroes elsewhere, and vice versa. If each family does home teaching, problems of mixed cultures, even languages, are eliminated.

A second benefit of home teaching on the mission field is that children are a part of the work in which their parents are involved. They can learn the village language and appreciate and know individuals they are serving. They can have their own special ministry in that community.

A child who only comes home to his parents for holidays may see himself as detached from the parents' work and not part of the village. He may even become bored on his visits home and long for the boarding school. Or he may resent the whole missionary project

---

[1]Editor's note: This is a portion of a longer paper which was scheduled to be presented at the Quito ICMK but was instead made available in Paul Nelson's "Home School Movement and Missions" presentation. His paper is in volume 2, *Planning for MK Nurture.*

and feel victimized. Surely this is a dangerous situation. What sort of identity will he have when he is sent to the homeland for college?

Our Pakistan Model

I have worked in Pakistan for two years. While there I became involved to some extent in the home-school situation and had the opportunity to observe the following model.

Parents of young children serving in Sind province in southeast Pakistan have chosen to teach their children at home. Most have correspondence courses or home study programs from their own country. There are Britons, Australians, New Zealanders, Americans, Canadians, and one Norwegian family.

These families are serving under various missions and are scattered over the semidesert areas of the province. A few families are in the city of Hyderabad.

School Weeks

The Sind Elementary Education Programme has organized a two-week period of "school" every eight weeks; that is, the children spend six weeks in allocation with their parents and work on their lessons with them at home. Then everyone comes to Hyderabad, where most missions have some sort of guest accommodations. There we hold "school" for two weeks. Meetings and/or workshops are often planned by various missions for the parents, to coincide with school weeks. Doctor and dentist appointments, shopping, banking, and other things are also done during school weeks. Our main thrust is group activities which children lack in their allocations. Sports, folk dancing, drama, group art projects, field trips, and games are part of the excitement. We do also have time for the "three Rs" and some children bring their correspondence course assignments.

On the final afternoon the pupils put on a program for the parents and display their work. All workshops, meetings, shopping trips, and other business activities are halted to free everyone, whether or not they have children in the "school," to come to the program, where each child has a part to play.

There is also opportunity each day for any parents who wish to do so, to come to the school, join in the activity, or just observe. Before the parents leave, they can also discuss any matter pertaining to the school, home teaching, or their child, with the teacher. A few special sessions for parents, with teaching tips, suggestions on how to deal with specific problems or incidents, and time for free questioning, have also been held during school weeks after school hours. At least one parent from each family usually comes to Hyderabad for the full two weeks while both parents will certainly attend the final performance.

Library books can be exchanged by the children and a supply taken out to the allocation for the six weeks they spend learning at home in their mud houses.

We have found these school weeks to be a time of supporting each other in home teaching, in the running of a Christian home, and in general fellowship as workers together in the Gospel.

During the six weeks that parents teach their children in their allocation, a teacher is available to help out when a parent is sick, discouraged, or has met some difficulty. Home teaching is hard work, and there are times when a helping hand is appreciated. But the rewards are great.

24

Field Education System

Kay Ringenberg, Larry G. Noack, Sharon Haag
Wycliffe Children's Education

Rationale for the Field Education System

Larry Noack: The Field Education System began as a program to address certain new realities in missions. First of all, the mission community is becoming increasingly multinational. People from more than thirty different nationalities are part of Wycliffe. Their children need an educational system which is somewhat rid of cultural and national biases.

Secondly, young couples are expressing strong feelings about not sending their children to boarding school. We need to look at ways in which we can help those families with the educational needs of their children and encourage them to use the gifts they have.

Thirdly, candidates are going to the field later in life, taking with them their older children. This can be a traumatic experience for those children, particularly when they get into the junior high and senior high years. If we can alleviate some of the fears that these folks have about what will happen to their children as far as their education goes, it is one step toward making them successful in their ministry.

The fourth reality is that more missionary families are working in culturally isolated settings. This is going to be a continuing trend over the next few years, but it is not practical to start schools in all the places these people are working. That's an impossibility. On the other hand, we could say, "Well, if they're going into culturally isolated situations, they can send their families to boarding school." This also may be impractical for them because of the separation factor and because of the tremendous amounts of money it costs to send their kids back and forth between school and home.

It was our idea to address these situations with a new alternative, one which would allow the families to work in culturally isolated situations while at the same time keeping their children with them. This led us to what we call the Field Education System. The main purpose of the Field Education System is: (1) to keep the families together as long as possible (through eighth grade); (2) to give the children the advantages of a formal education; (3) to develop those children to the fullest extent possible by giving them an individualized program which uses their gifts and abilities.

Philosophical imperatives

In designing the Field Education System, we felt that there were certain philosophical imperatives which must be a part of this system. We felt that the Field Education System must:

- Be an individualized program to meet the needs of each student. We explore the learning styles, interests, and gifts of each student in order to develop them. Along with that, since they are living in a rather unique situation, we use the rich environment in which the children are living, and make that part of the total educational package.

- Provide the maximum amount of time for the family to be about their ministry. We view an education system as a means to an end, rather than an end in itself.

- Have course content that is appropriate for a multinational student population. We do not see it as practical to set up different systems to meet the needs of kids of each different nationality.

- Be built around a multinational curriculum. We have gone to great lengths in our core curriculum to remove elements which are for a specific culture. We've done this by having people from Australia, England, and Singapore take a look at our curriculum to see whether it agreed with their philosophy of what should be in an education program. We will continue to assess that.

- Include opportunities for social and academic interaction with peers.

- Be logistically practical for families and teachers.

- Be financially realistic. We have tried to keep it in line with what it would cost a family to be involved in a correspondence course.

Kay Ringenberg: There are three basic components which allow the Field Education System to function as a viable schooling alternative for these special children in isolated settings.

- The teacher is trained in diagnostic and prescriptive education.
- The Core Curriculum is thoroughly understood by teacher and parents, who work together to monitor and evaluate the child.
- Regularly scheduled group classes are held during the year to foster group study and group social skills.

Core Curriculum

Thematic flow

There are three focal areas: science, humanities, and fine arts. Each focal area contains nine themes. The student will study three themes a year, one from each focal area. The scientific focus is based on the progression from Creation through the first Sabbath. Major science topics are woven into this progression. The humanities focus covers social studies from an anthropological point of view. It covers the study of man in his varied cultures and physical world. The fine arts focus covers chronological periods from before creation to the current age. Looking at fine arts around the world in these time slots incorporates many learning techniques. By using this thematic flow, the body of knowledge contained in textbooks can be studied in a fresh new way.[1]

Each child is in an individualized language and math program which is consistent with his home country. Language arts and math activities are included in each theme, but basic sequential instruction comes from the individualized programs.

At first it was thought that all instruction would be on the computer. It soon became apparent that good education includes many types of media.

As the Field Education System has been developed, particular attention has been given to trends in education of the gifted. Wherever possible, gifted curricular issues have been incorporated into the

---

[1]Editor's note: The Core Curriculum has now been revised to run on a four-year cycle with the students studying one theme a year from each of the following three focal areas: science and math, history and geography, and fine arts and P.E.

Core Curriculum. The higher-level thinking skills, creative problem solving, independent learning skills, and product-based evaluation are integral components of the Field Education System. However, since the program is highly individualized, it is also appropriate for the child who is not gifted.

We use lots of hands-on activities, lots of inquiry learning, and lots of research. Those activities are constructed around Bloom's higher level thinking skills — analysis, synthesis, and evaluation. (The higher levels imply that the lower levels — knowledge, comprehension, and application — are also in place.)

Noack: The Field Education System was designed first of all to operate on what we call a 15/45 cycle or three-week/nine-week cycle. At the beginning of the year, we have the families come together at a central location which we call an Educational Resource Center. Many of the families are working on the same kinds of activities in translation, so we try to locate our Educational Resource Centers in places where workshops can be conducted for the parents, while the children are brought together for evaluation and orientation.

After the initial three-week period, the families go back to their village locations, where they spend nine weeks or forty-five school days and the children carry out the schoolwork that was assigned to them. After that nine-week period we bring them back again to the Educational Resource Center for three weeks of social and peer interaction, and new assignments. Then they go out again. That cycle occurs three times during the normal school year.

There was some resistance to that schedule initially, but we have seen some beneficial side effects. It has helped those families set some short range goals, and they have become more productive in their work. However, we recognize that a three-week/nine-week cycle may be impractical in certain situations.

When we bring them together, we're not responsible for the boarding of the children. We're not setting up a boarding school. We're trying to remove the burden of responsibility for education from the parents. We're not trying to take them totally out of the picture, but we're trying to remove that responsibility by giving it to professional teachers.

The professional teacher is responsible for planning and overseeing the education of the child, keeping accurate records, introducing the learning, and evaluating how that child is doing. The student then has a personalized learning plan designed to meet his or her particular needs. The parent in this system serves more as a monitor of the child than as a teacher, and also provides reinforcement to what that child is learning. He becomes a resource for that child. Then the teacher and the parent consult about what that child is doing, whether changes need to be made in the program or not.

Ringenberg: The curriculum needs to be carefully designed so that the child is on task during the structured time of schooling. Ideally, if the child is working to maximum potential he has formal schooling for three hours in the morning and informal or nonformal educational activities for the remainder of the day. If the activities are constructed properly, then the parent is free during much of that formal time to work on something else, because the child is gainfully working on the activity without parental assistance. How much the parent is directly involved depends upon the level of the child. Obviously a child who is able to read the activity and is able to take ownership in the learning process takes much less of the parents' time than a nonreader or a child who is not highly motivated.

We do use some commercial curriculum materials, but in trying to be truly multinational and individualistic, and in working our materials around one theme, it has been necessary for us to construct our own materials. We brainstorm; we prepare activities; we field test them; and we revise. It's a lengthy process, but children are advancing and parents are happy.

We take into account the teaching and learning styles both of the teacher and of the student in constructing our activities. We do a very careful evaluation of the child. We have teachers who are very aware of their own learning and teaching styles so they can truly be consultants to parents to help them understand how they prefer to teach and learn. That is going to help the parents' relationship with their child's educational process.

Responsibilities of the Teacher

Sharon Haag: Our FES program is based at the Christian Academy of Guatemala, which is a parent-run school of about 115 children representing thirty-three different mission groups. The program now includes first through sixth grades. Possibly the program will expand up to eighth grade. This year we have thirteen children from eight different families and three different missions.

We have two teachers this year. Each is responsible for six or seven children. If we make the number of village visits that we like to make, one teacher can only handle four families.

One of the big responsibilities of the teacher in the FES system is to maintain good relationships with the mission entity or the school at which they're based and arrange use of facilities, how finances and budgeting will be handled, and how materials will be acquired.

Another responsibility is to get to know the families in our program. It's a team effort, so it's really important to build trust and confidence between the families and the teachers who will be working with the children.

Another responsibility of the teacher is to gather materials that are appropriate to the field where the school is located, and appropriate to the families that will be involved in the program. In Guatemala, we have gathered materials about Guatemala's national symbols and about Guatemala's history and development. We have also gathered materials that tell about the home countries of the families that are involved. We want the children to learn about their parents' home culture as well as to develop an appreciation of the place where they grow up.

How FES Works in Guatemala

At the ERC

With the FES curriculum, all the children study common units. Small group instruction is given at different skill levels. In studying the plant unit, all of the children cover many of the same concepts, depending on their level. Level one would cover more elementary concepts regarding plants. Level two would go beyond that. We do experiments together and give them an overall introduction to the concepts that will be covered in the unit of study.

Reading, math, and writing skills are more individualized. Individual instruction is given in skills that they will use when they go back out to their villages.

A lot of the activities at the Educational Resource Center are done with all the age levels together. The children need to learn how to get along as a whole group, to listen to each other, and to share appropriate things on a topic. That is something that is hard to teach an isolated child studying on his own out in the village, so we do as many group activities as possible. Since we're centered at a school, we join in their regular P.E. program.

We do special arts and crafts projects that they might not have the materials for out in the village. We try to use films and videos and other kinds of instructional material to help introduce concepts.

We like to take advantage of our surroundings that are related to our topic.   For example, we took the children to visit large-scale farming outside the city, so they could compare that to how farming is done in their village area; we took a trip to a lake to see how plants are used in decorative landscaping; we went to see a ceiba tree, which is the national tree of Guatemala.

There is evaluation of the individual child's learning skills and learning style in each area of study.   After this the teacher plans out the lessons for that child to do in the village.   We then go over those materials with the parents before they take them out to the village.

We're developing curriculum units so that we have a file of level one things, level two things, and level three things that can just be pulled out and sent with each child according to his skills.

We have orientation sessions for the parents to introduce them to the next unit, so they can begin to think, "What in my village area can we incorporate into this unit of study?"   The parents are free to come in at any time and see how we work with the children and how the materials are used.   We also get them started on projects that they will continue with when they go back to their village.

In the village

During the nine weeks that the family is in the village, the itinerant teachers try to make two one-week visits to each family.   During that time I feel the main responsibility of the itinerant teacher is to encourage, to see how things are coming along, and if there are any problems, discuss those.

I usually send out plans in reading skill development and math development for just up until the time when I will make the village visit.   Then I see how well the child has come along and ask about the pacing.   "Has it been too fast or too slow?"   While I'm there, I plan out the next chunk of lessons.

Another thing I do when I'm in the village is to take over the teaching so that the mother will have a break.

I like to see what resources are available to those children in the village.   What is their daily life like?   What is the culture of that particular village, and what parts of that can be explored by the children?   In planning the next unit, we can suggest projects that will go along with their interest area and take advantage of the environment they are growing up in.

Another responsibility of the itinerant teacher during this time is to encourage the children in developing independent study skills and doing their own special-interest projects. A big emphasis is given to putting what they've learned from the environment in a form they can report on.

We try to get across to the parents that even trips to the market and other daily activities are great learning experiences. Learning doesn't have to go on only at the desk.

Back at the ERC

After the nine weeks in the village, the children and families all come back to the center again. They bring their boxes full of projects and work they have completed. A big goal for this time together is reviewing all that they have learned. They synthesize what they have learned from their particular area of the country and share that with each other. They draw conclusions and evaluate why things are different in one area or another. They really learn to appreciate the differences that they see around them. We hope that will help them be observant and appreciative of their home culture also.

We also include projects which encourage them to compare and contrast the village where they live to where their parents have come from.

When the kids are out in the village working on things, it's a big motivation knowing that they're going to share their projects with everybody else. That is a great improvement over just doing a correspondence course all by yourself.

One second grade boy expanded his rock collection to a whole science project, and then he presented that in the school science fair and won first place. He can hardly write three sentences without wiggling off his chair, but because of his special project, he received a lot of appreciation and recognition for his interest in science.

During that first week when they come back from the village, we always have a culmination party. The kids choose a couple of their favorite projects or activities to present to the parents and families that attend.

The next two weeks, we evaluate again, introduce them to a new unit, and get their plans prepared for the next nine weeks.

Discussion

Noack: We aren't developing FES just for Wycliffe, but for any mission that can use it. Our desire is to serve all.

Has any thought been given toward planning for families that find it hard to pull up from their village area and come to a central location?

Haag: Two families have a few difficulties with that kind of thing. In one case, the mother comes in with the children. She's the one responsible for the teaching, anyway. It really is important for the person who is responsible for the teaching to come in. In the other case, the family lives close enough to the city that they commute each day for the three weeks.

How much more parent involvement is going to be necessary in families where English is not the mother tongue?

Ringenberg: The value of the Field Education System when we're working across languages is in confidence building. Because the instruction during the group time is in English, the teacher can evaluate what is occurring in the mother tongue by evaluating the child's application in English.

Part V

MK IDENTITY FORMATION

25

Being a Third-Culture Kid:
A Profile

David Pollock
Interaction

I trust we'll be able to deal with the idea of third-culture kid without too much emotional involvement or disagreement. Terminology is often inadequate. It's important that we don't get hung up on terminology, but recognize that there's something behind it that we need to address and be concerned about.

The term *third-culture kid*, though it has not been used to a great extent, is not a new one. It originated about thirty years ago with Dr. Ruth Useem, who was a sociology professor at Michigan State University. She and her husband were doing intensive work with U.S. business and government families. While working with the adults, she also had an opportunity to observe the kids. She said, "There's something different about these kids. They function at a whole different level. They think differently. They have a different base, and a different point of reference." She coined the term *third-culture kid*.

A sociology professor who disagreed with the term *third-culture kid* said, "It's a terrible term, and it doesn't meet the demands of the definition." But the term, though it may be inadequate, has given us a base for at least identifying a particular group of people. Whether we can call this group a culture or not is open to question, but they certainly share many common characteristics.

I was doing a seminar with foreign service kids a couple of months ago, and one girl said, "When I sit down in the public school in Fairfax, Virginia, everybody else is saying, 'I went to such and such a place during the summer vacation.' But when I say, 'When I was in Paris in July . . . ' the conversation comes to an end. But that's where I was in July! If I'm going to talk about my life's experiences, they relate to where I've been. They're a part of the geography. I'm not trying to be smart or put anybody down. I listen to everybody else share their experiences, but I can't say anything, because when I do, it either stops the conversation, or somebody backs off, and I realize that I've made another social faux pas. It really hurts."

She was in a group of thirty-five kids packed into a very small living room, absolutely delighted because she could do what any third-culture kid can do with another third-culture kid. She could say, "When I was in . . . " and the other kid said, "And when I was in . . . " and nobody threatened anybody. One of the delights of being a third-culture kid is finding other third-culture kids.

Problems with the Term Third-Culture Kid

The general working definition for is a young person who has spent a sufficient period of time in a culture other than his own, resulting in integration of elements from both the host culture and his own culture into what we have called a third culture.

Now let me shoot that down. First of all, the word *third*. There are many people who have become "global nomads." They have moved from place to place and from situation to situation. They have picked up bits and pieces of a multitude of different cultural experiences that have influenced their lives, their dispositions, and their values. They are not just third culture but are multicultural people.

Secondly, the word *sufficient* is ambiguous. What does sufficient mean? We don't know how long it takes an individual to become a third-culture kid. There are a tremendous number of variables that influence the process of an individual taking on this identity. International students and AFS students often take on some of the characteristics of a third-culture kid within a year. Neil Grove, who is the director of AFS, has given accounts of exchange students who within a year have taken on enough characteristics of their host culture that it has been almost impossible for them to identify with their home culture when they return. We do know that something happens. We don't know how long it takes. So "sufficient time" is a very individual thing.

We have to look at the individuals. We have to recognize that no matter how we define a group, people in that group do not look like, act like, or think like every other individual in that group. We don't expect all monocultural kids from the United States to act alike or function alike, or even to have been affected alike in terms of the culture. When we use the term *third-culture kid*, we're using a term that groups people together because of similarities, but we have to recognize that they are, in fact, individuals. There is no way to say, "This is the way every third-culture kid functions." We can say, "Here are some points of commonality that seem to tie this particular group together."

One variable is the length of time and intensity of exposure to the other culture. If we were to divide North American third-culture kids into four general categories, we would talk about Department of Defense, international business, foreign service, and mission kids. At least three of those categories would be common to every other country and culture. United States Department of Defense employees are the least exposed to foreign cultures. The American bubble is carried wherever the military goes, and people function under that bubble. It's only incidental that it happens to be in Germany. Somebody may wander outside the bubble and see a road sign that's written in German. That may be almost the extent of the cultural exposure. The Diplomatic Corps generally has a little more exposure to the foreign community. International business generally has a bit more than that. Probably the greatest exposure, though there are variables, is within the missions community.

Another variable is the developmental period when the individual is in that other cultural situation. A person who has been in Ecuador from the age of one to the age of seven is not going to have the same impact made on his life as the person who has been there from age one to eighteen. The individual who comes at seven and leaves at eighteen will be on still a different footing. The period of development when that person was in the other culture will determine the extent of the impact.

You really can't have your own culture. By definition *culture* suggests a corporate relationship. To talk about an individual having his own culture as he blends these individual experiences and elements is inadequate.

Going home for the third-culture kid, as his parents perceive going home, is not going home. If they go on furlough for a year, he doesn't go home till the end of that year. Mom and Dad have gone home, but he has been in a hiatus experience. At the end of that year he feels, "Ah, now I go home."

Now that will make us all paranoid about ever using the term *third-culture kid* again, but until somebody else comes along with another term, we probably are stuck.

I told the sociology professor I mentioned earlier, "I don't particularly like the term either. It doesn't really say what we want to say. Can you help me?"

He said, "Yeah. They're marginal people."

I said, "That's going to be a little hard to sell. I really don't want to do re-entry seminars for marginal people. Somehow I think that is a little offensive." What he was talking about, however, is that the individual faces two cultural experiences and he finds himself stuck somewhere in the middle of those two.

Obviously third-cultureness is very hard to define. If anyone comes up with a term other than *marginal*, I certainly would be interested.

In the Middle

One gal at Wheaton College several years ago wrote a paper entitled "I am Green." She said that she was neither the blue culture of her home nor the yellow culture of her host culture, but she found herself somewhere in the middle.

There are other people who often find themselves caught in the crack, touching both cultures, identifying to some degree with both, and yet not having a sense of ownership in either. A third-culture kid often belongs everywhere and nowhere all at the same time. When he steps into one situation he has the sense that he's away from home. He makes the change, moves into that other one he thought was home and he's away from home again. He's always kind of away from home.

A person may be a former missionary or a former foreign service person or a former international business person, but their kids will never be former third-culture kids. That identity doesn't stop because Mom and Dad go back to Hometown, USA. Pain often results when an individual returns to his home country at the age of twelve or thirteen. By the time he is in high school, he is far enough away from that experience to decide that he no longer can identify himself with third-culture kids. If he happens to be on a college campus where third-culture kids have a group that meets, he may stand on the edge of that group, having the sense that somehow he belongs there, but saying, "I don't belong."

> I met a fellow who came to one of the seminars that we were doing in the Midwest on third-culture kids. He said, "That's me. I'm a third-culture kid. All the lights went on. But I really am not, because I was twelve when we came home."

I said, "That doesn't change anything. You're still a third-culture kid." (He is no longer a kid. That's another problem with the term.)

He said, "Do you mean that I really am a part?"

After the session I went into the lobby and sat down, and third-culture kids came from all over the place. As the fellow I had been talking to walked into the room, he hesitated at the back of the group for a moment, then made his way through, and sat on the floor right in the middle. He was as happy as a pig in the mud. He joined the conversation and talked about his experiences of coming home, and how painful it was not to go back or to have had a chance to say good-bye, and on and on. He came up to me afterwards and said, "This is the first time since I was twelve that I have felt free."

That's something we have to watch with third-culture kids. Our tendency is to think that children are resilient. You can do anything with kids and they bounce and they adjust. Sure they do. We're all made to adjust, and adjustment does take place. Whether or not it's good adjustment, and whether or not it leaves a residue of pain, is a whole different matter. When that little kid at five years of age is taken away from an *ayah* and brought back to the United States, he may have suddenly lost someone who was extremely important to him. That *ayah* may have played a role in the child's life that was very close to, or maybe superceded the relationship with the mother. We have to bear in mind that these are real live people who have real live feelings and real live memories.

It's also important to emphasize that third-culture kids have the same needs as every other human being. They are no different from anyone else. Being very mobile and living in a cross-cultural setting creates complexities in the meeting of those needs.

There is a third-cultureness that can happen inside the borders of one's own country. I was doing a seminar in Addis Ababa, and a Nigerian who is in foreign service said, "I was not ever outside my country as a teenager, but my dad was involved in government, and we moved from tribal area to tribal area. This sounds like me." I think when you've moved from Massachusets to California you've moved from tribal area to tribal area. There's a lot of third-cultureness that's built into that experience.

Let me go to the Department of Defense as an illustration. Even though the American bubble is carried along with the military, there is a military culture and there is the American culture. That individual finds himself crossed between those two cultures. Basically it's still American culture, but the subculture of the military presents a whole different set of values that influence the individual. He is the product of those two influences on this life.

There's a certain percentage of third-culture kids who try not to identify with other third-culture kids in their home country because they are a reminder of some of the hurts that they carry with them. Some try desperately to fit in, because someone has communicated to them that it's really not OK to be a third-culture kid. "If you're going to go back to your own country, be like the kids there."

We are in the process of developing an organization called Global Nomads. Norma McKaig, who is herself a third-culture kid, has begun this organization. We've been talking about a conference that NASA and some other groups would help co-sponsor. The theme that has been suggested is "How to be at home as a global nomad." I think that's a concept we need to look at. It's really OK to be a third-culture kid and to be at home wherever you are, at least in terms of your comfort with who you are and what your background has been.

Points of General Commonality to Third-Culture Kids

Positive characteristics

Linguistic ability. According to some research quoted by Ruth Useem a couple of years ago, ninety percent of third-culture kids are conversant in at least a second language. The other ten percent have an easier time than they would have had otherwise, learning a second language.

Cross-cultural skills. You can't ask a third-culture kid to sit down and give you a list of his cross-cultural skills. He may not quite understand what you're looking for. He just does it.

Third-culture kids, for instance, tend to be excellent observers. You learn how to be an observer when you move from place to place and decide that it's not particularly smart to put your foot in your mouth on the first encounter with a new group of people. So you stand on the edge and observe. As a result, monocultural people tend to think initially that third-culture kids are a little dull because they don't jump right into a situation. They observe and figure out what's happening. Then they make their move and participate.

If we could train people who are moving into a cross-cultural situation how to be good observers, we wouldn't have all the grief we often have.

Compliance. The TCK tends to be compliant. He does not necessarily compromise his position or his values, but having once observed what's going on, he discovers how to fit in and how to be a part of that new situation. Often that means that he bottles up all the special knowledge that he's got inside. That's part of his being compliant. He finds ways to fit into sometimes very mediocre situations because he has learned how to get along.

World-view. There are a variety of cross-cultural skills that are very good and very usable. A TCK may use them for a lifetime and never be able to define them or determine where he got them. His world-view is bigger than a monocultural's. It is a three-dimensional view, rather than a two-dimensional view. A monocultural person is often stuck with a view of the world that relates to a television screen or a picture in a magazine, but the third-culture kid reads the headline in the newspaper and forms an in-depth picture. He can visualize real people who breathe and laugh and get sick and hurt and love their kids and have angry moments. Even if he hasn't been in the particular place that's talked about in the headline, he is able to perceive the bigger world as three-dimensional.

View of God. Out of the third-culture kid group, missionary kids and other kids who come from a Christian background often have a larger God-view as well. They have seen God at work in the lives of their parents, their peers and the people around them in ways that the monocultural kid may not have.

Maturity. Finally, the TCK tends to be more mature. The third-culture kid tends to be two to three years ahead of his monocultural counterpart at the time of graduation from high school. That's why the third-culture kid feels so much more comfortable in college with juniors, seniors, and faculty members than he does with freshmen.

I mentioned this one time in a seminar, and two third-culture kids sitting at opposite ends of a row looked at each other, and one said, "See, I told you." They were both in their late twenties and they had been talking earlier about the painful experience of being freshmen in college and being forced to relate to other freshmen.

We are encouraging colleges to look at a big-brother / big-sister program using third-culture kids who are juniors and seniors as the big brothers and big sisters. This will allow a TCK immediate exposure to another TCK and to an age group that is comfortable for him.

There are other positive characteristics of TCKs, but let me move to some negatives. Let me preface this by saying that not all the negatives have only down sides.

Negative Characteristics

Rootlessness. When an individual moves to a different country and settles in for an extended time (eight times in his first eighteen years is the average), he tends to find it a little difficult to identify with a geographic location. Some kind of rootedness and some sense of belonging to a place can be established, but it's not a full sense of "These are where my roots are planted." The sense of rootedness is more in relationship than it is in geography.

It is interesting to hear a foreign service kid who has never been in Egypt, but whose parents were posted there after he left, answer the question "Where are you from?" by saying, "I'm from Egypt." He's never set foot on that soil, but Mom and Dad are there. Relationship is the basic issue in terms of his rootedness.

How does that rootlessness affect his life? It affects his college career. Third-culture kids tend to be very mobile as far as their college careers are concerned. One girl came to our re-entry seminar two years ago having just graduated from Simpson college in California. She graduated in three-and-a-half years and had been to seven different schools.

Another fellow took a little bit longer. He took four years and went to seven different schools. I asked him what he was going to be. He said he was going to be a guidance counselor. He said that he knew most of the colleges and could tell people where to go and where not to go.

That rootlessness affects the individual's vocation. He may move at the wrong time and move himself out of development in his own career. Probably the most severe and serious aspect of that is the impact it has on his marriage. I was speaking at a school reunion in September. A foreign service kid came up after I had mentioned this and said, "You know what? My wife and I have problems every eighteen months. My dad was posted in a new place every eighteen months while I was growing up. As a result of that, I changed all my friends, my location, everything every eighteen months. It wasn't until today that I realized why my wife and I have been able to chart our problems. Every eighteen months I decide I'd like a new wife. I haven't done it, but I have this tremendous urge not only to move, but to change everything."

I call it the lemming instinct. All of a sudden you have an urge to move. You're not sure why. You go out and swim around the ocean until you drown. It's a strange pattern that develops in the life of an individual who has moved often. Foreign service kids and international business kids have a tendency to be even more mobile than MKs, and that certainly has an impact on a marriage. I encourage third-culture kids to consider this very carefully before they get married.

I don't think there's been any research done on whom a TCK should marry, and I don't think there's any way to nail that down, because there are some very adventuresome monocultural kids. In fact, sometimes the roles are reversed. There is a percentage of third-culture kids who say, I'm going to put roots down here, and I'm never going to leave."

I met a gal who had grown up on a farm in Iowa and had been absolutely nowhere. A guy who had been all over the world with his parents breezed into town and proposed. She got all excited. "I'm going to travel and see the world." He settled on her dad's farm and has never moved.

Insecurity in relationships. There's the sense that no relationship lasts very long. If an individual has been in boarding school since the age of nine, the relationship that seems to have lasted the longest is that nine years with the parents. Then the individual makes a move that most monocultural kids don't make until they are about eighteen. Somebody's always coming or going, mostly going. If you're not going, they're going. You're always saying good-bye. Even dating relationships are very short term.

There are some relationships that last a lifetime, and TCKs work at maintaining those. But there are a sufficient number of short-lived relationships to convince the TCK of the high probability that the person he's with at this moment will probably leave.

Ruth Van Reken's book, *Letters I Never Wrote*, talks about this from the perspective of a missionary kid. She talks about her own perception of her relationship to her husband Dave at the time they became engaged. When she said "Yes" to his proposal, she thought to herself, "At some point he is going to break the engagement." When she finally concluded that he wasn't going to break the engagement, she said, "He'll probably die before the wedding." When they were married, she expected that at any moment she would hear that he had been in an automobile accident or had been killed.

Her point was this: "I did not become a basket case. I didn't go over in the corner and dissolve in tears. I just maintained a margin of safety that allowed me emotionally to say "relationships come and go."

There's a paradox to this in that third-culture kids also make intense relationships rather quickly, scaring monocultural kids. A

TCK guy often get a reputation for being a heart breaker. He meets a monocultural gal and starts to talk to her. He's open and friendly. He gets to know the gal, and she says, "Oh, this guy's been all over the world. He loves me." She assumes the next thing he'll say is, "Will you marry me?" Then she discovers he's talking to another girl the way he was just talking to her, so the guy gets labelled as a heart breaker. He thought he was just being friendly and developing relationships. After all, you've got to do it fast, because it may dissolve tomorrow.

Third-culture kids support the post office, the airlines and the telephone companies because they work at maintaining relationships. One third-culture kid told me, "My view of heaven is having everybody I know in one place. That's what heaven is going to be about. I dream about it at night."

Loneliness. Along with insecurity is the issue of loneliness. For those of you who are parents and have the opportunity to counsel other parents, I believe one of the most dangerous times in the life of a third-culture kid is the year after that person graduates from college if he has not become engaged or married. That is the time when he loses all the support and all the communities. He's had the boarding school perhaps. Then he moved on into college and people were still around him. Then all of a sudden, when Mom and Dad are seven thousand miles away, he's all by himself. That probably is one of the most dangerous times in the life of an individual.

People ask, "When should I go home and be available to my kids?" We tend to think that if an individual gets to be twenty-two or twenty-three, they're well on their way and everything's OK, but that may be the year when they need Mom and Dad the most. Snap decisions are made at the end of college because they realize that next year's going to be lonely. Of course, that happens with monocultural kids, too. It's called senior panic.

Unresolved Grief. Another major concern is sadness and grief. Every human being experiences grief. That is not unique to the third-culture. Unresolved grief is not unique to the third-culture kid. However, the third-culture kid tends to experience grief in multiples.

Graduation is a good illustration. The wettest graduations in the world happen on international school campuses. Some schools have been very sensitive to this and have provided a rite of passage. Dalat School in Panang, Malaysia has a sea wall they call the wailing wall. At graduation, everybody lines up there and says good-bye. At Alliance Academy, they line up in the gymnasium and ruin the floor with tears. It is a very intense emotional experience when people say good-bye. It's important for us to provide those rites of passage. As adults, we need to find ways to allow kids to say good-bye.

To prepare a kid for re-entry, make sure you encourage him to resolve any old interpersonal conflicts, whether it be with a teacher, with his own parents, or with an old boyfriend or girlfriend. One of the major impediments to adjustment is the baggage of unresolved broken interpersonal relationships.

Also encourage him to say good-bye to all the significant people and even ones that may not be on his list of significant people. He may realize afterward that they were more significant than he thought. Find ways to say good-bye to everybody, and find ways to say good-bye to places.

After Walt Stewart's older daughter graduated, he took her on a tour of all the places where they had lived and vacationed during her growing-up years. She saw them all again, and she said good-bye. Those places are important to kids. They are a part of their history, and they need to say good-bye to them.

Saying good-bye is critical to the process of adjustment. Resolving grief involves saying good-bye, even with tears.

Off balance. Off balance is that sense that there's something that you ought to know but you don't. Everybody collects cultural trivia. You grab bits and pieces of everything that surrounds you, and you put it in your bag of trivia. When a question pops up later, you have the answer somewhere in that bag. The frustration that the third-culture kid has is that he collected his trivia someplace else in the world.

Probably the worst game in the world for third-culture kids is Trivial Pursuit. There are two ways that he deals with it. Either he doesn't play, or he memorizes all the cards. The problem is that life is a Trivial Pursuit game. There are all kinds of questions and issues that you have to have answers for. The third-culture kid has all kinds of information, but it just doesn't fit the questions. He always has this sense that there's going to be an important question asked, and he's not going to know the answer.

Out of phase. Ruth Useem indicated that she had seen what she felt was latent adolescent rebellion in third-culture kids. At the age of twenty-three or twenty-four the individual made choices that absolutely shocked and broke the hearts of his parents. She thought this was probably latent adolescent rebellion.

I'm certainly not going to argue with Ruth. But I have another theory that I would like to throw out for your consideration. Imagine an individual suffering unresolved grief who is stuck at the anger level.   Having just finished college, he is now going through a lonely stage. He is on his own, and he decides at age twenty two that he no longer has to be compliant. He perceives an opportunity to do something that he thinks will relieve his pain. These circumstances coming together at just the right moment could result in an explosive combination. I have a sneaking suspicion that what we have thought is an "out of phaseness" is simply the coming together of all those issues.

Another problem for some is the matter of delayed social development. Kids in the United States who have been dating since twelve may have a different view of dating and of male-female relationships than somebody who has lived at a boarding school where there has been a tendency to view classmates as brothers and sisters rather than boyfriends and girlfriends. This may result in a TCK going through some stages of development and change in his early twenties or late teens that somebody in a monocultural situation may have gone through much earlier.

Let this be a basis for thinking.

26

MK Identity Crisis: Fact or Fiction

Fran White
Wheaton College

I chose to address the problem of identity because I see it as the sickness of this age. I'm finding as I do therapy with different families, that identity is the big problem, not just with MK families, but with families around the world. We're seeing people today who lack a sense of inner substance. More and more I'm hearing young people say things like, "I'm empty." "I feel like I've got walls, but there's nothing inside." "I don't exist." "I'm not connected." It is the greatest suffering. It is much better to be in pain than not to feel.

Consequently young people with this problem tend to create dramatic situations that will help them at least have feelings. Oftentimes they'll be our suicide people, because suicide gives them a lot of attention. I have clients calling up and saying, "I just overdosed." Of course that means I'm to rush to their house and do something. They'll do anything to get rid of that terrible emptiness.

The other extreme is to get depressed, depending on the nature of their personality. This type of person also acts out. By "act out" I mean, they can't express their feelings. They don't know what to do with that emptiness inside, so they go on drugs, or they become promiscuous, because that gives them a sense of feeling. Theft, stealing, pickpocketing, and things of that sort become pretty common among this type of person.

I'm really concerned about this lack of a sense of inner substance and positive identification among young people. They lack a consistent sense of self, a sameness, a predictability of their moods and feelings, a sense of being put together and not being controlled by all kinds of forces. Without this, young people cannot face the many changes that are taking place in the world today. Newness, unpredictability, challenge, excitement are very scary to them. They don't have a sense of inner identity that allows change to take place. They fear they'll disappear; they'll exist no more.

Paying the price

This is a phenomenon going on among many young people. The spirit of this age seems to be a lack of commitment, a lack of connecting with someone or something meaningful. I think we can account for it by what's going on today. We are paying the price for the many divorces that have taken place. I often wish I could lecture people before they decide to divorce and convince them to work harder at marriage. Blended families, where a man and woman marry and bring their respective families into the new relationship, cause endless problems. I think that is one reason incest is on the increase. Natural boundaries aren't there that are present with your natural children.

Parents are not home because of dual careers. Parents are caught up in the energy and excitement of their work, leaving children with different types of baby sitters. There's often no consistency. We hear and read about the increase in incest, wife abuse, child abuse. All these things have given us instability. We hear of wars, terrorism, alcoholism, drugs. There are changes in our school systems. I'm not making a judgment on these things. I'm not talking the pros and cons of divorce or the pros and cons of dual careers. Some women do better with their children if they have outside interests. I'm just describing some of those things that have resulted in this lack of a sense of connectedness on children's, adolescents', and young people's parts.

As God's grace falls on all of us, so does the effect of sin. It affects God's norm for all of us. There are more and more mission-aries who are applying to mission societies today who have been affected by these types of backgrounds. I do the psychological screening for about seven different mission boards. An enormous number of families come through our particular organization, and I see their profiles. I am aware of how much they have been affected by what's going on in the world today, and how their own nuclear families have played a role in their lives. They've become victims of sin.

I keep thinking of that verse in Exodus, "The sins of the fathers shall be visited upon the children to the third or fourth generation." It isn't always their fault, but they've been affected by that. Needing the love and security that children do need, they reach out to get it some way, any way.   They, in turn, often become victimizers.   If they've been abused, you'll see them abusing.   If they're from alcoholic parents, you'll see some effect of what it means to be a child of an alcoholic parent.   You see things repeating themselves generation after generation.

I often have my students in school do what I call a *genogram*, a psychological history of their family four generations back.   It always astounds me to see the patterns that repeat themselves.   I always say, "There's a second part to that verse.   It says that God's mercy and grace fall on those who will turn to him.   We can break that pattern. We don't have to pass it down to our children."

I am alarmed by the number of candidates who are coming out of these types of backgrounds.   Many of them have been miraculously saved, truly so, and they've known tremendous deliverance.   Yet sin has its effects.   Overcoming the effects of scars and wounds in our lives is a process.   I don't ever want to underplay what the Lord in his mercy did for them, but in spite of the fact that they've become Christians, they still have the effects.

Overcoming the effects

Oftentimes there's terrific buried anger that they don't know about.   There's terrific anxiety.   There's an expectation to be rejected because they have always been rejected.   There's loneliness because they've never had parents to whom to attach and belong.   I could go on and on. They're still functioning with that.

I remember one candidate I screened just last year.   He was going to be a house parent.   Fantastic fellow.   But as I looked at his profile, every test showed a very high score on anger.   So I asked him, "What do you do with all this anger?"

"I'm not angry.   Don't tell me I'm angry."   I have to admit I stirred up the anger to check it out and see how deep it really was.

To make a long story short, he decided to stay behind and come into counseling to work through that anger.   We looked at his background.   He had parents who gave him absolutely conditional acceptance, who did not see him as a child in his own right.   He constantly had to please them.   As we worked through that anger, he went through some terrible weeks having to go off by himself to feel it and know it.

He worked through that.   At times it creeps back, but at least he knows about it.   What you know about yourself you can do something about.   What you don't know about yourself controls you.

He said to me, "Fran, if you hadn't stopped me, I'm sure I would have murdered a child. I was just that angry. I've often wanted to do it to my own children, even though I love them."

I think of another fellow we interviewed whose mother was extremely busy in her career. She was a terrific musician, known throughout the country in Christian circles. His father was in another profession, and very heavily invested. He was sort of left to raise himself.

When I asked him if he had faced the issue of being single, he said to me, "I want so badly to get married. I'm thirty years old. But somehow I feel like I can't connect. I don't know what it is. I get so close, and then I jump back. I get scared."

We had a long talk and he decided he would try to get some counseling about this.

Both fellows received help. It took awhile. It wasn't one or two sessions. In the beginning they said, "I'm going nowhere." They got to that middle part of therapy where they were very agitated and facing the issues and saying, "Boy, therapy made me worse." Eventually they could work through these issues. They're both on the field doing a tremendous job. The second fellow is married and has a very happy relationship.

In both these cases, there were intimacy problems. In the beginning something went wrong in forming the ability to develop close, intimate relationships. I'm not just talking about sexual relationships. Intimacy is many faceted. These are also forms of intimacy: recreational intimacy, aesthetic intimacy, affectional intimacy, and intellectual intimacy where your spirit speaks to someone else's spirit. You connect and you have a terrific fellowship together. You belong to each other in a special way. I always like to emphasize that there are many types, because if four-fifths of the kinds of intimacy are met in your life, you have a pretty fulfilled life. This gives a lot of hope and encouragement to single people who can experience the richness and depth of connecting with other people. Yet as I find this ability to connect missing, I am realizing the terrific suffering of all concerned.

I see intimacy as the ability to relate to others in a connected way without fear of being absorbed or losing identity, and yet being free to separate from those people at given intervals without fear of being abandoned. It's the ability to connect with a meaningful other without fear of being absorbed or losing who you are or to be separate from that person at intervals without fear of being abandoned. The fear of abandonment or being absorbed, and the sense of inner substance involves being neither a rule-bound prisoner inside yourself, nor chaotic in the sense that you're flying all over the place with no inner controls.

A second and frequent source of problems is a lack of inner consistency, inner structure, or inner substance. There are two extremes: the inability to function in a consistent way without being bound by inner sanctions, and chaos with no inner control.

Development during the First Three Years of Life

I would like to discuss how healthy identity develops. What are the weaknesses and strengths to promote healthy identity in a cross cultural situation? How can missions facilitate healthy identity and help prevent unhealthy or deficient identity?

We first have to get back to what happens in those first three years. Healthy identity is tied in very definitely with the child's early emotional attachment to Mother or a mother substitute. For healthy identity, it's absolutely essential that the attachment be developed.

God has made us with the innate drive to connect emotionally to a parent figure. It is not a choice. In order to really feel human as God intended, a young child must connect with a mother figure, because she is the principal care giver. This connection is part of how we develop our own person. It starts at conception and continues through intra-uterine life. It continues after birth and takes a new form at each developmental stage.

At birth the umbilical cord is snipped moments after delivery. There's no glue that ties the baby to the mother. There's no physical attachment any longer. Yet by virtue of the way God made us, the attachment process continues. It's something invisible within us that causes us as babies to build an identity through an intense emotional attachment to Mother. It is a process. It is not something that happens immediately at birth.

I know there's a lot of talk today about bonding. They talk about a maximal moment but what I'm talking about is a process that starts at conception and goes through life.

One thing we're sure of is that attachment is a lifelong process with its foundations laid in the way a child relates in the first three years of life. Let me go through some of those early stages to explain what happens.

From birth to about twelve weeks, a baby is symbiotically tied to Mother. That simply means that a baby does not know he's separate from Mother. As he feeds on Mother's breast, it's just as if Mother and he are one. He doesn't see himself as a separate individual.

At about eight weeks to twelve weeks, continuing on to one year, he starts to see himself as different. As he starts to explore Mother — reaches up to her glasses, pulls on jewelry, reaches out to her hair, pulls away from the breast to look over the world — the baby is starting to realize he isn't one with Mother. He is actually a separate individual in this world.

What he does not know yet is that Mother exists even when she is not present. If Mother goes out of his sight, it is as if Mother disappeared. The game peekaboo is so delightful to these young children, because in their eyes when Mother covers her face she is no longer there. Then she reappears and they squeal with delight. When the baby starts enjoying peekaboo, you know he's starting to be an individual in his own right.

At about seven months, a child's sense of being separate starts to peak. Now all of a sudden, he screams when Grandma comes and picks him up. He's starting to recognize Mother as a separate person, and Grandma is not quite enough, because when Mother is not there, she has disappeared. It happens when you leave a child in the church nursery. He's always been willing to stay there, but all of a sudden he screams his head off when you leave him. He's starting to see himself as a separate person, with his mother just having disappeared.

Then we look at the child from about one year to about two and a half years. That is an extremely crucial period when the child is realizing bit by bit that Mother and Father are separate. That's when he really starts to cry when Mother leaves, because she has disappeared and may not come back.

Bit by bit as he reaches two and a half years, he starts to explore, but always with Mother as a line of reinforcement. Those of you who have children know how the child crawls away but turns around to see if Mother is still there. He might go around the corner, but pretty soon he reappears, running up to you. He might get right up to your arms and then run off again.

At about three years, the child more fully realizes that Mother will not disappear. Even when Mother is not present, she'll still be there. He's free now to start to reach out to others, to realize that others have feelings, goals, interests. He doesn't think this. He's too young. But he feels it.

What has happened? Mother is now part of him. He has internalized Mother inside of his head, his feelings, his being. That's how a child forms a self-concept. He must internalize the mother figure. She becomes part of him, so he knows she's there even when she isn't present.

Role of Father

What's the role of Father in all of this? There's a lot of research on fathering. Children tend to attach to fathers in different ways. Oftentimes fathers show affection by bouncing babies, tousling them, throwing them up in the air. It gives the child the feeling of another sex. This is Father; this is Mother — sexual differentiation.

Father also mitigates the intensity between the mother-baby relationship. It isn't just mother-baby, but there's somebody else who's very important to Mother, who plays a role. You're starting to set boundaries that are such a big part of identity.

One of the things I'm finding in counseling is that young people today don't always recognize boundaries. They don't know where they end and the other person begins. I notice that, even on the college level. Sometimes when I'm talking on the phone, students will come right in and almost take part in the phone conversation. I have to say, "This is confidential." They come up when two professors are speaking and enter into the conversation.

It says something about who that person sees himself as. Does he have his own boundaries around himself? Do other people have boundaries around themselves? Father helps set those boundaries. The spouse subsystem is different from the parental subsystem. Mother-father are not the same as husband-wife. Children start to realize that through the way Mother relates to Father.

It's that relationship of mother and father which gives a child sexual identity or sexual differentiation and helps him to realize there is a difference between husband-wife, mother-father. It gives an additional sense of security, a more intense sense that he belongs to someone who is special to Mother and someone who is very special to Father.

I don't know if you've realized this, but people often tend to marry someone who has very much the feel of their opposite sex parent. They can look very different. You say, "This person is nothing like my father," or "She's nothing like my mother." It isn't in the outward accomplishments, but deep underneath there are often some of the same feelings. It's at this point that children are starting to build a sexual type of attraction. A certain determination in the kind of person who appeals to them is being formed. It's important for young people to work through some of the problems they've had with parents so that they don't take those problems into marriage and treat that spouse according to the anxiety and hurts that were inflicted by that particular parent. It's what I call finishing up the unfinished business of your past.

At the same time the child is forming this ability to know Mother loves him even when she's not there, he's also forming an inner sense of substance. He's taking his parents' values and their ways.

We give messages to children in all sorts of ways. Even the way we hold them says something about their worth. You can give either a critical or a nurturing message. You can say, "Johnny, that report card's fantastic! You only got one C, and the rest you've really worked well in. Maybe that's your weak point." Or you can say, "How come you got that one C?" It says something to a child about his worth, his value, his ability.

The child all during this period is building his belief system, his value system. We're giving it in a very unaware way. The consistency you show, the predictability you have, the rules you have in your household, the way you schedule—all help to give the child inner substance.

I've worked with parents of foster children, and I've always said to them, "You can't always give these kids love. They've been rejected so often. Just when they loved a foster parent, they got put into a new home. They're not going to accept your love. But what you can give them is an inner sense of substance. You can give them structure. You can give them rules. You can give them predictability. You can give them your value system. And love without that is not love. Both intimacy and an inner sense of substance are needed for identity."

Implications for Missions

What's all this got to do with MKs? The quality of attachments in these first years of life play a role in determining how that child is going to develop socially, intellectually, and emotionally. It also prepares him for the later ability to attach and separate. When you think of all the attachments and separations the MK has to make, you can realize how important it is that this base is laid. Being able to relate deeply to a house parent, to Mother, to Father, without fearing loss of self-identity or feeling abandoned when he goes off to school, depends on that base that is laid. It enables him to attach to a house parent or a teacher, and yet be able to separate, come back home, and reattach without feeling he has been abandoned.

This base also gives the foundation of values, the shoulds and oughts, the organized inner sameness. Without the sense of intimacy and the sense of structure or sameness, you have character disordered people. We don't call them character disordered any more. We call them antisocial. They're not mentally ill people. I'd rather have a counselee who has a bad value system that I can work with and help him change, than a counselee who has no value system, who pretty much does his own thing. That's what frightens me as I work with some of these young people from broken homes, from abused backgrounds, and alcoholic families. Because MKs face so much change, it's important that a healthy base be laid. We must program our value system into our kids' heads. The feelings that are built into them very early give them a conscience.

What are some of the implications for missions? First, I think it's extremely important today that we evaluate the prospective candidate in his family setting. After testing the candidate, I want the whole family in for an interview. I want to see how they function together, their patterns of intimacy. Their patterns of structure or substance show up in the family system. It gives me clues as to how this process took place in early years.

Family intimacy: enmeshed, disengaged, or interdependent

In patterns of intimacy, there are two possible extremes that could be unhealthy. These are the enmeshed family and the disengaged family.

The enmeshed family is a family that has too much togetherness. It's not real intimacy. It's not real closeness. There's too much we-ness, to much us, ours. They're all intertwined. There isn't the possibility of being independent. Children from an enmeshed home are very, very dependent because they're not allowed to move without Mom or Dad's permission. Differentness is seen as something wrong.

Adolescent kids want to close their bedroom door and put a sign on the door saying, "Keep Out." The parents think, "Come on, we've always had bedroom doors open around here." They say, "How dare he do that? We can't have any separateness." That's the family that's uncomfortable with separation. Probably in a family like that, the parents were brought up in nuclear families that did not know separateness. Probably the parents tend to be very dependent on one another.

At the other extreme is the disengaged family. Kids from this type of family are too independent, too detached. They're not given enough rules, not given enough *us*-ness. There's too much *I*-ness, too much *mine*. They're not even aware of their dependency needs because they were never allowed to have them. They had to be too independent too young.

It's really a dependency-independency issue. Most of us move appropriately across that line. There are times when a family has to be more enmeshed. When your kids are young or when there is a crisis, you have to be more dependent on one another. There are also times when you have to be more disengaged. You need to have your own interests, do your own thing. Hopefully you are interdependent most of the time. This means you appropriately move to either polarity, but most of the time experience a combination of dependency and independency. There are times when you are together. There are times when you are separate. A healthy person can be relaxed with both situations.

Family regulation: rigid, chaotic, or flexible

Another thing I look at is the way a family regulates itself. There are two unhealthy polarities I look for in this dimension. I look for a highly rigid regulation or a highly chaotic one.

The highly rigid family is the one that has so much structure that there's no room for individual differences. It's highly authoritarian, highly, "This is the way we do it. I am the leader here." The children don't get a chance to express themselves, to give input. "This is the way. That's it."

At the other extreme is the family that has no rules. Everything is chaotic. You don't know what time you're going to eat. You don't know if Tommy has a soccer game. There's not the caring. The children grow up not knowing their needs.

In the middle, we have the flexible family. Sometimes you have to be more rigid; sometimes you have to allow more space, but most of the time you're in between the two.

There's no ideal family. I love the term the "good enough" mother. There's also the "good enough" family. That means that fifty percent of the time you're doing the right thing; your kids will be all right. We're not perfect. I'm concerned about the families that aren't good enough, that always function at one extreme or the other. If I see a house parent candidate or a teacher or a family going out to the field operating at either of these extremes, I recommend remedial work before they go. If the remedial work isn't effective, maybe they should not go.

Family communication patterns

As I evaluate the family, I also look at their communication patterns. Are they open? Are they able to express feelings? Are there a lot of double binds where parents say one thing but do another? That double bind is one of the most dangerous kinds of communication you can give children. I'm not saying it's the cause of schizophrenia, but we see it in schizophrenic families. Parents say one thing, but they do another. They give Johnny a brand new shirt. They say, "Johnny, you never wear that shirt." Johnny comes downstairs with the shirt on and Mother says, "You don't want to get that shirt all dirty. Take it off." The child is confused and isn't quite sure of what to expect next.

Handling change and separation

Something else I look for is how the family handles change and separation. Do they know how to give their children some stability? How much change has there been in the family? Has the father been able to stay at a job more than six months or a year? I hear mission directors say about some missionary candidates, "Oh he's fantastic. Look at the experience he's had. He's done this, this, and this." The candidate may be only twenty-three or twenty-four years old.

I say, "Wait a minute. Is there an authority problem here? Why has Father not stayed more consistently at a job and adjusted to the bad as well as the good of that job? Has he learned to put up with what he didn't like? Has he been able to accept some of the things the boss said and learn from them?"

Family boundaries

I also look for boundaries in the family. Do the children have their own little subsystem where they can be brothers and sisters, doing their arguing and fighting without Mom and Dad always interfering? Is there a spouse subsystem that the children have no right in? Is there a parental subsystem where the children do belong? Does Father sometimes align with one of the children and do something special? Does Mother? Do they know what boundaries are all about?

Healthy family functioning

It's really important that we look at these things. Families from healthy backgrounds produce children who are more cooperative as opposed to being noncompliant. When families function on any of these extremes, particularly the detached, disengaged family, where the child has learned to do his own thing, we tend to see children who are more noncompliant. Healthy families tend to produce children who are more persistent, as opposed to children who give up; children who learn age-appropriate tasks through the life stages, as against those who tend to default on them; children who understand others, as opposed to those who tend to be self-centered. This has terrific implications in predicting what will happen on the field.

Those who have had this healthy early background are more able to face some of the vicissitudes of life later on. It does not mean you are not going to have problems, but it means you have that basic sense of security and identity that will help you eventually work through those problems.

It's important that we help families on the field be aware of what healthy family functioning is. What we know about, we can do something about. What we don't know, we can't do anything about. I think it's more and more important that we have pastoral counselors on the field, people who are trained in healthy family dynamics, strong in it, and who can help families to work through some of the difficulties that arise. If we can keep missionary families from going home before furlough time, we have saved them tremendous trauma.

Life Stages

Let's look briefly at life stages. Think about evaluating house parents according to these factors. Have they gone through these developmental stages healthily? Have school teachers done this? Have parents?

Preschool period

This is a period when kids can incorporate a lot of guilt. If there are too many separations or hard things, or if a parent dies, a child often feels guilty because somehow he feels responsible for what happened. It's so important to give the preschool child as much sameness as possible. I'm not talking about travelling or changing countries. I'm talking about the sameness within the family—your rituals and ways of doing things. Keep the child in touch with the familiar.

School age

This is the age when a child develops the skills that are going to help him through life. If he doesn't develop these skills, there's going to be a sense of inferiority. It's the age when kids take in all kinds of knowledge. They give and take with others. They can lose and win. They learn to control and manipulate the environment. They form same-sex friendships, which are so important for later relationships.

I'm always concerned about the child who does not have same-sex friendships. Sometimes you see kids in college taking up immediately with the opposite sex and never really getting to know people of the same sex. This lack of same-sex friends can place a tremendous load on the marital relationship, since no two people can meet all of each other's needs.

What are the implications? One is the need to develop an educational program that gives the opportunity for social interaction. I don't want to take a position on home schooling. I see a lot of pros, but somehow we must program into it the possibility for social interaction with peers. I know Wycliffe has satellite schools where parents do teach young children yet bring them in for that social interaction periodically. Young children have the security of Mom or Dad, but somewhere along the line, the opportunity for social interaction to develop their own identity is built in.

Now the attachment to Mom and Dad is growing less and less intense. It's still strong but it takes a different form. They need an adult who's interested in them. Missions can start to learn to pair children at boarding schools with someone on the field who is significant to them, someone who will take a special interest in them.

I'd like to see workshops where specialists come in and help parents, house parents and teachers to know how to separate. What can teachers do to help with the separation? What can house parents do to get the kids to express their feelings? I'd also like to see workshops that foster a knowledge of developmental tasks, which help parents, house parents, and teachers understand individual differences, and that teach them how to listen to kids, to their hopes, to their joys. I would also like workshops on recognizing symptoms of learning problems and what to do to ameliorate these problems.

Junior high

If problems are going to surface, this is the key point. One day junior high kids can be such little angels. Even though the teacher is not a bit prepared, the lesson goes over tremendously. Another time the teacher is well prepared, but when the kids come in, everything falls apart. Elastics on the braces go flying across the room. A contact lens goes down under, and the class falls apart. It's an unpredictable age.

It's the time when their peers start to be more important than parents. The child who always made his bed and kept his room clean, suddenly forgets it because the opinion of peers is starting to be more important than parents' opinions. They form heterosexual friendships, but still need adults.

The late developer. Boys tend to develop later than girls. If you get a boy who's a late developer, he can get a reputation that stays with him through secondary school. In a year or two, he will have caught up with his peers. But meanwhile, he's still a child while the others are becoming teenagers. He'll burst into tears at something when the other boys are no longer doing that. He might not be as good at athletics because he hasn't developed the coordination yet. We need house parents and parents who are aware of this and ready to help these late developers so they don't develop a negative self image.

The aesthetic boy is one we want to keep our eyes open for. Somehow that isn't always OK. Everybody has to be good at sports. It has nothing to do with homosexuality, but somehow it gets labelled that way, and that's the child who needs special help. That's when we need outsiders to come in. We definitely need counselors at junior high level who can pick up on the beginning of some of these problems.

At the beginning of junior high you need to ask yourself, "How is my child adjusting?" Are there particular problems that he should have special help with? Is this the time to go home? I am a firm believer that if your child is not happy and is not adjusting, and if every possibility on the field has been tried and has failed to remedy the problem, you need to consider changing that environment. The child must be able to adjust as he begins senior high.

Junior high kids act out. When they're upset, they don't tell you about it. They do crazy things. They start stealing. They start drinking. They're the kids who get on drugs. They're the kids who cause the sensation. You need to say, "There are some real hurts in there that we have to work on."

Later adolescence

Secondary school is the time of identity consolidation. This is when you as a parent ask if you should send your kid to a national school. It doesn't seem to matter so much in elementary school.

They seem to do OK. In secondary school they consolidate their identity through their peers. You have to remember, if you send your high schooler to a national school, the child must internalize the culture. He must identify with those cultural values of his peers, or else he is going to stay detached from his peers and never form close relationships. Is that the culture you want him to identify with? Are these the peers you want him to have? Are these the people you want that child to date? Some children do very well and become bicultural and bilingual. For others, it's a complete failure. You need guidance at this time from people who visit the field and are willing to help you with some of these decisions for your particular child.

College

This is the age when young people try things on for fit. They're developing their goals. The first two years you're going to get letters saying they switched majors, dorms, and jobs. They were going steady with someone but they broke up. You think, "Are they ever going to settle down?" It's a time of experimenting. Toward the end of college, young people need to have their career goals straightened out. It's better to make some kind of decision, even if it is not exactly the best for that child, than to make no decision at all. At least that decision can be redirected and changed, but no decision keeps them floating.

Another thing I find with MKs is the tendency for them not to work part time. I think one of their adjustments to the new culture is to learn the work world of America. I see MKs going back to the field every summer for short-term service. Some of it is good, but somewhere along the line, the child should have the work experience in his own country, earning and handling money for himself. Some MKs do it fine, but some do not.

Until college, the MK community tends to guide the MK's decisions. Perhaps it's necessary that they start learning to make some of these decisions on their own. They realize there's a bigger world beyond themselves, and they need to become their own person.

If your young person is not adjusting to college, you need to look at why. This is the time he is going to make his psychological break from you. It doesn't mean he's giving you up. But instead of relating to you as child-parent, it's now going to be more of an adult relationship. If your child is having trouble with that adjustment, there may be the need for you to be home during those college years. That is not true for all missionaries, but I would highly recommend that there be at least one significant other, perhaps a parent

surrogate, that your young person can go to and can be close to.   It's
the last developmental period when the child can work through in a
natural way the unfinished issues he has with you.   After that it
becomes much more difficult.   Some children work them through on
their own.   Others need you there.

Some of them visit fields during the summer, which I think is an
excellent idea, but perhaps not every summer.   Sometimes it is wise
for parents to take shorter furloughs and be home a couple months
every so often with the children.

MKs tend to diffuse their intimacy needs all over the place.   As
they come to the end of the college years, technically they should be
narrowing in on fewer, but closer, friendships.   They often need each
other at the beginning as that line of reinforcement to reach out to
others.   But is it happening?   Are they reaching out to others?

Another area is self-reliance versus commitment.   Because college young people are often in the States without their parents, they
have to be more self-reliant, but somewhere along the line, you must
teach them the commitment of staying put, adjusting to the States,
accepting the good with the bad, learning that their own country isn't
ideal, but that it doesn't have to be.

After college

I'd like to suggest that an MK not consider going back to the
field until he or she has made a healthy, comfortable adjustment in
the States.   That doesn't mean he's giving up his MKness.   That
doesn't mean he's not part of the third culture.   He'll always have
that special identity.   There will always be a nostalgia, but he must
learn to accept the good and bad of his own country.   Before he goes
back, he must learn to overcome the feelings of "I can't stay here," so
he is free *not* to go back.

I think the MK who is not free *not* to go back to the field is not
going to be the most effective missionary.   Someone who has a
career, a profession, something to go back with, who has learned to
be comfortable with people who perhaps don't completely understand
his background, is free to really hear the Lord's calling and know
whether he's to go back or not.   Then he or she is free to marry an
MK or a non-MK.   The MK who marries a non-MK and has never
made that psychological break from the field (which is a little like the
psychological break from the parents) could be creating problems.

I see so many missionaries on the field who are there because
they don't know what to do if they come home.   What will I do?   I
have no work.   I have this terrific position here.   What would I do at

home? The importance of having a career, having a skill, a talent, a trade before you go out to the field becomes very important to one's identity.

The MK has much more international understanding than most of the world. The more heights and depths the Lord gives you in life, the more richness, the bigger that difference is going to be. We have to have some fellowship with people who share our understanding, but we all must learn to meet people where they are without cynicism, boredom, or lack of respect, and be comfortable there, all the while knowing there's something richer.

Your ability to connect to others, to commit to others, is going to determine your children's background. As the MK marries and reproduces, or goes out as a single person and regenerates himself or herself in others, he is going to pass on all the unfinished business and all the healthiness of his background. Face it now so that you may pass on your heritage in a way that glorifies your Lord.

27

MK Identity in Formation: Cultural Influences

Daniel Barth Peters
Link Care Center

My perspective on MK identity formation is not so much from a psychological perspective as from a cultural perspective. Most information about identity formation comes from the psychological field. However, I want to make sure that we place the MK as a whole person in as broad a context as possible. Therefore, I'm focussing on cultural identity and the relationship of cultural information to personal identity.

The definition of culture that we will be using is "the acquired knowledge that people use to interpret experience and generate social behavior." (James Spradley, *Ethnographic Interviewing*) I want you to focus on "interpret experience" and "generate social behavior." Clifford Geertz (*The Interpretation of Cultures*) says that culture is "public and transacted symbolically.... Man is suspended in webs of significance he himself has spun. I take culture to be those webs.... The study of culture is not an experimental science in search of law, but an interpretive one in search of meaning."

Many of the folk theories regarding MKs are polarized around two contradistinctive myths that either posit MK's as wonderful, the future of world missions, having the experience of a lifetime, or as screwed up, psychotic nerds who are bitter, resentful misfits. Both of these are folk theories. Depending on who you know, you will be given "true stories" about MKs as evidence to support one of these positions. Examples that do not fit the position are treated as anomalies.

My assumptions are:

1. MKs are individuals, and neither myth can be generalized.

2. MKs reflect the larger evangelical world in denying personal pain. I've had adult MKs come up to me and say, "If you had asked me at twenty-two what it was like to be an MK, I would have given you 'the line.' I'm now thirty-five and have a baby, and I'm beginning to come in contact with the pain of my experience." (This is one of the true stories that I'm using to validate my folk theory.)

3. All people in all ages and all cultures experience pain in life. However, that does not eliminate the Christian community's responsibility to minister to its own kids in their pain.

If the Christian community is going to take the biblical authority to send families into the uttermost parts of the earth, then we as the Christian community need to be accountable for our use of that authority.

Models of Understanding the MK Culturally

I have real problems with the third-culture kid model. I don't buy all of it. And the parts that I don't buy come from my background of culture studies.

A pretty standard definition of third-culture kid goes something like this:

> A third-culture kid is one reared in a host culture different from that of parental origin. It is two dominant cultures blended with personal experience to produce a unique and distinct third culture.

Historically the TCK model was the first attempt to understand the MK in terms beyond the fact that he was attached to missionary parents. It was a major paradigm shift in understanding the experience and the personalization of missionary kids. I don't want to denigrate it on that basis at all. It was very positive. It was a step forward.

Its real strength has been in giving MKs an explanation for understanding themselves as different, without attaching a judgmental value to whether that difference is negative or positive.

TCK was kind of a neutral term that explained that there are children who grow up outside of a dominant culture. Therefore it was a model that a lot of people liked to use, just because it was not negative.

It appears that the functional use of the term TCK has been separated from its original meaning. We are now using TCK basically to mean a kid raised outside of his own dominant culture. We're using it as a descriptive term of where a person was raised, rather than as a model for understanding them culturally or explaining their cultural experience.

I want to deal with the implications of the words *third culture*. First, it assumes significant exposure to more than one culture. That's not true of all missionary kids. You can't have third culture unless you have more than one culture, right? So, I have a problem at that point.

Secondly, TCK assumes some sort of synthesis between those two cultures. You cannot assume cultural synthesis. Culture studies find that there are people who hold contradictory cultural information, and that cultural information can be processed into personal identity and still be in conflict. That synthesis never occurred.

A New Model—The Multicultural Kid

I'm going to propose a new model, the multicultural kid. I don't want to propose that we use this term to replace TCK, but *third culture* assumes synthesis. *Multicultural* doesn't.

A multicultural kid is a child reared outside of a dominant monocultural context. It's a descriptive word without implying what his cultural experience is. He's outside of a monocultural context.

Distinctions from TCK

We should not assume significant exposure to more than one culture. The MK may be raised monoculturally within the evangelical foreign mission culture. There are MKs who have no national language, no national culture, and no contact with nationals. Don't tell me they are part African.

Not only may they not have been exposed to national culture, they may never have been exposed to American dominant culture either. We have missionary kids growing up with no primary experience of dominant national culture. They only have secondary information they get from their parents or wherever.

To me these are important distinctions when we're talking about the term *third culture*.

Let's assume that the MK does have cultural experience in more than one culture. In that case, the MCK may *not* synthesize the information he's given into some kind of harmony or blend in order to produce a third. In the absence of synthesis, there may, in fact, be cultural conflict. One of my assumptions is that some of the psycho-logical problems by which we have been interpreting missionary kid behavior are not pathological. They are cultural.

Types of cultural involvement

Let's look at cultural involvement using a model of linguistic involvement that I've worked out with Donald Larson. There are three basic levels of linguistic culture transfer—independent bilingual, interdependent bilingual, and dependent bilingual. We switched it over to culture:

Independent biculturalism. In any situation the bicultural per-son is free to act, think, respond, or choose from either culture. Very few of these people exist anywhere in the world. That means in any situation, they feel totally whole and comfortable responding out of either culture, A or B.

Interdependent biculturalism. Most people who have cross-cul-tural experience have interdependent biculturalism. In any situation the bicultural person acts, thinks, and responds within the present cul-tural rules governing behavior. If you're interacting in the village, the cultural information that you have defines what is appropriate.

Dependent biculturalism. The third, which is the experience of a lot of missionary kids who are not truly third culture, or who don't have two sets of culture information, is dependent biculturalism. Cul-ture number two is always processed through the informational screens of culture number one. Culture number one would be home culture, or the culture most reared in—a person's primary culture. For some MKs, that could be the evangelical foreign-mission subcul-ture of American evangelical culture. I don't believe evangelicalism is a belief system. My assumption is that it is a cultural system with a lot of truth in it.

Applications to MK identity formation

I would like to take this model and apply it to developmental psychology, so we get cultural influences on MK identity formation. We know that as children grow up they form identity or self-concept. We know that there are some environmental influences—physical, geographical, and also sociocultural—in self-concept formation.

I want to give an example of a kid who goes overseas with his family at age two and lives in a national neighborhood. He has all national friends. Later he goes to a national school. The family stays there over an extended period of time. He has a lot of bicultural information. He has secondary American experience from his folks and some of his own experience from the neighbors next door. Basically the cultural information he's getting from both sides is putting pressure on him in his self-concept development to do something with that information if it has conflicts in it. The sooner and the longer the contact, the deeper the level of cultural information processed into identity formation.

I was about twelve years old when I went to Vietnam. I interpreted the Vietnam War and my experience there as an American child. We lived upstairs from a Vietnamese family. I learned a lot. I began to speak the language. I had a lot of cultural experience, but it did not form my self-concept.

Concepts of the "good"

In my culture theory, every culture has a concept of the "good" it is heading towards. It orders itself in its social stages to make progress towards that good. There are conflicting cultural definitions about what is good. Conflict can come when resolution or synthesis has not occurred.

For example, every chart I've ever seen on Western and non-Western characteristics shows the West as individualistic and the East as communalistic. A person from the West raised in an Oriental culture can have cultural information that says, "Community is the good," and cultural information that says, "Individuality is the good." This is known as cultural dissonance and motivates the holder of it, whether a whole group or an individual within that group, to seek resolution.

In this light, some MK "problems" that have been historically interpreted as psychological problems may be a psychological expression of cultural conflict or dissonance.

Levels of cultural information

One of the things that we have not dealt with when we're talking about the cultural experience of missionary kids is the different sources from which cultural information comes.

1. There is "self-culture," your inherited, God-given personality, talents, abilities. That's you, no matter what your cultural context is.

2. The earliest information we get that forms self-concept is from family. My family has some definitions of the good that define my world-view distinctly from my wife's.

3. The third area I would call a parochial area. This includes ethnic, geographic, and religious backgrounds. Simply stated,

a New York Italian Catholic is going to have a different set of cultural information, and thus cultural identity, than an Eastern-Oregon cattle-rancher Church-of-Christer.

4. At the next level, there's national or dominant culture. You can have conflicting cultural information at this level, and when you overlap another national set of information, you get more conflict.

I'm not saying that all missionary kids have cultural conflict. I am saying that not all missionary kids are third-culture kids.

When a kid goes overseas at age twelve, his basic enculturation process is finished and his self-concept is basically formed. What is introduced into his system is not cultural identity, but anomalies that contradict what he knows to be life.

I grew up in the Bay Area. When I was twelve years old, I rooted for Willie Mays playing center field for the San Francisco Giants, built forts in eucalyptus trees, the whole bit. Next day, I was in Saigon. People were suffering. I was hearing people die. I was seeing houses blown up. We almost got killed. I was seeing war orphans with open sores digging through our garbage. It didn't fit anywhere in my cultural information and all the good that I was headed for, growing up to be a nice-personality youth pastor some place. It didn't fit.

What I had to deal with then was not an identity problem, but "How does my belief system account for this anomaly?" That was eighteen years ago. I still have real struggles. It did make a significant impact on my life.

Understanding Age Patterns

Another way I think we can help re-entry MKs is understanding that age can be broken down into areas other than just chronological. Chronological age is different than biological age. For example, I am thirty-two, but my body may be pushing forty because of Southeast Asian diseases to which I was exposed. There are examples of seven year old kids who are eighty years old biologically. Don't assume that chronologically and biologically age is the same. Neither should we assume that emotional age, social age, vocational age, educational age, or cultural age is the same. When a kid is raised in a foreign culture, his cultural age, that is his ability to deal with pluralistic groups of people, may be advanced.

I was sixteen years old, I was flying around the world by myself. I was going through customs, changing planes, no big deal. But I'd never had an adolescent peer. My emotional and social ages were still twelve.

When I came back, I had never held a part-time job. All my nieces and nephews in the States in high school pump gas and work at Wendy's. I came back and I was concerned for the state of the world — and my parents sent me money. Vocationally, I was five.

A person's age pattern is directly related to his self-perception and identity, for it is a group norm against which to measure his own "normalness." The complexity of age patterning is a key in understanding MK re-entry, for it is only then that the MK may become aware of deviance from dominant cultural patterns.

Difference at this point does not reflect need for therapy. What is needed is support from that community of people to encourage and nurture the MK through a socialization process into a more matched age pattern.

The Adult MK Issue: Where Is Home?

Where am I from? Between the time I was twelve and the time I was fifteen, we moved fifteen times due to the war situation. Right as I was entering junior high, the adolescent group formation and all the stuff that was supposed to happen, completely fractured. We sold our house; I got rid of my bike, all my toys, all my sports equipment; all my brothers and sisters went away to college or got married — everything was gone. There was no past. We got to Vietnam — totally new life. That raised the question, "Where am I from?"

I need to know that I belong to someplace or to somebody — that I fit in a larger system. Part of what has made the term *third-culture kid* so popular is that it deals with the fact that I don't feel like I belong. I'm third.

Developing a sense of belonging

There are three components to developing a sense of place, a sense of belonging:

Geographical. There seems to be some relationship between a person's sense of belonging and the physical environment in which he was raised, whether it's concrete in the inner city of New York or the side of the Swiss Alps. Studies are beginning to show that people who are raised in a certain context are more comfortable in that environment. It's a physical relationship that relates to the jar of dirt that immigrants bring and kissing the ground and all sorts of things.

I feel great when I get back to the tropics. It's humid and I can smell the diesel fuel. There's a part of me that responds to that physically.

There's an interesting book called *Number Our Days,* by Barbara Myerhoff. She did a study of a Jewish senior citizens' center in Venice. Most of them were from Eastern Europe. There was an amazing amount of grief and pain in those people's lives over the fact that for some, their home town no longer existed after World War II. There were now trees growing where they had their first date. The town where they had their first child no longer existed.

Ideational. Your ideational system is basically your cultural system and your belief system—your world-view and your religious beliefs. Some MKs are so fractured that the only thread they have left is the hope that they have in Christ. They identify a sense of place ideationally—"in the arms of Jesus." I don't want to denigrate that; not having a sense of home causes pain.

Relational. Relationship is basically belonging to a people. It is through family, peers, friends, community, church youth group, that people define their sense of place in the world relationally. I have some sense of belonging and know how I fit in because of my group membership in a very special group of people at Link Care. It's part of my relational sense of place.

A lot of psychologists will say that MKs have an overdependence on family. Where is home for the MK? Wherever Mom and Dad are. Their sense of place and balance is weighted to the relational component because there's been no geographical stability. There may have been no ideational sense of place because MKs are so often exposed to multicultural sources of information, and oftentimes, because of their experience, they question their faith.

The problem comes when they're twenty-eight years old and married, and they still can't redefine their sense of place in the universe outside of their parents. They are weighted to a relational sense of place in the world.

People with the strongest roots are generally from a small community with a high degree of commitment to a central belief system. A Swedish Lutheran from a village in Minnesota has *home.* He is in balance. He has a strong sense of his identity. He knows that people are still eating lutefisk, and they are going to drink peppermint schnapps while they ice fish. He knows the climate, the geography, the type of schools. He's very different from a missionary kid who has had four short-term assignments and every time he is back in his home culture is on deputation.   A sense of place just does not develop for that MK.

In her plenary address, Ruth Van Reken said, "If I'm TCK, I'm alone. If I belong to the missionary culture, then I have a sense of belonging." It is a relational sense of place. I think that is one of the reasons a lot of MKs stay in the missionary community. It is no different than any other ethnic person not wanting to leave their ethnic roots.

I'm not saying it's bad. I'm saying it's just life. It also might be the way God works.

Whenever there's an immigrant population that moves or changes culture, they always have a Little Saigon or a Little Italy. In a foreign place, they bond with their ethnic group. You can change group membership; I'm not saying you can't. But in an enculturation process, there's always home.

The community of believers is an invisible community of belief. The missions community is not taking the primary responsibility for caring for the kids raised in it. We are saying that some other community should take care of our kids — either the host culture or the school culture. I want to see us as a community deal with our responsibility to own our kids.

I was talking to a missionary kid from India, and she said she was very alone, very much in pain, not understanding what happened to her. I shared with her little illustration I heard my father preach.

> A young child is in his crib and doesn't want to go to sleep. The parents go out, shut the door, turn the TV down, and wait while he cries.
>
> Finally they come back in and say, "Look, you know that Mommy and Daddy love you. We'll just be in the next room."
>
> He says, "I know Mommy and Daddy love me, but I'm afraid."
>
> After everything else fails, they come in and say, "You know Jesus is with you."
>
> And the little kid says, "I know Jesus is with me, but I want somebody with skin on him."

I think what we need to do is be the skin of Jesus, and be the arms of Jesus. That will give our kids a relational and ideational sense of place. Even if they never have a geographical sense of place, they will still know they belong.

Answers to Questions

If you're going to make the cultural assumption that the children you raise overseas are going to come back, go to U.S. schools, marry U.S. girls and boys, then I think you owe it to them to provide them a sense of belonging in the U.S. culture—grandparents, home town, home church, whatever. I've talked to a lot of people on furlough; it has been very successful for them to go "home" first, and spend four weeks or whatever. They may even leave the kids there if they have to do some deputation. They put the kids in the local school and work with the local church missions committee on keeping those kids in contact with other kids in the church.

If possible, develop a sense of geographical place. Right after I identified the importance of the house in Fresno that we had come back to every time from the war, that house came on the market. Last year we bought it, and by God's grace I feel I can go on with my life in much more whole ways.

Broaden their relationships. There are dependent relationships and independent relationships and obviously growing up is moving from one to the other. Looking back on my missions experience, I would have forced socialization on me.

28

MK Values and Ethno Relationships

Ray Chester and Dave Sanford
Arizona College of the Bible

Chester: Our statements are highly biased. We hope that they are true to the word of God because that is our absolute authority. I hope that is your absolute authority. If so, then you are in the minority among evangelicals today. That is one of our biases.

Sanford: It is also our understanding that if you disagree, that's fine. In fact, it is at points of discussion that we can learn from each other.

American Values

We want to start out looking at our own values. Why do we do the things we do? Why do we think the way we think? We may help you discover some of your own values and motivations.

One value in the United States is *self*. How do I have value in myself? The work ethic is very much a part of this because the American value of self is wrapped up more in what I do than who I am. Does this carry over into the missionary community?

Look at the terms we put around ourselves. The term *missionary* is a good word to help us establish our personal identity. What happens when that term no longer fits you? You must find some other way of describing yourself or identifying yourself, because in America our value of you as a person is greatly dependent on what you do.

We have known several missionaries who have had problems when they retired. After thirty-five years as missionaries the title was no longer there. One couple was in tears because they did not sense they were of value any more, because their title was gone.

This is a typical American value. Do we buy into it? Does this carry over to our kids? Is it biblical? These are questions we need to think through, because values are passed without thought, generally. We need to dialogue with our young people about these values.

Chester: One of the things we ask parents or students who are planning to be parents is, "Do you know explicitly what your values are, and have you delineated those values? Are you specifically teaching very definite values to your children? Do you know what you want those values to look like twenty years from now?"

Normally we get the response, "What values?" Our values haven't been defined. There are just things we like doing and things we don't like doing. But there are subtle values that we teach constantly without saying anything and most of us never give them a moment's thought.

Are there values that can be instilled at a young age by your verbal expression and your lived model that will build a child up so that some of the issues we must now deal with in the therapeutic community or the education community would no longer be issues?

Sanford: Another strongly held value in America is youth. Once we get beyond youthfulness and can't jog around the mountains any more or put enough makeup on our faces to look young, our self-worth begins to slip. This is typically American.

Chester: Going to a high school football game in the United States is a fascinating experience. I can sit in a football stadium and watch the parents' pep club all night. They are reliving what they once had.

I wonder if we do not do that within the missionary community. Why aren't we focussing on the aged missionary? I've never heard of a conference on the aged missionary? That doesn't fit into our concept of what we do.

We're not saying it's wrong to focus on youth, we're just asking, "Why are we doing it?"

Sanford: Often we pass this value on to our families even while living in a culture where age and wisdom are highly valued. We have to be aware of both value sets. If we are not, we create tension. Our children may see youth on one side and age on the other. They don't know where they fit in if we are not dialoguing or helping them through this with a Biblical perspective on age as identity.

Another typical value in the U.S. is individualism. If you've read any national writers reflecting on the missionary community in any country of the world, you will probably find some of their first impressions of us deal with strong individualism.

There is something in that that has value, but I think we have honed this particular value to a point now where it is devastating, even within the missionary community. We often think attitudes and actions cause conflicts, but basically we conflict with one another, because our value of self has so heavily emphasized my doing what I want, when I want, and how I want. I don't sit down and think, "I want to be an individual today, so I'm going to be stupidly individualistic." No. I do it because that's the value that gives me a sense of worth.

It's within this environment that our kids are raised. They are learning those values.   We transmit them without thinking them through. Have we helped our young people see that these are typically American values, honed to excess? Talk about it with your kids.

Chester: Let me read you a definition of individualism by Conden and Yousef in the book *Introduction to Intercultural Communications*. "The sense each person has of having a separate but equal place in society. The independent U.S. self must never feel bound to a particular group."

Sanford: The premise of the book is that if we are to relate well to people of other cultures, we must understand value bases — their values, our values. We must be alert in order to become good internationalists, able to adapt, to adjust, to see, to understand, and not conflict without knowing what we're conflicting about.

Chester: Notice, "The independent U.S. self must never feel bound to a particular group." Think about that with regard to yourself for awhile. How loyal are you to your group? "I'll only stay here as long as it is advantageous for me to be here. If I have a better offer over there, I'll go."

Now think about this with regard to Japanese culture. When a Japanese man goes into a bank and signs up to be a part of that bank, the concept of retirement or change is not existent. He signs up to be there for the rest of his life.

My father-in-law, who was Vice President of Lloyd's of London, feels that is ridiculous. You don't do that. That's not an American concept. How long do you plan on staying at the bank? Until a better job opens up at the next bank.

See? We can never be bound, ever, to a particular group. That's a deeply held American value.

Sanford: We're not necessarily saying it's right or wrong. Cultures are different. And different is different, not necessarily wrong. The "necessarily" is very important. We have to see if it goes against a biblical absolute. To say that we're going to change and be typically

Japanese is not any better than saying we're going to be typically American.

Our point is that we must recognize how strongly we hold our American values. They come out without our thinking.

Values Concerning God

Did you ever reflect upon the U.S. evangelical values expressed concerning God? Who controls whom? The prevailing reaction that we have seen is that man is in control of God.

Chester: That's a hard pill to swallow, but that attitude is prevalent in the evangelical community. We are the determiners of the actions of God.

Sanford: We live as though we are the controllers of God.

> I was sitting in a missionary prayer meeting. There were only about thirty missionaries in this African city of a million and a half people. There was a very small struggling national church with need for leadership and encouragement, but there was no mention in that prayer meeting of any of the Christian community. It was totally "God, do what I want you to do for me and my family." I was aghast.

I listen to my prayers more now. Who is controlling whom? Is God really God for us any longer?

Chester: Lack of discernment is destroying the church in North America today. There is a total inability to discern right from wrong. We have no standards.

Dave and I talked in Dallas at a conference and had a very knowledgeable person with all the degrees ask, "How can you say there's a right and wrong? There are no absolutes."

> I was visiting a Sunday School class at a large, independent evangelical Bible church and the Sunday School teacher just happened to mention, "There really are no absolutes in Scripture."
> I said, "Let me talk to you about that." I opened my Bible, which he hadn't done yet, and I started pointing out a few acultural statements in Scripture.
> He said, "No, Ray. You don't understand. It's only an absolute if you and I agree on it."
> I looked at him and said, "That makes you God."

He didn't particularly appreciate that comment, but it's true. He had become the absolute of Scripture. His is a commonly held belief today. It is never written, because it would be heresy to do so, but we have been living it as an unexpressed value for a long time.

Sanford: This is not a values seminar, but we're trying to raise your awareness of your own values. They come basically from your base culture. As we communicate with a different society with different values, we have noticed some clashes. In the process, if we're aware, we're more able to adjust, to understand, and then to resolve some of these issues. It is our desire that within the missionary family these things be understood and discussed so that our children learn the skills to enable them to analyze what they are doing and to have some biblical bases for their actions.

Chester: It's a difficult process for those who are so locked into the values expressed by their culture, that they even interpret Scripture through cultural values.

I was speaking at a large seminary. The person right before me was a missionary who said he had become distraught because husbands and wives didn't love each other in that European country. They didn't hold hands. So he had gotten trained in Marriage Encounter and was now going back for his next four year term to teach those people how to biblically love each other.

In my talk I opposed the cultural value he had expressed. I am commanded in Scripture to love my wife. That is an acultural command. No matter what culture you deal with, that command is there. However the expression of that love may be culturally determined.

I was talking to another missionary who was horrified that the wife in a Brazilian Indian tribe would walk three steps behind her husband. He said, "You don't love your wife."

The elder of the church said, "Of course I love her."

He said, "No you don't. If you really loved her, she'd walk next to you."

He said, "No, the way I demonstrate my total love for her is by having her walk behind me. I'm her shield. The only women who walk next to men are prostitutes. You don't want my wife to be a prostitute, do you?"

The missionary had taken a biblical absolute, and made it cultural. He never could see that there was an absolute statement there that was acultural.

People hold much of their truths in the light of how they were enculturated. We look at absolutes and see that they can be expressed in various ways culturally. It is a lifelong process.

Sanford: It is a pilgrimage. It is a walk with the Lord by the power of the Spirit of God, who gives you discernment.

Training Our Children

What do we teach our kids? Are we letting them know, from personal life as well as our teaching that God is sovereign; that God is God?

Chester: There is a desperate need in the evangelical community today to know who God is. We don't know. And that's exactly what we teach our kids—we don't know who he is. We have set ourselves up as God. Then we wonder why we have all of these horrendous problems. As Shakespeare said, "Oh, the tangled web we weave when first we practice to deceive." Yet we are the ones who are deceived. Read Jeremiah 10, where he talks of "the discipline of delusion."

Sanford: God had become their creation rather than they being the creatures of a sovereign God. He said, "Your gods are the works of your own hands." How often we, even within evangelical leadership, worship the work of our own hands.

We would never stand before our kids and say, "I am God." We would shudder, because that's blasphemous. Yet, often in the way we live, we communicate that message to them. There is not a strong basis for their believing, "God is God in my parents' life. Therefore, I can trust that same God to work in my life." We should pass on that heritage of confidence in values based upon biblical principles that our children refer to when they make decisions. If we have let them know how we have come to hold those values and if we have taught them the process of examining their own values, then their chance of effectively living out a biblical lifestyle is very high.

> **Chester:** A young lady came up to me on campus. She had met my older son. She said, "He must be having some real problems in the dating scene. What are your rules on dating?"
>
> I said, "We don't have any."
>
> "What? I mean, a professor, I mean, especially at a Bible College, with no rules on dating?"
>
> I said, "We started at a deeper level, teaching our sons values so that when they got up into the teen years, we didn't have to come up with all the regulations on the dating process. He already has a set of values that he believes in very strongly, and we don't have to come in with all the barbed wire, the alarms, the lashing machine."

We started teaching our sons skills and helping them to identify values at an early age. Instead of unplugging the TV and throwing it out the door, we tried to use it as an educational tool. We would look at a commercial and dissect it. I'd say, "Who's the target? Why do they use those colors? Why that vocabulary?"

We went to a church, and my son who was seventeen went to the youth program. When he came out, I said, "Eric, what was it like?"

He said, "It was like going to a secular high school, except different terminology."

I had to throw in another dimension to his thinking. I said, "I appreciate that you could focus and see some of the negative stuff, but did you also notice any young people in there who really did love the Lord?"

"No, I forgot that one, Dad."

"Well, next time you walk in, don't focus totally on the negative." There are some young people who are desirous of walking with the Lord. And there are some parents who are desirous of teaching their kids right from wrong.

Friendship Patterns of Missionaries

Chester: : David said, "My friends are those who wholly follow thee." Who do you put around you as intimate friends? Do you choose people who foster your own ethnocentrism?

Sanford: Whether you understand them or not, your friendship patterns within society help determine the dating and courtship relationships that your young people are going to pick up. They learn the values that you express by the way you speak, the way you relate to one another. The family influences children long before the schools ever do. Here are three postures we defined:

Chester: First is **isolation**. We stay within ourselves. We send our kids off to the MK school. We let them play only in our home. We don't want them playing in the nationals' back yard because they might get a disease. We keep them within the shelter of our own little house. We put them in the car we brought with us and take them to the missionary school. Total isolation from the national or accepting community.

Sanford: Do you see a value in that concerning the supernatural and the kind of value your kids form without your ever saying it? You might preach a God that is sovereign, but you live as though you are sovereign in their lives. You are the total protector. You will keep them from disease. You will keep them from harm. You will keep them from the influences of this dirty society. You are their sovereign when they are one, two, and three years old. Then you wonder why they react against that God that you preach verbally. Do you see how your lifestyle is opposed to what you preach?

Chester: If you want to create a problem in your family, teach discrepancy. Live one way and talk another. If you want to disintegrate a family, do that. It's a guarantee.

Sanford: Dissonance must always be resolved. We cannot live with dissonance, where one thing is spoken and another thing lived. If you are in a mission agency or a school where one thing is said and another thing lived, there is a tension that must be resolved. Kids don't recognize that it is a dissonance that must be resolved, but they do resolve it. Kids recognize that we stand before people as the mouthpiece for God, who is sovereign. Then they watch us live a totally different belief. That's dissonance. When word and deed are in harmony, there is a phenomenal impact upon life. Not many reflect on the importance of passing on to our kids a heritage of God's faithfulness and sovereignty and grace.

Isolation is one posture that we can take as we make the transition into our host culture. It will have an impact on all of the other relationships that our kids have with that community.

Sanford: A second posture is **participation**. We are friendly participants in this host culture. We move recognizing our base, recognizing their values, and being able to interact with them.

> **Chester:** I was riding from Moody to O'Hare airport one time with an evangelist friend from India. He had once been a very wealthy man. He had gotten into politics before he became a Christian in order to have Christian missionaries kicked out of India. I asked him why.
>
> He said, "Did you ever wonder why we have so many religious beliefs within India? One of the reasons is because in India there's a basic value that says 'You can believe anything you want to believe as long as you live it.' The moment you don't live what you say, you're out. All I could see among missionaries was they talked big but they lived nothing. So we wanted you out."
>
> Through that process and his export business, he did come to know the Lord as his Savior. He went back to India and is now a missionary to India cross-culturally in some of the poverty ridden sections.
>
> He did find a few missionaries who actually lived what they taught.

Sanford: So, when we speak of participation, it is harmony between life and action — understanding where we have come from and who the people from the host culture are, and being able to live in that community and participate with them — as Paul said in I Corinthians, "Becoming all things to all men." As Christ was sent by his Father to speak the words of his Father and do the works of his Father, we have been sent to speak his words and do his works. We can participate with members of the host culture, alert to differences, for the glory of God.

Third is **integration**, or as some have called it, "going native."

I remember one old missionary fellow who wore a Quichua hat and pony tail, and shoes made out of rubber tires, but the natives still called him Patron. He asked, "Why do you still call me Patron? I walk like you, talk like you, smell like you, and live like you."

"You don't have an Indian mother."

You can't change that. Yet he was so desperately wanting to integrate.

While on the field, we had opportunity to have students from America in our home. One so desperately wanted to be a part of the community that he married an Indian wife, because he thought, "That way they will look at me as if I am an Indian."

He wouldn't use his shower because the Indians bathed in the river. After he married, his Indian wife bathed in the shower and he bathed in the river.

He would never eat cake because the Indians didn't have ovens. "I can't eat cake because they can't eat cakes."

She said, "OK, I'll make cakes and you just sit out and have your tortilla or whatever."

He wanted so desperately to integrate and to be one of them. They all knew he couldn't. They told him, "If we had a shower we'd use one. The only reason we go to the river is we don't have a shower in our house. This is not an expression of who we are. This is an external." This "primitive" Indian girl he married began to transform his life by helping him recognize that he could never become an Indian.

The rest of his life has a price tag on it, because his folks' grandchildren live in the jungle. They will never really know their grandparents. The community also paid a price helping him through a learning process when he entered their community thinking, "I've got to integrate totally and be just like them." I think they were probably more helpful than he understood they were.

This is a neurotic longing to be accepted.

Chester: I would say that the predominant group are isolationists.

Sanford: I am hurt that there is too much of the isolationist model around. Superiority complexes and racism unfortunately still do exist.

I was in one location in Africa a couple of years ago and was hurt by the isolationism of the missionaries there. The only blacks who ever came there came to sell or to serve. We asked the missionaries, "What is the community like? Can we walk down the street? Can we go into the market?"

"Oh, no. They're very hostile people. The political situation is bad."

My sister-in-law, who speaks Swahili very well said, "Let's go walking." We encountered a fantastically friendly group of people, but the missionaries that we were staying with had isolated themselves from the community. Their belief of the community's hostility had kept them from even greeting the natives.

Chester: Isolation of the nuclear family is a growing phenomena today. The total worship of a nuclear family unit is probably one of the most unhealthy things I've seen happening.

"I can't allow anyone to interfere with my family because . . . . " Obviously because "I am God over my family."

Sanford: There is a growing concern for participation, for mutuality and reciprocity in the body of Christ. I guess from optimistic desire, I see that to be a healthy, growing phenomena.

I think all of us should be learning the skills to be able to participate anywhere. I'm concerned that our students acquire the skills to function anywhere.

Price Tags of Choices

Chester: You are aware that every decision you make has a price tag? The discerning person looks at the price tag. Am I willing to pay that? Is it profitable and biblical? Is it something I can afford to pay? Or am I like the average American who is now $13,000 in credit card debt? "I just buy it and hope I can pay for it somehow."

Every decision has a price tag, whether you go in as an isolationist, as a participant, or as a total integrationist.

Sanford: We are particularly looking at the price for the family.

Chester: What might be a price tag for an isolationist on entry?

- *Loneliness*
- *Lack of language acquisition*
- *Not forming intimate relationships with the other culture*
- *Fear*
- *No response to the message we have to share*
- *No support system*

Sanford: The kids are watching their parents as they go through the transition.   They are learning their procedure for entry into another society from them.   What are the price tags of a participating family?

Chester: A young couple who came to candidate school wanted to totally integrate.   They went through a course in their college that promoted going native as the best way to do things. They were all excited about going to the mission field.   They were going to let their kids run wild.   They had a utopian concept of what it was going to be like out there.

I said, "When you retire from the field, assuming you make it to retirement, where are you going to go?"

They said, "Back to Indiana."

I said, "Are you going to make sure you have enough money for tickets to go back down to that village to visit your grandchildren?"

"Huh?"

That's one of the price tags they'd never even considered.

"What will you do then?"

"We'll isolate.   We just won't let them date."   That's the answer to that one!   We come up with external laws, again.

Sanford: Some of the host culture's values may be "forced" upon you.   Privacy is as good an American value as individualism.

Chester: Have any of you ever gone home and tried to describe the experience of being at a party with eighty Indians in a 6' x 8' living room?   Try describing that to a North American with an eight bedroom house and a forty-eight-million-square-foot living room?

Sanford: We took one of our pastors who had been raised on a big ranch in Colorado and his wife and eighteen-month-old child with us into Mexico City for eight weeks.   They lived with the pastor of a local church.   The apartment had a living room and a bedroom, both about eight foot square.   The pastor and his wife had four kids.   There were twenty people living in the apartment below them.

Rick had to have space.   One Sunday morning he got up, and some other people had been invited for breakfast.   There were about fifteen people around a little table in one little room.   He got ready for church and got in his car.   If anybody has a car in Mexico City, everybody goes in that one car.   So there were about twelve people in a six passenger car.

They got to church.   People don't like to sit by themselves, so in a pew for seven, there were fifteen people, and Rick was squished up in the end.   He was about ready to go berserk.   After the service, everybody was hugging everybody else, and he just couldn't wait to get back to his bedroom, close the doors, watch a football game or something, and get away from people. He got back in the car with all twelve people, got back to the little apartment, walked inside, only to find they had invited another family of about ten people for lunch, of which I was one.

Rick was sitting on the davenport watching an American football game, with Spanish commentary. All of a sudden he shot to his feet, rigid as a telephone pole. He said, "I can't handle this any more," and went into the bedroom and pulled the covers up over his head.

That's one of the price tags for participation. After that incident, he was all right. He is in Ethiopia today as a pastor. He loves Latin American people because of his experiences. You give something up, but you gain, too.

Chester: There are many who go with the concept of integration and end up as total isolationists, because it doesn't work. It's what I call reactionary Christianity. The only reason I'm where I am is because I don't like where you are. I never stop to check where I am. The only thing I'm interested in is, "This is not there."

Sanford: By dividing these positions into three categories, we confuse the issue. Most of this is very dynamic. You may experience all three within a three year period of time. It is a dynamic experience rather than a division of life. Life can't be categorized quite so easily.

Our entry posture, sometimes is not ours to decide. We don't carry the total agenda. The host culture does. If we are really participants, we go and work under their agenda of what it means for another cultural person to enter their society.

I was talking about this with a friend in Liberia who said, "We have tribes in Liberia where you must live at the border of the tribe for at least six months before they even acknowledge you are present so that you can come into the village. The American agenda says we're supposed to live with them and bond, but it doesn't work there. So we live according to their agenda. By doing that, we're participating in their society. These are the norms they are setting up for our entry and we live with them."

Sanford: We're talking about entering and continuing the enduring kinds of things like marriage. What happens if your kids or even some of the missionaries do marry? All of a sudden you have an enduring relationship with that society that you have to learn to adjust to.

A lovely young lady came to Ecuador to work, and an outstanding young man in the city of Guaranda came to know the Lord. Sooner or later there are some natural processes that take place, and it was our privilege to participate in the wedding ceremony as they came to be husband and wife. He's an ob-gyn specialist in Indiana today. There were some prices paid by both families, but there is also an enduring relationship.

Chester: If somebody wants to date cross-culturally, we instantly come up with "This is how you should do it" or "No, no, no, you shouldn't do it." We never ask the question, "Why do you want to date in the first place?"

A student in my office awhile back told me, "That girl is nice. I'd like to date her."

I said, "Why do you use the word *date*?"

"That's a stupid question, Ray. Everyone uses the word *date*."

I said, "I know that, but I want to know why you use the word *date*."

He said, "You're going to make me think, aren't you?"

I never said one thing pro or con about that girl. All we talked about were the values he had learned that would lead him up to the place where he felt like he had a need to be with another person. He had never thought through any of that before.

We get caught up on the ABCs of trying to answer kids' questions of "should I or shouldn't I?" instead of addressing the values leading them to make some of these decisions.

Sanford: When we leave a culture, there are some price tags, depending on how we went in. There are relationships that are built or destroyed.

As we learn how to evaluate our own values and learn how to enter into these societies and make transitions, we are expressing those values by our lives, as well as by our language.

Those who are having troubles returning to the States are perhaps the same ones who had trouble going from childhood to puberty. They've had trouble transisting along the way. Maybe it's because we parents and leaders have given models that have a little too much dissonance. We would like to encourage you to examine, evaluate, articulate the values that are motivating and pushing you in your ministry. Then be able to transmit those in a cognitive way to those you are working with. Let them know. Let them ask questions. Let them determine their answers. And support them in the way they are doing it. Let them know there are prices to pay. Share the price tags you have paid in making your entry, your stay and your exit.

Chester: That is, by the way, an explicit command in the Old Testament. Psalm 78 is one that comes to mind. Fathers are to instruct their children in rights and wrongs, how they have blown it, how they have honored the Lord. Why? So they would not be a stubborn and rebellious generation.

What are you teaching? Do you really know what you teach? Paul knew. In I Corinthians 4 he says he is sending Timothy. Timothy was a son. He says, "When you look at Timothy, just watching him and hearing him will remind you of me, Paul. Then you will remember that every place I went, every church I went, no matter what I said or did, it all matched. I provided a consistent, solid model reproduced in Timothy. Watch Timothy. Timothy will remind you of me. And then you reproduce it yourself."

Paul laid himself on the line. In I Corinthians 11:1, "Mime me as I mime Christ."

The most challenging verse to me in this area is I John 2:6. "If you say that you abide in him, you ought so to walk as everyone else in your culture walks." Right? Well, "...as everyone else within your Christian community walks." Right? That's not what it says. No matter how you read it; no matter how you take it apart, "If you say you abide in him, you ought so to walk even as he walked." The reverse of that, if you don't want to walk like Christ, keep your mouth shut. That's what it said to me: "Ray, if you don't want to walk like Christ, keep your mouth shut. Lock yourself in a closet."

Sanford: The price tag of that one is in Hebrews where he said, "Consider those who have been your teachers." Consider what? Their youthfulness? Their vigor? Their vitality? No. "The end of their life, and follow them." So there is a place for those of us who are parents, grandparents, teachers, those who are setting an example of godliness and sharing those values.

Chester: As you work with these kids, I hope you can say with John in III John 4, "I have no greater joy than to hear that my children walk in truth."

29

The Role of Significant Others in the
Life of an MK

Ron and Barb Cline
World Radio Mission Fellowship

Ron Cline: Any person in the process of growing up needs significant others. These are people, usually outside your family structure, who care for your welfare and contribute to your development. All of us need them. In fact, I would go so far as to say a person who doesn't have one of these people is somewhat disadvantaged in the growing process.

As we become adults, we can become a significant other to those who are still in their developmental stages. This seminar is on how to be a significant other.

Barb Cline: These young people on our panel are just a sampling of the many MKs that I have had the privilege of interviewing in the last few months. They are all about the same age. They all come from Ecuador. I think they have some really good things to share with you.

Kathy, when you first came to the dorm in fourth grade, was there someone who was a significant other to you?

Kathy Sevall: I remember my Pioneer Girl pal. She used to buy little gifts for me, and take me over to her house—fun stuff.

Barb: Then you came back in seventh grade. Was there anybody during that time of your life?

Kathy: My sister was here that year too, and we used to go over to the home of some close family friends for meals. I think that was neat, just to get in a family setting. They gave me a baby-sitting job, and having that responsibility made me feel good, too.

Barb: Jill, when you came to the dorm to live in Quito during your high school years, what kind of significant others did you run into?

Jill Blakeslee Gilbert: There was one lady who always looked out for me when there were mother-daughter banquets. She either took me herself or made sure that someone else would take me. She did that for a lot of the other dorm girls too. I knew I could stop by her office any time and say, "I'm really having a problem." If she was busy, she'd say, "Well, I have to get a paper out, but we can talk for a few minutes. Can we get together later?" I never felt like I was totally imposing. I knew she was busy, but I knew she had time for me.

Also, I was involved with the Christian Service Outreach. Our group did things together, and that was real special. We met with our Sunday School teachers, the Clines, every week. Just knowing we had people to interact with every week meant a lot to me.

Barb: Was there a time, Jill, during these high school years that you felt alone, or felt that you didn't have a lot of input from a significant other?

Jill: Yes. I've been reminded of that since I've been teaching. I was, I think, basically a good kid. I kind of conformed to everything that was expected. I got involved in the right things. But because I wasn't a problem, because I wasn't really outstanding, lots of times I felt a little bit lost in the shuffle. I knew that those people I mentioned were there, and that they cared, but looking back, I don't remember a whole lot of people saying, "You have a real talent in this area. You ought to pursue it," or anything like that. That might be typical—if you're a good kid, sometimes you get a little bit lost in the shuffle.

Barb: I think that's an important thing for us to hear. The kid that's always in trouble is going to have lots of people looking after him. The kid who's an athlete, or a superstar, or a tremendous leader, usually gets quite a bit of attention too. But what about the one that just goes along, does well, doesn't cause any waves? Have you reached out to anyone like that?

Now Rich, I remember the trauma of coming to the field with a fifteen-year-old, and how California looked better and better that first year. Then you went back and decided Ecuador really was your home. What helped you to adjust during the last three years of high school? Were there significant others for you?

Rich Cline: The most significant people in my life, probably first and foremost were friends that I made in high school, fellow MKs. I was a complete stranger, so I was amazed how they went out of their way to be friends with me, and let me in on their secrets, and let me in on all of their little schemes and everything that was going on. That was really important for me. That made the transition a lot easier.

But there were others too. I'm thinking of two couples in particular. They had organized times when MKs could go to their homes. We would just sit and play games and talk and stay there practically half the night — very relaxing times. They were married adults, but they came down to our level. They were just part of the group. The thing that was most important to me was that their homes were open all the rest of the time too. We could go to their house any time, day or night, and just bang on the door. They would come to the door in their bathrobes and their slippers, and they'd invite us in. They'd make popcorn, and we would just sit around and talk. They were willing to deal with us on our own level. They were never inconvenienced by us. That was something that really stuck out to me, and it's something that I'm trying to do now as an adult for other kids.

Russ Cline: In Ecuador, along with friends who were significant came their parents. A lot of families of my friends always had their houses open for meals or things like that. As I developed relationships with their kids, I developed relationships with the parents at the same time. But probably the person who had the most impact on me in high school was a basketball coach who spent many, many hours watching me run laps, or making me run laps, or just being a friend. He taught me a sport; he taught me how to relate to other people as a leader on a team; he taught me how to be a friend. He was always there, ready to listen and give advice, while he watched me run laps.

I had another significant family, in the States, even though I was thousands of miles away in South America. When I was a sophomore, they sent me a plane ticket and said, "Come up and work with us for the summer." They gave me a job and a vehicle to drive. They paid everything and let me live with their family. That was great. They continued to do that for two more summers during high school and college. They invested a lot of time with me, and they became very significant to me as a family. Even though they were far away, they still gave me a lot of input.

Barb: Kathy, as an MK transplanted back into the States, have there been people who have been significant to you there?

Kathy: Again, I think it's the people who open their homes and allow you to be part of their family. That means a lot. I'm thinking of one of the counselors at school. Every year he has a picnic for all the MKs. We go over and play games outside and eat and share and have a good time. It's always good to get off campus and to be in a home with other MKs.

Barb: Kathy, your family has taken another young person into their home so that she could go to school here. How has that affected you as a family? Would you recommend that?

Kathy: First of all, I think it's been neat for my sister to have a little sister. It's good that they have each other for companionship, going places, fighting, and all those kinds of things that I had with her. Secondly, I think it has been good for Karina. She lives in the Galapagos Islands, and there aren't many people out there. Her dad owns a ranch, and she knows a lot about animals, but not a whole lot about socializing. Not only is she still near home, but she's with an American family, and a Christian family. It's been neat for us to be significant others in her life. Hopefully this will really help her as she grows up.

Barb: Jill, you have talked about your role as a teacher. How are you trying to be a significant other to your students?

Jill: Watching the kids grow in different areas, encouraging their strengths, and encouraging them in their struggles is what I'm trying to do.

Barb: That probably comes from not having had a lot of encouragement. Being able now to do that for the people in your charge is significant.

Rich, what stands out to you as one quality that we need to develop if we're going to be a significant person to someone else?

Rich: Basically coming down to the level of the MK, being a human being and relating to them as a person their age, not as an adult to a child. Probably one of the most significant people in my life after leaving Ecuador was a college professor who was very honest with me about his feelings. I called him by his first name. He invited me to his home, or we'd go out and do things. On my papers that I would hand in to him, he would write very personal notes. It wasn't a teacher / student relationship; we were friends. As a result, I learned more from him, even regarding the subject, than I would have ever learned if he had just been a lecturer in a classroom.

Barb: That's important. Russ, can you think of a quality that stands out?

Russ: I think the one thing that people who were significant to me did was push me. They could see through all the problems and frustrations I was having. They saw some good in me, and they really encouraged and pushed. When I got to college, a lady who knew I was a missionary kid took a chance on me, because she thought that maybe I would do OK. Through that experience I learned so much more and was given so many different opportunities to work and minister. She became significant because she took a risk. I think one of the most important things is that we be willing to take risks on kids. Give them a chance, and know that there's a lot of good inside of them even if it's hard to see. You've got to push them, take a risk, and make yourself vulnerable.

Barb: That's an important word—risk. I heard that over and over as I interviewed people. One adult MK who is about my age said that a lot of people took a risk on him. Now he is working as a missionary, and whenever he has the opportunity, he goes back to those people and shares with them what's happening in his life, so they can see that the risk they took really paid off.

Ron: As missionaries, sometimes we think that all of our time with young people needs to be spiritual. Rich, did these people you dropped in on have a Bible study for you? When they had an activity and had games, did they close it with a devotional? Did they sense a need to have a spiritual tag put on the activity?

Rich: Not at all. They were giving us an example of how to live Christ every day. They were showing us that having the doors open was an important part of being a Christian. Without their saying it, we got the message.

Barb: In their conversation with you, did they ever share about their own spiritual struggles, or did you know where they stood with the Lord?

Rich: Sometimes they would talk about some of the things that they were working through. But I wouldn't say that we ever got into any deep spiritual conversations. Sometimes we would get into a discussion about something we had heard in a classroom or in chapel that day at school. We would talk about that, not as a teacher and a learner, but as friends. That's why those people were significant to me.

Ron: Did any of you get discipled by somebody who became a significant other in your life? Positive or negative.

Russ: I had a negative discipleship experience when I was in junior high with a guy who really wanted to disciple. I know his heart was right, but as junior high guys, that's not what we were looking for at all. Every time we got together, it turned into a church service with a message and a sermon. We wanted someone we could be friends with, and who would open his house to us. Instead we got message after message, and scolding after scolding, and preaching.   It was really a negative thing.

Most MKs have Bible class every day and chapel at least once a week.   They've got church and Sunday school that they're required to go to, and they kind of get overloaded with spiritual teaching.   When they see someone who lives a spiritual life as an example, they tend to grab onto that and really learn from that, because the teaching is almost too much.

Ron: The role of significant other involves:

1. Taking time.   It's going to cost you some time, even in your bathrobe maybe.   But kids have got to go some place, and you'd rather have them sit in your living room than out behind the building some place.

2. Showing interest.   How do you know when somebody is genuinely interested in you?

Jill: I found that I would kind of test people.   Inside I really wanted them to be interested in me, but I'd kind of put them off a little bit, by what I'd say, or by being a little uncooperative.   If someone is willing to overlook that, then he is interested in me as an individual. I think MKs get the feeling that people are interested in who your parents are, what you've done, or what group you're involved with.   I think a key is to be able to focus on the individual, and to persist a little bit even if they're not the most lovable one or the one with a great shining potential.

3. Being an example.   Let the MKs know some struggles you're having.   That doesn't mean dumping on them, but it means being honest with them, and letting them know how you solve problems.   A lot of MKs are away from the model of Mom and Dad.   They have dorm parents, but that's an abnormal situation.   They don't get the true relationship with the dorm parents that they might get in the home.   They may pick you; see how your marriage works; see how you handle differences; see what kind of process you go through in conflict resolution; see how you deal with priorities.

Barb: A word about dorm parents.   I had a number of dorm kids who said, "Sometimes my dorm parents are so busy.   I know they are busy because they're running the dorm.   They have to shop, they have to do all of the things that have to be done to run that dorm.   But I would much rather just have them.   I'd like for them to get somebody to do those things so that they could spend time with me and be available when I need them, not just when it is structured."   I thought that was a good word, not just for dorm parents, but for parents also. We get very, very busy, in our active missionary life. Are we willing to allow somebody else to help us or to let some things go in order to have that time to be available?

Ron: Let me just add this, if you're a significant other for a dorm kid, keep the dorm parents informed of what's going on. You don't have to be sneaky and tell tales, but you can work together many times to help the dorm parent.

Discussion

Ron: What other things would you add?

> *Write to them even after they've left. Answer their letters to you. They know you're busy. When one of our mission executives wrote to me and followed up, that had a tremendous impact on me. For him to take that kind of time showed me the interest that he had in me.*

Ron: Remember when you write, give them all the latest gossip— who's going with who this afternoon, and what's happening. They're interested in that too.

> *At the Alliance Academy, the chaplain has arranged for each dorm kid in all five dorms to be adopted by a family. He designates one Sunday near Thanksgiving as a day they go and spend with that family. He also encourages them to get together for birthdays, Christmas, or other special occasions. We've found that a real change in our relationship with the two boys we "adopted" occurred when we visited their home. Once we visited where their parents work, it made a big difference in how the two boys related to us.*

> *We don't have a lot finances as missionaries, but I found that being willing to spend some extra money is helpful. On one occasion when I knew that one of the girls who was in another country needed to talk to someone, I made several long distance phone calls. It cost me lots of money, but it was very significant for her. When the Lord blesses you with extra money, be willing to share it with some of these kids that are in need. Even when they're in college, send them a gift. The Lord will bless and return.*

> *I'm a parent of three MKs, and I have to constantly remind myself of the need to let my kids have significant others in*

their lives and not be threatened by it. I have the hunch that maybe some dorm parents need to be reminded that they are not the only significant others in the lives of their dorm kids. As a teenager I had some very important significant others, but they were very much a threat to my parents. I vowed that as a parent, I would not allow that to happen, but it's easy to follow the same pattern.

My wife and I work with the church youth group, and one of the most beautiful things that I have found in working with them is to be able to say, "I don't know," and "I don't have all the answers. I don't pretend to, but I'll try to help you find them." So many times it seems like my pride wants me to give them some kind of a spiritual answer, but a lot of times, when you say you don't know, they will open up more, because they realize that you're not going to bluff them.

If there's a parent that's coming to visit their boarding kids, and I'm involved with their children, I like to have them stay at my home. Being able to communicate with those parents gives me a lot of insight into those kids.

Ron: In the story of the good Samaritan, Jesus uses the word *compassion.* The Samaritan put himself in the wounded man's shoes and asked, "If I were the one attacked and in the ditch, what would I want somebody to do for me?" Look at that obnoxious MK and ask, "If I were that MK, what would I want somebody to do for me?" That's compassion. Compassion is not easy. Sometimes it's costly.

Another word Jesus used was *care.* Milton Mayeroff, a man who wrote a little book on caring, says, "Care is when whatever you come in contact with is better as a result of that contact." That's a good thing to think about with MKs. Are those kids better off because of our contact?

I think it's very important to admit when you're wrong, and to ask forgiveness.

Barb: I think a lot of people feel they don't have anything to offer. They are either intimidated by kids, or they think, "What can I give that kid?" I want you to leave today, knowing that you can be a significant other in the life of an MK or other people. You have the resources. Give of yourself and your time. Everyone of you can be a significant person.

Russ: The only thing I would like to add is, when you invest yourself in an MK, it's not always just you giving everything. The MK will probably give a lot back to you. I remember when some of these people moved, we would be the first ones there to help them carry their furniture out of the house. We were the ones that would baby-sit in an emergency. When they needed to shellac their kitchen cupboards, we would all go over there in a big group and help them out. It was because of their investment in our lives that we felt a part of their family. We were free to go over to their house and help them with anything they needed help with. I never regarded any of it as work. I remember scraping a kitchen floor. The grouting was kind of dirty between the tile. We were all down on the floor scraping, having a great time, and we didn't notice that it was awful work.

Ron: Thank you, MKs. You've been good teachers.

Part VI

MK RE-ENTRY

30

Bridging the Gap: Re-entry for Elementary Students

Karen Wrobbel
TEAM, Madrid, Spain

I teach at a day school in Madrid. Recently a twelfth grader who had gone to Spanish schools from kindergarten through ninth grade was doing a math problem for me. According to my way of thinking she was doing her division backwards. I couldn't find anything in that problem, because she had learned to write it differently. She was able to explain her method to me, but when a teacher asks a third grader, "Where in the world did you learn to divide?" you have a little bit of a problem.

Our missionaries in southern Spain live too far apart to have a day school together, so we developed a program to use an itinerating teacher. The children study three days a week under the parents' supervision, one day a week with the teacher in the home, and one day a week at school.

When we were developing the program we asked the parents, "What are your needs?"

Some said, "We want a full American program."

Others said, "We want to leave our children in Spanish school, but we really worry about when furlough time comes, and the children don't know how to read English, and don't know anything that will prepare them for the States."

So we developed a prefurlough re-entry program to help elementary school age kids. This includes teaching English skills to those who are in Spanish schools. In order to make this program as intense, practical, and valuable to the child as possible, we save it for the final year before furlough.

Prefurlough Re-entry Studies

Right now on our field we have all American families, so this program was designed to meet their needs. However, you can readily adapt this to whatever homeland your children might have. These skills can be taught in an MK school classroom, or they can be used by an individual parent.

U.S. money

The student will be able to:

1. Identify U.S. coins and bills by name. I don't want my children calling a penny a *peseta*. (Introduction level: K; Mastery: 1+)

2. Tell the value of American coins and bills in dollars and cents. They need to understand that a quarter is twenty-five cents or a quarter of a dollar or that a five dollar bill is five hundred pennies so that they can make change. (Introduction: 1; Mastery: 3+)

3. Demonstrate an understanding of the value of money and its use in purchasing. They'll look pretty stupid in the school lunch line trying to pay for their lunches if they don't know what money is. (Introduction: 1; Mastery: 2+)

4. Make change correctly for a purchase with American money. Our teacher has a school store to help teach this skill. She has a jar full of American money. By doing certain skills the children earn points and can buy things from the math store. Last year my daughter would come home saying, "I have twenty-five cents in the math store, so I can buy a pencil. Then I'm going to hang onto some of my money to get a better thing later." She was beginning to learn the value of money. (Introduction: 1; Mastery: 3+)

Non-metric measurement

The student will be able to:

1. Use a ruler or yardstick, to measure length. (Introduction: 1; Mastery: 2+) In most countries the metric system is used, but our children could look pretty stupid in an American school if they don't even know what inches or feet are.

2. Convert yards into feet, into inches. We're not trying to teach them to convert yards into meters. (Introduction: 3; Mastery 5+)

3. Weigh objects in pounds and ounces instead of in kilos. (Introduction: 1; Mastery 2 +)

4. Convert pounds into ounces.   Again, not converting kilos back and forth, but knowing there are 16 ounces in a pound. (Introduction: 3; Mastery: 5 +)

5. Measure liquids and solids in cups, pints, quarts, and gallons, instead of milliliters, liters, etc. Our teacher assigns cooking projects to teach these concepts. (Introduction: 1; Mastery 2 +)

6. Read a thermometer using the Fahrenheit scale instead of the Centigrade scale. (Introduction: 1; Mastery 3 +)

7. Tell the boiling point, and the freezing point of water, normal body temperature, typical winter and summer temperatures in his home state, using the Fahrenheit scale.   If you're a teacher, agree with the parent on what state to work with. The child then learns, "Where I am going in Illinois, it gets into the 80's and 90's in the summer. And in the winter it gets as low as 0, and sometimes below 0. It's very cold in the winter and hot in the summer." It is especially helpful for kids who have a spring-like climate all year. (Introduction: 2; Mastery: 4 +)

8. Demonstrate an understanding of the term "dozen." (Introduction: 2; Mastery: 3 +)

Geography

The student will be able to:

1. Name thirty of the fifty states by identifying them on a U.S. map with state boundaries marked. I want my children to be able to find where our home's going to be, where our relatives live, and where they are going to travel on furlough. They can begin to get a picture of what's going on by learning where those states are in relationship to each other. (Introduction: 3; Mastery: 5 +)

2. Identify the capital of their home state. When I started this with my children, I had to explain that the United States is a group of states, and that each state has a capital. That really took them by surprise. (Introduction: 1; Mastery: 1 +)

3. Describe features of their home state, such as climate, major rivers, mountains, deserts, and major places of interest. For instance, I want my children to learn that Illinois has the Mississippi River on one side, that Abraham Lincoln is from

there, and that it is called the Land of Lincoln. If you're from California, you'll want your children to know about Disneyland, Knotts Berry Farm, and the Redwoods so they can begin to look forward to visiting these places when they're on furlough. One of the exercises that we do with the kids is to make a travel folder on a trifold paper. The kids fill out the name of their state, the names of friends to visit there, things to see, etc. Even though they have roots in their foreign country, we also want them to have some ties with the States. (Introduction: 1; Mastery: 3 +)

History and current events

The student will be able to:

1. Identify major figures in American life, both past and present, and describe their importance to our country. They should not only know who George Washington and Abraham Lincoln were, but they should also know who the current President is. (Introduction: K; Mastery: increasing with age, as more people are studied.)

2. Outline major events in U.S. history as studied in class. In other words, they should know that there was a Revolutionary War, but that it's not the same as the Revolution in the country where they're living. They should know there was also a Civil War a long time ago, and it had to do with slaves and the North and South trying to separate. (Introduction: 3; Mastery: 3 + , according to studies.)

3. Discuss events of current interest in the U.S. with understanding. (Introduction: 1; Mastery: according to their level.) If a child was shortly going on furlough after the Challenger crashed, they would have needed to know what a Challenger was and what happened. Boys should probably know something about sports. It helps them be able to converse about what's going on relative to their level.

    It is also helpful if they are familiar with currently popular toys and television shows. What's a Transformer or a Gobot? Who is Sheera?

    It's good to have someone that can lovingly but honestly tell your kids that they look like a bunch of missionaries just fresh out of the bush. My husband's family had this kind of relationship with one missionary family. Whenever that family would go on furlough, they would spend the first couple of weeks with my husband's family, who would help them reintegrate. "No you can't do that." "No you can't wear that." "This is what's popular."

> *We've got friends who are missionaries in Africa, and they were quite concerned about their children's re-entry for furlough. The mother really worked getting them the right clothes so that when they got of the plane they wouldn't be conspicuous. But when they got off the plane in New York City, they were all stared at, and there were a few chuckles. The mother turned around, and all her children were carrying their suitcases on their heads.*

Calendar skills

The student will be able to:

1. Write the date in the accepted form (month/day/year). Perhaps in your country they write day/month/year. (Introduction: K; Mastery: 2)
2. Read and interpret an American style calendar. In Spain, the calendar starts with Monday. Sundays are at the end. (Introduction: K; Mastery: 2)

We believe that this program will provide the student with practical skills to make smooth transitions. It does not teach everything the student may need or want to know, but it does give the student a common base of experiences with his American peers.

Ideas from the Participants

Things to include in prefurlough preparation

- *Idiomatic expressions*
- *Orientation to the local church: Awana, Pioneer Girls, and youth groups*
- *Table manners, hours of eating, and different foods*
- *Greetings*
- *Spelling differences between Commonwealth countries and the United States*
- *How to use escalators*
- *How to use water fountains (You can drink the water from water fountains!)*
- *How to use a library*
- *How to view television objectively*

- *Music and choruses that you'll be singing at church   (Sending children's tapes could be a good project for a church group.)*
- *Acceptable church behavior*
- *Understanding the value of American currency in relationship to the value of the local currency*
- *Understanding that other Christian families may have different values than we do, and that we may not always agree with them*
- *Preparation for physical safety in different situations*

How a receiving school, church, or family can help MKs adjust:

- *Study the culture of the country where the child is from even using the missionary parents to help with that.*
- *Send photographs to the field in advance, of the home, the church, the school, so the children begin to see where they're going to be.*
- *Send videos from the States, complete with commercials. Then the kids will know some of what's going on and some of what's popular.*
- *Get current pictures of family members out to the field, so you know who cousin so-and-so is, who's in the family.*

Suggested Resources

Duplicating masters:

American History, Hayes School Publishing Co., Wilkinsburg, Pa. 1972. (Grades 4-8)

Famous Folks: Comprehension Skills, Frank Schaffer Publications. (1028 Via Mirabel; Palos Verdes Estates, CA 90274) 1980. (Grades 3-4)

Know Your States, Frank Schaffer Publications. 1981. (Grades 3-8)

Learning about U.S. Geography, Frank Schaffer Publications. 1985. (Grades 2-3)

Learning about Your Country, Frank Schaffer Publications. 1983. (Grades 2-4)

Learning about Your State, Frank Schaffer Publications. 1984 (Grades 1-3)

Other sources:

Money Books A, B, C. Useful Mathematic Series, The Continental Press, Inc., (Elizabethtown, PA), 1982

Measurement, Books B, C. Useful Mathematics Series, The Continental Press, Inc., (Elizabethtown, PA), 1982

Map Skills for Today, Weekly Reader Skills Books, Columbus, Ohio.

31

Using the College Selection Process in Career Decision Making

Gary Sinclair
Director of Counseling, Southfield Christian School

I've been concerned over the last five or six years that there has been no Christian school counseling organization anywhere. In Christian schools in the States and often in mission schools, there is a terrible lack of school counseling. The Association for Christian School Counseling and Career Stewardship was begun to help people around the country, and hopefully around the world, have a resource for Christian school counseling.

Several years ago our school put together a book called *A Guidance Manual* to help people who are trying to get a guidance and counseling program started in their school. It includes our goals, our objectives, how we try to meet those objectives, and resources and practical tips on how to get a school counseling program going in your school. We'd like to make it available to you if you would help us with the postage and the cost of putting it together.

I am the director of counseling at Southfield Christian School. I would not call myself a career guidance expert, because as a high school counselor, I don't think I ought to be a career guidance expert. I think that high school is a time to prepare, but it is not a time to make a lot of big decisions about the future.

I believe that as we plan for careers, God gives us wisdom, God gives us insight, and God gives us guidance through his Word. God does have to be vitally involved in this process. And yet, it does involve us. It does involve work, it does involve planning, it does involve thinking.

Foundational Principles

Build a strong academic foundation

High school is the time to build a strong academic foundation which will allow the student to pursue a variety of career options. It is not the time to specialize.

> We had an excellent student who applied to MIT a few years ago. He went to an interview, and the interviewer looked at his transcript and said, "This is quite good, young man, but I have one concern. How come you don't have college writing on here?"
>
> "College writing? But I have calculus and I have advanced physics."
>
> "Listen, we'll teach you to do calculus and advanced physics. You need to know how to write."

Provide opportunities to learn about careers

High school should provide career exposure and not require career choice. I hope that your school is able to have career days. You say, "Career days on the mission field?" I would think so. I do not pretend to be an expert on missions. But you have some tremendous opportunities to expose your young people to ideas and situations that will provide a rich foundation for their future.

In our career days, we use mostly our own parents. These parents have been involved in a lot of work situations. We use people from our own community. It's a great rapport-building idea. It's a way to introduce our young people to a variety of careers.

How about asking some of the people around you who are in full-time Christian work to participate in a Christian career day? What's the ministry like? What's it like to prepare for missions? What would they have done differently? What would they do the same? What do they like about missions?

Here in South America there are people in the oil business you could invite into your classes. Let the students find out now what the world out there is like.

One of the things we ask the parents who come in to our career days and to our career projects is, "Please tell us what it's like to be a Christian in your situation." That has been rich, folks. It has been exciting to hear an engineer say, "Do you realize that the other day my boss asked me to undercut the budget? Do you realize that happens to me regularly, and as a Christian I need to deal with that?"

Others said, "Do you know the opportunities I've had to share Christ in my engineering office, or in my advertising business, or as a lawyer?" "Do you realize some of the struggles I face as a doctor today, having to make moral decisions about life?" That kind of exposure is terrific for young people.

I would suggest that you allow them to work, if possible. At the Alliance Academy, they are beginning to allow their students to work at radio station HCJB, giving them some finances, and giving them some opportunity to get job experiences. What a great way to introduce them to the world of work!

Keep current information available

To most effectively use the college process to assist in career decision making, the secondary school must have an adequate supply of college and career materials and have regular correspondence with the major colleges and publishers.

I hope that if you don't have some sort of pipeline for getting materials to your school from American and other publishers that can help you in the area of colleges and careers, you'll develop one. One of the reasons we began the counseling group that I mentioned, is to become a resource. I would love for our organization to become a resource for materials for some of you.

Consider unique life experiences

We must assist our young people with learning to bring their whole life experience to their career decision making. As Christians, we ought to be bringing together all our experiences, talents, abilities, and spiritual gifts, and saying, "Lord, what would you have me do with these?" I see the mission field as a terrific place to do that with young people. Let these kids know how special they are and what unique experiences they have had—cross-cultural experiences, speaking other languages, meeting other people, learning to communicate, learning to be on their own. They have a whole wealth of skills and abilities that could be a part of their future. "You mean that's something God could use in a career other than on the mission field?" Yes.

I use a questionnaire, and I encourage you to develop one at your school. I ask all of my juniors and seniors to fill it out before they meet with me. It asks them, "What do you see as your greatest strengths; what do you see as some of your weaknesses?"

I ask them to look at Scripture passages on spiritual gifts and ask them, "Do you have any sense that maybe you have some strengths or gifts in this area?"

"What unique experiences have you had?"

"You've travelled to a foreign country. You've been a missionary kid. You speak another language. You've gone cross-country on a bicycle. You love to work with young people. You play a lot of sports."

As we sit and talk and as we begin to pull those things together, I've seen a lot of eyes kind of light up. I say, "Did you ever think about the possibility of doing this, which would combine your ability in that and your skills in that and using it in full-time Christian work?"

I'm not trying to talk them into a job. I'm just saying, "Have you thought about that?" They take notes and take the questionnaire with them. They begin to probe and explore. I pray that God will use those kinds of discussions to direct them in a way that would use their whole life experience.

I hope it excites you to think about the possibilities of working with your young people as whole people, people to whom God has given a unique set of experiences and abilities.

Practical Considerations for Students

In addition to personal counseling, I work a lot with students in getting ready for college. We can use students' thinking about college as a way to look at careers and to plan ahead and to think through the future.

I realize this section does not address the question of what we do with those students who are not college material. I have some concerns and frustrations with that, too.

Make use of furloughs

We need to urge families to use their furloughs to give MK students adequate college exposure. Many special college programs are available which can provide information on a variety of career options. I realize that missionaries only come home every so often. Maybe you'll come home during that student's sophomore year, or maybe you'll go home during their eighth grade year and miss all of high school. But I still think you need to begin to familiarize that student as much as you can with the idea of college, if that's a part of his future.

Wayne State University, in Detroit, offers "Meet Wayne State." They have a day for medicine, a day for engineering, a day for social work and psychology, and a day for all these other things. I encourage my students to go to that program. "Whether you want to go to Wayne State or not, I don't care. You're going to learn about engineering. You're going to learn about medicine. You're going to learn about the requirements for a whole lot of things."

Those kinds of programs are available. I realize that MKs and their families are going to have to work a little bit harder at that kind of thing, but I encourage you to go to that counselor and find out what opportunities are available, whether the student is in the eighth grade or the twelfth grade. Take advantage of those opportunities when you're able.

Look for colleges with multiple options

Limit college choices to schools that will provide students with several career alternatives. Help your students look at schools that will give them a variety of options.

I have students say to me, "I want to be a doctor. I found the best school I can find." That sounds like a good idea. The problem is, what if they can't cut it or don't like it? Are there other alternatives at that school, or are they going to have to transfer because there's nothing else?

Take advantage of college programs

One of the ways that colleges can be of tremendous help is by using their internal programs to introduce students to careers. This is happening in the United States more and more. Things like:

Co-op programs. Many students can now alternate going to school for a time and being off for a co-op session. During that co-op time, they're working in their major field for an actual company. They're also, in a lot of cases, making money doing that.

> At the University of Detroit, an engineering student three years ago was making $1500 a month. He did that for three months at a time. He had a year's experience when he came out of school and $18,000. That's unusual, but it's out there. And it's one way to help reduce the financial crunch.

How great to have a student actually get some work experience during college! After the first three months or the first week, he may say, "I hate this. This is terrible. I don't want to do this." What a great time to find that out! What a terrific way to do it!

The majority of the students who find it is something they want to pursue, have a job when they get out of college. So it's terrific either way.

Look for schools that have those options if possible. Some schools are doing it in every major field.

Internships are a similar kind of thing. They're usually shorter term and are often available during the summers.

Overseas studies. Some colleges in my area require students to go overseas. Your student may not want to do this. "I've been overseas. I don't want to do that again." But some of those are work-related opportunities, and they're worth looking at.

Music and ministry opportunities. If you have a sense that students are going to be ministry people, get them into a school that's going to use that. I love music. I'm a musician. My college experience was rich partly because I had opportunities to be involved in ministry groups and special gospel teams. That convinced me that was something I wanted to pursue.

Campus-based exposure to the world of work. Some schools have right on their campus programs like counseling, child care, and tutoring, that the students can be involved in so that they get exposure to the world of work.

Check on job placement services of colleges

I got my job through my college. They were a tremendous help to me. Check the school out, however. Find out what percentage of their students are getting jobs in their major field. That will tell you a lot about the school.

Keep an inventory

Keep a regular inventory on the student as the year goes on: likes/dislikes; favorite courses; special skills/abilities; unique experiences; character qualities; spiritual gifts; specific work experience; academic skills/strengths. Ideally this type of information could be kept on a computer file in the counselor's office. Some computer-assisted programs such as *College Entry*, which runs on an Apple II computer, would be ideal for this. It's a way to keep records on college students.

It would be great if you began even as early as the eighth or ninth grade to start meeting with students, finding out what their likes and dislikes are, and pulling all that together, so that when you meet with them later on, you have some things you can talk about.

Use testing and inventories only as a tool

I think tests are valuable, but be careful. A lot of people say, "Here, take this test and it will tell you what to do the rest of your life." It's not that easy. But let me suggest a couple that might be particularly helpful.

> Differential Aptitude Test is usually given in the eighth or ninth grade. It also contains a "Career Questionnaire," which is correlated with the students' scores on the test. This is an excellent "first exposure" to a student's career possibilities.

> Strong-Campbell is a long-established interest inventory which helps students see career areas that would fit their interests, likes, dislikes, etc. A weakness is that it does not consider ability at all.

> Armed Services Vocational Aptitude Battery is offered free of charge by the U.S. military branches. It tests ability in several career clusters and provides a print-out showing the student's strengths and weaknesses.

> ACT. The American College Testing Service provides a "World of Work" map on the back of its test results that shows the student where his/her interests tend to be.

Consider some of the computer-assisted college and career software now available.

Dan Peters: Your mission and your kid's school provide perfect opportunities to teach management and operational skills. There are schools which have the students participate in the budget decision process in order to teach them management principles. They get to sit in on the meetings. They struggle with "Do we have a soccer field or a new science lab?" They wrestle with values. If it has a title, it can go on a resume. However think about how vulnerable you're willing to be with your "territory" in order to give students career information.

The MK's field experience is very broad. Sit down, think about it, list all of the types of skills and interests and values that your MK cross-cultural experience has produced. You'll come up with hundreds of experiences and interests that you have had that other people haven't had that are definable and useable in the job market.

Often the career exposure in the MK community is limited to the current careers of the adults around him — missionary, teacher, doctor, nurse, radio operator, etc. All of those people have been dish washers, youth pastors, truck mechanics — all of those are valuable career resources to your MK. Don't let that person put lesser value on the other career experiences that he has had. What you want is the information about what it was like, not whether it was better or worse than his current vocation.

Resources for College Counseling

The College Handbook. College Board, Box 886, New York, N.Y. 10101, 19___. $15-20. This book is the clearest and most complete of the major college reference works. Each entry contains basic information about each college including curriculum, admissions guidelines, etc.

National College Databank. Karen Hegener, ed., Peterson's Guides, P.O. Box 2123, Princeton, NJ 08543-2123. 800-EDU-DATA. A book of lists categorizing colleges by scores of characteristics—i.e. offer co-op, have intercollegiate sports, etc.

Barron's Profile of American Colleges. Barron's Educational Series, Inc., Woodbury, N.Y. 19___. Similar to the College Handbook above. Different style. Ordered alphabetically, which is not as helpful for state-by-state use.

College Blue Book. "Degrees Offered by College and Subject" (a MUST!), "Scholarships, Fellowships, Grants and Loans." These two are part of an expensive three-volume set, but they are well worth it. Macmillan Publishing.

College Times. College Board Publications. $10-15 for 50. A newspaper format with lots of practical helps for students and their parents on choosing a college, financial aid, deadline schedules, etc.

Christian College Handbook. SMS Publications, P.O. Box 1668, Evanston, IL 60204-1668. Usually you pay only the postage for these ($1/copy) and it is an excellent handout for your students. Has a helpful grid showing which colleges have various majors.

Writing Your College Application Essay. College Board Publications, $8-10. A must for students planning to attend colleges where essays are essential. Practical with lots of samples of different types and styles of writing.

America's Best Colleges. U.S. News and World Report, Sisk Fulfillment Services, P.O. Box 463, Federalsbury, MD 21632. An annual listing of colleges by size and type based on a survey of college and university administrators. Every counselor ought to have at least one copy of this in the office.

Peterson's Four-Year Colleges. Peterson's Guides, Dept. 8828, P.O. Box 2123, Princeton, NJ 08543-2123. Similar to other four-year guides listed above.

Consider a Christian College. Peterson's Guides, covers seventy-five Christian colleges of all sorts of persuasions. Helpful, but not as complete as it might be.

Financial Aid

Octameron Associates, P.O. Box 3437, Alexandria, VA 22302. Write for a brochure on their numerous helpful books on everything from Innovative Tuition Plans to Writing Your College Essay. Here are two musts:

The A's and B's of Scholarships. A listing by college of what academic scholarships are available at each school along with their requirements, deadlines, etc. Excellent!

Don't Miss Out. A compilation of information on general financial aid, scholarships from private and little-known sources, co-ops, etc. $8-10.

The College Cost Book. The College Board. Good book, simple to use. Goes out of date quickly, so you may need one every other year at least. Order in tandem with the College Handbook, and you'll save a little bit.

Need a Lift? The American Legion, P.O. Box 1050, IN 46206. $1. Very helpful on both federal aid programs and private sources. Includes a summary of all the states' requirements for residency. Not very well organized, but remember, it only costs a dollar.

How to Finance Your Child's Education. The College Board.

32

College Admission and
Financial Aid Strategies

Wayne MacBeth, Houghton College
David Morley, Westmont College

Wayne MacBeth: Choosing a college is really a process, it's hardly ever a point-in-time decision. We are going to talk about some of the strategies we think would be helpful in thinking about college.

Consider a Christian college

We think it would be wise for an MK to seriously consider attending a Christian college. There are a lot of other options, but we think a Christian college is a good option for several reasons.

1. A world-view which is Christian inside and outside the classroom. A Christian college is committed to the fullest development of the whole person, whereas the secular university or state school to some extent excludes, and in some cases may be antagonistic to, the spiritual.

2. Christian faculty members to work with students, to challenge them, and to affirm them.

   I know a fellow at Houghton who has skirted the edges in terms of rules. He's had some struggles and has been vocal about it. But after three years at Houghton he said, "You know Wayne, it's been rough for me here, but it was a good choice for me, because I needed some structure. I don't think I could have said that or even understood that as a freshman. I know I've stretched to the limit in some cases here, but it's been a good experience for me."

   We did some videotapes recently, and some of the students' testimonies underscored this point about Christian faculty. Again, and again students seemed to indicate that the opportunity to interact with, not just study under, a faculty member is really an ideal arrangement, and can more likely happen in a Christian college than in a large secular one.

3. A Christian student body to provide an opportunity to build relationships and friendships with others of similar values and beliefs. It's important to form friendships in a college context to help solidify your identity and rootedness. One overseas student said to me recently, "In many ways being at Houghton has been like coming to a much larger version of the school that I have been at. I have good opportunities to build relationships with other people." I think that's an important factor that a Christian college can offer.

Consider an accredited college

It is important to consider an accredited college. Graduate schools will not allow, in most cases, students to enter their programs unless they have appropriate degrees from accredited undergraduate colleges. You can usually determine if a college is accredited by simply looking at the information in the school's catalogue.

An accredited school gives you the option of transferring credit from one school to another. If accreditation isn't there, transfer problems can pop up all over the place.

Consider the supportive environment

Think about the supportive environment academically, socially, and spiritually. Academically we think you should look for a well-qualified college, based on information from alumni.

Socially, MKs and many other students are best off if they have some kind of network to plug in to.

The first six weeks of college are really the most critical. If a student makes the transition the first six weeks, he's really on his way. But the first six weeks are also the most volatile. When you work with someone, encourage them not to wait a year but to begin to start right away to plug in—to find a job, to find a friendship or two, to build relationships with others, to become part of a group.

We encourage our currently enrolled MKs to write to the MKs who write to us. Then we get someone else to be in touch with them, too, in order to help them develop a relationship or two even before they arrive on campus.

Spiritually, what is the climate like? It helps most people if they can visit campus, but if you are two to ten thousand miles away, that's very difficult. A videotape is really a nice way to get at least some visual sense of campus, and to hear some student testimonies from a distance. Many people do plan ahead, and whenever they're home on furlough, they take their children to visit campuses. Even if it's early on, ninth or tenth grade, it gives the students some sense of contact. "I've been there. I know a little bit about it."

You can pick up some information about the spiritual climate by asking alumni what it is like. You can look in the catalogue. Do they have a chapel program? What Bible courses are required? What outreach organizations and opportunities for Christian service do they have? Are they voluntary or required? There's much about a college that one cannot pick up from just the catalogue. However, I think you need to start there. The catalogue is very important, and you can use it to preselect.

Consider finances

The MK and his family obviously need to be fiscally responsible in planning. It is possible these days to accumulate a lot of loans. A loan is appropriate as a way to help close the gap. Let's say you get a grant, you get some assistance from the college and the federal government, and you have some family resources. Maybe the loan is that last resort that helps to close the gap. That's fine and can be appropriate, but it has a price tag. It has consequences after graduation, and you have to take those into consideration.

Christian colleges are more sensitive to the needs of the MK than about any other kind of institution. That's another positive reason to consider a Christian college. Even though college education is more expensive than ever before, it is possible for MKs and their families to plan for and fund an education that will be worth what they spend.

Dave Morley: As the expense of higher education continues to escalate, it becomes more and more important to plan ahead. Choosing a college may be one of the most important decisions anyone makes in his lifetime. Colleges are a lot like people. No two colleges are the same. They have personalities all their own. And the nature of the MK requires perhaps even more special care as that whole process of selecting a college takes place. So we would encourage you to encourage kids to think early about that process. By starting early and by gathering all the information, students are going to make the very, very best decision for themselves. It is so sad to meet students who made bad decisions because they didn't have the information.

Many students don't know what their career field is going to be, so the decision about where they are going to go to college becomes very complicated. They become paralyzed because they don't know what to do. We often say to students, "Hey, don't look at this as necessarily a four-year decision, if that's what's paralyzing you. Kids are mobile now. They move around. If you make a mistake, and if you've chosen an accredited college you can take the work that you've earned and move someplace else."

Students need to ask the right questions in choosing a college.

- What about choosing a college that has primary concern for the undergraduate student? If you look at the budget of most of the Christian colleges in the country, you will find that their primary purpose is working with undergraduate students. They're not graduate institutions. Most of them don't have teaching assistants or graduate assistants teaching classes. They have their best faculty teaching undergraduate students.

- Is it a residential college? I think that is of particular importance to the MK.

- Does it take a liberal arts approach to learning? Maybe more than ever before, the importance of a liberal arts college is emerging in terms of a balanced approach to life.

- Is there a deep commitment to the Christian faith?

- Does the school have the vision of producing world Christians?

The purpose of this is not to promote any one college, but to try to get kids to think about asking the right kinds of questions in their college decision process.

Guidelines for College Selection: A Self Directed Search, by Wayne MacBeth, answers many questions regarding the college experience. Let me suggest a few other questions:

- What is the percentage of commuting students on a campus? On many campuses, a large percentage of students leave on the weekend, but MKs are likely to be there seven days a week.

- What is the percentage of students at that college who graduate in four or five years?

- What is the percentage of students going on to graduate school?

- What is the housing availability on a campus?

- What is the typical financial aid package? Can that campus give you an idea of an average financial aid package for all students, and then an average financial aid package for MKs?

(Most are using computers to some extent now, and most can provide that kind of information for you.)   What is the percentage of students receiving financial aid?

- What about the average size of a class?   Faculty-student ratio isn't always an important indicator.   In the State University system in California the faculty-student ratio is about 17 to 1.

Some guides like *The College Handbook*, the Barron's Guide, and Peterson's Guides, will give you some idea of the profile of the student that attends a particular college.

Financial Aid

State residency does mean quite a bit, depending upon the state where the college is located.   In California, if the student's family income is $48,000 or less a year and the student's grade point average in high school is a 2.8 or above, that student automatically qualifies for about $4,600 from the State of California to go to any private college in the state.

Establishing state residency is not a black-and-white issue.   It's a matter of degree.   You need to build a case for your state residency. It's not inappropriate to deliberately make a stateside residence change as long as it is a legitimate change.

You do have to plan ahead to do that, because usually you have to be there for one or two years.   You can write to a financial aid officer at a college in the state you are interested in for information. I would think if he doesn't provide much support, you might not be very interested in that college.

The rules regarding independent students are changing.   Any one who's twenty-four years of age or above is automatically independent.   The guaranteed student loan rules are changing, and it's going to be more difficult to qualify.

Deadlines to remember

First, I think it's pretty important for anybody overseas to obtain their applications to the college they're interested in by December 1 of the year before the fall they want to attend.   The admission office won't see the transcript of the senior year.   That's OK if the student is good academically.   However if there is any question or concern, the application could still be submitted and the transcript from the school could be sent after a semester or a quarter is completed to give some senior year information.

It's an individual issue as far as deadlines on campuses are concerned. Students interested in the University of California have to apply during the month of November. December 2 is too late. They won't get in. The Christian colleges encourage you to apply in the fall, but some will certainly take applications later than the month of December.

MacBeth: The second deadline that I'd really emphasize concerns financial aid. A lot of the Federal and State programs are open-ended. If you're eligible you will receive it. But institutional money does run out after a certain point in time. Early on you will get the maximum aid that you will be eligible for.

It makes sense to apply in the fall so that in the spring, you can obtain the FAF (Financial Aid Form) and mail it. This will be the basic document to mail to the school you're interested in. Even if your family has to estimate income, you ought to try to get it in the mail by February.

You really can't know what financial aid you might be eligible for until you apply. The important thing is choosing a college where you really think you're going to grow the most as a person, choosing a college where you really feel the Lord wants you, and then applying for financial aid and seeing what's possible.

33

Understanding MKs: Why Their Actions (Sometimes) Don't Fit

Edie Bakker
Wycliffe MK, Papua New Guinea

Sometimes returned missionary children exhibit behavior which is socially unacceptable or inappropriate in the United States. What is not always noticed is that much of this behavior may be perfectly acceptable and even admired or respected in an MK's subculture on the field where he was raised. The same action which is considered normal overseas may, in the U.S. culture, appear irresponsible, immature, offensive, or even emotionally unstable.

Many times wrong conclusions are made in counseling MKs because of the inability of the counselor to recognize the MK's inappropriate actions as being based on his different ethics, rather than being psychological problems or abnormalities. *Ethics* is defined in *Webster's Dictionary* as "beliefs which deal with good and evil or moral duty and practice." Ethics determine his moral alternatives. *Values*, by contrast, are things a person "prizes, esteems, or rates highly, things he believes to be a better alternative." I will be focusing on behavior based on ethics.

Counselors are trained to look for personal conflicts which may be causing a person to act inappropriately. When the person is of a different culture, however, his actions may not be the results of personal conflict at all. They may, in fact, be perfectly acceptable, if not the only moral alternative for someone with his background.

To try to find a reason behind the culturally different MK's behavior other than good conscience or belief can compound his problem of adjustment drastically by causing the MK to think he is sinning when he is really doing what he believes is right. This is a major source of false guilt for the MK. If he listens to the advice that his behavior is wrong, he will feel guilty whatever he does. This is because what is right in the new culture is wrong in his mind, and what is right in his own culture, in his mind and conscience, now becomes wrong! Are you confused? So is the kid.

When this situation is repeated often enough, it may cause him to feel that he cannot do anything right. In addition to the obvious drastic effect this will have on his self-esteem, the feeling of not ever being able to do what is right is for many people a first step away from faith in God.

A person's ethics may be very deep and difficult to change. In addition to being directly tied to his sense of morality, they are usually hidden in his subconscious. For example, most Americans would not be able to say why they think it is important to work hard for one's pay when one can receive enough money to live by other legal means such as welfare or grants. Yet this ethic is so deeply ingrained in them that to purposely do otherwise would be a serious breach of conscience. Before choosing to leave work and live on welfare, most Americans would probably need to think through why they believe they should work for their money, and why they could or should change that belief.

The MK is in that same position when he must try to live differently than the way he believes, in order to live appropriately in the new culture. The problem is compounded by the fact that his subculture is not just any culture. It is missionary subculture. Therefore, he is even more convinced that his ideas are the closest to the gospel truth.

Here are some examples of misunderstood behavior based on different MK ethics and values. They are fictional in that I did not want to copy any one person, but these are things I have seen many times.

Jim — Ethic

Jim is a twenty-year-old in his second year of college. He returned to the United States at eighteen. He is about to lose his fourth job because of his habit of continually skipping work. He usually spends this time with his friends, particularly with his girlfriend Nancy, with whom he does not even claim to be serious.

Jim's parents' and/or a counselor's incorrect conclusions might be:

1. Jim is not interested in his job and has been unable to find his true interests and settle down.

2. Because of a very low self-esteem (possibly due to living in children's homes or the absence of parents), he is seeking love from his friends and girl to the extent that he is neglecting his other responsibilities.

3. He is lazy and is leading Nancy on, living a carefree and irresponsible life.

4. He is bitter at his parents for having left him and is therefore subconsciously retaliating by being careless about his responsibilities.

5. He was never given enough experience at a regular job on the field and so does not know what is expected of him.

6. He has always had money given to him and so does not comprehend having to work for it now.

Many of these conclusions are logical and could sometimes be true. In Jim's case, however, as in many MK cases, the reason behind his behavior is a common MK ethic. Jim is acting according to his deep convictions, and to act differently at this point would cause much guilt and confusion.

Jim's ethic: People's needs always come before work. Never neglect a need in a relationship for the sake of material gain or secular responsibilities. While work is important, it is not usually as important as the needs of friends. (I have asked many MKs how they feel about some of the ethics I have written, and they agree, "That's what I was thinking and I didn't know how to express it.")

Explanation: This ideology carried to Jim's extent may seem ridiculous from our cultural point of view, but consider the following:

1. As Jim grew up observing his parents, he watched them regularly and consistently interrupt important translation work because a friend (villager) needed to buy a mosquito net for his new baby, wanted advice about selling his coffee, or asked them to come to a party (cultural feast). The work was gladly set aside for this aspect of ministry, which in Jim's eyes was only meeting the needs of one's friends.

2. The people among whom Jim's parents worked very likely believed relationships should come before work, since almost all tribal peoples do.

3. Jim's understanding was then solidified by the talk of grown-ups and Sunday sermons on the importance of relating to people this way and its effect in spreading the Gospel.

4. Jim's belief was further solidified by his understanding of Scripture, because those verses which stood out to him were

those which made the most sense from his cultural view. For example, the Sermon on the Mount lists important aspect of Christianity, all of which deal with relationships, not self-provision, and indicate that this is the real way to have your needs met.

Matthew 5:23-24 states, "If any of you has aught against a brother . . . go to him immediately." The implication there is to drop everything for the sake of a relationship. Other verses on the relative value of work vs. relationships include Matthew 8:28, Matthew 22:39-40, Mark 14:3-9, Luke 10:38-42, and I Timothy 6:10.

It could be especially difficult to see that Jim's behavior is primarily motivated by his conscience if any or all of the following situations occur:

1. Jim himself may not have any idea why he believes it is more important to meet his friends' needs than to remain at work every day, just as an American doesn't know why he believes the opposite.

2. Jim may not be a very spiritually-oriented person, so it may be difficult to imagine that he is basing his actions on something that he believes is morally right. Still there are a lot of nominal Christians who act on what they believe is morally correct.

3. Jim may indeed have problems in his life (perhaps even some of those listed earlier) which may cause him to behave inappropriately even from his own cultural point of view.

To add to the confusion, Jim's values or ethics could be causing him to behave inappropriately in several areas at a given time. He may be exhibiting a whole range of inappropriate behavior at once, giving the illusion that his problems are quite severe. All of these things could make it extremely difficult to see that Jim's behavior may be the result of his very deep and not easily changeable convictions.

Mary — Value

Mary is an eighteen-year-old MK in her first year of college. She seldom dresses up and is mostly seen in jeans. She has only had a trim, never had a real haircut. Her face is never made up, and she docs not wash her hair frequently. It occasionally appears oily.

Possible conclusions of her pastor or relatives

1. Mary doesn't care about herself at all and is suffering from low self esteem.

2. Mary has not been taught how to take proper care of herself.

3. Mary is exhibiting typical teenage rebellion against society.

4. Mary is obviously miserable inside as shown by her unkempt appearance and is probably not right with the Lord. (Many kids have told me they have heard that last one.)

Although these answers might be true in some instances, the chances are that, since Mary is an MK, she is just acting according to her own convictions.

Mary's value: Beauty is found on the inside, not on the outside. Outward appearance is unimportant or is at least a lower priority than many other things.

Explanation:

1. As a child, Mary may have had only second hand clothes. If she was raised in a village, her parents may have found many activities to be far more important than choosing what their little girl should wear. Her clothes may have been far better than any the nationals wore. Meticulous combing of one's hair has little purpose in the jungle. (This does not constitute suffering. She would agree with her parents that these were not important.)

2. Later at school, none of her friends could afford to get haircuts or makeup. Neither did they see it as important since there was no TV to bombard them with glamorous made-up images. In a small close group with little outside pressure, competition for popularity tends to depend more on behavior than on looks. For Mary, this meant that at school knowing what to say, when, and to whom, was what attracted friends, not how one dressed.

3. Parents on the center paid little attention to looks and there were no aunts or grandmas to say "My word, how pretty you are in that outfit today!"

4. This became an even stronger value in light of her understanding of Scripture. I Peter 3:3-4 says, "You should not use outward aids to make yourselves beautiful.... Instead your beauty should consist of your true inner self, the ageless beauty of a gentle and quiet spirit, which is of greatest value in God's sight." Other Scriptures on the same theme include, I Samuel 16:7, Isaiah 3:16-24, and Matthew 6:25-30.

Although Mary could be unhappy inside, or rebellious, or uneducated, it should be realized that Mary's way of dressing reflects a cultural value and not her state of mind. (In fact for Mary, dressing up may be a sign of rebellion, just as it was among American Christians two generations ago!) Many MKs feel there are more important things to do than to spend an hour in front of the mirror every morning. For instance, one could spend the time in devotions or in extra sleep before a long day.

Evaluating MK Behavior

One major complication involved in analyzing an MK's ethics, values, and therefore his motivation, is that MKs come from many different backgrounds and subcultures. Each missionary takes on a few of the host country's values, and each mission adds its denominational views. Children are especially apt to pick these up since their minds are still in the developing process. The result of this multicultural situation is that it is impossible to describe exactly what any particular MK may value or believe. Further complicating the issue is the question of just how "MK" an MK is. An MK who has had a short stay on an overseas field would naturally remain far more American in his beliefs than one who had been raised overseas.

In both of the examples above, normal counsel could have dangerous results since Mary or Jim could be led to feel bad about the way they are. In order for them to change, they must first be accepted as they are, and then be shown biblical or logical reasons why a new way of acting may be better in this cultural setting.

The MK could also be shown gently and objectively, using as much concrete evidence as possible why his action is inappropriate. However, depending on the strength of his convictions, it may still take time and prayer before he is ready to throw out the old way. In fact, often a compromise solution is best, rather than a complete change, since the MK's belief may indeed be the more scriptural, and may be of real value to society. Thus a knowledge of some of the ethics and values commonly governing MK behavior can be useful for improving one's understanding of MKs, even though it cannot be used as a guide for diagnosing specific causes of behavior.

Viewing the MK's behavior as different rather than wrong will help him to put it in the proper perspective so that instead of seeing himself as a failure he can see his lifestyle as perhaps inappropriate in the new setting. This frees him to change since it is not personally threatening, and it also frees him to let God work since he can approach the matter with a clear conscience.

It could be useful to MKs to study their own ethics and values and to think about why they believe the way they do. In doing so, they will grow in those areas in which their perspective is correct, and they will also be able to see for themselves how certain of their beliefs might not apply in the United States. Such a study can bring much spiritual growth, wherever one is from, as one carefully considers what part of his belief system actually comes from God and what parts are simply cultural.

This is the story of Jim as if I were relating it to a fellow MK: Jim is a twenty-year-old in his second year of college. He has had four different jobs because of some misunderstandings with his boss and being laid off when there was not enough work. Jim's friend Nancy has been having a real hard time lately. She has trouble with homework and has been misunderstood at church. Several times she has needed help that only Jim could give. No one else could understand her. Knowing he could trust God to provide for his financial needs, he took off time from work to help her. Jim's not sure why everyone keeps asking if he and Nancy are serious. He really hasn't thought about the future at all, and he doesn't see her as nearly so close a friend as the friends he has had in the past. He is concerned about her as a sister. His taking time out to help her has nothing to do with romance.

Sue — Values

Here's another common example, which shows how long this can go on and how several things work together. Sue is a young married adult MK and has always had lots of friends on the field. Now she has a few acquaintances who call her occasionally on the phone. However, no one ever comes to her house or does anything with her, so she feels very unpopular. A few times someone asked her to lunch at a restaurant, but as both she and her friends were on a tight budget she thought this was a strange thing to suggest, so she declined, stating that she could not afford to go out. Getting up all of her courage, she decided to go back to the way she had always made friends in the past. She tried walking up to someone's door and knocking. When Jill answered the door, she was extremely embarrassed and kept apologizing about not having vacuumed. Finally after some awkward silence, Sue left apologetically. Jill never returned the call. Sue tried this two more times with other friends and gave up.

Values in conflict

- The American value of casual friendships versus the MK's desire for very deep friendship in which you can share very personal issues.

- Time values would include making an appointment, but an MK would drop a business appointment for a friend.

- Calling ahead versus knocking on doors unexpectedly.

- Eating out versus doing something that is free. Most MKs, when they first come back, are not used to doing anything that costs money. They wouldn't consider eating out a form of recreation.

- Avoiding uncomfortable relationships versus confronting. The friends didn't call back, and say, "You came over to my house and that really hurt me because I wasn't ready. I don't understand why you did that." That would have given the MK some idea of where she had gone wrong, so she wouldn't have done it two more times.

What Can Happen When the MK is Misunderstood

I'd like to show you what you can do to help with this problem, to alleviate it, and how far it can go.

First Year — Stage A

Activity: Going to a party, the MK doesn't bring money. Everybody decides to go out for pizza, but he doesn't have the money for pizza.

American response: They think he's a freeloader or poor.

Activity: The MK is invited to relatives' for dinner. Afterwards the relatives are sitting around watching football. The MK gets up and excuses himself and leaves.

The MK felt like the activity was over and now they were snubbing him. It's as if you're having a conversation with someone, and all of a sudden you pick up a novel and start reading. "What is it? They don't want me here? Why didn't they tell me to go home?"

American response: They think he's a snob or antisocial.

Activity: At a church picnic the other kids are playing ball, eating and talking about records, but the MK is canoeing, hiking and feeding the animals. The MK may be very good at canoeing. He may not be good at other very simple things like skating.

American response: They think he's a show-off, or they feel jealous.

Second Year — Stage B

He's now into his second year. What would be the response of the MK as a result of the response he got during his first year here?

He's going to experience some frustrations and a little bit of rebellion. He feels people don't like him. He's going to want to pull away and do more of his type of activity because he still doesn't understand what's happening. They're not communicating to him what he's doing wrong.

Now, instead of walking out during the football game when his relatives invite him over, he simply turns down the dinner invitation and says, "I've got an exam tomorrow."

Since he is not good at skating or bowling, he finally gets together with other MKs and takes off on a motorcycle trip for about six weeks. They travel around the country. It could be something besides motorcycles. I know kids who have hiked across America. Guys may get into daring stunts like sky diving, because they're feeling frustrated. They did some pretty neat things on the field, but now they're just the kid on the block that can't skate.

Girls are not free to express this as well because they can't go out on their own. The MKs I've talked to agree that you can't see this stage in MK girls as well. They feel it, and it hurts them. I think that's why girls sometimes end up more emotionally damaged because they can't get out and do these things. They may go to another church or not go to young people's meetings.

Another possibility is that MKs will get involved with off-the-wall groups. Anyone I have seen getting involved in a cult or strange group has been at this stage.

What would be some American response to Stage B behavior?

- *Push him away.*
- *"He doesn't like us."*
- *"He is socially maladjusted, rebellious."*
- *"Let him go. He's not worth the effort."*
- *"Let's have a prayer meeting for him."*
- *"Cliquish with MKs."*
- *"Irresponsible."*

After Three or Four Years — Stage C

Real psychological problems now exist in Stage C. Now every time he walks into church people are praying for him and nobody is understanding him. He's going to start saying, "I'm different. I don't fit in anywhere."

By now he's not thinking "I fit in back on the field." He's just thinking, "I don't fit." He's asking, "What can I do with my talents and my future?" He's feeling a loss of self esteem because of all the criticism.

What's the American reaction to seeing a kid with these types of feelings and problems?

- *They avoid him.*
- *"He's not a Christian." They can't see any fruits of the Spirit.*
- *"He has lots of emotional conflicts to resolve." They're not going to see them as cultural conflicts.*
- *"He's not normal; he's strange."*

In order to understand what happens next, the biggest ethic that I have found to differ between MKs and Americans is that Americans measure success by money or lifestyle. MKs feel that success is defined by doing something well or adjusting well.

If a non-missionary were to contemplate a job overseas, he would ask himself, "Is the lifestyle going to work out?" Or, "How much money will I make?" Those are going to be the criteria as to whether or not he goes overseas. The MK would ask, "How well am I going to adjust when I move?" and "How well will I do at the job?" I think both criteria are worldly, and they strongly govern what we do. An MK looks more at fame, and an American looks more at fortune.

Now, the MK who doesn't fit in has lost his self-esteem. He doesn't know what he's going to do with his future. Everybody's telling him he needs therapy. He didn't adjust well. He's going to feel that he is a failure at his two goals in life, doing something well and adjusting well. This is where some of them do end up having a nervous breakdown or wanting to give up.

We have a gracious God, and he prevents most kids from going this far. But that's the direction they're headed.

Ways to Respond to the MK

We can see how at any point we can cut back this process, if not stop it completely. Instead of looking at him as a snob or antisocial, understand that the problem is cultural. We can provide some MK activities that he can do so he can get an occasional respite and feel comfortable.

- Get some MKs together and let them have a canoe race.
- Give him an opportunity to learn some of those sports which the other Americans are doing, without being embarrassed.

If you're the only one in the bowling league that doesn't know where to put your fingers, that can be terribly embarrassing. If you take MKs out and teach them to bowl, you can give them a head start.

- In every phase, always expect the best of people. That comes from I Corinthians 13:7.

- Be patient, or explain to him what he's doing wrong.

- Look for things that you can learn from him. Instead of looking down on him because of his cultural differences, accept him. He is going to adjust. It might take awhile, but he is going to eventually. Just by accepting him you can keep him from going further into the cycle.

- If he is in the second stage provide MK activities. I think they need this escape. Let them plan a cave exploring trip or something.

- We need education for them. Re-entry seminars explain what Americans are doing. It is hard for Americans to explain that. You almost need an older MK that has fought against the different values one at a time and says, "Oh this is what they mean by that."

- Again, expect the best of them.

34

Transitional Missionary Kids

Grace Barnes, Russ Cline, Esther Whitaker
Azusa Pacific University

Grace Barnes: In this session we are going to talk about the trip the MK takes from birth through life. Our main focus on this trip will be Re-entryville. The City of the Fifth Dimension is our origin.

City of the Fifth Dimension

As human beings we all live in a three dimensional world. The fourth dimension represents cross-cultural, international, and world experiences which many who travel, or who live overseas incorporate into their lives. The fifth dimension is unique to the MK, and profoundly impacts the other dimensions of his life. Some characteristics of this fifth dimension are:

- **The birthmark of the MK** is the overlying spiritual environment that the MK is born into.
- **The compound view of life.** Traditionally missionaries have lived in some sort of group which the MK feels a part of. The compound view of life can sometimes communicate separateness from the national, perhaps a superiority. A lot of times a missionary will feel very rich in an international community and very poor at home. These messages can present problems to MKs as they grow up.
- **"Hand-me-down" faith** is the experience of the MK in a world where there are lots of right answers, high standards, and expectations with strong spiritual values. The MK senses that a he must be good and conform throughout his life. Sometimes this can produce a supersaturation, a sense of wanting to be released and a tendency to want to break away. All of us have needed to process our faith through

questioning and doubting. The MK needs to know that this is OK and is a part of his own cognitive development.

- **The MK image** comes from the belief that MKs have certain characteristics, qualities and attitudes. Often the missionary has been put on some kind of pedestal by churches at home and by the national. The MK may feel he has to live up to those expectations, too.

Esther Whitaker: When someone says, "I'm an MK," immediately a picture comes to mind, and with it, certain expectations. Recently I did a small survey of college MKs to find out some of the expectations they felt were placed on them:

Expectations of parents

- *I am expected to be an example! Everything I do reflects my parents' ministry. If I do something wrong it could affect the nationals. I'm very much held up as an example. It puts a lot of pressure on me.*
- *Do well academically.*
- *Be involved in youth group and church.*
- *Love the church.* (I didn't like going to church when I was a kid. Sorry.)

Expectations of "home" church

- *They expect me to be like my parents and be a missionary.*
- *I'm categorized with my parents and not allowed to be a 'normal' American kid.*
- *I'm expected to be all together, definitely strong in the Lord and not have any problems.*

Expectations of the missionary community

- *It was expected of us to be good and do well. Therefore, it was hard for me to be honest when I had doubts or questions about spiritual things.*
- *I often felt there was a tendency to spiritualize my problems.*

Expectations of peers in the United States

- *I sometimes feel like a rare gem that is to be polished and looked at. They want to hear stories. Some do care.*
- *I'm expected to be stronger spiritually than my peers.*
- *I'm expected to have it all together emotionally and spiritually.*

MKs' impressions of God

Many MKs have very positive feelings about God. Even if they were working through some questions, they still felt that he was there as a provider, a protector—very real and personal.

MKs impression of life as an MK

- *I loved it!*
- *I'm very glad to have grown up overseas as a missionary kid.*
- *It was adventurous.*
- *It was a positive experience.*
- *On the whole I liked it.*
- *The positives greatly outweighed the negatives.*

MKs' thoughts about future missionary service

I asked them, "Would you like to be a missionary?" Their responses were mostly the same, and reflect my feelings also:

> *"I'd be open to being a missionary. I don't necessarily feel that's what I'm called to right now, but if the Lord were to call me, I would be open to it."*

Re-entryville

Barnes: As he gets to Re-entryville, the MK tends to experience culture shock and college shock together.

College shock is that phenomenon which takes place within the family between parent and child when a kid goes off to school. There are many changes that take place during this move from dependence to independence. Tendencies are that if a child has grown up in a very rigid, authoritarian background and is then set free, some very strong counterdependent things will take place.

When culture shock takes place along with college shock, it can be quite painful. There's a lot of leave-taking. There are a lot of new beginnings, a lot of things to learn, and there can be a loneliness.

Culture shock/college shock

Russ Cline: My freshman year was miserable. I went to school to be with my brother, but he went to the mission field for six months and left me there all by myself. It was tragic.

My culture shock/college shock did not hit me until I came home to Ecuador for Christmas my freshman year. The family was all excited to see me. I was an adult now, coming back to my home town. But all of a sudden, I didn't have a car to drive, because it was Mom and Dad's car. I'd never been able to drive in Ecuador before, but I thought, "Since I'm an adult, I'll be able to drive."

I was back with all my friends from high school. Some were still in high school, and some had come back for Christmas. All of a sudden, I found that I was a kid again. That was great, but the six months of growing I had done meant nothing.

When I went back to school after Christmas, I suffered my college shock and my culture shock. I asked myself, "Where do I belong? Where do I go? What do I do?"

I realized I had to make a decision. I decided that my home was going to be the school for the next four years. I decided I needed to be involved in things and make friends. I decided I needed to learn to be independent. After that, I began to feel that I could be myself. I felt like the transition went really smoothly.

Whitaker: I had a really hard first year. In fact, I hated it. I did go to college right away, but I didn't enjoy where I was. I missed many of my friends. It seemed to me like everybody had somebody. I was very lonely. After that first year, I ended up going to another school. Everything went smoother. I was more willing to accept the United States and what it had to offer, too. I'm American, but I was very prejudiced against Americans when I first came. It was neat to realize that my prejudice was leaving and to realize that I was not such a wonderful person. I just had a different experience, and I'm really grateful for that. Now I have some very close American friends.

Barnes: Statistics show that during their first semester, most students determine whether they are going to stay in college or not. Fifty percent do not finish college. The crucial time for the MK is that first year, and primarily that first semester. Our support systems need to be strong in those first few months. Some MKs have a tendency to want to go back to where they're from, or to isolate themselves. Others become so involved in the new that they reject where they've come from. It's difficult not to do that. It's almost like you have to say, "I've got to say good-bye to the past for awhile so I can get into the present." During those times it's important to have good support people who understand some of what is going on.

College is a time to be in a neutral zone. You're not totally responsible for your life yet, and you can have a good time. But you're also learning a lot and trying to determine what direction you're going. With graduation shock, you're dealing with "Where am I going to live? What kind of a job am I going to get?"—all of the things that mean setting up life in a world where you're going to have to leave most of the friends you made in college. If parents and family are a long way away, it can be difficult.

Vocationland

As we move from graduation shock into Vocationland, we start dealing with, "What am I going to do with my life?" Generally speaking the MKs tend to incorporate their world experience into their life work, even if it's not a missionary calling. They seem to get involved somehow with international people, and use that background. Some love to travel. There is a strong service component to growing up in the missionary community.

We forget sometimes that vocation is a process. If we're partners with God in this world to further the Kingdom, it's going to take on a lot of different expressions. If Naisbitt, the author of *Megatrends*, is correct, we will change careers several times in our lifetimes. We are going to continually need to be educated and trained for new things. Starting out on this journey of vocation can be a scary thing. We need to help kids learn to develop their own support systems. A lot of times we expect the support system to come to us. It's not so important where you live, as who you have as your support system.

Cline: I decided at a very young age that I wanted to go into the ministry, not knowing what that was. I was probably four when I made that decision. Throughout my lifetime, having incredible parents as role models, I saw ministry and serving God as a very positive experience. I don't remember a point in my life when I didn't believe that was something I wanted to do. So I went to college and became a religion major.

I got to the middle of my junior year, and all of a sudden I thought, "Whoa! Is this something that I for sure want to do? Have I even looked at other things?" So I decided to take an accounting class, because I was a disaster at accounting. I found out I loved business. My last year, I finished my religion and took all business classes and picked up a double major in business administration.

I got to March of my senior year asking, "What am I going to do? Do I want to go into religion, which is something that I've wanted to do all my life? Or do I want to go into business, which is something that I've learned that I love?" Through a lot of prayer and counseling from friends and support groups, I decided that my calling was really in the ministry. But I find that the business side has really helped me in my calling.

I'm a youth pastor in a church in Los Angeles. It's everything I expected, but there are a lot of other things that I didn't expect. One is that I'm scared to death about settling down. This is the first time I've felt like trying to establish a home. I live on my own. Trying to afford an apartment in the San Fernando Valley is incredible. During college, you have financial aid and parents and missions organizations that send you money. But then it's just incredible when you don't have that income.

Finances is one of the biggest things I struggle with. As missionary kids growing up, we had everything we ever needed, but not always everything we wanted. All of our lives we lived from people giving us money. All of a sudden I have to earn my money, and it's a different thing. I go to church, and I want to pass the offering plate and take the money home. It doesn't work that way any more. That was something that was very hard for me. I realized that if I was going to survive, literally survive, by putting food on my table and gas in my car, and paying my phone bill, I had to work for it. That's something that I didn't understand until now.

The other thing I struggle with is in the area of friends. My friends from Alliance Academy are spread all over the United States, all over the world. We still have a unique bond. We call each other and support each other and pray with each other. All of us have reached the graduation point, and all of us are in different areas. One of my best friends is a pilot. He lives in Chicago. He said, "Russ, after four years of college, what I really want to do is come out to California and be independent for about a year. I want to get on a motorcycle and travel. I want to play. I want to experience things, because I feel like we've been locked in for four years. Let's go out and play."

Then I called another friend who just joined a missions agency and is working in Spain. He said, "Russ, with your talents, you need to think about full-time service. Don't waste time. You need to go back to school or get into the ministry right away."

I find myself asking, "What am I going to do?" I love what I'm doing, but at the same time, I want to play. I want to get some other experiences. I miss travelling. I have to work hard to get to Ecuador for Christmas for a couple of weeks or to get excuses to get off work. That's really tough.

It's so frustrating for me working and trying to make a living. I'm working in a church that supports missionaries, but that's the extent of their ministry. Do I stay there and work it out so I get experience and time, or do I need to get out? Do I need to find a missions organization I can work with. Do I need to find another church? What do I do?

I feel pressure from people saying, "Come back to the missions field, Russ," or "Russ, if you go back, it's a cop-out." The easiest thing for me to do would be to go to the mission field right now. That's where my heart is, and that's where part of my talents and skills are. Do I need to take that easy step, or do I need to stick it out?

Whitaker: I remember just a little before graduation my parents saying, "Well, honey, you're on your own." They did help me afterwards, and I knew they would, but it's knowing you have to provide for yourself. I don't like it.

I just continued working where I had been in school. I've had a ball. Being an MK has given me a real feeling for the internationals I work with. I'm thankful for my parents' teaching me about Jesus Christ. That is essential to me, and I'm thankful for that.

Right now I'm wondering what I'm going to be doing. I have this restlessness inside of me. I love to travel. I love to be with people and have a chance to see what's inside of them. I'm open to going to other countries. But in my heart, I want to work with internationals. I love them very much. I'm interested in the Moslem world, but that can be a dangerous world. I'm wondering if I'm really willing to sacrifice my life. I don't know. I'm in a time of questioning and change.

Developing a Support System

Barnes: A support system ties into how well you are able to relate to people quickly. It also has to do with the ability to know who you are and what you have to offer. Wherever I go, I start developing friendships where I am. I find people who are attracted to me and that I am attracted to, and I develop those relationships. They end up becoming a support base. Also, if there are people, like MKs, that I am concerned about, I will introduce myself as a support person. If they want to take advantage of that, fine. If they don't, they don't have to.

Cline: One of the toughest things my MK friends and I faced in college was not having a support system. Everyone needs to have a support system. It takes a lot of time. You're not going to develop a relationship with people and have them be a support system right away. It took me four years to get a group of four guys. We have met every week for the last three-and-a-half years. Because of all that time together, we're as close as can be. That's my strongest support system anywhere. We all know relationships take a lot of time. You need to be willing to invest that time. The beginning is always tough. You'll want to cancel out; you'll want to skip a week. It's like doing devotions. It's hard to have the discipline to do it, but it pays off in the long run.

A lot of missionary kids have those groups in high school, but we separate and go all over the world. We wonder, "Is that support group still there?" Most of us discover that it still is. When we happen to run into somebody at a conference or in the airport, we realize that that relationship and bond are still there. Because we've put in the time and commitment, the love will always be there.

Whitaker: I encourage people to introduce themselves and believe in themselves and continue pushing until people start to respond. Eventually they do, because we all have good qualities.

Barnes: In a missionary family who has lived totally by faith and had everything given to them, there can be the tendency for the MK to believe, "I'm always going to be taken care of by someone else." That can be a false illusion. We need to help our students even before they get to school to realize that no one in life is obligated to be their friend. The first time I went to a Young Life staff conference, I figured people ought to come up to me and make me feel welcome. Nobody knew that I was new. Somebody said, "You just have to go up to people and let them know who you are and that you're here. Then they'll be very open and welcome and supportive of you."

I think what we need to do as supporters and companions is to allow kids to go through a process. Let us encourage them to take advantage of their past, as they attempt to make the present and the future an honest expression of all God has given them.

35

Loneliness and Life Adjustment

Lynn Moss
Wingate College

What is loneliness? It has been described by some as a state of dejection or grief caused by being alone. But do you always have to be alone to experience loneliness? I don't think so. Others have proposed that it is caused by a need for companionship or an intimate relationship. Robert Wyse divided it into two categories. There are some who experience an emotional loneliness, which is the lack of intimate contact with another. This can happen after a divorce, a separation from a loved one, the death of a loved one, or the end of a dating relationship. Social loneliness, on the other hand is experienced when a network is missing from your life; you don't really have roots.

In Western society in particular, the fear of loneliness more than actual loneliness gets people into a state of frenzy. Many times people will overschedule every moment. How many people do you know whose every waking moment is filled with activities?

Many people try to numb their senses. Rather than feeling aloneness, they'll watch television, or turn on the music. How many people do you know who as soon as they walk into the apartment turn on the TV? You ask them, "Why do you turn on the TV?" "Just for the noise."

How many people do you know who try to numb their senses with alcohol, drugs or food? There are so many ways we try to disguise these feelings of loneliness and try to overcome them.

One of the most difficult and significant transitions in the Western world is that from adolescence to adulthood. It entails moving from an age graded society to a social status graded society. It's a time when you move from needing acceptance by parents to needing acceptance by peers. Adolescence is a critical time of life regarding loneliness.

In college, there is a continued struggle for identity. For many students, it is their first experience away from home, and loneliness is compounded. One study showed that seventy-five percent of all college students polled said they were lonely. Many times your popularity, your standing in the community, your athletic achievements, your academic achievements are meaningless when you go from being a big fish in a small pond to being a very small fish in a very large pond.

There are actually three levels of loneliness that a TCK can experience: first, the adolescent transition; secondly, the experience of starting college; and third, the adjustment to a new culture where they don't know anyone. In my study, I found that MKs not only experienced the same problems that international students did, but in many cases had even more. In the areas of church, social, personal development, financial planning, and student activities, they were equal to or had more problems than international students. They were much more lonely than American students but experienced about the same amount of loneliness as international students.

Themes of Re-entry

Robert Downey identified five themes of re-entry in his dissertation:

Social identification

When I was standing in the registration line at Mars Hill College, I was feeling rather depressed because I had just left home and had to come back to the U.S. by myself. A girl in front of me turned and we started up a conversation. She said, "Where are you from?"

Not wanting to be too proud I said softly, "Zambia."

She said, "I know how that is. I'm from a small town, too."

"Where are you from?" is a Catch-22 question. You know you're either going to appear cocky, or you're going to be kind of strange.

A hesitation in relationships

You don't want to get too close, so you wait a little, because there's no telling when you'll have to leave or when they will leave.

Culture shock

Culture shock is a loss of a sense of when to do what. I had no idea who Ronald McDonald was when I started college. The other kids looked at me as if I had come from the moon instead of just

Africa when I admitted that. I stopped admitting things after awhile.
I learned. Never admit that you don't know something. Just smile.

The pervasive influence of the third culture

Third-culture kids lived in a social world that is relatively
enclosed. You identify most closely with those people who are peri-
patetic, who are global nomads.

Pinpointing home and roots

"Where are you really from? We know you grew up in Africa,
but where are you really from?"

Grief Process

Actually having to leave what many MKs and TCKs consider to
be where they're really from, the home where they grew up, precipitates a very deep grieving process. Sometimes it's ignored. I know I
ignored it for years. This process is very much like the process experienced by people who lose a loved one. The first thing that they go
through is shock.

My parents told me, "Lynn, you have to go to the States
to go to college. You are not going to the University of
Nairobi."

"Please let me."

"You can't."

In the back of my mind I thought, "Maybe the airport will
blow up, or something tragic will happen and I won't be able to
leave. I'm not really going." I got on the plane and suddenly
realized, "I'm leaving. I'm really leaving." I didn't want to say
good-bye because I thought, "There's an outside chance that I
really may not be leaving."

I faced reality when I was on the plane to Charlotte,
North Carolina. When I got off the plane, I had gone through
that whole reality stage. Twenty-eight hours gave me plenty of
time to think. I got there and realized that this was really real.
I moved quickly into the anger stage.

I got off the plane and met my grandparents and said,
"Look, get used to it. I'm only going to be here four years.
You can't keep me any longer than that. I'm an African. I'm
going back. I know I have to go to college here, but don't get
used to me being around."

My attitude was, "My parents made me come to college,
but I don't have to like it."

Manifestations of anger

Many times anger can be manifested as hurt, frustration, guilt, or fear of rejection. The presence of anger is not bad. In fact, many times it is needed to get into the actual grieving. It is so much healthier to go through the process of grieving than to repress it for years and then have it suddenly explode. Many times MKs will experience anger, and it will be focussed in a variety of places. They'll be angry at:

- Their parents. I was so angry at my parents for making me leave home.

- Their country where they grew up. "It's your fault I'm different. Why did you make me different?"

- Ministers and the church. "They are not really Christians. All they care about is their pews or the color of the choir robes."

- The United States. "This is a terrible place. It is so materialistic."

- Their friends. "They don't understand."

- God. "Why did you take my parents overseas so I had to grow up different?"

- Self. It comes out in a tremendous feeling of guilt, which is acted out in a variety of ways. Many people get caught in this anger stage. Sometimes it's manifested in sleeping, overactivity, being overly religious, being underly religious, or being involved in drinking, drugs, or promiscuity. They may be angry but are not able to put a handle on what makes them so angry.

Suggestion for Care Givers

What can care givers do for the MK who is experiencing transition and the loneliness that accompanies transition?

- Encourage them to take a trip home and visit some of those places, encourage them to say those final good-byes, to go ahead and cry.

- Listen to them. More than anything else, MKs, just like other people, need to be listened to. They need to be able to vent some of their anger. Listen without judging.

- Don't expect spiritual giants. I struggled with my own relationship with the Lord. I wondered when I got here,

"Maybe I was a Christian just because my parents are missionaries. Maybe I'm really not one. Maybe I went forward because all ten-year-olds go forward in our mission during the revival."

- Give them a place to get away. Give them a place where they have a den, a fireplace, a dog, and no pressure. Just a place to go to get away without being hassled, without having to answer questions, without having to be anything. That's probably one of the most important things that someone could do for an MK.

- Give them a place to go for Thanksgiving or vacations, especially if their parents are not home. Research has shown that MKs adjust better in the first year of college when their parents are home or when they have an older brother or sister to whom they can go when they have questions. Be someone that they can go to for answers to questions about American life.

- Let them borrow your car after they get their drivers license.

- Take them shopping. Find out what the college students are wearing.

- Take them to sporting events.

- Be there.

Mindset Affects Vision

Many times we enter situations with certain mindsets. Look around the room and name five things that are blue. You notice how blue jumps out at you when you have a blue mindset? I just bought a Peugeot, and suddenly I notice all of them on the road. When you learn a new word, you suddenly notice everybody is using this word. How come you never noticed it before? When you have a certain mindset, you will find what you are looking for. This is what I want to tell MKs. You will find what you are looking for. If you come back to the States thinking, "These Americans are so shallow, this is going to be such a bad experience for me; I'm not ready; I don't think that Americans are wonderful Christians," you will find what you expect. You will hear those racist comments. You will hear comments demonstrating myopic vision among your peers. You'll ask, "Wow, don't they care about what's going on in the rest of the world?" If you look for those things you will find them. But if you look for the good, and you look for the good in people, and you look for the good in the experience, it will be there.

My whole attitude was rebellion when I first got back. I thought, "I will never have good friends like I had overseas." When I got past that and was willing to go a little outside of myself, I met some normal American people who had never been overseas, but who were curious and warm and interested in my life. In fact, I have taken one friend home with me to visit. There are people who care. You just have to find them.

Part VII

THE ADULT MK

36

The MK Song

Daniel Johnson
MK, Ecuador

It hurts so much to know the pain you're going through.
And know just how you feel 'cause I have been there, too.
No one seems to understand, and no one seems to care;
No one takes the time to listen or just be there.
People are interested in only where you're from —
They find out what they want to know, and then they're gone.
Sometimes they put you in a box and won't let you out.
No one takes the time to find out what you're all about.

A wanderer without a home, and nowhere to go;
So many memories I just can't let go.
Slowly you realize you never can go home —
How long can you keep going running all alone?
Even if you go there, things will never be the same;
You grew up and times have changed, but who's to blame?
Everyone says change is good; you should be glad;
But how can you be happy when you're hurting so bad?

And you know, Jesus loves you —
You've heard it all your life.
And when you were young
Jesus made his home inside you.
And he knows you,
And He'll always understand.
Heaven is your home.
Jesus is your friend forever,
And he'll never let go of your hand.
You'll never be alone — you'll always have a home
With him.

Slowly time goes by; the hurt begins to heal.
Everything that happens proves God's love is real.
No one ever understood like Jesus understands;
No one loves the way he loves you, with His hands.
You've learned so much from all your past—
At last you understand
That everything that comes to you is from God's hand.
Now you see the reason for the way that you've come
So much more to do and be until he takes you home.

And you know that you're here
So you can glorify your King,
And you're just a passing through.
This world is not your home forever.
Jesus loves you and He'll always understand;
Heaven is your home,
Jesus is your friend forever.
And He'll never let go of your hand.
You'll never be alone;
You'll always have a home with him.
No, you'll never be alone.
You'll always have a home in Him.

37

"Going Native," or
An Alternative to Re-entry

Randy Borman
Wycliffe MK, Ecuador

I'd like to present an alternative to the famous "MK problem" of integration into the U.S. mainstream culture. That is, simply stated, the concept that the MK is uniquely qualified to continue as a missionary in the country or culture where he or she has grown up. I suggest that this alternative should be treated positively by the missionary and church community.

The MK or the TCK typically grows up with his feet in two cultures. This usually equips him or her with an extra language, and frequently, with a base of friends, an understanding of ways of thought, a resistance to local diseases, and the ability to get around in the culture—how to handle the bureaucracy, for example. This also often serves to give the MK an intense love and loyalty for his or her country of residence and its peoples. In spite of this, a terrific amount of pressure is applied to the MK to reject this training and "return" to the culture of his or her parents. I am one of the few who did not return to my parents' culture, but I can testify to the pressures that were placed upon me to do so.

Let me briefly describe what I do now. I am a *rivereño*. I was born in the Ecuadorian oriente, quite close to the Pastaza river. I grew up in the Cofan village of Dureno on the Aguarico river, and at Limoncocha, the SIL center on the Napo river. I learned Cofan and English at the same time, and received educations in both the missionary sub-culture and the Cofan culture. I went to the U.S. after completing high school at the Alliance Academy in Quito, I got a job in a factory. This was followed by a year at Michigan State University, where both my grades and an intense homesickness reflected the "typical" MK problems of "re-entry" that we hear so much about.

After my first year of college, I came down to Ecuador to do a research project. At the end of the summer, I was supposed to go back to Michigan State, but I saw a real need with the Cofans to get their land title and start working on the boundaries. I presented that to the SIL director, expecting him to say, "Go back and get educated. Then come back and help these people."

Instead he said, "I think it's a wonderful idea that you should go out there." He gave me a lot of encouragement.

My parents were on furlough, and all of my high school friends were gone. It was an excellent opportunity to see my country and its cultures without the "sweetening" of friends, family, and security which MKs and others, so often confuse with a love for a place and its people. It's typical when you move out of the nest, to remember the nest with a lot of nostalgia and longing. When you go back as an adult, you often find out that it's very different from what you expected.

After six months in Ecuador, I returned to the U.S., re-entered school, and in spite of continued homesickness, pulled excellent grades, made friends, and managed to appear a proper and upstanding American. But I still felt a strong pull to return to Ecuador to try to find a niche there. At this point, the missionary and church community offered me three culturally acceptable alternatives: (1) return to live in the U.S., pursue my education, and become a professional, (2) live in the U.S., get a job, and settle down to a middle-class suburban existence, (3) become a missionary or professional Christian worker in the traditional sense of the word. The third possibility was the only one which really made much use of all my years of training and living in different cultures and places. Yet as a "native" rather than a "foreigner," I felt there were a lot of things I'd do differently from the way traditional missions were equipped to work. In this I received very little encouragement or guidance.

After several years of "on-site training" if you will, I found myself deeply involved in the progress of my hometown of Dureno, and concerned intimately with the material and spiritual lives of people up and down the Aguarico river system. Yet in spite of my growing ministry among these people, often meeting needs which a "foreigner" never could meet, I found that my original "family" of missionaries and church people had a very hard time accepting what I was doing. I heard "cop-out" more than once, and people would make references to "when he settles down" and "what do you plan to do with your life?" It wasn't until I began to make "American-style" money as a tour guide that I really felt that the pressure began to ease.   This, incidentally, came especially from my parents' home churches and my stateside friends.   The mission community was a lot less worried about that, but I did feel it a little from them, too. Somehow, even though a bit eccentric, I was a success, and the missionary community no longer had to shake its head sadly and say, "Too bad, another mixed-up kid with problems."

At present, I am making good money as a tour guide and am highly successful in American terms of being well known in my field, and sought after for my knowledge of the Amazon and its peoples, animals and plants.   I mention this with a touch of irony, because I feel this is the least important thing I'm involved in.   My contacts with tourists and scientists have been a rewarding ministry.   The money received allows me an independence I value, as well as the power to purchase basic necessities, not just for myself, but for projects I want to do.

My main focus is the river community.   I live on the same level as my fellow *rivereños*.   I plant my own fields, hunt my own meat, catch my own fish, saw my own boards.   I eat the same foods, live in the same style house, do the same work as my neighbors.   These things are not things which an outsider can readily pick up.   Even should one manage to become proficient in them, one could still not be accepted in the same manner as someone who has grown up in the culture, in full view of everyone.   The outsider will almost always remain an outsider.   (I have seen situations where an outsider has been fully accepted, but this is rare.)

I find that in spite of being accepted by the natives as a native, my skin color sets me apart.   Yet this can be an advantage.   In my case, I found that the Western education I've received is extremely valuable in helping guide both spiritual and material progress, and the fact that I stand out because of skin color has made it easier to assume a leadership role.   Incidentally, the decision to take any sort of leadership role was not easy to make.   I had grown up in the atmosphere of "let's try to work under cover."   You want to influence what's happening, but you want someone else to actually do it.   This is necessary when you're a missionary in a foreign country.   You don't want to be directly involved in the political structure or do anything that is going to have national ramifications.

On the one hand, I was finding it difficult to "slide under the rug" and work from under cover.   On the other hand, I was receiving credit — and being blamed for — attitudes and events which I had had very little or nothing to do with.   I decided that if I was to be blamed, it might as well be with reason, hence the part I take in the social and political sectors of river life. As an Ecuadorian, I can get away with this. There have been problems, and I have no doubts there will be more, but I face these as a concerned citizen, not as a nosey outsider. If you will, this constitutes "license to tamper," something missionaries are often accused of doing without license.

The sum total of it is that I feel my birth in a country different than that of my parents and my training as a missionary kid were unique preparations by a God who doesn't make mistakes, for a unique ministry in Ecuador. The love God gave me for this country, this river culture, and these my friends and neighbors here, was not merely to better prepare me for a life in the U.S. but was part of God's call to this ministry in my home country.

I think that with a little thought, most people will recognize that the MK has a rare opportunity to affect his or her country as a lay person. However, I see very few kids returning to pursue a ministry of this sort. There are a number of reasons for this. One is simply the fact that it almost always means a cruder lifestyle than they could achieve in the U.S. This doesn't mean merely sacrificing a few little comforts like hot water from the tap. This involves medical and dental care, education for one's children, perhaps the difficulties of living in a country where the liberties Americans take for granted may not be available.

A second problem is that of time for one's ministry to one's neighbors when one has to work at a "secular" (Is there truly such a thing?) job. Certain forms of ministry become almost impossible. For example, Bible translation is a full-time missionary activity. I don't think you could hold down a job and be a Bible translator at the same time.

Because we are of a different skin color, there is the likelihood of personal danger from people who oppose what we are doing. We're a target that stands out.

I wonder how many MK's would be more than willing to accept these risks and sacrifices if they received the slightest bit of encouragement and support from their Christian communities. I'm positive that I'm not the only one who became deeply involved in local cultures as a kid, and I'm sure I'm not the only one who felt a deep homesickness for and desire to help the people of the country where I grew up. Yet most of us are pressured to move away from that. To return to "your" country, even as a traditional sort of missionary, is to somehow be "copping out," to be "trying to get back into the womb"—a recognition of failure to make it. Why?

I may be overly bold to put it so bluntly, but I feel the chief reason is that Satan has a very strong interest in not having these specially trained warriors sent to the places where their training will do the most good. If you're a military commander fighting in the forest, you don't want to fight people who grew up there, especially if they've received additional special training which could make them even more formidable. If you must face these elite warriors, let it be in the desert! Their training will still make them dangerous opponents, but at least they won't know intimately every trail which leads behind your lines! You hope the city people are sent to the forest, where they'll be lost from word go. This is plain sense. And Satan knows it. Obviously there will be strong attempts to put these elite warriors out of commission by any means possible. And what better than to get their own team to put pressure on them to go elsewhere?

Obviously this is not the whole story. Perhaps there aren't many MKs that have been prepared for this sort of life and work. I definitely don't want to convey the impression that I think it is wrong to go to the U.S. and become a "success," whatever that means. But I feel that our Christian community as a whole, and our missionary community most especially, should be aware that it is a potentially valuable alternative for an MK to return to his or her country. I suggest that we turn the emphasis around and actively work to prepare kids for a potential ministry in their country. At the very least, we should try to understand and encourage kids who do try it.

As a community, we should give more than lip service to Jesus' rejection of man's concept of success. I shouldn't have to be earning middle-class American wages before I stop hearing that I have an adjustment problem because I'm not living an American lifestyle with American goals. Above all, it should be recognized that the love an MK feels for his or her country of residence is often God-given. That love should be encouraged, even when it means sacrifice.

I decided to present these thoughts because I see so very few MKs coming back to "their" countries, in spite of superb training they received living in them and dealing with the people. Most missionaries spend several years just learning how to get along in a country, and may never really learn to live and think as the "natives" do. Even when they eventually learn the ropes of the local culture, they are still frequently enigmas to the people they work with. They are seen as a group of people of a different language and culture who, for some strange reason, came to live elsewhere. They generally seem very rich in comparison to the people they live with, but never seem to do any "work" as understood by the natives. This was the case with my dad. He was never out there hunting. They knew he was messing around with papers, but that wasn't something they could understand. Luckily the group was real tolerant of other cultures, so it wasn't as big of a problem as it could have been. But I have seen other groups where it has been a problem.

The MK comes equipped with all the education and (potentially) all the vision of a foreign missionary. The MK also comes fully equipped to handle the culture. What a combination! Let's stop throwing it away by directing all our efforts toward "re-entry" into the American mainstream. At least let kids know that this can be a legitimate alternative. As a community, let us, at the very least, stop standing in the way of those who do feel this route to service is what God would have for them.

Some examples of what some MKs have done along these lines: (1) married local people, taken active part in the church and community; (2) set themselves up in business in their country; (3) entered Christian service as pastors or teachers after receiving training in their country, rather than, or in addition to, outside training.

We have a lot of people who are willing to go to the U.S. or elsewhere, but I see very few missionary kids going through seminary in their country, even when there are seminaries. A cousin of mine is a Brazilian and went through seminary in Brazil. He's gone back to the States to get additional training, but he will return to Brazil shortly as a Brazilian trained in Brazil with a little bit of supplement from the outside.

Questions and Answers

[Questioners expressed concerns about citizenship, military service, and friendships in which deep sharing was possible. These are not problems for Randy. They were also concerned about those who had started out as Randy had but had given up or had become bitter. He felt that the biggest factor is knowing God has called you to be there. Other questions follow.]

Most missionary kids who experience the same sort of yearnings that you did have few role models, other than second generation missionaries to the same country as their parents. How big of a pain in the neck would it be for you for an MK to pick your brain about what it's been like?

That's a ministry I could see as a real positive one. I'd be willing.

*Without being aware of other options for service, kids may
mistake a call to live in their home culture for a call to missions. Would you agree?*

The biggest difficulty for this sort of ministry is to find a niche in your
country. With tourism I have ten to twelve trips a year. It's a little
more than I would like. I am involved about half the year with the
tours themselves and maintenance. Usually I have one to three
months with absolutely no trips. I try to bunch all the tours during
rainy season when there's nothing else practical you can do. To have
a job that leaves you that sort of spare time is really hard to find.

I know my sister struggled with this because she didn't have a
niche she could fit into here. It's much harder for a single girl than a
single guy.

*How do you deal with the argument, "It'd be too easy to go
back. Why not go where the challenge is going to be tough?"*

It depends on what your ministry is going to be. It was easy for me
to go back in many respects, but I think that's because God prepared
me for doing that. I looked around at the other things I could be
doing, and my criteria was, "Is there somebody else who can handle
this situation? Is there somebody else who can handle what I'm doing
down there now?" I believe it was God's preparation that made it
easy for me, because it's not an easy life by Western standards.

*It doesn't only take someone who is willing to give up their
privileges for ministry, but it takes someone spiritually sound.*

God is good at handling situations. If we wait until we're spiritually
sound to step out, I'd still be waiting, I'm sure. It's a process.

*When you fly, how do you keep the people from being more
attached to the airplane than they are to Christ?*

I'm not using airplanes. That's why it takes me six days to get from
there to Quito and back.

*A tour guide is between cultures. Would there be legitimacy
in moving into a village, hunting, growing a garden, and
being a part of the culture?*

I did that for a couple of years. The main problem was gringo community pressures. Also, it is frustrating when you are pinching your
pennies trying to get back enough to buy a new kettle. There are a
lot of situations where you can't help your neighbor, because you're
needing help yourself. Now I work with a group, and we have four
outboard motors going up and down the rivers. We take river people

basically for free or charge them a minimal fee for the goods they carry. We let them know very clearly it's because we have this tour operation which allows us to do it. Some form of outside income cuts down on the amount of work you have to do just to stay alive. In my case it is also helpful in remembering how to speak English.

> *Looking back, do you wish your parents had sent you to an Ecuadorian school?*

No. School was the problem, not the Alliance.

> *My heart is with you, but I am wondering about complications involved in marriage and a family.*

Yes, I've thought about that a lot. It's in God's hands.[1]

> *How are you different from us MKs in secular jobs who have a heart for the people we are working with and for God's kingdom?*

The only difference I feel is that you're living Christ in the business world, and I'm living Christ in a situation where most people can't. An MK can fit into a place where he can live Christ because of his background in the other culture. We have access to the Western culture with all of our Bible studies and books. The Quichua man on the river, in spite of the fact that he's a Christian, doesn't have access to that. Because of my access, I can minister in a way that he can't.

The point is not just that this has happened for me. But I think it could happen for a lot more people with a little bit of encouragement and a little bit of help. I would be willing to write letters to people who were interested.

---

[1]Editor's note: Randy is now married to a Cofan woman and has a son whom he plans to send to the Alliance Academy when he is school age.

38

The Role of the MK in International Affairs

Richard Gathro
Christian College Coalition

The American Studies Program of the Christian College Coalition takes forty students from any of our seventy-five colleges to study public policy and to intern in government-related positions for a semester in Washington. We try to help these students develop a biblical view of public policy.

They are some of the best and brightest from our colleges, but they do suffer an incredible inferiority complex. Every semester I have some of these students come back to me after their first day of internship shaking. "Oh gosh, there's a Yale student interning with me. Am I going to make it?" The truth is, at the internship sites our students are preferred over the Ivy League students. They're brighter, more balanced, less egotistical, and have a better attitude. They're more teachable, more diligent, more excited and enthusiastic. I challenge my students to try to get past the "Ivy League Syndrome" and realize that some of our colleges are offering an education that is absolutely outstanding. They couldn't get anything better anywhere else to prepare for a life work.

Need for a vision

My experience in working with students for more than fifteen years is that they need a vision for their lives. Many of the greatest movements are a result of the ability of the leaders of those movements to stir the sense of the heroic in the lives of young people.

I read a lengthy analysis of the Nazi youth movement. One of the leaders of the youth movement said, "You have to understand we were looking for something, and Nazism provided it for us." Our youth are made for the heroic. We are made to give our lives to

Christ.   We have such an inferiority complex that we don't realize how exciting it is to be an evangelical.

It's estimated that by the year 2000, there'll be 6.8 billion people in the world, 5.3 billion of them unreached for Christ, 83 percent of them in countries that are not open to traditional missions.

I want us to think about broadening our sense of the mission field and broadening our sense of mission alternatives. I want us to think strategically. If we're going to reach the world, we're going to have to be a little bit more creative in how we equip our young people for missions. I think adequate equipping is epitomized in Acts 8:4 where it talks about how God's people were scattered, and they preached the gospel wherever they went. It doesn't say that they were trained and sent out by a mission board. They were scattered, and as they went, in whatever professions, they shared the gospel. That is the vision I want us to have.

A lot of our students have a problem with seeing that wherever they are, they are evangelists. Do our churches every fall, as they send their students off to state universities, ever lay hands on those students, pray for them, and send them out as missionaries to those campuses? No. We need to broaden our vision. Our own students don't have any idea that they can do anything until they are all trained and prepared.

Going beyond that, I think that one of the primary ways of penetrating those closed countries is the training of people to be the fragrance of Christ in international business, international trade, education, the foreign service, the Peace Corps, the Agency of International Development, and other development organizations that are welcomed in those host countries.

In the church we've created a strange thing called full-time Christian service. That has done a disservice to the church, because it has told a lot of people that they're not in Christian service — that their only job is to be faithful to their spouse, teach Sunday school, and to support those who are out there in full-time Christian service.

None of us, no matter what we do, are part-time Christians. It's all or nothing, in or out. We need to communicate that to our young people. They need to be released from that burden of either-or and realize God is calling them and shaping them. They are in full-time Christian service no matter where they go.

I have a friend who worked for a while with Campus Crusade in Yugoslavia. He would kind of sneak in and out of Yugoslavia and do his clandestine work, because, of course, it's a closed country.

Suddenly his eyes were opened. He discovered he loved business. Why not go into international trade? Now he works as an import-exporter, speaks Yugoslavian like a Yugoslav, and has the freedom to move about Yugoslavia. He builds churches while he does his business. There's no pain, no sense of sneaking around. It's a way of moving in and out. He doesn't have to have an address in Vienna.

It's a little less adventurous, but he feels so much more like he's up front and straight forward by doing it that way.

Requirements for overseas careers

There are three requirements that most of the authorities on international careers agree on for a person going into overseas careers: (1) interdisciplinary training, (2) intercultural understanding, and (3) being multilingual.

Interdisciplinary training is probably where formal education comes in the most: to have an understanding of policy, economics, sociology, philosophy, business; to get a broad training; to be all things to all people. Intercultural understanding is the ability to get in somebody else's shoes, the ability to understand somebody else. Most of our MKs as they think about an international career are equipped with two out of three of these requirements. They've got a tremendous head start because of their intercultural understanding and their bilingualism. And of course, if you are bilingual, it's a lot easier to learn other languages. Think about how well-equipped missionary kids already are!

Developing a biblical world-view

I think there ought to be for us, as kingdom people, a fourth requirement—a biblical world-view. A lot of our evangelical young people are now feeling permission to enter business or law. Some people are rejoicing over a new conservative swing, particularly in the United States. However, there's a problem with that. That conservative swing isn't so much social and moral as it is economic. "Me. Make bucks. Make bucks."

Choosing a career for love's sake

I've had a number of conversations with some of our students who want to go into business or law particularly. If you really press them to find out why they want to do it, it's not because they feel called to it. It's because they see some security there. "My father was unemployed once, and I don't want to ever be unemployed. I want to make money." There's a beautiful scene in *Chariots of Fire*, where Eric Liddel said, "God has made me fast, and when I run, I feel his pleasure." It's not a sense of, "God has made me for business; when I do business, I feel his pleasure," but a sense that "This is where I can build security."

We need to be giving them a vision to be MBAs for love's sake, to be in trade for love's sake, to be into policy for love's sake. That's the real starting point. That is where a biblical world-view comes in.

Understanding of calling

Secondly, we need to give them an understanding of what calling is all about. For me, there are two kinds of calling. There's a general calling to love God, to love our neighbor, and to be righteous people. That's what God is mostly interested in. But most of my students think calling has to do primarily with what they are going to do with their jobs and who their mate is going to be. God is far more interested in the kind of people we are, and how we love and live, than he is in who our mate is going to be and what our job is. That's the starting point.

But there is a specific calling. I envision God as sort of a master chess player. As we read the Scripture, we see that he is carrying out his work in history. All things are going to come together in Christ. He is over all things. All things revolve around Christ. And, in terms of specific calling, he is shaping us as his chess pieces.

There are different kinds of chess pieces. He's called some of us to be pawns, and some of us to be rooks, and some of us to be queens, and some of us to be knights. He can move us around that chess board to carry out his history. Now we're not robots, obviously, but there's too much anxiety over what's going to happen with our lives. We forget that somebody is in charge and ordering our lives.

Lynda Peters in her seminar on career counseling [pp. 417-425] pointed out that in our specific calling, we need to take into consideration our talents, skills, values, temperament, personality, physical abilities and limitations, interests, educational background, and spiritual gifts. The fact is, God who is sovereign is shaping us as clay and giving us all of those things for a purpose. We need to help our young people discover that there is a strategy for their lives, and to see the different kinds of options that God is shaping them for. A specific calling isn't always so much to have a specific profession as it is to be a certain kind of person. We need to give young people an idea of where they'd be more useful, helpful, and capable, and where they wouldn't be.

One young person came in who was working in a law firm. After a lengthy discussion about all of these elements, I said, "What are you doing in a law firm? It's going to drive you nuts. You're an artist! Do something creative. You like to make and create."

Well, she now works for a catering company. Simple.

Let's help our young people have a sense of what they are and how God is shaping them. It struck me as Rachel Saint was sharing about the problems the Aucas are facing right now [Chapter 5], we need a broader vision of people being called to all professions, so we can address darkness on every level. We need people there among the Aucas, but we also need people who have responsibilities in other areas in Ecuador who can confront other evils that those Aucas are facing, whether it's a government action, a corporate action, or a societal action. It's a total package. We need to discover that our identity is Jesus Christ. We need to know him, the fellowship of his suffering, the power of his resurrection.

One time we took a group of young people rafting down the Shenandoah River. The rapids were dead that day, so I decided to make things lively and created submarine warfare with the rafts. As a consequence, I got a double ear infection from the polluted water and spent almost two weeks in bed. I was angry at God. "God I have so much to do for you out there."

A friend of mine came by and said, "Look, God knows where you are. Your job is to know him, the fellowship of his suffering, and the power of his resurrection. Stop having a false sense of your own abilities. Relax about your own importance."

I wept as I realized I wasn't placing my identity and security in Christ. I was placing my identity and security in the things I was doing.

When I wept and repented of that, the Lord sent a fellow I had gone hunting with to see me. I had wanted to tell him about Christ but it just had never worked.

He said, "I'm here to accept Christ."

I said, "Are you sure?" It seemed so easy. I think the Lord has a sense of humor and decided that was a good time to send him.

The Lord wants our security and identity to be in him, and he wants us to take that identity to whatever we do, wherever we go. That is what allows us to be world Christians instead of only American Christians or Ecuadorian Christians. It gives us a freedom and a release.

Larry Crabb, who is a psychologist at Grace Seminary, draws his three concentric circles and says that we have three areas of need in our personal lives. We have the outer circle of basic or casual needs: to be fed, to have a roof over our head, to be clothed, etc. If those needs aren't met, we're consumed by them. The next circle represents critical needs: relationship, a sense of significance, a sense that we mean something. These needs are natural, normal needs. God has created us for relationship. The problem is, that we get so consumed with our critical needs of wanting relationship that we forget our most crucial need, and that's to be one with God.

The greatest sin that we're warned against in the Scripture is idolatry. "Thou shalt not have any other gods." But how often do we fall prey to other gods? Even good causes. So very often we'd rather give ourselves to a good cause than to Christ. Sometimes we'd rather give ourselves to evangelism than to Christ. We can make an idolatry out of evangelism, out of social action, out of making money, out of our own nation. There are many idolatries, and we have to have a sense of where our God is. If God isn't our God, then we create some other god. So we have to have our security in Christ, and our identity in Christ. That's our starting point; that's our base.

Shalom

The goal is that great Hebrew word *shalom*, peace. In English, *peace* is a kind of oversimplified word. In Hebrew, *peace* means whole, complete. It's that vision in Colossians 1 when Paul says, "Let's strive to make every person complete in Christ." Whole, healthy. In the Hebrew it means to be at peace with God, to be at peace with our neighbor, and have peace between nations. To be at peace with ourselves, to be at peace with the earth, the environment we live in. Wholeness. Completeness. Peace. Shalom.

One way to work toward shalom is to develop an understanding of justice and righteousness: knowing what is right and doing it; knowing what is wrong and trying to set it right. In the Psalms it says, "Justice and righteousness are the foundation of his throne."

Once I marked every passage in Psalms and Proverbs that dealt with justice, injustice, righteousness, and governments. I was overpowered with the sense of God's concern for things being set right, for justice, for breaking the barriers of oppression wherever they might be found.

Another concern is for the sanctity and dignity of human life. We should look upon people as Christ looked upon the rich young ruler who was bragging about how he obeyed all the commandments: "And Christ loved him."

Do we see people as image bearers? When we lived on Capitol Hill, that was hard. It was hard because a major percentage of the population of Capitol Hill is homosexual. It was hard because a major percentage of the population is caught up in materialism and power. It was hard because there is a significant percentage of Capitol Hill dwellers that are very poor and prey on the rest of us.

Particularly with the homosexuals, I had to keep reminding myself, "These are perverted image bearers, but they are image bearers. They've been created in the image of God." Do I look past that homosexuality and desire them to have shalom, to be made whole? Am I broken for them? Or do I join my buddies who call them names? Do we see them as image bearers?

Do we have a vision for the value of life that goes into the womb? We read in the Psalms about being fearfully and wonderfully made in the mother's womb. Evangelicals have finally caught up to the Catholics and decided that there's something wrong with abortion.

There is something wrong with people starving to death, people committing suicide because they've gotten old, things like that. We need a whole pro-life ethic that is concerned about anything that destroys human life. I don't want to make human life an idol. Some of us do that. But do we see human life as image bearing?

Another dimension is stewardship. We, as God's people, have been given responsibility for the care of the earth that's around us, for our abilities, for what we have in our possession, for how we spend our money, for how our government spends its money, for how people are used in life. On and on. This is part of the vision we need to be constructing for our young people as they go into the world for love's sake.

Other requisites for international careers

There are some other requisites for international careers that I want to briefly mention.

- Writing and communication skills. Please, as you're working with young people, help them learn to write. Ninety percent of the success of our Washington internship students depends on their writing skills, their ability to construct a sentence. It's atrocious how poorly so many people write.

- Knowledge of events. They need a knowledge of past events, present events, a certain sense of what trends are, where we're going, a sense of context and an ability to look at that bigger picture. This is something MKs can particularly offer.

- Economics. They need to understand economics. When foreign service people talk to my students about careers in the foreign service, our students' jaws drop when told, "You must know economics." The bottom line is not diplomacy, it's economics. So much of our relationship with other nations involves economics — knowledge of public policy process, how governments work, how policy is formulated, what interest groups are — those kinds of things.

In personal qualities and relational skills, you need curiosity; humor; intelligence; hunger to read, study, learn, and grow; and ability to build rapport with people.

Those are additional kinds of qualifications you want to be equipping your young people with as they think about international careers. MKs have developed some of these skills already, particularly those primary ones that I've mentioned.

Resources

There are a variety of resources that I want you to be aware of as we seek to counsel our young people. There are a variety of things we can be doing on the educational level.

The Pacific and Asian Christian University has now developed a whole program of field ministry internships in medicine, youth ministry, agriculture, art, social work, law, and journalism, throughout Asia to equip and train people.

Eastern College has implemented a wonderful new idea. They have an MBA program that specializes in international development. They say to these young people, "We're going to give you a lot of the same basics you would get at Harvard for an MBA, statistics, economics, and so forth. But we're going to equip you to have a theology for international development, and give you a six-month internship in international development abroad in Kenya, Haiti, or a similar place, where you can get field experience to enable you to develop enterprise abroad."

One of the greatest needs around the world is for people to be free from their own economic chains. If you teach a person how to develop his own little business, and get it started, chances are he'll have something left over after he feeds his own family which he'll need to spend. That creates a need for other businesses and other services. This is a simple, basic free-enterprise system. This program gives the students a theology for business and skills in international development.

On the undergraduate level, the Christian College Coalition has two programs that I want to mention. The program I work with in Washington is called the American Studies Program. We have internships in everything you can think of. Students build the biblical world-view I'm talking about, and get hands-on experience in the world of public policy. Now the Christian College Coalition has started the Latin American Studies Program. Students from our colleges can go to Latin America for intensive language study. They learn about the culture, politics, and economics, do service projects, take field trips, and so forth. They get hands-on experience.

In international careers you are asked more about your experience than your education. We are too preoccupied with degrees and not preoccupied enough about what people can do. Never let going to school get in the way of our education, folks.

The U.S. government has federal internships. There are organizations like Global Opportunities and Tentmakers International that are trying to provide opportunities for jobs. There are people that are now doing more and more networking, making a life of connecting people interested in international careers with the jobs.

There are a couple of books that I want of mention. *Careers in International Affairs*, published by Georgetown University, contains all kinds of informations on careers in international affairs. This book is a little more substantive and detailed than *The Overseas List*, published by Augsburg Press. This is written by people who have a more Christian bent and a broader view of the kinds of opportunities that are available.

I recommend both of these books. I think these are two musts for exploring international careers. Also, the State Department publishes *Foreign Service Careers*.

Let's all work together and have a strategy for our MKs, for them to go into the world to reach people for Christ for love's sake, in all phases and all careers, all of them in full-time Christian service.

39

The Cult Appeal:
Is the MK Susceptible or Immune?

Margaret W. Long
MK, Guatemala

As a teenager growing up in the 1960's, I heard about cults, mainly the major ones like Jehovah's Witnesses, Mormons, and Christian Scientists. I wasn't particularly disturbed or threatened by these cults, since I knew I had been given firm, solid doctrinal training as a missionary kid.

In the 1970's amidst the unrest of the Vietnam War and the general unrest in the United States, all sorts of new gurus and messiahs seemed to appear out of nowhere. I wasn't particularly threatened by these people, either, since I knew that I was not susceptible to the lure of some weirdo in an orange robe with a ridiculous haircut. During this time, I learned about an MK that I had grown up with who had joined David Berg's Children of God cult. That disturbed me a little bit, but I quickly dismissed that as an isolated instance and figured that one of the reasons she had been susceptible was that she had not gone to boarding school and had not gotten the wonderful doctrinal training I had gotten.

I probably would have been a little more disturbed had I known that Berg's father was an evangelical pastor, a teacher at Westmont college. I would have been more disturbed had I known his mother was a radio evangelist for the Christian and Missionary Alliance church; that Berg himself had been a Christian and Missionary Alliance evangelist. I would have been very disturbed had I known all about what Berg stood for, and that he encouraged his followers to engage in prostitution and all manner of incestuous relationships.

The 1974 kidnapping of Patricia Hearst and her subsequent criminal activities did not particularly bother me. I did not think of the Symbionese Liberation Army as a cult at all, since it was

372

politically oriented rather than religiously oriented. I also thought that the whole business about her having been brainwashed was a clever ploy by the lawyers. When she was sentenced to prison, I figured that spoiled rich kid deserved what she got.

In November 1978, the mass suicide of 913 people in Jonestown, Guyana, grabbed my attention. I began to ask more questions and do a little more reading, but I still had only a casual interest and curiosity. I would have been much more concerned had I known that the person who had been second in command at Jonestown was Tim Stone, a student leader at Wheaton College. I would have been very disturbed had I known that he had been a staunch Baptist. One of the leaders was Bonnie Kielman, the daughter of an Assemblies of God missionary to Brazil. Other people had solid church backgrounds. Ironically, less than eighteen months after that incident, I unknowingly steered my own brother into a destructive cult.

I started studying the Bible with a colleague of mine who happened to be a member of the group that my brother later joined. I was fortunate enough to move to another city and away from the group, but my brother became deeply involved. His extended involvement and my brief involvement dispelled many myths that I had had about cults.

For the purpose of this paper, I am going to define a cult as a highly manipulative group which exploits and sometimes physically and/or psychologically damages its members and recruits.

Dispelling the myths

Myth #1: My loved ones and I are immune. Obviously we were both susceptible.

Myth #2: MKs are immune to cults due to their solid biblical training. We were both MKs.

Myth #3: Knowing the "real thing" guarantees the ability to spot a counterfeit. At least initially, the counterfeit looked a lot more like the real thing than the real thing did. There seemed to be much more commitment and dedication to studying the Bible and witnessing than in any American church or in many international churches.

Myth #4: People are susceptible because they are either weak-minded, pathological "weirdos," seekers, or suckers. Although we were susceptible to a cult, I don't feel that it was because of any of these factors. We were both college graduates who had full-time careers. Neither of us had a history of pathological behavior. We weren't looking for some exotic group experience, but rather a serious

Bible study experience. Neither one of us was considered particularly gullible or the inveterate sucker.

There are three hypotheses I would like to propose today.

- The MK population is highly susceptible to the lure of today's cults, particularly aberrational Christian cults or self-improvement cults.

- Aspects of the MK's experience related to his family, life-style, values, environment, educational system, and re-entry to his parents' culture may make the MK prone to cults.

- MK susceptibility to cults will increase unless there is a concerted effort on the part of the mission community to build up MKs' immunities and reduce the risk factors.

Common Characteristics of Cult Members

Researchers have shown that there is no one personality type that gets involved in a cult. Two major elements that almost always appear are a lack of awareness of the bottom line when they joined the group, and secondly, ignorance of the power of mind control or coercive persuasion techniques that were used to recruit and indoctrinate them. Most were normal individuals prior to involvement in the cult.

Traditionally we've thought of cults recruiting people in their late teens and early twenties, but the cults of today are actively going after younger kids, as well as people in their thirties and forties. Even the elderly have become prime targets.

Studies have found that most cult members were good students prior to their involvement. In one study, 77 percent of those who got involved had B averages or better. Most were in college or had college training or degrees. Most came from families who attended church regularly. Most came from middle to upper class families with 40 percent having annual incomes in excess of $30,000. Most came from *un*broken homes. In short, the typical cult victim seems to possess average or above-average intelligence and education, and appears to have a solid, church-related family background.

Most cult victims are highly idealistic. They want a sense of purpose in their lives. Cult recruiters capitalize on that idealism and offer the highest sense of purpose. In my brother's case, he was intrigued and attracted by the enthusiasm and the devotion to Bible study that he saw among the members of the group.

Most cult victims are dissatisfied with themselves. The idealistic person is usually dissatisfied with some aspect of himself and his current life. Cult recruiters are very good at discovering early on what the person is dissatisfied about, making him feel powerless to change that, and then offering him the opportunity to make everything better by joining the group. My brother and I were most dissatisfied by our lack of serious Bible study.

Most cult victims are disillusioned with society or some aspect of society. Besides wanting to better himself, the idealistic person usually wants to fix the things around him. That would include fixing things in his church. My brother and I, having experienced the enthusiasm and dedication of an overseas church, were pretty disillusioned and alienated from the church that we attended in North America, which seemed to be apathetic, lukewarm, and uncommitted.

Researchers tend to agree that people are susceptible to cults when they are in states of transition or when they are experiencing normal crises or stresses in their lives. Everyone has the normal transitions or stresses, and as Darryl Christiansen says, everyone is susceptible to cults for at least a short period of time. But it only takes a short period, sometimes even one day, to enter the pipeline into the cult industry. In my brother's case, transition and stress factors included being new to a community, being new to a job, experiencing the recent death of his mother, and breaking off an engagement.

What are the appeals of a cult? Many people are drawn to a cult for the very same reasons that others are drawn to a particular evangelical church. The cult offers to satisfy one's basic needs such as the need to have an identity; to belong to a community; to belong to an exclusive group having truth, spiritual depth, and meaning; to be deeply committed; and to submit to benevolent leadership.

Risk Factors for the MK

The MK's philosophies

First, MKs tend to have a heightened and ingrained idealism. They are very supportive of their parents' profession, which they tend to idealize. As a result, they have high ideals for themselves. With missionary parents as an example of commitment to doing God's work, it stands to reason that when put into a cult setting and asked to give up everything for God's work, they're likely to think that's a very similar thing to what their parents have done. The MK's idealism, then, and his sincere desire to make the world better and improve people's lives, can be used as a powerful tool to get the MK to join a cult.

MKs have very high expectations of themselves. When the MK's actions do not fit his idealized expectations for himself, he exists in a state of cognitive dissonance. He is always trying to figure out if he should change his actions. Maybe he can't change his expectation. As long as he experiences that dissonance, he feels guilty and dissatisfied with himself. The cult offers him a shortcut way to resolve that dissonance. My brother was able to keep his career as an industrial engineer, and he was able to be a missionary in his own environment.

When the MK returns to his parents' culture, or re-enters, he feels alienated. He can't easily accept the culture of his parents as his own. This alienation opens a wide door to any group or community that says it also condemns the same things. My brother liked the international flavor of the group he joined. He liked the emphasis on sacrifice versus materialism. He liked the warm atmosphere versus a cold atmosphere. He liked the commitment versus apathy. He liked the idea of selecting a marriage partner on the basis of spiritual attributes rather than physical assets. Note that things he liked in the group were opposites of things MKs usually condemn about American culture.

The MK's periods of vulnerability

The average individual experiences many transitions in his life, such as moving from one place to another or changing schools, going from high school to college. However the typical MK experiences many more. If he's not born on the mission field, he goes from the home country to the mission field, from the home environment to the boarding school, from the boarding school back home. From the mission home he goes on furlough, from furlough back to the field, from the field to college, or whatever he chooses to do, and so on.

The trauma of that re-entry experience is so great that some researchers have likened it to that of a returning POW. The MK often never accepts the United States or his parents' culture as his own home. In 1976, a researcher named Sprinkle asked MKs the question, "Has the US become home for you?" Two-thirds of the kids could not say "yes." The problem is that the MK rejects the culture of his parents, but he's not truly a person who belongs in the culture of the mission environment. In a sense, he is in a lifelong period of transition, which means that in some way or other he is in a lifelong period of susceptibility to cults.

Separations, which are related to transitions, cause stress. Stress or crises have been shown to increase one's susceptibility to cults. The MK has to go through separations from parents, from friends, from relatives, from home, from boarding school, from the third culture, from his parents' culture, and so on. He is constantly involved in a separation of some kind. Whether he's on the mission field or in the home country, he is separated from somebody who is significant to him. These separations multiply the times when an MK is susceptible to the lure of cults.

Conversely, the MK is used to dealing with separation, so when a cult causes him to become isolated and separated from others, he may not find that as unacceptable as your average American would. "What do you mean, you're making me say good-bye to my parents and friends?" The MK has said good-bye all of his life. He may not find that difficult to do.

The MK may also be so comfortable with having an extended family, that he may not find the cult family something to consider strange, unusual, or unacceptable. He may even welcome that cult family as being very similar to what he knows. In my brother's case, he was not actively seeking an extended family, but he found it very easy and natural to add Missionary Peter, Missionary Sarah, Missionary Samuel Lee, and all the other missionaries and people in the group to his already huge surrogate family of aunts and uncles.

The MK tends to find social adjustments somewhat difficult. The cult offers the instant intimacy and instant friendship that he might have known on the mission field, and that may seem very attractive to him.

Also, the MK is accustomed to making decisions without consulting his parents. He may join a group like that quite easily without consulting them first.

Appeals to the MK's basic needs

The lure of a cult is its promise to meet very basic needs. The MK may have heightened needs. In that case, his desire to meet those needs may be heightened. There may be similarities between his missionary environment and the cult environment that prevent him from seeing the dangers involved in a cult. I'll talk about five of those needs:

Identity. The MK, as others, must go through the process of deciding who he is, of determining what his identity is. This can present some unique problems. He might experience identity diffusion because of his multicultural experiences. He might experience identity confusion because of his re-entry experience. The cult offers a focus to his identity as well as the chance to resolve that confusion. The MK might fully adapt to his parents' culture, but most researchers believe that he doesn't adapt — he merely adjusts. Unfortunately, because the MK functions in a state of identity diffusion and identity confusion, and never really fully adapts to the culture of his parents, he is susceptible to the love bombing of cults. Think of the MK needing someone who can't wait to hear more about his experiences overseas, who understands exactly what he's saying, who has an awe and a reverence for what he's experienced, and who makes the MK feel totally special and appreciated. Most MKs would find it very hard to resist that sort of love bombing.

Community.   The MK tends to believe that he belongs nowhere. Lacking a permanent place to call home and a culture to call his own, he is susceptible to any community or group that offers him stability and a subculture that he can claim as his own. The cult offers him a community that seems even better than any community he has ever known before, including that third-culture community.

Cliff Schimmels feels that the third-culture community is different from most U.S. communities. He talks about it being a body-life community, and about being impressed by everyone calling him Uncle Cliff. The MK exposed to this positive community environment may see the cult as a logical extension of that community. He's experienced that extended family relationship of closeness and caring and protection. He has experienced the rather privileged nature of an MK environment. When he leaves that environment, he may feel a great void, and the cult may seem like a logical replacement for that community.

The MK also experiences the negative aspects of the third-culture community. One is a built-in temporariness; people come and go quite frequently. (They tend not to have old people in the third-culture environment, since missionaries often retire.) So when the MK experiences the cult and sees people coming and going, maybe rather abruptly, he may not question that; it may not send out any alarms to him. The third-culture community tends to be a very adult world. Membership is determined by the adults. Values and rules come from adults. Rebellion from kids isn't tolerated very well. So when the MK becomes involved in a cult community, he may not find it unusual that rules and values come from the leader, and that rebellion is not tolerated. He may not even spend all that much time considering the pros and cons as to whether he should belong, since he is used to automatic membership in a group. He may even leave his membership in the hands of the group leader, who then uses it to manipulate him.

Need to belong to a group with depth and meaning. The third-culture community may be very exclusive, so when the MK encounters a cult community that claims to be the only possessor of the truth, the only group accomplishing God's purposes, he may not react negatively.

In the overseas mission environment, the mission community is highly visible. Missionaries are the elite. Given the nature of that environment, it may be very difficult for the missionaries to allow the MKs the freedom to be themselves and the right to be different. The MK may be pretty tightly restricted on his freedom and on his expressions of diversity. As a result, the highly restrictive environment of the cults may not seem all that unusual, and may be acceptable to the MK.

When a group like a mission community becomes so concerned with being spiritual and pure, it develops a spirit of separation and elitism that can degenerate to a list of dos and don'ts. Dividing actions into pure and impure, dos and don'ts, spiritual and unspiritual, can cause one to forget Ephesians 2:8-9, "By grace are ye saved through faith, and that not of yourselves. It is the gift of God, not of works, lest any man should boast." If the MK hears all about salvation by grace, and yet everything around him speaks of salvation by works, he will not hear the internal warnings when exposed to the cults that claim to believe salvation by grace but demand absolute, unquestioning obedience. Failure to understand the difference between grace and works can almost guarantee that the MK will find the cult an acceptable alternative to the Western church.

Need for commitment. Being fully committed and involved in one's work is almost synonymous with being a missionary. Cults similarly promote total commitment and the importance of doing God's work at the expense of all else. It was missionary-style commitment that caused my brother to devote so much of his money to the group that he had little money for food. Commitment caused him to lose his job as an industrial engineer. Commitment caused him to devote so much of his time to the group that he had no time for family or friends and almost no time to read or watch television or to interact with the outside world. Commitment caused him to never have the time to attend church. And finally, it was commitment that caused him to get very little sleep and have no time or energy to evaluate what was happening to him.

Need for leadership and advice. In 1981, Jordan, who did a dissertation on TCKs, found that TCKs upon returning to their parents' homeland tend to seek an adult mentor. If they don't find an adult mentor, they experience loneliness and a sense of estrangement. This need for an adult authority figure plays right into the hands of destructive cults.

While firm discipline, rules, and strong leadership are essential for success of both families and schools, there is a danger of substituting human power for God's freedom, and substituting legalism for the good news of Jesus Christ as the Savior of sinners, not perfect people.

In 1983, Doland described a fundamentalist evangelical college that exhibited control patterns which she labeled as totalitarian evangelicalism. She defined totalitarian as 'a society's desire to produce a standard, approved, human product through rigid control of thought and action'. Since the conditions she described existed in a closed evangelical setting, she labeled it totalitarian evangelicalism.

It's important to consider the characteristics she described. Perhaps one finds some of these in the MK community. Ask yourself these questions: Is order maintained for the purpose of control versus the purpose of doing things in a decent, orderly manner? Do the school's energies mainly have to be spent on controlling? Do you seek to develop uniform behavior that is reflexive? Do you instill the idea that the individual and his needs are subordinate to the school, the group, or the family? Do you have unnecessary rules that are designed to condition the individual to obey? Do you attempt to evaluate the individual's attitude as well as his actions? Do you use severe and humiliating punishment for disobedience? Do you discourage questioning, suggesting, and critical thinking? Are you isolated from the outside world? Do you instill the idea that the outside world is evil or bad?

All of these characteristics existed in the evangelical fundamentalist college that Doland described. I believe they also existed in the boarding school that my older brother attended some twenty-seven years ago. If very many of these questions received a yes answer, then you are training the MK to be a perfect cult member, since the cult is a totalitarian institution. The individual who has been exposed to earlier training that could be considered totalitarian would be unlikely to possess or heed the internal warnings that might aid him in seeing that there is something wrong with a cult.

Why Is the Traditional Study of Cults Inadequate?

I'd like to describe what I consider to be the traditional evangelical approach to cults. I'd like to particularly deal with the definition of a cult, the standpoint from which cults are taught, doctrine as one's defense against cults, and the attitudes towards cult victims that are promoted by the traditional approach.

The word *cult* is a very value-laden term. If you look in the dictionary, you find such things as "excessive or fanatic devotion," "veneration of a deity" or "a group of followers". That doesn't distinguish between the People's Temple, the Unification Church, Southern Baptists, or Assemblies of God. I assume that we find those definitions unacceptable and impractical. A definition that seems to characterize the more evangelical approach to the study of cults would be that of Dr. Martin. He calls a cult "a group, religious in nature, which surrounds a leader or a group of teachings which either denies or misinterprets essential Biblical doctrine." I'm not against this definition. I think it's a very helpful definition from the standpoint of someone who is analyzing a group and has lots of information available to him to analyze. But when you're trying to tell the MK about a cult, I don't think it is very helpful, and I'll tell you why.

First of all, the focus is on the teachings of the group. It obscures the fact that most people, especially Christians, who join cults do not do so because of the teachings of the group, but because their basic needs are met.

Also, it excludes groups that aren't religious. An example of cults that would be excluded by this traditional definition include self-improvement cults, new age cults, therapy cults, political cults, and even sales cults. All of these would be excluded even though they have the same characteristics of groups that call themselves religious. However, it would include all the world's major religions, such as Islam, Buddhism, and Hinduism.

Finally, this definition does not mention anything about the deceptive or manipulative techniques that are used to recruit, indoctrinate, and keep members. If the MK doesn't learn to watch for those things, he might be deeply involved in a cult long before he knows much about the doctrines of the group. When deception and coercive persuasion are not taught, the victim's guilt is implied from the standpoint that if he had evaluated the doctrines of the group well enough, he would have discerned something wrong with them.

At the beginning, I defined a cult as "a highly manipulative group which exploits and/or psychologically damages its members and recruits."   This definition enables you to see the similarities among groups, regardless of their purposes or goals. Although the definition does not mention doctrine, that does not imply it is not important. Even though it is not specifically mentioned, if you analyze a group that could be called a cult by that operational definition, you will find doctrinal aberrations. For example, by this definition, cults enslave the individual. Scriptures teach that you shall know the truth, and the truth shall make you free. There is obviously a doctrinal problem with groups that enslave the individual.

Finally, waiting to decide if a group is a cult or not until you can analyze the doctrine is both impractical and dangerous. In some cases, a person may be involved in a group for a long time before he knows the true doctrinal position of that group. At this point, the likelihood of his perceiving the problems and being able to leave the group are severely diminished by the fact that he is very psychologically enslaved by the group.

The Standpoint from Which Cults Are Taught

Bussell has said that in the traditional approach to teaching cults "most available books, workshops, and seminars are built around the we-they mentality that contrasts their heretical doctrines against the truth upon which we stand." The major problem with this we-they mentality is that it creates a false sense of security or immunity. As many evangelicals can attest, including my brother and me, evangelical Christians are susceptible to cults, and particularly to Bible-based cults.

A second problem with this traditional we-they mentality is that it ignores the important similarities that exist between evangelicals and cults. I don't feel that evangelicals can afford to use that we-they mentality. The similarities between cults and the evangelical, traditional church are just as important to know as the differences. Most of the cults that aren't Eastern-based come from within traditional churches.

Let me give you some examples. From the Congregational Church we have Christian Science and Jehovah's Witnesses. From the conservative Presbyterian Korean Church we have the Unification Church and the University Bible Fellowship, which my brother belonged to. We have from the Methodist Church the Unity School of Christianity. From the Grace Brethren Church, we have Faith Assembly. From the Nazarenes and an interdenominational church and the Disciples of Christ, we got the People's Temple. From the Christian and Missionary Alliance, we got the Children of God. From the Reformed Church, The Way International. From Campus Crusade for Christ, the Northeast Kingdom Community. If I missed some denominations, it's because there are too many cults to mention. Bussell says, "If in our minds we think we are not susceptible to cults, we are the most vulnerable."

A final problem with the we-they mentality is that it ignores the fact that cultic tendencies can begin within one's own church. Not only historically but today also, the MK and all evangelicals need to see that vulnerability to cults comes from within one's church as well as without. The MK needs to be taught to watch for cultic tendencies in his church and to be prepared to challenge abuses of authority and the lack of accountability and other such things that may be occurring in his group or his church. The traditional approach to teaching this, includes the study of one's doctrines as well as the study of the doctrines of various cults. The rationale being that if you know the real thing you can spot the counterfeit, and by studying the heretical doctrines and teachings of a cult you will be prevented from joining that group.

There are problems with this. A fairly modest estimate of the number of the cults in the United States today is somewhere around two thousand. Obviously there is no way to immunize the MK against all of these cults. There is no way to know the names, much less the doctrines of all these cults, and the fastest growing ones are often the ones about which nothing has been written. Many cults do not have doctrines that are available for study and discussion. Some have no written statements at all. Some may have written statements, but they don't really represent what the group actually teaches. Some have doctrinal statements that are revealed only to people who have already joined. Misrepresenting one's teaching or practices is almost a standard operating procedure of a cult. In other words, the ends totally justify the means. Therefore, if I want to recruit you or save you, it doesn't matter how I do it even if it takes lying, cheating, stealing, or anything else. I will do it.

Finally, the person who has doctrine as his only way of determining whether or not a group is a cult doesn't have enough of a defense. When my brother was questioning whether or not to study the Bible with the leader of the University Bible Fellowship, he dutifully asked all the doctrinal questions he felt that he should ask. When he got rather standard answers that you would hear in a traditional church, he didn't have any other defenses, even though at the time, he saw things that weren't quite right. He assumed that he had checked everything that he needed to check.

James Sire wrote a book called *Scripture Twisting: Twenty Ways the Cults Misread the Bible*. University Bible Fellowship frequently uses as least ten of those techniques. Unfortunately, it took four-and-a-half years for my brother to recognize the doctrinal problems of this group, and then he was able to do so only with intervention from the outside.

The we-they mentality then, in the sense that if you knew enough about your doctrine you wouldn't get involved in a cult, blames the cult victim, and incorrectly assumes that the cult victim had all the facts and full information and consent when he joined. That is not the truth. It promotes myths about cults and who joins them: (1) The weirdo theory—obviously someone who joins the cult is not like me; therefore that person must be psychologically unstable. (2) The weak minded theory—the person is too unschooled and doesn't understand about cults. (3) The seeker theory—the person was looking for something and was so rebellious he tried anything, and he got what he deserved. (4) The sucker theory—he was so gullible he would join anything just to be a part of a group.

If the MK is taught with the traditional approach, he will tend to blame the victim and not think of himself as being susceptible. On the other hand, if he understands the cult victim as being a victim of deception, a victim of intensive thought reform, and a victim of enforced dependency, he'll see his own susceptibility and take measures to protect himself from the lure of a cult.

What Should a Curriculum on Cults Include?

A curriculum should dispel some of the myths and then teach about mind control. Give a "generic brand" idea of cults. By that, I mean general principles and characteristics of cults, so that no matter what kind of group a person comes into contact with, he will have an idea of how to spot one and what to do about it when he does.

Also talk about the types of cults that the MK might be likely to join. I don't usually see MKs joining cults that are very different from traditional Christianity. I do see them joining cults that are not billed as religious, and aberrational Christian groups that just look like an off-brand of Christianity.

In 1982, the delegates to the national Parent Teacher Association of the United States submitted a resolution to promote education on cults. I suggest that we join with the PTA in committing ourselves to providing each MK with information and training that will help him resist being lured into the negative nurture of the cult communities.

The cult community that my brother joined offered to nurture him and help him reach his full potential more than the local church did. But the cult community took his idealism and his missionary-style commitment and deceived him into thinking that the group leaders were just like those missionaries he had known on the mission field. They put him through an intensive thought reform program that ate away at his self-esteem, that shut off his emotions, that distorted his sense of right and wrong, that distorted his notion of salvation by God's grace, that exploited his physical, material, emotional, intellectual, and spiritual resources.

As you think about what steps can be taken to help prevent such negative nurturing, it is crucial that you understand that during the four-and-a-half years that my brother was a member of this group, he never wavered in his desire to serve God. He never wavered in his desire to help others. And he never wavered in his commitment to Bible study and witness. Exploitation of this kind of commitment and dedication that typifies so many MKs is something I hope we will all be committed to preventing. The life of even one MK is too valuable to waste.

Recommended Books and Resources

Appel, W. *Cults in America: Programmed for Paradise.* New York: Holt, Rinehart and Winston, 1983.

Barro, J. *Shepherds and Sheep: A Biblical View of Leading and Following.* Downers Grove, IL: InterVarsity Press, 1983.

Bussell, H. *Unholy Devotion: Why Cults Lure Christians.* Grand Rapids, MI: Zondervan Publishing House, 1983.

Cialdini, R.B. *Influence: Why People Agree to Things.* New York: Quill, 1984.

Dinnamon, K., and Farson, D. *Cults and Cons: The Exploitation of the Emotional Growth Consumer.* Chicago: Nelson-Hall, 1979.

Dellinger, R.W. *Cults and Kids: A Study of Coercion.* Boys Town, NE: Boys Town Center, 1985.

Doland, V.M. *Totalitarian Evangelicalism.* Christian Century, May 4, 1983, pp 429-430.

Edwards, C. *Crazy for God.* New York: Prentice Hall, 1979.

Enroth, R. *Youth, Brainwashing, and the Extremist Cults.* Grand Rapids, MI: Zondervan Publishing House, 1977.

Friesen, G. *Decision-Making and the Will of God* (Critical Concern series). Portland, OR: Multnomah Press, 1980.

Heller, R. *Deprogramming for Do-it-Yourselfers: A cure for the Common Cult.* Gentle Press, 1982.

Langone, M.D. *Destructive Cultism: Questions and Answers.* Weston, MA; American Family Foundation, 1982.

Lifton, R.J. *Thought Reform and the Psychology of Totalism.* New York: W.W. Norton, 1961.

Martin, W. *The New Cults*. Ventura, CA: Vision House, 1980.

Sire, J.W. *Scripture Twisting: Twenty Ways the Cults Misread the Bible.* Downers Grove, IL: InterVarsity Press, 1980.

40

Career Counseling for Mature MKs

Lynda Peters
Link Care

In the past, career planning and guidance depended on a knowing person. It was kind of a doctor-patient approach, so that the high school student was very dependent on the government or the high school counselor to point the way. In recent years that thinking has changed to more of a do-it-yourself attitude. More material has come out so that you are not dependent on one person to help you through the process and give you information. The idea now is to teach you how to get the information yourself so you're not dependent on anybody else.

Effective career planning is a systematic process based on a series of three steps—introspection, selection, and connection. It is important to complete each step before you go on to the next step.

1. Introspection

Introspection is the self-examination stage. Its purpose is to answer the questions, "Who am I? How has God made me? What are my talents? What are my values? What are my interests?"

Talents/skills

A talent is a natural ability. It's something you seem to have a flair for, and as far as you can remember you've been good at it. Probably the best way to make a decision about career planning would be to base it on your talents and skills. But in my years of career planning consulting I have found that instead of basing our career choices on talents, we go by values and interests. From a biblical perspective it would probably be safer to go with the talents, because that's what God has given us. That is probably where we ought to start in order to be a good stewards.

We need to broaden our horizons when we think of talents. We might think of art, music, sports, and even math, but we need to think in terms of a lot more natural abilities, for instance the ability to initiate something. You may have worked with people in the past who are always starting up projects. They may not be the world's best finishers, and they may not be the world's best planners, but they seem to have a knack for having an idea, getting other people enthused about it, and actually getting it off the ground. A lot of times an organization will suffer because it was started by an initiator who doesn't have the planning and the managing talents to run it. The organization tends to falter unless that person is willing to relinquish the controls to a manager. Being an initiator would be something I would consider to be a natural ability. It's something that person was not trained for. They are just naturally good at it.

Planning seems to be a natural ability. The person who always plans social events or weddings seems to have a knack for knowing what to do first, and what to do next, and so forth. Things run smoothly when they're in charge of planning the event.

Skills are abilities that you have learned to do, like driving a tractor or nursing skills.

There are two or three sources that are good for helping you determine what your talents and skills are. In my opinion, the two best and most complete resources available for career planning were done by Christians.

The Career Kit, put out by Intercristo, costs about $60. It's a workbook that begins by discussing talents and how to determine what they are. It takes you through the entire process and ends up telling you how to approach employers, how to talk to an employer about getting a higher salary before you get the job — really detailed information. It's very helpful. It has a very Christian, very godly perspective. It might be a little bit advanced for high school students, but you would be able to use some of the exercises with them. It would be helpful for anyone dealing with career planning for more than one person to work through it himself in order to understand the basic principles of career planning. If you want a crash course in career planning, this is probably a good place to start.

Career Match, by IDAK, runs a little over $40. To my knowledge, the *Career Match* is the only standardized or computerized instrument which matches talents with career opportunities, job titles, or ministry titles. Others match values, interests, personality, or temperament, but the *Career Match* is the only one that matches talents. You fill out an extremely exhaustive form, which you mail in to them. They send back a ten or twenty page print-out which gives you a listing of work settings, positions, and duties.

The problem with any standardized or computerized test like this is that you don't have the opportunity to change as you get feedback from the person who is doing the matching up for you.

I would like you to encourage your students to remember that we all tend to accept something in print as more true than if it is just told to us or something we come up with ourselves. The natural response is to think that because you fill out this little form and send it in to the computer and the computer sends you a print-out, it is more true than what you come up with on your own. That is simply not the case. The very best way to determine what your talents, interests, and values are is through self-reporting exercises.

The best way to determine those things is to look at your past and ask, "From as far back as I can remember, what have been the kinds of achievements and enjoyable activities that I have performed well and enjoyed?" You're always looking for two factors—anything that you do well and that you enjoy. Any time you find those two things together, that's a good place to start looking for a career that will fit. The best way to get that information is to examine your past. *Career Kit* and *Career Match* take you through that process. That's why I'm very impressed with them.

An advantage of the *Career Kit* over the *Career Match* is that many people can thumb through it and get some use from it, whereas that would not be true of *Career Match*.

The *Quick Job Hunting Map*, by Dick Bolles does pretty much the same thing only on a much briefer level. It helps you pick out your favorite achievements, and then gives you a grid of several hundred skills that you cross-section against those achievements. That enables you to come up with a list of skills that you have demonstrated which is the best way to determine career options for you. It also gives you a couple of exercises on interest and values. If you're thinking of something to buy for a whole class, this is the way to go. I suggest that you get one *Career Kit*, perhaps, and a whole passel of these.

If I were starting from scratch right now, I would probably go through all three. They are well worth the money.

Values

Values are what is important to me. Is it important to me that I have an office with a window? Is it important to me that I have a boss who listens to my feedback? Is it important to me that I have regular raises like the government gives, that I don't necessarily earn, but that just come with inflation?

Best sources for discovering values are the *Career Match* and the *Career Kit*. The Strong-Campbell Interest Inventory is a good standardized form for high schoolers. It is a computerized form that gives you a print-out. They categorize people by a combination of values, personality, and interest. They do not address the issue of talents or skills. Once they determine what your type is, they list different occupations from your very best choices to your very worst.

Another form that helps you with values to some degree is the *Self-Directed Search*. This is not computerized. It is good for the mission field because you fill it out and get the results right there on the spot. It is very inexpensive, about $5 per student, and it does give you a nice list of occupations to consider and then matches those occupations with six personality/value/interest types.

Temperament/Personality

The psychological-emotional reality which you bring to the working world is an important factor to consider in career planning. It can change with age, but there is a pretty strong degree of stability in that.

If you're teaching a class on career planning, it's not a bad idea to have the kids sit down and make a list on themselves first of all, and then get feedback from each other. Susie makes a list of Joe's personality traits—cheerful, aggressive, hard worker, that sort of thing. Besides such exercises, the standardized personality tests like Performax or Meyers-Briggs are helpful.

Interest

Interests are those things which attract me. Every time you hear a certain word you perk up and start listening. Maybe you're in a crowd and you hear somebody say, "Horses." All of a sudden you start moving over to hear what they're saying about horses. Your interest could be photography, or a color, or banking, or a particular type of mission or ministry. The best sources for discovering interests are the same as for values.

Physical make-up

There are physical characteristics that affect our career choices. You cannot be a 6'2" woman and be an airline stewardess, but you could be a basketball player.

You can't have poor vision, even if it's corrected by glasses, and be an airline pilot.

Educational background

This is just a list of education. Don't forget, if you're doing this yourself for a resume, to include seminars and workshops and conferences that you have attended.

Spiritual gifts

This may or may not be appropriate, depending on if you're working with the body of Christ.

Other Resources for Career Planning

Guerilla Tactics in the Job Market is a very inexpensive little paperback that takes you through the whole process of career planning from beginning to end. It is loaded with exercises that help you through this process. Instead of having to be dependent on computerized tests, it gives you a lot of different exercises that are not in *Career Kit* or *Career Match*.

The main mover and shaker in the change to do-it-yourself career planning is Dick Bolles, the author of *What Color is Your Parachute?* This book is wonderful reading to help you reshape your thinking about what the career planning process is like in the United States. It doesn't give you a whole lot of specific help. If you have a real extrovert, outgoing, hustler type of personality, that book will work for you. But if you're analytical, scholarly, timid, it won't do the trick.

Ralph Matson and Arthur Miller, authors of *Finding the Job You Can Love,* discovered that every time they would give the assignment to write down the top seven or ten achievements of your lifetime and then pick out the skills that you used doing those, there were certain motivational drives that appeared at the end of each of these assignments. If you took Joe Blow and looked at his favorite accomplishments and achievements from age four through age fifty-four, every one of those achievements would have certain common factors. There would be one motivational drive, and it would be something like to gain recognition, to be the key contributor, to meet needs, to excel, or to conquer and prevail. That's really key information in determining what's going to bring you satisfaction in a ministry or a career.

They also determined that that same kind of information was true of the kind of circumstances you enjoy working with, the kinds of relationships you like to have. Did you enjoy relating to people as a coach, or did you enjoy relating to people as a dictator, or did you enjoy relating to them as an associate? That would always be consistent. In my own practice I have seen the same thing.

The *Occupational Outlook Handbook* comes out about every two years. It lists jobs in the United States and gives about a page and a half description of each, how much money they typically pay, and what kind of education you need to get into that kind of work.

The *Dictionary of Occupational Titles* contains over 30,000 titles of careers available in the United States. It gives a paragraph on each of those. These are $15 to $25 and can be ordered through the Federal Government.

2. Selection

This answers the question, "Where is the job or ministry that matches me? Now that I know who I am, what kinds of jobs would be appropriate for me, and what kinds of employers do I want to be hired by?"

Reading

The first thing you do in the selection process is read everything you can get your hands on about career opportunities. Probably the best resource is *Vocational Biographies*, a collection of books containing interviews of people about their jobs. The whole set costs over $1,000. You can get yearly supplements which cost $200 to $300. You don't have to start out with the whole set. You can start with just the most recent set. If I were on the mission field today teaching career planning, I would do everything within my power—I would take a cut in salary—to get a library of these. They are extremely readable, while most monographs that you get in college career libraries are real boring. Even people who struggle with reading will still find these fun. They are generally accurate and include a more interesting variety of jobs instead of just nursing, teaching, and that sort of thing. They are very up-to-date.

High schoolers should not be making career decisions, but they should be doing a lot of reading and information gathering.

Field surveys

Field surveys are absolutely crucial. They are the most effective and yet the most often-resisted step in the career planning process. If you do your field survey, your chances of achieving career/ministry satisfaction are greatly enhanced.

This is an interview with a person who actually works in the area which interests you. You probably cannot imagine calling a stranger up on the phone and saying, "Could I please come and talk to you about your job?" The fact is that most people are willing to talk about their work. They have very few listeners who are truly interested in their job, so it's fun for them to talk about it and it's extremely informative for you.

If I were teaching career planning to high schoolers today, I would show them how to do that. I would make it a homework assignment to practice on each other and on other people in the missions community. I would bring Gary Sinclair into the classroom and say, "Gary, you are Director of Counseling in a Christian high school. Tell me what that's like." I would go through this series of questions right in front of the class:

- How did you get into this line of work?
- What kind of education did you need?
- What is your job description, i.e., what tasks are you required to do, or what kinds of things do you do every day?
- What do you like best about this line of work? (Try to get information on tasks rather about their boss or co-workers.)
- What do you like least?
- What does a person have to be good at to do this job well?
- If I were interested in pursuing this further, what advice would you give me?
- Could you give me the names of two other people who could tell me more about this area/type of work?

A week or two later I would say, "Now your homework assignment is to do that same thing with a friend, your parent, or somebody close that you feel safe with." Then a few weeks later, I'd have them do the same thing with somebody they don't know quite as well.

I believe this is as far as the high school student should be taken in the career planning process.

Decision making

Each Christian makes decisions differently, the best he can. One book that has given me a brand new view is *Decision Making and the Will of God*, by Gary Friesen. He says that a lot of times our approach is to depend on some mystical revelation from the Lord when in actuality we need to use wisdom.

Connection

Now that I know what I want to do, how do I connect with somebody who is willing to pay me to do that?

Informal interviews

Just drop by to see someone and say, "I've been considering doing work in this area, and I'm interested in your company. What can you tell me about your company?" You don't go in and say, "Can I fill out an application form?" The best information about how you can do this is in the *Career Kit* and Bolles' *What Color is Your Parachute?*

Resume

Once you decide what company you want to work for, you write your resume. It is not very productive to make up 120 resumes and send them out to every organization in the world. You do not get the personal attention you need. Before you actually apply for a job, you need to know that you want to work there, or at least you need to have it narrowed down to a choice of two or three places.

Write an individual resume for each employer that you are addressing. Employers want to know specific information about you. The more specific you can be, the better. And the best way to be specific is to have done your research on who you are as a person and who they are as a company or ministry.

The best information on how to write a resume would be in the *Career Kit*.

Interviews

The best information on interviews would be the *Career Kit* and *What Color is Your Parachute?*

Decision Making

This is the final step.

Recommendations for High Schoolers

The field surveys of the selection phase are as far as I believe a high school student should be taken. The whole career planning process rests on the introspection section. If you don't know who you are, what your values are, what your interests are, how can you make a wise decision about a career? A young person simply has not lived long enough to know the answers to those questions. It is best to put off that decision as long as possible.

High schoolers can make a grid with the first seven steps: talents and skills, values, temperament, interests, physical make-up, educational background, spiritual gifts. They may include separate columns for talents and skills. As early as they feel able, they can write information about themselves in each of those columns. They can keep this chart the rest of their lives and add to it as they get older and know more about themselves. It will help them make sound decisions when they become exposed to the working world, and when they get ready to write a resume, they can use that information to convince an employer that they are the right person for the job.

Discussion

How does the list change as a person gets older?

Your talents will remain the same throughout your life, though you will probably discover more as you get older. Some of your values will remain stable but some will change. When you're eighteen you may want to travel, but when you're thirty-five and have three kids, that changes. But the need for good feedback probably will remain the same throughout your life. Interests will frequently change. Skills are learnable and acquireable. Temperament and personality remain fairly stable. Your physical make-up will change. Education can change. Your spiritual gift will remain the same as I understand the Scriptures.

Gary Sinclair: *If you're working in a school setting, you may be asking yourself, "When in the world would I ever get this done?"*

In our school, even as early as junior high, some of our teachers in a social studies class or an English class have taken on a small unit in an area like this. It can teach writing skills, organizational skills, or planning. You'll probably have to take it a little at a time in some settings.

41

TCKness: Impact on
Marriage and Career

Dave Pollock, Jim and Lois Stück, Kent and Sharon Foster

Dave Pollock: This panel will begin to take a look at the impact of third-cultureness on marriage and career. My role is that of a catalyst. We are going to open this session with each of these people sharing a little about their background.

Lois Greenlee Stück: I feel I've had the best of both worlds. I've spent years both as a non-TCK and as a TCK. I sense that has had some real positive effects in my life. The first fourteen years of my life I was in a very missions-minded home. My father was a seminary professor. We constantly had missionaries and internationals from the seminary in our home. We made two extended visits to Colombia, South America. When I was fifteen, my parents became missionaries. They went to Colombia, and I came to the Alliance Academy in Quito, Ecuador. At that time in my life, it was the best thing that could have happened to me. It was wonderful. The experiences I had at the Academy helped my personality to blossom. I don't have time to go into all the positive things that happened to me.

I also met Jim Stück at the Academy. We have now been married for ten years. I was a book editor after graduating from college until the birth of Philip three years ago. Now I devote myself to caring for Philip and my husband. I also work on the board of Interact with Dave Pollock.

Jim Stück: I was born one block from this hotel. I went to the dorm here in Quito at age six. I'm sadly close to the stereotype of the MK raised in the jungle. I first learned of deodorant when I was in junior high. I remember going to a banquet and wearing white socks with black shoes when I was in high school. After Alliance Academy, I was one of two in our class who did not go on to college. I travelled for four years to see the world, but I had a legitimate cover. One year I was at a Bible school in England. The other three years, I went to Spain, India, and Nepal with Operation Mobilization.

When I married Lois, my life changed forever, for good. I went back to the States and went to college. For the last six years I've been working in New York City in the financial district.

Sharon Foster: I am the only monocultural person on the panel. I grew up in the Detroit area, where I still have seventy close relatives. None of my family has moved or travelled. I had not travelled until I met my husband, Kent. We've been married for eight years. We have three children, ages seven, five, and one. I received my education at the University of Michigan, where I majored in education. I'm a homemaker now.

Kent Foster: I'm the oldest of three children. My father was in radio and television, and was hired by the State Department on a temporary basis. I left New England at the age of seven when my family moved to Greece. Everywhere we moved after that, our whole family had to learn the local language. We generally lived away from Americans, and generally associated only with the locals. We basically fully adapted to the culture we were living in, which I think is unusual for foreign service types.

In 1962, we moved from Greece to Iran for language training for a year, and then on to Afghanistan, where a lot of my growing up years occurred. In 1967, when my father was assigned to the American Embassy in Saigon, it was decided that my brother and sister and I were not really American enough, and if we didn't go back to the United States, we'd lose all touch with who we were. We moved back to New Hampshire, close to my grandparents. I experienced re-entry in a rural elementary school and a rural junior high school. I'd have to say that the two years we spent in New Hampshire were very frustrating for me, because I never felt like I fit in.

We left in 1969 to go to Ghana, West Africa, where I spent a year in the British school system. In 1970, my parents decided that the British system was going to really mess up my education, so I should finish my last two years of high school in an American boarding school. To improve my French, I spent the summer working on a peach farm in the mountains outside of Lynell, France. Then at the age of fifteen, I went to boarding school in that city, where I finished high school. It was also at that school that I had a personal encounter with the Lord Jesus and gave my life to him.

I attended nine schools in all before I went to the University of Michigan in 1972, to study Chinese. I had childhood fluency in Greek and Persian or Farsi, and I presently speak Chinese, French, and English.

I joined an interdenominational community in Ann Arbor with about two thousand adults and one thousand children. It was there that I met Sharon. I travelled extensively while I was at the University of Michigan. I went to India, where my folks were posted. I experienced re-entry trauma each time I went back to Ann Arbor. I was feeling more at home in New Delhi than I was at Ann Arbor.

Sharon and I were married in 1978, and I've lived in Ann Arbor for the last fourteen years.

My TCK experience always was considered interesting, but not really useful for anything. I've experienced very few intense relationships with friends overseas. We didn't have time to get to know one another. It was particularly dramatic when I went from New Hampshire to West Africa. It had taken me two years to break the ice in the school I attended in New Hampshire. In one day in the community in Accra, Ghana, I knew everybody and felt welcome. I always felt off balance in the United States, out of touch with what was going on, and a certain kind of loneliness, like I didn't fit in there. I really want to go overseas again.

My younger brother had just the opposite experience. He doesn't like being overseas. He went through trauma in his twenties. He's been drifting ever since.

My sister had a positive experience. She got me in touch with Dave Pollock through a master's thesis she did last year at Columbia, called "Global Nomads." She's currently in Manila working with NBC. She has turned her TCK experience into something positive.

The thing that really helped me through it all was knowing that we all have our citizenship in heaven. That's been the stabilizing thing for me.

Dave Pollock: We have asked the panel to discuss how they perceive TCKness or lack of TCKness has affected their relationship to each other, and also to comment on observations they have made of other couples who are in similar situations.

Sharon Foster: I'm the monocultural one. At age twenty-two, after completing my college degree, I met Kent, and I was very attracted by his TCK qualities. He had a world-view. He had lived in exciting places where none of my friends had been. He had instant rapport with all the members of our Christian community. He was flexible. He could do anything. He still can. He can sleep anywhere, any time, which I find very difficult. He was mature both as a young man and as a Christian. All these things were very attractive to me, who had spent my whole life in the same city.

I never thought that his experiences would affect our marriage. I was in love with him and not with his experiences. We began our outreach to internationals about three years ago. The issues which touch TCKness just came up within the last year, after seven years of marriage. That's an important date to remember.

In our marriage we deal with two-year changes. Every two years we either have a baby, move, or Kent changes his job. I experience a lot of the me-and-the-children versus the internationals that Kent seeks to serve, and the outwardness that he always has towards the other people in our community and in our city. I am concerned how our children would be affected if we do end up living overseas. I also realize that my children could experience difficulties if we stay in the States. That's why I feel it is very important for me to remain in the will of the Lord. I desire to have Kent reach his full potential, to come to grips with his TCKness, and to find a positive way he can use his experiences in our life together.

We bring the internationals in our city to our home to care for them there. We do a lot of hospitality. We help the Chinese find homes, food, and different services that they need in our community. Kent can help them because he understands exactly where they are coming from. For me, it means being honest with the Lord, with myself, and with Kent as to how I feel about all these people in our house and how we deal with the TCK qualities that Kent is coming to grips with.

The Christian life is one of slow crucifixion, and marriage is not exempt. The passage I've been clinging to during this conference is from Psalm 37. "Delight yourself in the Lord. He will give you the desires of your heart. Commit your way to the Lord. Trust also in him, and he will do it."

Kent Foster: I married Sharon because I felt that she really understood me. I grew up not feeling understood, not feeling like I fit in. As a TCK, I had always been more interested in relationships than in pursuing the American dream of two cars in the driveway and all that stuff. I never had any desire to buy a house and settle down. After living a number of years in Ann Arbor, the encouragement from friends and Sharon's parents went along the lines of, "You really ought to settle down. You ought to buy a house. You ought to have the things that are normal for an American family."

Sharon's father builds and wires houses. I was not a fix-it guy. We always had servants in our house, so I never had to do any of that stuff. We did end up building a house, so it's been a learning experience for me. We've had a steady stream of internationals coming through our house. It's been a source of tension for Sharon, because the brunt of the cooking and hostessing falls on her. People drop in at all hours of the day and night.

Sharon and I had a discussion a couple of weeks ago about how my Saturday priorities were out of whack. I wasn't going down the list of things that had to get fixed. I was just talking to one international after another who dropped in.

My first experience of putting my TCK background to some positive use was with international students in Ann Arbor in January of 1984. I went around the room talking to people from every continent and was able to identify with them. We started getting involved with them, particularly with mainland Chinese, because I spoke their language.

We didn't really experience a crisis with our international student ministry until about a year ago, in the seventh year of our marriage. From year five to year seven we had had a pretty positive experience. In September of 1985, my company surprised me by giving me an opportunity to move to Hong Kong and work there. I said, "Boy, this must be the Lord. It's all coming together." During the next six months I was going to Massachusetts for lots of interviews. Then all of a sudden the door shut.

After that, Sharon admitted to having feelings of great concern and fear about what the move would have meant for our family. It was then that my sister gave me her thesis and introduced me to Dave Pollock. The next thing I knew, I was sitting at a re-entry seminar in Farmington Hills, Michigan, finding out I was a TCK, which I hadn't known before. There I saw a movie called *Welcome Home Stranger* which really hit me—the image of the family coming back after living overseas for many years and not fitting in.

We came to a moratorium on our international student work in September of this year due to questions it was raising about the priority I needed to give to my wife and my children. It came to a crisis point. Since then I have felt that something has been dying inside of me. In November of this year, I had a chance to meet for the first time some people I had lived with in Afghanistan twenty years ago. I don't know why the Lord is doing all this this year, but the next thing I knew, Dave was saying, "Come to Quito," and I said, "Why not?"

The TCK experience has been a source of tension, but as Christians we're committed to working through these issues with God's grace. Even if it hurts, the Lord is here to help us.

In the career area, I'd have to say that my Chinese studies degree and my TCK background have never been considered very useful. When I was in college, I was steered away from teaching English as a Foreign Language, which is something I was really interested in doing after a summer job working with internationals. I got into the computer field through the back door. I had been working as an accountant for a local church. I joined Digital Equipment with the idea that I could work for an international company and perhaps be a tentmaker in some other part of the world. The biggest revelation to me through all this has been discovering that the TCK experience is no accident. God in his providence allows us all to experience things for some purpose.

Lois Stück: I can't possibly separate the impact of TCKness on marriage and career because at this point my marriage and family is my career. My whole life is wound up in that.

We also have a constant flow of missionaries, internationals, MKs, and assorted friends through our home. We love it. We chose to do that. We're glad the Lord has allowed us to do it. Sometimes it's very hard. I get tired of changing beds and preparing meal after meal. Sometimes we want some time alone together when we can't have it. But even when it's hard, it's what we want to do. It's a joy, and it's something we feel we can do for the Lord. It's very important to me, because when I went to college as an MK, there was no home I could go to. There was one family that ministered to me, but they were a four-day trip away, and I had to make a strong effort to go there. I want to be that someone for other people. I use the family that helped me so much as a model. I try to think, "How did they make me feel so loved and so welcome?"

When we met the Fosters on Sunday night, we talked until midnight. We met as four very different people. We have four different personalities; we have very different backgrounds. And yet, I was amazed that the four of us found that the stress points in our marriage were virtually identical. We were laughing as we told each other stories. We would start to talk about an incident, and the other couple would say the same thing. Some of those are because of the male-female differences, but I think the TCKness of our husbands has caused most of the stresses on our marriages. I won't name all the issues, but the one that is most important to me is something that occurred after we had been married seven years.

At that time, Jim developed an interest in North African Mission and started talking to me about joining and going to North Africa to work with Arabs. That's something I believe in very much, but I had no inclination. I felt nothing about it in my heart. Jim, being the typical TCK, was ready to step out, ready to pack up our bags and our brand new baby, and go learn two new languages. It was a new challenge. It was exciting to him.

To me it was very different. I developed a very strong feeling of guilt for not having the same desire he had. I believe that guilt was very strong because my parents are missionaries, Jim's parents are missionaries, our four brothers are all missionaries, and most of our friends and loved ones are missionaries. If you're a Christian, you're a missionary, right? I believe in missions. I'm encouraging friends to be in missions. Yet, somehow I was not given any peace that this was for us at this point. I was dealing with a husband who seemed to be talking to the Lord about this, and I was cut off. We went through two years of struggling with this. We applied to the mission and filled out all the forms. It was torture for me. I felt very alienated from Jim.

We had had seven years of complete unity. It was the first time Jim ever wanted to do anything I didn't want to do. It was very, very hard. I felt abandoned by God. I felt cut off because I was pleading for peace. I knew if I had the peace, I could do it, but nothing ever spoke to me, and I felt a terrible abandonment. It reached a climax when I found myself thinking, "If I were killed in a car accident, this whole thing would be solved and Jim could go. God would be pleased, and it would be over." That was an extreme that had to be dealt with. It's been two years. I didn't want to get up here when Dave asked us to be on a panel because the process isn't over. I can't say the healing is complete. The healing is taking place. That's very good, but it still hurts.

Whenever one spouse has painful memories from the past come up, both spouses have to deal with it. The whole marriage is affected. It's not Jim or Lois dealing with something. It's us as a couple. We've found that when that happens, in some cases we've drawn closer to support each other and to unify. In other cases, it has been extremely threatening to our unity and has been very difficult to deal with. As I said, during the first seven years of our marriage, everything had always been easy. Being a Christian was easy. God and I always wanted the same thing. My pastor has said, "Prayer is not magic," but up until that time, it seemed like it was, because everything always went well.

I often wish that it could be easy again, that I could go back to the happy, carefree Christianity that floated along. But I know that there has to be growth. There is pain, and sometimes there's alienation along the way, but the healing brings you to a new level.

Jim Stück: I've divided my life into four segments: travel, marriage, education, and profession. The four years of travel after I finished high school is an extreme example of one of the dominant characteristics of a TCK, mobility. During those four years I changed countries each year.

Second, marriage to Lois, an MK, was the first of two great steps toward healing. That was the first time I could relax. Someone knew who I was and loved me. It was a nail in the coffin of niggling alienation from my background. In marriage I responded to a woman with a world-view. That's characteristic of TCKs. They look for friends and mates that have a world-view.

Then I went on to college and got a graduate degree in international relations and another graduate degree in business. My college years reflect another strong characteristic of TCKs, adaptability. I went to four colleges in six years. We're adaptable. We can make those changes.

Some friends of our have been compiling a summary of all the dissertations, theses, research papers, and books that have been written on TCKs and MKs. I'll mention two things they have found. One has to do with education. TCKs and MKs tend to go much farther in education than the U.S. norm.

I think the most obvious aspect of a TCK is reflected by our professions. TCKs worldwide tend to go into service careers as opposed to industry. My areas of consulting and investment banking are people oriented. After we moved to New York City, I was an international bank officer for two years. Then I was a management consultant for two years. Now I'm in investment banking. In September, after about eighteen months of that, we'll make another change. Do you see the pattern? Like Kent, my family moved every eighteen months. I was always in Ecuador, but we moved stations.

One of the most obvious advantages of the TCK is having cultural and the linguistic skills. With Chemical Bank I handled the Mexico desk. I knew Latin American culture, and I spoke Spanish.

So often the weaknesses of being a TCK correspond to the strengths. I'd learned flexibility and mobility being a TCK. Every move I made was an advancement. The flip side of flexibility is restlessness. Every eighteen to twenty-four months, you want to move on to something more challenging. It has affected both Kent's and my lives. He was thinking of going to Hong Kong, and I was thinking in terms of North Africa Mission. It was around that seven year period when we had this crash in our idyllic marriages. Our families paid the price.

The down side of mobility is rootlessness. We've lived in six homes in ten years of marriage. New York City has to be the ultimate center of rootlessness. It draws TCKs. We feel very much at home there. It also draws others who have been outsiders in their culture. Many of my friends and the people who have responded to me are people in the gay community, the American Jewish community, and internationals. They're not part of the majority in the American scene. The strong bond of friendship with these others is interesting. I am an outsider, and they're outsiders, and we're in a dominant culture that's different from ours. We have to adapt and to play games.

Included in the credit training program for Chemical Bank were preppie types—old money, prep schools. Here was this jungle missionary kid. (You can take the boy out of the jungle, but you can't take the jungle out of the boy.) These guys felt at home with me. We had instant good friendship. It blew my mind. I began realizing that to them the boarding school experience was the most significant part of their lives. They left home earlier than most Americans. Their friends are from their boarding school. They were sent overseas for summers. They were bilingual and trilingual. Travel was no big thing for them. Many times they had relatives overseas. God has a sense of humor. I went to Alliance on grants because my parents were under the poverty level. You take the lower financial level and the higher financial level, and they have certain similarities.

When I was thirty my first child was born. Up to that point my first year of school was just a blank sheet. Somehow through my son's birth, I started reliving what had happened.

This summer I went to a re-entry seminar that Dave Pollock was holding. There were about twenty eighteen-year-olds from Africa, Latin America, and Asia. It was emotionally charged. I was surprised to find myself fighting back tears. On the last day I saw a missionary from Africa and his big strapping eighteen-year-old son embrace. I lost it. I went out to the beach, and for forty-five minutes I was weeping, groaning, and choking. The only thing that went through my mind was, "I want my Daddy. I want my Daddy."

For the first time I became a six-year-old back in the dorm, all alone, the oldest in my family and the first to go to boarding school. I had godly dorm parents, but I was reliving twenty-seven years later the incredible terror that my mind had blocked out. I never thought I had any problem with unresolved grief, and then all of a sudden I found I had bucketfuls of it.

As a Christian I would like to speak of knowledge versus wisdom. Knowledge can be dry and impotent. We can understand our TCKness and look at the salient points in our marriage and careers, but that doesn't help us change. Wisdom, which the Bible talks about, is living and powerful. That's what is going to make the changes we should go through.

42

Caring for the Adult MK

Ruth Van Reken, MK, SIM International
Ruth Ostrander, MK

When I was asked to do something for the conference, I sent out a survey to other adult MKs, to find out if there are MKs who share some of the same feelings that I do.

The survey asked questions about age, sex, marital status, country of birth, separation from family, relationships with siblings, death of family members, departure from host country, subsequent visits, relationship to authority, feelings about boarding schools, and becoming a missionary personally.

I sent the survey to about 860 MKs. I got back almost 300 responses. People from twenty-two to seventy-five answered, talking of their struggles and their healing. It was wonderful to see healing in process. There is a lot of health in our community. Many people could talk about their struggles and still say, "I'm glad I'm an MK."

On the other hand, there are some MKs who are totally defensive. "There shouldn't even be a study like this. We don't need it. It's just a waste of time. Conferences like this are silly. I made it; everybody else should, too." There's yet another group that thinks missionaries shouldn't even have children. Six people said missionaries should not have children because the pain for the children is too much. There was a wonderful span of response that made me feel like I had heard from the hearts of a lot of people.

I expected to find that more older people had been born in the home country because there weren't hospitals in the host country. Instead, I found the opposite. People used to go to the field when they were young. In my parents' generation, if you weren't out by the time you were thirty, you didn't get to go. It was a lifetime commitment. They had a long term and didn't get home frequently.

Older MKs went for much longer periods without seeing their parents. When I was young, we would normally go four years and never see our parents. That was life for missionary kids. My parents left when I was fourteen. They returned when I was eighteen. I went from freshman in high school to freshman in college. It was routine. It was our system. For those over forty, the average time for not seeing parents was 3.6 years, while those under forty averaged only eleven months. There's a terrific difference in the amount of physical separation.

I asked how many siblings or parents had died before the MK was eighteen. As a kid, it seemed like everyone had a sibling who had died. My mother had six kids. I knew one of us was bound to die. There was cerebral malaria and other things that are treatable now. In fact, 22 percent of the earlier group did experience loss through death as compared to only 9 percent of the younger ones.

I asked if as an adult they had been able to visit the place(s) where they grew up overseas. I was surprised how many of the earlier ones had, though many had gone back as missionaries. The trend is up. Kids go back more often to see their parents.

I asked how old they were when they left their host country for the last time during their growing up years. In our generation, we didn't have high schools on the field. Most of us left at eleven, twelve, or thirteen. The average for those over forty was 12.23 years. I think it affected our identity. The younger, under-forty group, were sixteen on the average. Most of them finished high school on the field. They expressed far more bondedness to their friends. The loss of friends is talked about much more deeply than in my group, because when you lose your friends at eleven or twelve, you haven't formed the same closeness. All of my friends from that time went to different places. I've lost track of all of them. Our mission is now trying to form an alumni group.

I asked how they would describe their current relationship to their brothers and/or sisters. In the older group there is resolution. They talk about a process. This is the group that was in the war. A lot of people were left at home when they were two to four years old. They were separated from their siblings and seem to have a much less close relationship. A lot of this group did not experience family in the way that some of us did.

I asked how multiple separations had affected them. Both groups had a fairly even curve on this. I have discovered that a lot of processing doesn't start until about age twenty-five. That's when life starts to hit. If you had asked me in college, I would have said none of this affected me at all. People who have had multiple short separations still struggle with the same distancing as those who have the long separations.

Instead of sharing all the case studies with you, I have asked Ruth Ostrander to tell us about her adult MK experience. I think she is representative of the broad group of people I heard from who are not against missions, who are willing to say, "I've had some struggles, and there's a process that is going on."

Ruth Ostrander

When I was three years old my parents went to Japan. I went to a Japanese kindergarten. I went to first grade in the military school. From second grade on, I was in a hostel or with another missionary or in a dormitory setting. I had eight different sets of house parents growing up.

My first separations were really difficult. I recall coming home for Christmas vacations and having a weeping session, telling my parents all the things I felt were unfair in the hostel and all the things I was struggling with. After multiple separations, I came to realize that there wasn't a whole lot they could do for me. I had to learn to be strong on my own. I didn't feel comfortable sharing things with my house parents at the time, so I pretty much kept them to myself. I knew the letters that were sent home each week were read through before they were sent, so I didn't really tell my parents, on an ongoing basis, what I was going through. I realized I was going to have to fight my own battles. Every time I left my mother, she had no tears. She was very strong, and it telegraphed to me that I needed to be strong, too.

I always knew that my parents loved me, and I clung to that. Intellectually I knew they were doing the best thing for me. They explained to me that it was the best thing to be sent away from home. But in my heart, I didn't feel like they loved me. I couldn't match up my thoughts with my feelings, because they were never there when I needed them. They weren't there during the hard times.

In high school, I threw myself into sports. I threw myself into drama. I was a cheerleader. I was known as always having a smile. It was my goal to be a good MK, to make my parents proud of who I was. I knew there were so many advantages to being an MK. I didn't disregard that. In fact, I was looking forward to going to college and sharing those experiences that were different than those of all my colleagues'.

But when I got to college, my first shock was that nobody could relate to my experiences. They didn't really care about the positive aspects, let alone about the hurts. My hurts really didn't come up at that time, because I knew that I needed to survive. I could be tough. I was tough all along. I was just going to make the best of it. If you were to ask me in college how I felt about my experience as an MK, I would have given you all the positive things.

I was more mature than everybody else. I felt I knew where I was going. I could cope with being away from my parents when most of my colleagues had never been away from theirs. I was looked up to as being strong. I carried some leadership. The moment I set foot on campus, the basketball coach snapped me up and put me on the varsity team. That was my identity. I threw myself into basketball.

It wasn't until my senior year that things came crashing down. I had gone back home during the summer session. At that time I felt that I needed to talk some things through with my parents. I knew that I hurt, but I didn't know how to bring it up or how to approach them about it. I expressed to them that I hurt, but I realized that they were really down and struggling during that time. Later on I found out that they were expecting me to cheer them up, because they were having such a struggle. So we just didn't click, and I didn't get to talk to them about my feelings at that time.

My senior year was a real paradox, because I was thrown into deep depression. I had a hard time getting out of bed. I didn't know how to face graduation. I didn't know what I was going to do afterwards. My parents were still in Japan. I didn't have anybody I could really relate to. I had a hard time making it through final exams. I didn't know where I was going to turn. At the same time, I was being awarded Who's Who in Colleges and Universities of America, and everybody was saying how fantastic I was. Deep down inside I knew I was a basket case. I felt like I was a living lie, and I had a hard time facing that.

After college I pulled myself together. I used the teaching credential I got and taught for two years in a private school. Eventually I ended up in the Parks and Recreation system in Los Angeles designing programs for the handicapped. I was really successful in my career. During that period at various times I decided to see some psychologists. I went to three different therapists. I discovered that I had a lot of anger towards the way I was brought up, because of the separations. I had anger towards God. I had anger towards my parents. I needed to deal with that. I needed to learn how to express my feelings. We'd never talked about feelings in our home.

Incidentally my mother had never talked about feelings while growing up either, so I can't blame her. She didn't know how to do it. I didn't learn how to do it. I worked through a lot of my problems in therapy. In fact, I thought I had worked through them all.

Two-and-a-half years ago I committed myself to marriage. It took me thirty-one years to be able to commit myself to a person. I dated a lot of different people. I always feared being abandoned. I wanted to make sure this person was going to stick with me through life.

I committed myself. I started out feeling, "I have it made. I won't need to struggle any more. This person is going to love me." He loved me dearly. He still loves me dearly. He loves the Lord dearly. He expresses his feelings. He tries to get me to express my feelings. He's willing to allow me to express everything I'm going through.

I established a good marriage. The problem was that about a year ago, all these feelings came up again. It surprised me, because I thought I had gotten ahold of them. There were two things that triggered it. First of all, my husband and I started talking about having children. A lot of fears came up. I began thinking about my childhood again. I realized that there were still some struggles I had that I hadn't worked through with my mother. I felt I needed to work them through before having children.

The second thing was that I was on the missions committee at our church. I attended a missionary conference and heard Carol Richardson speak on the role of a missionary wife and mother. Afterwards, I went up to her and surprised myself. I completely broke down. I was hurting all over again. I was saying, "Lord, I thought I dealt with this." I'd prayed. I'd searched through Scriptures. I sought comfort through the Psalms. I thought I'd dealt with it.

She was wise enough to encourage me to write to Ruth Van Reken. I had never heard of Ruth before in my life. I took her address in Africa, and I wrote a letter.

In the meantime, New Year's came along. One of my New Year's resolutions was to get this settled. I really wanted to be healed the following year. I prayed that the Lord would heal me. I didn't know where else to turn. I'd been to psychologists. I'd done everything I could think of. I'd even approached my mother several times saying, "I really hurt. I need to talk this out." I needed to know that she could recognize my hurt, but my mother had a difficult time with that.

She made comments like, "You know, you've got to go on. You can't hang on to this all your life. You need to put this aside. Don't dredge it up again. Let's get on with it, Ruth. What's your problem?"

I realized that really what I was asking her was to admit that it hadn't been right for her to send me away to school. She couldn't do that. And I knew why she couldn't. To say that would be saying it had been against God's will for her to send me away. I knew that it hadn't been against his will. He had given me so many positive things in my separation. I had grown in so many ways. Most of all it had made me grow closer to the Lord. My mother had given me all the spiritual principles I needed in my life. She had given me a closeness with the Lord, and she loved the Lord so dearly. I realized that it took a lot of strength for her to give me up. But I just couldn't connect those two things. She couldn't hear about my hurts, because in a sense it was admitting that she was a failure as a missionary. So we were stuck there.

Then, in the Lord's grace and perfect timing, I heard a sermon. Our pastor shared that when the Lord Jesus Christ hung on the cross, he was completely separated from his father. He was abandoned in a sense. He suffered total isolation from his father. It was such a comfort to me to know that he suffered and that he hurt and that he could understand me and understand my hurts. I'd heard that story many times before, but it just never hit me that way.

Beyond that was the fact that when he was hung on the cross and he was completely rejected, his first words were, "Father, forgive them, for they know not what they do." Right away I thought, "My parents didn't know what they were doing." Afterwards, I shared this with my husband.

He said, "It's interesting, because Stephen identified with Christ and followed Christ's example. When he was being stoned to death, the Pharisees thought they were doing God's will. They thought that he was a blasphemer. His words were, "Father, forgive them for they know not what they do."

I'm not trying to say my parents were Pharisees. I'm just saying that I realized in order to truly identify myself with Christ, I had to follow his example and forgive my parents completely and not hang onto thinking they did the wrong thing by sending me away. They felt they were doing the right thing. And I believe that they did do the right thing in God's sovereign will. I just needed to forgive them unconditionally and not wait for them to ask for my forgiveness. It was really comforting to know that Christ could feel what I was feeling.

A few weeks later, I received a letter from Ruth. She sent me one of the original rough manuscripts of her book. The first night I got it, I read the first letter. I read, "Dear Mom and Dad, . . . " and at the end it said, "Love, Ruth Ellen." My name is Ruth Ellen, too, and my maiden name is Van Scooten, so that in itself was a bond. I just broke down. It took me over two weeks to get through that book, because it triggered so many repressed memories, so many things I hadn't dealt with. It gave me the liberty to grieve through all those things I had not allowed myself to grieve about before.

That grieving process has been so freeing for me. The verse says, "The truth shall set you free." That's the way it has been for me. Being able to suffer with Christ and grieve for that abandonment has really set me free.

After going through that, my husband suggested that I go back to my mother and talk to her again. He was with me at the time. Being married was a cushion for me. I knew that if my mother still could not accept my hurts, my husband did, and I could always rest in his love. When I approached her again, it was on a totally different plane. I wasn't blaming her. I had forgiven her, but I still wanted her to know where I was at.

When I approached her, it was the first time that she expressed to me, in tears, that it had hurt so much for her to send me away. I knew it had hurt, but I could never feel it, because she never let down her guard. She told me she had been afraid to do that. She knew if she did, she'd fall apart. Then I'd fall apart, and I'd never get out the door. It had to be done. We didn't have an alternative. But I needed to see that. I needed to know that she hurt. I also realized, that it hurt her so much that it took every bit of her energy just to make it through those times herself. It took all the energy she had to cope with her own feelings. She didn't have anything to give me. It still is very difficult for her to hear of my hurts because she has not, I feel, dealt with all of her own hurts. Until she can do that, it is very difficult to reach out.

I'm still in a growing process. Your process may be different. We all have to go through a healing process whether we're MKs or not. It's a process of maturing and growing up. I know that I have been healed a lot. It's living proof to be able to stand here. I still have more to go, but a year ago I couldn't have stood here without breaking down. I wouldn't have been able to get through the session at all.

Ruth Van Reken

The survey told me that story in different forms, over and over. It's also what's in my heart. If we're going to talk about caring for adult MKs, we have to understand it's a process. We have traditionally forgotten about MKs after college. Somehow after that we're on our own. If you are my family, that is ultimate abandonment.

My own particular mission is my superfamily. I belong to missions in general, but I have a real protective instinct towards SIM. In a sense that's my family, my home. If somebody in SIM rejects or hurts me, it hurts even worse.

Missions have to understand that they have some responsibility as family for the kids that have come through their own mission. Some kids are very hurt in a particular mission, so the healing needs to come through that mission as well as through the whole corporate body.

Most of us feel for our mission. We want to protect it. It's like a brother or sister. You may know that they're not perfect, but you don't let anybody else know it. That's one reason it's hard for us to deal with anybody else's pain which has been caused by the mission experience. I didn't want to deal with anybody's pain from my mission, because they were somehow attacking my family. That's why I let a lot of my friends go.

For the first time, last January I was asked to speak to a church about MKs. I realized that they had been getting many inaccurate messages. Churches want to interact with us, but they don't know how.

They said, "Can we write letters?'

I said, "Frankly, when my kids get fifty letters from the first grade class of XYZ, it's a blessing, but you sure don't know what to do. You know you should respond. You know you should be grateful, but how are you going to ask your kids to write to fifty kids they've never met?"

There are all sorts of things Christians can do about the care of MKs and adult MKs. I think each one of us has a responsibility to share with them some of what we've learned here.

Another issue raised in the questionnaire concerned MKs who return to the field as missionaries. Mission boards have to be aware of the experiences and knowledge MKs already possess.

My mission board didn't think I knew anything. I thought, "Listen, honey. I was born over here." When I went to candidate school they told me I was going to have culture shock. I thought, "I will not." And I did not. I thought the market was wonderful. I thought the smells were terrific. All of that made me feel, "I'm back home."

Something else that came through over and over in these questionnaires was the way missionaries react to nationals. I think an MK interacts with nationals easily. We grew up with them. Sometimes the missionary culture is a little exclusive regarding nationals. It hurts to say that because it seems disloyal to my community.

As an adult MK going back, I was not making a social statement by inviting nationals into my home. It was not an act of defiance or an act of trying to prove something. It was because I like them because they are my friends. I had played with those kids. I was criticized about how I was going to spoil people and how we don't do this and how we don't do that. The questionnaire revealed others had encountered similar criticism.

I think also there are unresolved issues from our childhood that are triggered when you hit the mission community. That's another issue that someone should research.

Another important thing Ruth is saying is that we need to start helping our parents if we are going to help the adult MK. In a lot of these questionnaires, the healing comes when the parent can sit down and listen, and when the mother can say what she felt, and the dad can say what he felt.

When I wrote my mother those letters, I didn't know at first if I could send them. "She's going to think I hate her." But I got back such a beautiful letter from her. She just said, "Thank you for sharing. I'm sorry for your pain." She didn't take any guilt. She didn't tell me she had been a bad, awful, evil, ugly mother. She said, "I'm sorry it hurt you or that you've struggled. If I had known, maybe I would have done things differently. But I can't change a thing. I just wish I could give you a big hug." That's all I needed. I knew she understood me.

When I was telling her how afraid I was to come to this conference, she said, "I suppose I could tell you to cheer up and trust the Lord, but I guess that wouldn't do any good, huh?"

I said, "Well, we're coming, aren't we, Mother."

We're able now to laugh about some of this. Part of my process has been saying, "Mother, just listen. Thank you very much." She can laugh back with me. That has become something special for us.

But there are a lot of parents who are very nervous and defensive. Some people who read my manuscript would say, "My children were happy. They're MKs. This doesn't apply."

I thought, "You've missed something. I'm happy I'm an MK. There's so much blessing, but there can still be these things we need to work out."

My main ministry up until now has been with Women's Bible Study Ministries. I work with women from broken homes, from alcoholic fathers, from incestuous situations. One of my good friend's first memories is of her father trying to kill her. Compared to that, I have such a wonderful life. But that's the hooker for me. Because my life is so wonderful, and it is, I don't have permission to talk about anything that is difficult.

When I was able to receive my pain and sort it out, God changed my whole ministry. It doesn't scare me any more that others have pain. I don't have to pretend I'm so pious that I can't feel with them. Now when they come to me and tell me whatever they tell me, I can cry with them. Somehow, when the Bible says I can share the comfort he's given me, I can do that because I received his comfort. If I never was able to tell Jesus what the hurt was, I couldn't ask him for the comfort. But when I'm able to say, "Lord Jesus, this is what hurt," then I am able to go back and grieve for it and receive him into it. Because it's past, doesn't mean it's impossible to change. God who is timeless is God of yesterday, today, and forever. If there's something in my yesterday that I need help with, he'll take me there.

I have learned to acknowledge my present pain and give it to God right away. I'm not going to have to spend twenty years grieving for today, because I have learned to process life and start moving on. But I can't get going today until yesterday is finished.

That's where a lot of adult MKs are. That's what they need to hear. It's not abnormal. We're just in a process.

How are we going to let each other know?

Ruth's story is our story. Start to tell it to people. I hope we're going to find out that when our own story no longer frightens us, nobody else's will either. We will be free enough to say to members of the global nomad community and the PK community, "Come and join us. Let us share with you what we have learned. Let's get on with life in the fullness of it." Jesus said truth sets us free.

Do you know that the first piece of armour is truth? Our biggest problem is that we've lived in untruth about what we feel.

That's why we've been so broken and so hurt. Truth is our first defense against the enemy, so let's be truthful.

I think God is going to raise up some way to connect us adult MKs, and he's going to raise up some way to let parents know that their kids aren't such weirdos. It would be helpful, if parents would quit panicking as we go through developmental stages. There must be no greater pain for a parent than to live with the idea that they have failed. When their kid doesn't make it with Christ, no matter what else they do, they feel like a failure.

We need to reach out to those who have been hurt. We need to let them know that we're not judging them. We need to reach out to the parents who have turned away from missions, because they've been told it was all the family's fault. We need to embrace each other.

Addresses of Speakers

Mrs. Robb Bakker
907 Peach St.
Duncanville, TX 75137

Mrs. Grace Barnes
MK Advisor, Operation Impact
Azusa Pacific University
Azusa, CA 91702

Mr. Randy Borman
Casilla 5080
Quito, ECUADOR

Mrs. Joyce Bowers
DGM/ELCA
8765 W. Higgins Rd.
Chicago, IL 60631

Dr. John A. Burgess
116 Conant St.
Beverly, MA 01915

Dr. Raymond Chester
5551 West Cortez
Glendale, AZ 85304

Rev. and Mrs. Ron Cline
World Radio Missionary Fell.
PO Box 3000
Opa-Locka, FL 33055

Mr. and Mrs. Kent Foster
2470 Parkwood
Ann Arbor, MI 48104

Mr. Richard Fowler
LeTourneau College
PO Box 7001
Longview, TX 75601

Dr. Marjory Foyle
Flat H
22 Bassett Road
London
ENGLAND W10 6JJ

Mr. Richard Gathro
2221 N. Vernon St.
Arlington, VA 22207

Sharon Haag
Christian Academy of
Guatemala
APDO 25-B
Guatemala City
GUATEMALA

Daniel Johnson
38 E. Main St.
Walden, NY 12586

Mr. and Mrs. Lester Kenney
PO Box 683
Marine Parade
Singapore 9144

Dr. Paul Kienel
P.O. Box 4097
Whittier, CA 91745

Dr. Margaret Long
5635 Bishop Ct.
Nashport, OH 43830

Mr. Wayne MacBeth
Houghton College
Houghton, NY 14744

Mr. David Morley
Westmont College
955 La Paz Rd.
Santa Barbara, CA 93108

Dr. Lynn Moss
Wingate College
Wingate, NC 28174

Mr. Larry Noack
Children's Education
7500 W. Camp Wisdom Rd.
Dallas, TX 75236

Dr. Dellanna O'Brien
Interfaces
P.O. Box 11233
Richmond, VA 23230-1233

Ruth Ostrander
56 1/2 Nieto Ave.
Long Beach, CA 90803

Mr. and Mrs. Daniel B. Peters
Link Care Center
1734 West Shaw Ave.
Fresno, CA 93711

Mr. David Pollock
RR 1 Box 23,
Centerville Rd.
Houghton, NY 14744

Dr. John Powell
1714 Linden St.
East Lansing, MI 48823

Mrs. Kay Ringenberg
6663 Nyman Dr.
Dallas, TX 75236

Miss Rachel Saint
a/c H.C.J.B., Casilla 691
Quito, ECUADOR

Rev. David Sanford
John Brown University
Siloam Springs, AR 72761-0000

Dr. Cliff Schimmels
Wheaton College
Wheaton, IL 60187

Dr. Esther Schubert
RR #1, Box 263
New Castle, IN 47362

Mr. Gary Sinclair
Southfield Christian School
28650 Lahser Rd.
Southfield, MI 48034

Dr. Alfredo Smith
Casilla 9455 CCI
Quito, Ecuador

Miss Saloma Smith
7 Duffield Rd.
Weston, Ont.
CANADA M9P 3C8

Mr. Walter Stuart
Heermann Burte Str. 1a
7842 Kandern, 1
WEST GERMANY

Dr. and Mrs. James Stuck
4007 Oak Grove Dr.
Valparaiso, IN 46383

Mrs. Ruth Van Reken
8124 N. Lincoln Blvd.
Indianapolis, IN 46240

Dr. Ted Ward
1209 Courier Court
Deerfield, IL 60015

Dr. Frances White
1272 Reading Court
Wheaton IL 60187

Mrs. Sharon Willmer
807 Howard St.
Wheaton, IL 60187

Mrs. Karen Wrobbel
Avda. de Aragon, 226, 4C
28022 Madrid,
SPAIN

Index

Values, cont.
  U.S. 54, 55, 280
Vocational training 87
  see also Non-college-bound
        MK

W

Work ethic
  of MK 267, 328, 341-343
Work experience
  as preparation for career 313,
        316
World Christians
  MKs as 57-60
World-view
  biblical 365-371
  of MK 403
  of TCK 247, 399

Y

Youth
  as U.S. value 281